COPING WITH FINANCIAL FRAGILITY AND SYSTEMIC RISK

edited by

Harald A. Benink

Assistant Professor of Finance
University of Limburg, Maastricht, The Netherlands, and
Adviser of the Banking and Financial Services Group
of Moret Ernst & Young

Parts of the book are reprinted from
the Journal of Financial Services Research
Vol. 9, Nos. 3 - 4 (1995)

ᴣ ERNST & YOUNG

Kluwer Academic Publishers
Boston/Dordrecht/London

FINANCIAL AND MONETARY POLICY STUDIES

Volume 30

The titles published in this series are listed at the end of this volume.

Table of Contents

General Conference Papers

Distributors for North America:
Kluwer Academic Publishers
101 Philip Drive
Assinippi Park
Norwell, Massachusetts 02061 USA

Distributors for all other countries:
Kluwer Academic Publishers Group
Distribution Centre
Post Office Box 322
3300 AH Dordrecht, THE NETHERLANDS

Library of Congress Cataloging-in-Publication Data

Coping with financial fragility and systemic risk / edited by Harald A. Benink.
      p. cm. -- (Financial and monetary policy studies ; 30)
  "Parts of the book are reprinted from the Journal of financial services
research, vol. 9, nos. 3-4, 1995"--CIP pub. info.
  Includes bibliographical references.
  ISBN 0-7923-9612-X
  1. Finance. 2. Banks and banking. 3. Risk. 4. International finance.
I. Benink, H.A. II. Series.
HG173.C678 1995
332--dc20   95-30695
                                                  CIP

Printed on acid-free paper.

Printed in the United States of America

Introduction

The questions of how fragile the banking and financial system is and, if it is fragile, what are the consequences for the stability of the system ('systemic risk') and how should public policy cope with it in order to protect the economy, are among the most important economic issues of the day. The rash of bank failures and large and well publicized losses in the securities and newly developed derivatives markets in the 1980s and 1990s in many countries throughout the world have refocused attention on these questions for the first time since the widescale bank failures during the Great Depression of the 1930s.

The papers collected in this volume are those presented at a conference which was held at the University of Limburg in Maastricht, the Netherlands on September 7–9, 1994. The conference was cosponsored by the Limburg Institute of Financial Economics (LIFE) at the University of Limburg and the *Journal of Financial Services Research*, with the financial support of Ernst & Young, Europe. The co-organizers were George G. Kaufman of Loyola University of Chicago and Harald A. Benink of the University of Limburg. The conference brought together leading banking experts from academe, public policy-makers, and financial institutions from both the United States and Europe to explore the issues related to financial fragility and systemic risk.

The first two days of the three-day conference were devoted to primarily academic analyses of the issues and attended primarily by academics. The last day included a wider range of both presenters and audience. This volume contains the papers and discussants' comments of all three conference days. Moreover, a special issue of the *Journal of Financial Services Research* (vol. 9, nos. 3/4) is published containing the contributions of the first academic days and two of the papers presented on the third day.

The papers presented during the academic part of the conference examine financial fragility and its potential consequences for both the private sector and public policy from a wide range of perspectives. The first set of papers identifies and discusses the sources of perceived fragility in financial institutions and markets and its potential consequences throughout the economy. Papers were presented by Hyman P. Minsky, George J. Benston and George G. Kaufman, Charles W. Calomiris, and Franklin R. Edwards. The discussants were Jacques J. Sijben and Stuart I. Greenbaum. The second set of papers examines private sector solutions to dealing with the fragility and mitigating the consequences. The authors are Franco Bruni and Francesco Paternò, Robert A. Eisenbeis, Seha M. Tiniç, and Charles R. Taylor. The third set of papers examines regulatory (governmental) solutions. Papers were written by Paul M. Horvitz, David L. Mengle, and Harald A. Benink and David T. Llewellyn. The papers on both private and regulatory solutions were discussed by Christian de Boissieu, Claudio E. V. Borio and Charles A. E. Goodhart. Robert Z. Aliber gave a summary of the issues discussed at the academic part of the conference. During the last day the conference had a more general, less academic scope.

H. A. Benink (Ed.), Coping with Financial Fragility and Systemic Risk, 1–2.
© 1995 *Kluwer Academic Publishers. Printed in the Netherlands.*

The lectures were given by Barry Riley, Jerry L. Jordan, Andrew D. Crockett, and H. Onno Ruding. The discussants were Marius van Nieuwkerk, Paul Rutteman and Anna J. Schwartz.

As co-organizer of the conference I would like to thank George J. Benston (Emory University), Franklin R. Edwards (Columbia University), Robert A. Eisenbeis (University of North Carolina), George G. Kaufman (Loyola University of Chicago), and Paul M. Horvitz (University of Houston), co-editors of the *Journal of Financial Services Research*, for their strong support in organizing this conference. Special thanks are offered to my co-organizer George G. Kaufman. His continuous attention and support has substantially improved the quality of the conference. Furthermore, I would like to acknowledge the kind secretarial support by Nathalie Jansen and Carina Wijnands at the University of Limburg. Finally, Ernst & Young is credited for its financial and organizational support. Especially, I would like to thank the following Ernst & Young partners: André J. Bindenga, Jules W. Muis, and Jan J. Nooitgedagt.

July 1995   Harald A. Benink

                                                                  Limburg Institute of
                                                                  Financial Economics (LIFE),
                                                                  University of Limburg

2

Journal of Financial Services Research 9: 197–208 (1995)
© 1995 Kluwer Academic Publishers

Financial Factors in the Economics of Capitalism

HYMAN P. MINSKY
*Distinguished Fellow, The Jerome Levy Economics Institute of Bard College, Blithewood,
Annandale-on-Hudson, NY 12504-5000, U.S.A.*

1. Overview

The conference's title, "Coping with Financial Fragility: a Global Perspective," implies that financial fragility is a meaningful economic concept. Its existence, not always but from time to time, is accepted as an attribute of capitalist economies. However the structure of the dominant macro- and microeconomic theories of our time, which are built upon the modern version of Walrasian general equilibrium theory, ignores the financial dimensions of capitalist economies.[1] If economic theory is to be relevant, for the intensely financial world in which we live, then an economic theory which fully incorporates financial factors into the determination of the behavior in the economy is needed. Such a theory should not hold that financial factors are "exogenous shocks" to the economy or explain whatever malfunctioning of the economy that takes place as the result of the incompetence of central bankers.[2]

Even though modern economic theory finds no place for financial factors in the determination of the course of the economy through time, modern capitalist economies use public powers, either through the Treasury or a central bank, (1) to prevent and contain financial instability, the danger of which is presumed to increase as the fragility and complexity of the financial structure increases; and (2) to pick up the pieces and fix the financial structure after an episode of instability damages financial structures.

Thus, a consensus exists that the public wisdom needs to be applied to create institutions and conventions so that capitalist economies can cope with the economic instability that is an apparently inherent attribute of capitalism. This consensus also holds that individual exertion, as aggregated into the behavior of markets, cannot be relied upon to ensure either the stability of economies with complex financial structures or a speedy halt to and recovery after a bout of instability. The rationale for intervention lies in the association of downside financial instability with serious depressions and of upside financial instability with serious inflations.

Thus, a discord exists between the economic theory that purportedly guides policy, which finds no place for money, finance, and endogenously determined instability, and economic institutions and usages, whose purposes are to contain endogenous tendencies towards financial instability and to offset the consequences of instabilities that do occur.

In chronicles of business cycles, such as those of Schumpeter (1939) and Friedman and Schwartz (1963), the differentiating factor between (Friedman and Schwartz's) mild

(Schumpeter's Kitchen) and (Friedman and Schwartz's) deep depression (Schumpeter's Juglar) cycles is the extent of financial involvement; deep depression cycles are characterized by financial crises (Schumpeter) or ı decline in the money supply (Friedman and Schwartz). A stylized interpretation of the information about the more serious business cycles of the capitalist epoch is that over a span of years characterized by minor cycles the financial structure changes so that a generalized "overindebtedness" arises. This overindebtedness cannot be sustained, and a more serious decline, accompanied by financial crises and decreases in the quantity of bank liabilities results.[3]

In capitalist economies a change from financial robustness to financial fragility happens over extended periods in which, in the aggregate, serious financial problems do not occur. Gain-seeking behavior by business men, bankers (financiers), and households is affected by the effect that success has in attenuating risk aversion.[4] The results are changes in observed portfolio compositions. Over a run of good times, the liability structures of households and firms change so that ever larger proportions of their gross cash flows (incomes) are prior committed to the fulfillment of obligations as specified in their liabilities. The evolution of household and firm liability structures during good times increases the exposure of financial intermediaries to a failure of their assets to perform.

A failure of the assets of financial institutions to perform leads to decreases in the flow of cash to, and increases the aversion to risk of, financial institutions. The result is a decrease in the financing of consumption and investment spending via financial intermediaries. This decrease in financing leads to decreases in investment and consumption spending, which, in turn, decreases the flow of profits and wages available to fulfill outstanding contracts.

Thus, financial fragility is not a characteristic of a structure of financial liabilities in isolation. It is a characteristic of an economy in which the funds available to meet payment commitments on liabilities are determined by income flows (gross profits for firms, and mainly wages for households), even as these income flows are determined by investment and consumption spending. Investment and consumption spending are "financed" by a combination of internal funds (retained earnings for firms) and borrowings.

Some statements, which are on the surface paradoxes, emerge from these interactions among firms, households, and financial units. One such statement is that "Investment takes place at any time because units expect investment to take place in the future"; another is that "the greater the investment financed by financial intermediaries, the greater is the likelihood that the assets of financial intermediaries will perform."

A decline in investment activity leads to a deterioration of profits of businesses and a decline in the wage incomes of households. In a heavily indebted economy

1. even minor declines in profits and wages can lead to increases in nonperforming assets in the portfolios of financial institutions.
2. even minor increases in interest rates can lead to increases in nonperforming assets in the portfolio of financial institutions.
3. even minor increases in wages can lead to pressure on profit flows and therefore to an increase in nonperforming assets.

4

As businesses, households, and financial institutions try to compensate for the shortfall in their cash flows by selling assets, i.e., as they try to make position by selling out position, a serious decline in the market price of both financial and capital assets can result. Such declines lower the mark to market net worth of economic units and adversely affect the demand for consumption and investment output.

If unconstrained, an adverse interactive process by which the path of aggregate demand is determined can lead to a collapse of income, employment, and asset prices; whereas a favorable interactive process can lead to an expansion of income, employment, and asset prices. However, in a modern big government capitalist economy, government deficits are an important determinant of aggregate profits. The relative size of government in an economy determines the sensitivity of gross profits to the pace of investment: the greater government demand and government financing of private demand, relative to the privately financed demand for investment output, the smaller the sensitivity of gross profits to the pace of private investment. If gross profits are sustained, or even increased, because government deficits, either built into tax and spending schedules or as a result of discretionary fiscal measures, increase whenever private investment declines, then the instability of financial markets is likely to be contained.[5]

Aspects of modern capitalism, such as the radical increase in the size and scope of government in the economy and the greater flexibility of central banks that are not bound by gold standard constraints, have diminished the likelihood that financial crises will emerge and have ameliorated the severity of crises that do occur. The current much larger share of government in the advanced capitalist economies means that aggregate profits cannot fall to the low ratios to gross product that occurred in earlier times.

An integrated model of the economy which makes financial instability endogenous can be set up in terms of two submodels. One is the submodel of the financial structure, which is taken up in the next section. The financial structure submodel is formulated in terms of the interrelated set of balance sheets and income statements of the economy, and the relation between flows of cash towards a unit and the commitments to pay cash that are embodied in liabilities. In a second section that follows, a model of how income flows, in particular how aggregate profits are determined, is presented. This is followed by a section in which the characteristics of a formal model which integrates the financial structure and the determination of incomes model are presented. The final section states some conclusions.

2. The financial struture submodel

Economies are complex multidimensional systems. Robustness and resilience are two attributes which a system may possess. Robustness means that small shocks to the system are absorbed without much difficulty; resilience means that a system bounces back after a shock. Fragility negates robustness and resilience: it therefore means that the response of the system to small disturbances or small changes can be large and that after a disturbance the system does not bounce back. We can set up the problem of fragility/robustness in terms of a line which stretches from robustness on the left to fragility on the right.

On any date, every economic unit can be placed at some point on this representation of the degree of robustness and fragility of its financial structure. Where a unit is placed on the robustness/fragility line depends upon the relation between the unit's cash flows (profits, wages, taxes, and cash flows from owned assets) and its payment commitments as determined by its liability structure. The placing of the units of an economy on this line leads to a frequency distribution of financially fragile and robust units.[6]

The argument will be in terms of an economic unit, which could be a firm, household, financial institution, or government unit. It is useful to divide the cash-flows-to-payment commitment relation of economic units into three classes—namely, hedge, speculative, and Ponzi financing units.

For hedge financing units, the income cash flows are expected to be large enough so that the contractual payments on account of both interest and principal on its liabilities can be met from its income cash flows during every period over an extended horizon. Inasmuch as equity liabilities do not commit payments, the larger the equity share in the financing structure of a unit, the greater the likelihood that the unit is a hedge financing unit. Equity and long-term debt financing are attributes of hedge financing units.

For the second class of units, that of speculative financing units, the cash flow earned, either from operations or from the way its assets perform, is sufficient to pay the interest due on debts, but insufficient to meet the payments due on the principal of its maturing liabilities. To meet its payment commitments, such a unit has to refinance, i.e., roll over, maturing debts. Speculative financing units are dependent upon the "normal functioning" of financial markets and institutions. Disruption of financing channels, such as occurs when banks fail, can adversely affect speculative financing units.

For Ponzi financing units, the cash flows, from operations or from the way its assets perform, are not large enough to meet both the interest payments on their debts and all payments due on their maturing liabilities. Such units not only have to refinance or roll over maturing debts, but they have to borrow funds to pay interest. Ponzi financing units capitalize interest on debts. On the balance sheet of private units, this means that the equity account is decreased and the debt account is increased: the debt equity ratio increases for Ponzi financing units.[7] As the equity account goes towards zero for a private Ponzi unit, the ability to Ponzi finance ends.[8]

Financial fragility and robustness (in the first instance) are attributes of the balance sheet and income statement of individual business firms, households, and other economic units. For an economy, the greater the ratio of hedge financing units, the more robust its financial structure, the greater the ratio of speculative and Ponzi financing units, the more fragile its financial structure. Financial institutions which hold the liabilities of firms and households as assets are propagation and amplifying or dampening factors in an episode of financial instability; such institutions need not be, though they may be, the triggering factor in an episode of financial instability.

In an economy where the rolling over of debts is a common characteristic of business processes, the continued viability of banking and financial market intermediaries is important for the income-generating process. The real bills doctrine, the commercial loan theory of banking, rested on the critical role of short-term debt which was rolled over during the course of trade and commerce. (Viner, 1937)

However, financial institutions which are short-term debtors and hold longer term assets are especially vulnerable to increases in interest rates. Large increases in interest rates can transform speculative financing units into Ponzi units. For Ponzi units, the higher the interest rates, the quicker the exhaustion of the equity as interest is capitalized. It is also worth noting that if long-term debts have a floating rate, then a rise in interest rates can lead to a need to capitalize at least some interest that falls due. When monetary policy leads to the very high interest rates, such as those which prevailed in the early 1980s, hedge financing units can become speculative units, and speculative units can become Ponzi units. The robustness of the financial structure can be undermined by excessively high interest rates.[9]

In order to get to the financial instability hypothesis from the hedge, speculative, or Ponzi financing structure of balance sheets, particular empirical generalizations have to be posited. One is that over a course of years during which a capitalist economy does well the rate of growth of private debts exceeds the rate of growth of the underlying income that supports such debts. In particular, payment commitments due to business indebtedness outpace gross profits available to support such payments. A second assertion is that a change in the composition of debts occurs over a run of good times, in that short-term debt financing increases relative to long-term debt and equity financing. Furthermore, financial layering increases as new financial institutions, with novel balance sheet assets and liabilities, emerge in response to perceived profit opportunities.

As a result of the growth of debt relative to incomes, and short-term debts relative to long-term debts and equity, an increasing proportion of units become dependent upon the "normal functioning" of financial markets in which debts can be floated or rolled over. Disruptions in these markets, which may be the result of nominal interest rates becoming greater than those that entered into the calculations of borrowers and lenders, can have disastrous and contagious effects. As high interest rates lower the prices of long-term assets at financial institutions, the equity capital of these institutions can be impaired.

Over a period of extended good times, changes in the way investment and positions in the stock of capital assets are financed occur. This leads to the closer articulation betweeen the cash flows to businesses and households which result from the performance in the economy, and the cash flows from these sectors due to payments mandated by their liability structures. Financial innovations and changes in financial practices are part of the process that increases the fragility of financial structures over the run of good times, even as legislation and administrative decisions, after a bout of fragility and instability, try to shut the door to any future replication of the recent instability.[10]

As was argued earlier, at any moment of time the economic units can be thought of as determining a frequency distribution on the robustness/fragility axis. The stylized facts about the changes that take place in balance sheets and payment commitments of economic units over an extended period of good times mean that this frequency distribution migrates to the right, i.e., fragility increases. With such a shift to the right, the likelihood of a serious disruption in financial markets increases.

3. The economic theory of a capitalist economy:
The determination of cash flows submodel

A modern capitalist economy is a different beast from the economy envisaged by those engaged in the project of advancing general equilibrium theory. When Walras sent his classic work to Henri Poincaré, Poincaré commented that Walras makes two critical assumptions:

> . . . you regard men as infinitely selfish and infinitely farsighted. The first hypothesis may perhaps be admitted in a first approximation, the second may call for some reservations (Israel and Ingrau 1990).[11]

Poincaré was willing to grant Walras's agents infinite selfishness, i.e., the maximization of utility as their sole objective, but he was not willing to grant them infinite (perfect) foresight. The assumption of perfect foresight remains the blocking point to accepting the Arrow–Debreau proof that an intertemporal general equilibrium exists and that this result leads to relevant propositions about the behavior of a capitalist economy. That a general equilibrium exists in a pure market economy, where there are no institutions which prevent disequilibrium or contain the consequences of disequilibrium, is accepted as an article of faith.[12]

Once Walras's general equilibrium theory, or some modern variant, is accepted as the "true" representation of the economy, the neutrality of money, i.e., the quantity theory of money, follows. One postulate of general equilibrium theory is the assumption that utility functions are "over the reals," i.e., that only real variables, such as goods and services, enter the utility function (Hahn, 1985). One aspect of the Keynesian break with Walrasian theory is the recognition that preference functions are over wealth as well as the reals. This implies that in a modern capitalist economy, where financial instruments, which are often offset in part by financial liabilities, are major components of household wealth, the current prices of assets and liabilities, as well as their ratios to the prices of current outputs, are factors determining both consumption and investment demand.

The alternative to beginning one's theorizing about capitalist economies by positing utility functions over the reals and production functions with something labeled K (called capital) as a variable is to begin with the interlocking balance sheets of the economy. Within a closed economy, every financial liability of any unit shows up on the balance sheet of another unit as a financial asset; in addition any entry on a balance sheet requires an offsetting entry either on the same or the other side of the balance sheet. A basic structural characteristic of a capitalist economy is given by the cash flows that the interlocking balance sheets generate together with the cash flows generated by the production and sale of the outputs of the economy.

The units of a closed economy can be conveniently grouped into businesses, households, financial institutions, and government. Every liability is a commitment to pay some form of money as stated in the contract which sets up the instrument. A liability is a commitment to make payments on principle and interest either

1. along a time axis as stated in the contract,

2. on demand, or
3. upon the occurrence of specified contingencies.

The third, contingent payments, is of importance in the explosive emergence of a liquidity crisis because long-term debt typically becomes demand debt when any default of payment commitments happens.

In contrast to the assumption of perfect foresight, which orthodox theory needs in order to demonstrate the existence of an equilibrium, the financial instability hypothesis assumes, as Keynes does, that units live in a world with intractable uncertainty: not only is their foresight imperfect, but sensate agents know that their foresight is imperfect. When the economy is tranquil, interest rates on short-term financing are lower than on long term liabilities, because lending units with imperfect foresight believe that they have better knowledge about the short-term than about the long-term prospects of borrowing units. In tranquil times, as risk aversion attenuates, units which have established mutually profitable relations with bankers for the short-term financing of short-term positions find it feasible and prospectively profitable to introduce some short-term financing of longer term assets into their liability structures. Bankers as merchants of debt are all too willing to teach customers with whom they have profitable relations how to use short-term debt to increase their "bottom line." Middle men of the commercial paper markets also find it profitable to teach customers how to use short-term debt for longer term financing. Customers find the use of short-term debt profitable.[13]

Even in the absence of the use of short funds for long-term purposes, the continued operation of a firm requires that short-term credits such as that for inventories be refinanced: the short maturity leads to the need to finance the principle amount in order to continue or to expand operations.

By the very nature of their demand liabilities, banks need to roll over their debts. Typically, new deposits, as well as the flow of cash as their assets perform, offset the major part of banks' losses through the clearings. In addition, banks keep secondary reserve assets which they believe that they can sell in broad markets to offset transitory reserve drains losses of funds through the clearings.

Short-term financing, which requires the regular refinancing of positions, emerges from profit-seeking, cost-minimizing behavior, and portfolio preferences of risk-averse individuals. Such rolling over financing makes borrowers vulnerable to changes in financing terms, such as increases in interest rates and insistence on collateral. For heavily indebted organizations, whose incomes do not increase as short-term interest rates rise, a rise in market interest rates can lead to total interest costs exceeding the income available to pay such debts. Then, either by not spending accruing funds to maintain capital assets or by borrowing to cover such interest payments, the firm runs down its equity base: it increases its debt to equity ratio.

4. Determination of profits

Although household and government debts are significant factors in the total indebtedness of a modern capitalist economy, the debts of firms and the income of firms—the gross profit flows—are of primary importance. In a capitalist economy, the total gross profits of firms are determined by the composition of aggregate demand. Capital assets are valuable, because aggregate demand is large enough to make them scarce; such assets are not valuable because they are productive. The values of capital assets are derived from the cash flows that are generated. The profits earned by specific capital assets as embedded in particular firms are determined by the comparative success or failure of these firms in the competition among capitals for profits and by the aggregate of profits as determined by the composition of aggregate demand. Our concern is with the determination of aggregate profits, not with the determination of the success or failure of a unit in the competition among capitals for profits.

Following Jerome Levy and M. Kalecki, we know that

$$\text{Profits} = \text{Investment} + \text{Government Deficit} - \text{Balance of Trade Deficit.}[14] \quad (1)$$

This relation is true under heroic simplifying assumptions to the effect that all wages are spent on consumption and no capital income is used to finance consumption; investment is financed internally by retained earnings and externally by selling bonds to banks; government spending is on current output, wages, and transfer payments; and the balance of trade is on goods and services.

In this equation, the government deficit is the result of taxing and spending functions in which the current level of profits and wages determines the deficit or surplus of the economy. The balance of payments, which includes receipts and spending on account of foreign investment and foreign debts, is not the relevant concept of the foreign balance for the determination of aggregate demand.

The wage bill associated with any level of aggregate profits is determined by the volume of output which needs to be produced so that, in the aggregate, the sum of the individual profits adds up to the total profits.

5. A formal model that combines the submodels

A simple recursive model, which is too complex for an analytical solution but which has been simulated, relates investment to internal cash and the ratio of capital asset prices and output prices (Delli Gatti, Gallegati, Minsky, 1994). An algebraic statement of the combined effect of the price (P) of capital relative to the price of investment output and the availability of internal cash upon investment behavior takes the form of

$$\text{Investment} = (a)\, P(\text{capital})/P(\text{investment}) + (b)\, (\text{internal funds}) \quad (2)$$

Internal funds are given by profits minus the payments on debts (interest plus payments on principle that are due).

$$\text{Internal Funds}(t) = \text{Profits}(t-1) - r\text{Debts}(t-1). \quad (3)$$

Debts grow by the difference between investment and internal funds.

$$\text{Debts}(t) = \text{Investment}(t - 1) - \text{Internal Funds}(t - 1) + \text{Debts}(t-1). \qquad (4)$$

Additional accounting equations, as well a simplifying assumption that all debts are to banks, that have money as their only liability, are part of the formal model.

The results of the simulations of this model depend upon the values assigned to parameters. One result using a priori acceptable parameter values is a four-phase business cycle. The phases are

1. A recover phase, where profits are increasing even as indebtedness falls;
2. A robust expansion during which profits increase as debts increase;
3. boom, in which indebtedness increases even as profits begin to fall; and
4. deflation phase in which debts and profits both fall.

Because of an assumed government deficit, which is kept constant over the cycle (for the sake of simplicity), the fall in total profits of phase 4 is contained. With somewhat different parameter values and without the support of the government deficit, the downside potential of profits and debts can become open-ended. As profits go to zero, the values of capital assets and investment go to zero. A debt deflation as described by Fisher is one of the possible results of this similar formulation.

6. Conclusion

The lesson from the modeling exercise for the understanding of financial fragility is that the overall fragility of the economy depends not just upon the course of financial commitments but also on the course of cash flows. One source of the difference between the behavior of capitalist economies in the post–World War II period and their behavior in the interwar and earlier periods is the fact that the much greater relative size of government in the postwar period than in earlier times has made it impossible for profits to collapse as completely now as in the past. In capitalist economies, stabilization policy is successful to the extent that it stabilizes profits.

Thus, the change in the importance of government has changed the fragility/resilience relations in capitalist financial structures. Earlier in the post–World War II epoch, during the era of active contracyclical fiscal policies, aggregate profits tended to rise during the recession phases of business cycles due to increase in the government's deficit. With aggregate profits stabilized and even rising, a reduction in private debts, induced by various "crunches" in financial markets, took place in an orderly fashion. Once the downside pressure on aggregate profits was reduced by the impact of the government deficit upon the aggregate of profits, the decline in financial and capital asset prices was contained. With the potential decline in asset prices contained, a regime of lower interest rates soon led to a revival of investment.[15]

The two main crises of banking in the United States since the establishment of Federal Reserve System were the breakdown of the banking and financial system over the period 1929–1933 and the crisis of thrifts and commercial banks in the late 1980s to early 1990s. In both cases the Federal Reserve was not the institution that reconstituted the key parts of the financial system which had broken down.

In 1933, the Reconstruction Finance Corporation, an agency of the Treasury, was the key institution in restarting the banking system after the bank holiday. In the recent crisis of the thrifts and of commercial banks, it was the deposit insurance facilities and ultimately the Treasury that prevented any pass-through of losses on assets to the liabilities of the depository institutions. Both of these crises were solvency crises, not liquidity crises. In the modern world, solvency crises are more dangerous than liquidity crises. The overall performance of the economy is enhanced by the ability of the Treasury to step in and sustain the solvency of critical financial institutions.

Because of the nature of the financial structures necessary for a successful capitalism, capitalism remains a flawed economic structure which is susceptible to cycles of financial expansion leading to financial fragility and therefore to the potential for debt inflations and deep depressions.

Because government needs to be big in order to contain thrusts to deep depressions, government and its institutions can do great harm, especially if their actions are based upon "Pollyanna" views of the wonders of markets and a "true faith" that markets always know best. Policy makers need to adopt a skeptical attitude toward claims that universal truths about economic policy (relevant for all economies at all times) have been derived from economic science.

The experience of the United States with the practical monetarism of the Volcker years (1979–1982) shows the error of the simplistic application of strongly maintained policy slogans. By only looking at one element of the balance sheet of banks and thrifts (the liabilities called money), the Federal Reserve during the Volcker years acquiesced in the stripping away of the equity of the thrifts. This meant that the only equity which the thrifts had was the value of the endorsement of their liabilities by deposit insurance funds.

For big government to be able to prevent great depressions, it needs to be able to stabilize aggregate profit flows by running large contra-cyclical deficits and to have sufficient muscle in financial markets so that it can refinance failed financial institutions. This requires that the credit worthiness of government be beyond question. This means that when the economy is functioning normally the government validates its debts by its income flows, i.e. there is no need to resort to inflation in order to reduce the ratio of government debt to gross domestic product. A government that is big enough to contain the depression proneness of capitalism needs a tax system which raises sufficient revenues so that over the run of good and bad years the ratio of government debt to gross domestic product remains in a comfort zone of from 25 to 50 percent of gross domestic product.

If successful capitalism requires government to be a large part of the economy, then it is important that government spending play a constructive role in the development of resources: government cannot be restricted to the financing of consumption.

Notes

1. The postulate of general equilibrium theory which ensures that money and finance are excluded from the core of the theory is that variables in preference systems are "real" goods and services.
2. As is well known, the revolution that Keynes believed he was bringing to economic theory has been transformed into special assumptions, such as price rigidity or peculiar asymmetries in information, which are added to the basic asumptions underlying the corpus of orthodox theory. In his introduction to the French edition of *The General Theory*, Keynes stated that his aim in writing the volume was to escape from the Quantity Theory of Money. As the general equilibrium theory, which dominates economic theory, has preference functions, production functions, and maximizing behavior determine outputs and relative prices, there is no place in this theory for money or finance to affect the critical variables of the economy. In Minsky (1975), Minsky (1986), and too many articles to recall, I have first interpreted Keynes's *General Theory* as setting out an investment theory of aggregate income and a financial theory of investment and then constructed what I have called a financial instability hypothesis interpretation of Keynes. This article presents and applies this hypothesis to current (1994–1995) concerns.
3. Irving Fisher started his exposition of what happens during a debt-deflation from an initial position of over indebtedness. He did not explain how overindebtedness occurs. This was an obvious weakness in his theory. Over indebtedness theories of great depression flourished in the 1930s (Hart, 1937; Clark, 1935) before Keynesian economics in the stripped forms pioneered by J.R. Hicks (1937) and A. Hansen and the econometric forecasting models took over as the dominant macroeconomic theory.
4. In this view the propensity of the agents in an economy to take risks is endogenously determined: it reflects the experience of the agents. The postulate anent the formation of risk aversion is that a run of good times (economic success) leads to an attenuation of risk aversion while any cascade of losses or a period in which asset prices fall (economic failure) leads to an increase in risk aversion. In an economy where aggregate profit flows are sustained even after a set of financial market disruptions that in themselves would tend to increase risk aversion, the increase in risk aversion seems to attenuate in a few years. The institutionaliza-tion of portfolio investments in the post-war era, as a result of the rise of pension and mutual funds in an environment characterized by shallow and short recessions, has led to the flows of funds seeking portfolio investments being sustained even during recessions. As a result financial markets are more resilient now than in earlier episodes.
5. In analyzing the impact of government deficits on aggregate profits, only that government spending that leads to the financing of domestic demand should be included on the spending side in the determination of aggregate profits. Thus the government spending caused by the refinancing of the savings and loans after their debacle cannot be considered as profit determining. In a similar way interest on the government debt that is paid to foreign owners of government debt is not part of the government spending that has a positive effect upon domestic profits.
6. This frequency distribution changes through time. A shift to the right of the frequency distribution repre-sents an increase in the fragility of the economy.
7. We do not draw up balance sheets for governments. Within the conceptual apparatus of the financial instability hypothesis, governments can be hedge, speculative, or Ponzi financing units. A "normal" deficit by a government unit takes the form of a rise in debts that is offset or even more than offset by asset accumulation. However, for governments that are Ponzi financing there is no asset accumulation to accom-pany the rise in debt. In the virtual balance sheet of the government, an increase in debt brought about by the need to capitalize interest must be offset by a decrease in equity.
8. In 1995, for many governments which are Ponzi financing, the deficit is less than the total interest paid on their indebtedness. If the growth of their tax bases, in the form of GDP growth and their willingness to tax, are sufficiently great, then the situation is sustainable even though it may not be good policy. If the total debt is large enough relative to GDP and the ability to tax is constrained, then the situation is not sustainable.
9. Over the long course of their history the savings and loan associations were ostensibly speculative units, but because of the interest-rate pattern that ruled they were in fact hedge units. It can be argued that there was an implicit contract between the savings and loan associations and the government that the cost of funds was not to be such that they would lose on the carry of their assets, long-term, fully amortized fixed-rate mortgages.

10. It is worth noting that the prohibition of market-determined margin requirements for household purchases of securities is one of the regulations set in place in the aftermath of the great collapse that is still in force.
11. Henri Poincare, as cited in Israel and B. Ingrau, *The Invisible Hand*, MIT Press, 1990. The source is W. Jaffe, *The Correspondence of Leon Walras and Related Papers* (3 vols.), Amsterdam: North Holland, 1965.
12. An alternative view to the effect that the basic economic process leads to intermittent breakdowns of the equilibrating powers of markets and that a semblance of tranquility results from the impacts of institutional rigidities and policy interventions is to be found in Ferri and Minsky.
13. In turbulent periods the current financial structure can lead to a bidding up of short-term interest rates. The rise in short-term rates will often not be accompanied by an equal rise in long-term rates. In part this reflects a belief that in time tranquility will be established. In turbulent times agents in the economy are more assured about the long-run than of the short-run behavior of the economy.
14. For an explication of these relations, see chapter 8 of Minsky (1986).
15. This was especially true when the impact of crunches was concentrated on the thrift industry and housing.

References

Clark, Evans. *The Internal Debts of the United States*. Twentieth Century Fund, (New York, The MacMillan Co. 1933)

Delli Gatti, D., Gallegati, M., and Minsky, H.P. "Financial Institutions, Economic Policy, and the Dynamic Behavior of the Economy." Working paper No. 126, Jerome Levy Economics Institute, Bard College. 1994.

Ferri, Piero, and H.P. Minsky. "Market Processes and Thwarting Systems." *Structural Change and Economic Dynamics* 1, (1991).

Fisher, Irving. "The Debt Deflation Theory of Great Depressions." *Econometrica* 1 (Oct 1933) pp. 337–57.

Friedman, Milton, and Schwartz, Anna, *A Monetary History of The United States* 1867–1960 (Princeton, Princeton University Press, 1963).

Hahn, Frank *Money and Inflation*, (Cambridge Mass. MIT Press. 1985)

Hansen, Alvin. *Monetary Theory and Fiscal Policy,* (New York, McGraw Hill, 1949).

Hart, A.G., *Debts and Recovery*. Twentieth Century Fund (New York, The MacMillan Co, 1938)

Hicks, J.R. "Mr. Keynes and the 'Classics': A Suggestd Interpretation," *Econometrica* 5 1937.

Israel, G and Ingrau, B *The Invisible Hand* (Cambridge Mass. MIT Press, 1990)

Kalecki, Michael, Selected Essays on the Dynamics of the Capitalist Economy (1933–1970) (Cambridge, Cambridge University Press, 1971)

Keynes, J. M. Preface to the French Edition of the General Theory, *The Collected Writings*, Vol. 7, (New York, St. Martins Press 1973)

Levy, SJ and Levy D *Profits In the American Economy*, (New York, Random House 1986)

Minsky, H.P. *John Maynard Keynes*. (New York, Columbia University Press, 1975).

Minsky, H.P. *Stabilizing an Unstable Economy*. (New Haven, Yale University Press, 1986).

Schumpeter, J. A., *Business Cycles*. (New York, Mc McGraw Hill, 1939).

Viner, Jacob *Studies in the Theory of International Trade*. (New York Harper and Brothers, Publishers, 1937).

Wolfson, Martin J. *Financial Crises: Understanding the Post War United States Experience. (Armonk, New York. M.E. Sharpe. 1986 1st ed. 1994 2nd ed.)*

14

G21   u.S.   15 - 46
E42
E58
G28

Journal of Financial Services Research 9: 209–240 (1995)
© 1995 Kluwer Academic Publishers

Is the Banking and Payments System Fragile?

GEORGE J. BENSTON
John H. Harland Professor of Finance, Accounting, and Economics, Emory University, Atlanta, GA 30322, U.S.A., and member of the Shadow Financial Regulatory Committee

GEORGE G. KAUFMAN
John F. Smith Professor of Banking and Finance, Loyola University of Chicago, Chicago, IL 60611, U.S.A. Consultant, Federal Reserve Bank of Chicago, and member of the Shadow Financial Regulatory Committee

In his introduction to *The Risk of Economic Crisis*, a compilation of papers presented at a conference sponsored by the National Bureau of Economic Research (NBER), Martin Feldstein (1991, p. 1) recognizes that, despite the inability of less developed countries to service their debts, the massive collapse of savings and loan associations in the United States, wide swings in currency exchange rates, the increase in corporate and personal debt, and the stock market crash of 1987, we have not suffered an economic crisis in recent years. Nevertheless, he asserts:

> But the risk of such an economic collapse remains. As Charles Kindleberger's distinguished and fascinating book (*Manias, Panics and Crashes: A History of Financial Crises* [Basic Books, 1978]) has ably demonstrated, economic crises have been with us as long as the market economy. At some point, greed overcomes fear and individual investors take greater risks in the pursuit of greater returns. A shock occurs and the market prices of assets begin to collapse. Bankruptcies of leveraged individuals and institutions follow. Banks and other financial institutions fail in these circumstances because they are inherently leveraged. The resulting failure of the payments mechanism and the inability to create credit bring on an economic collapse (Feldstein, 1991, pp. 1–2).

He goes on to conclude:

> The public interest in avoiding the failure of banks and other financial institutions argues strongly for government regulation and supervision of these institutions. Even Adam Smith explicitly advocated the regulation of banks because he recognized that their failure would have damaging effects on the economy more generally (Feldstein, 1991, p. 2).

The authors are indebted to participants at the Conference on Financial Fragility at the University of Limburg, Maastricht, The Netherlands, September 7–9, 1994, and also to Douglas Evanoff and Paul Horvitz for helpful comments.

15

Feldstein explains further his argument for regulation, as follows:

> The banking system as a whole is a "public good" that benefits the nation over and above the profits that it earns for the banks' shareholders. Systemic risks to the banking system are risks for the nation as a whole. Although the managements and shareholders of individual institutions are, of course, eager to protect the solvency of their own institutions, they do not adequately take into account the adverse effects to the nation of systemic failure. Banks left to themselves will accept more risk than is optimal from a systemic point of view. That is the basic case for government regulation of banking activity and the establishment of capital requirements (Feldstein, 1991, p. 15).

These statements by a distinguished economist (chair professor at Harvard, President and Chief Executive Officer of the NBER, and former chairman of the President's Council of Economic Advisers) which are repeated in substance by many other economists, bankers, legislators, regulators, members of the general public, and in particular by central bankers, serve to motivate this article. Is the banking and payments system unusually fragile? Are depository institutions (hereafter, simply called "banks") really prone to failure more than are other firms, and, if so, is the failure of one or several banks contagious, giving rise to banking panics, the collapse of the financial system, and severe damage to the macroeconomy? Do losses suffered by depositors in bank failures have more adverse impact on either other banks or the macroeconomy than losses suffered by creditors in the failures of nonbank firms have on other firms in the same industry and beyond?

Furthermore, has banking become increasingly subject to international contagion? This concern was well expressed by the then president of the Federal Reserve Bank of New York to the Seventh International Conference of Banking Supervisors: "the speed, volume, value, and complexity of international banking transactions have introduced new linkages and interdependencies between markets and institutions that have the potential to transmit problems and disruptions from place to place and institution to institution at almost breakneck speed" (Corrigan, 1992, p. 6).

In section 1 we consider the theories that appear to underlie Feldstein's and many other observers' belief that the banking and payments system is inherently unstable and prone to failure. Fractional reserve banking, discussed in section 1.1, has long been identified as the primary reason for this instability. In section 1.2 we describe and anlayze the sources of fragility in fractional reserve banking that may threaten the survival of the banking system as a whole. Four sources are identified, each of which implies somewhat different public policies: (1) excessive expansion of credit; (2) asymmetric information resulting in inability of depositors to value bank assets correctly, particularly when economic conditions worsen; (3) shocks originating outside the banking system that are independent of the financial condition of banks and either cause depositors to change their liquidity preferences or cause reductions in bank reserves (high-powered money); and (4) institutional and legal restrictions that weaken banks, making them unnecessarily prone to failure. In all of these scenarios, deposit withdrawals produce instability in the banking system only if they cause a reduction in aggregate bank reserves. If the withdrawals are redeposited at other banks, there may be costly churning and some deadweight losses, but no threat to the survival of the banking or payments system.

We review much of the empirical research on the sources of bank failures and banking panics in section 2. This review leads us to conclude that the primary causes of past failures have been reasons (3) and (4): exogenous withdrawals of bank reserves (largely gold), and institutional and legal restrictions (primarily on U.S. banks). Thus, we do not view banks and the banking system as inherently fragile. Nor, in the absence of poorly operating central banks or undue imprudent restrictions on bank activities, do we find that bank failures are any more contagious or any more costly than failures in other important industries.

The evidence on bank problems being contagious and spreading quickly and indiscriminately through the financial system and beyond is reviewed in section 3. The evidence does not support this concern.

Bank failures, though, might be costly, such that the benefits from preventing them with government action might be worth the cost. We examine these costs in section 4. In section 5, we discuss the role of the lender of last resort, either as a direct lender to individual banks experiencing liquidity problems or as a supplier of liquidity to the banking system.

From our review of the evidence we conclude in section 6 that banking is not a "public good" and that the fragility of the banking and payments system should not be a public concern, other than for preventing actions, including those by the government, that either directly or indirectly increase the risk profile of banks or the potential losses from bank failure to other banks or the government (taxpayers). It is losses to taxpayers through government-provided deposit insurance and other noncontracting third parties (externalities) from bank failures, not bank failures per se, that are of primary public concern. These adverse externalities can be virtually eliminated by imposing an adequate capital requirement on banks, made effective by a system of structured early intervention and resolution. Other presumably prudential restrictions on banks' activities should be removed, as these make the banking and payments system less efficient and individual bank failures more likely and more costly.

1. Theories of banking and payments system instabiliy

1.1. The potential instability of fractional reserve banking

All firms might fail. Firms fail when they invest in products and processes that turn out through time to generate a smaller cash flow than the amount required to pay bills and service debt, so that eventually their net worth declines below zero. Some failures are the result of frauds. For example, the promoters or managers of nonfinancial firms may claim that they have made potentially very profitable discoveries that do not, in fact, exist. Nonbank financial firms may practice a Ponzi scheme, where they pay early investors high returns to entice new investments which are used to pay the high returns, until the scheme collapses. None of these situations is new, and all continue to the present day and, most likely, will be with us in the future.[1]

Banks differ from other financial institutions and nonbank firms in several ways that may make them more prone to failure. They are funded predominantly by short-term and demand debt (deposits) primarily to satisfy the demand for such par-value securities by households and business firms. They usually hold assets that cannot be sold quickly except at substantial discounts from par (loans) or that have fixed-interest rates and longer maturities (bonds and mortgages). Because banks typically hold relatively low levels of capital, rapid withdrawals of deposits (runs) that force equally rapid liquidation of assets or declines in the value of assets for other reasons can render banks economically insolvent. Thus, banks are more fragile than financial or nonfinancial firms that are proportionately less funded by short-term debt and more funded by equity (less leveraged). Each of these sources of potential instability—deposits and assets—is considered in the next two subsections. The relevance of these concerns to countries with deposit insurance or an effectively run central bank is discussed in the third sub-section.

1.1.1. Instability of deposits and bank currency.   If banks are perceived to be generating losses that threaten their net worth, creditors (depositors) can withdraw their funds very quickly. In response, because banks operate on a fractional reserve basis, holding only small amounts of cash, they might have to sell assets quickly, even if they have made borrowing arrangements with other (correspondent) banks. To the extent that some of their assets are not highly liquid because they have longer maturities, lower credit quality, and are customized, fire-sale losses are likely to be incurred.[2] Because banks typically hold relatively small amounts of capital, these fire-sale losses may render them insolvent. Thus, a liquidity problem may turn into a solvency problem.

In the normal course of events, the holders of bank liabilities (henceforth, depositors) have no reason to fear that their demands for repayment would not be met; if they did, they would not have deposited their funds in the bank. However, if depositors believe that their bank has or even might experience a loss in asset values that would be sufficient to render the bank insolvent, they have incentives to withdraw their funds immediately, i.e., to run. Because fears of insolvency at one bank raise concerns about insolvency at other banks, runs are widely perceived as being contagious. When many depositors run on many banks at once, a "banking panic" is said to result.

It is depositors' ability and, perhaps, propensity to run that is the basis for many people believing that the banking system is fragile. Because banks' deposit liabilities frequently serve as the means of payment (bank notes in earlier times, demand and possibly savings and time deposits in the 20th century), the presumed fragility of banks implies a concomitant fragility of the payments system.

As banks increasingly process payments among depositors in countries around the world, concerns have also arisen about the vulnerability of domestic payments systems to bank failures in other countries. A foreign bank might fail, and thus not transmit payments for funds for which domestic banks already have given depositors or other banks credit, as occurred in the failure of the Herstatt Bank in Germany in 1974. Conversely, the receiving banks might be unable to pay other banks with claims on them. At the least, a costly unraveling of claims might be required. Thus, a domestic payments system might be disrupted because a foreign bank failed.

1.1.2. Instability of bank lending and losses on bank assets. Banks that invest in long-term fixed-interest obligations subject themselves to interest-rate risk, to the extent that these obligations are funded with short-term and demand liabilities. Should interest rates increase, the value of the banks' assets will decline more than the value of their liabilities, and they could be rendered economically insolvent. Such was the situation for U.S. savings and loan associations and mutual savings banks in 1979–1981.

Some contemporary observers, such as Minsky (1972, 1977, 1991) and Kindleberger (1978), believe that commercial banking is inherently unstable because banks can and do fuel an euphoria-driven over expansion of credit that bids up asset prices (and is bound to crash) and money, by holding lower ratios of reserves to deposits than is prudent. (Monetary expansion, though, cannot occur without the concurrence of the central bank.) When (and if) some of the businesses or projects to which banks presumably over extended credit fail, asset prices decline sharply, and banks' assets are reduced in value. Knowledgeable depositors attempt to withdraw their funds (as described above). Such a run, ignited by the bursting of an asset bubble, may be contagious, either because many banks overextended credit at the same time or because depositors cannot or do not find it economic to distinguish among economically solvent and insolvent banks.

Kindleberger (1978) provides copious examples of financial collapses in one country that appear to have been transmitted to other countries, occasionally through the collapse of asset prices and banks. Eichengreen and Portes (1987, pp. 11–12) suggest an international linkage running from the default of foreign debt to the failure of banks holding that debt, or depositor withdrawals in anticipation of a foreign exchange-rate devaluation.

1.1.3. The relevance of banking instability to countries with deposit insurance or an effectively run central bank. A fractional-reserve banking system is not unstable if depositors who withdraw their funds either redeposit in other banks or purchase safe securities, such as government obligations, and the sellers deposit the proceeds in banks. If the funds are redeposited, total bank reserves do not change, as the receiving banks' reserves are increased to the same extent that the losing bank's reserves are depleted. As long as banks have approximately the same voluntary or required ratios of reserves, the money supply is not affected. Nor is total lending affected, other than some deadweight losses from a possible reshuffling of bank-customer relationships. This conclusion holds even if depositors shift their funds to foreign banks, as the foreign banks now have deposits on the original or another domestic bank.

However, some depositors might "run to currency" and keep their deposits out of the banking system, in the form of specie (gold and silver) in earlier times and government-produced currency in later times. Such a run to currency would reduce the reserves of the banking system, and some banks would be more likely to fail. Consequently, in the absence of actions by the central bank, if there were one, there could be a multiple contraction of the money supply. As Friedman and Schwartz (1963) demonstrate, when prices do not adjust quickly to the lower quantity of money the result usually is a business recession or depression. The situation is exacerbated when banks are forced to call in or forbear from renewing loans so that they can meet the decrease in deposits from decreases in assets (Bernanke, 1983).

However, central banks can and generally do offset the decrease in bank reserves with open market operations or direct (discount window) lending to banks. Thus, even a run to currency need not and should not result in a banking panic or general economic disaster in modern developed economies.

Furthermore, credible deposit insurance removes many depositors' incentives to run to currency, even if the bank were thought to be insolvent. Although uninsured depositors still have incentives to run, they are very likely to transfer their deposits to other, presumably safe banks. Almost all of these depositors with large deposit balances (over $100,000 in the United States) must use checks or wire transfers rather than currency to pay their bills. Furthermore, keeping large amounts of funds in specie or currency risks loss through theft. Lastly, these depositors often have loan relationships with the bank which are valuable and costly to replicate elsewhere, and their outstanding bank loans can be used to offset deposit losses. Hence, a run to currency in the present day in most developed countries appears to be an unlikely event.

Nevertheless, those concerned with the expansion and sudden contraction of bank deposits and loans claim that banking is unstable whether or not total bank reserves or reserve ratios remain the same. These observers believe that, when demand for bank loans is high, banks shift from secondary reserves to loans. In bad economic periods, even when depositors do not run to currency and even when the central bank offsets depletions in bank reserves, bank loans decline as some banks fail and other banks refuse to make or renew loans that appear to be risky. Thus, these observers believe that the banking system (and therefore also the payments system) is inherently unstable and cannot be controlled sufficiently well by a central bank to obviate difficulties in the rest of the economy.

1.2. The sources of instability in fractional reserve banking

It is important to distinguish among the sources of presumed past and possible future instability of the fractional reserve banking system, since alternative explanations imply different public policies. Four alternatives are analyzed: (1) excessive expansion of bank credit (which calls for controls over bank lending practices); (2) asymmetric information resulting in the inability of depositors to value bank assets accurately, particularly when economic conditions worsen (which calls for greater disclosure, or effective "inside" monitoring arrangements); (3) shocks originating outside the banking system, independent of the financial condition of banks, that either cause depositors to change their liquidity preferences or cause reductions in bank reserves (which is no longer relevant for most countries, unless their central banks act inappropriately, or which necessitates the provision of credible deposit insurance, either of which offers strong reasons for believing that banking panics should not occur); and (4) institutional and legal restrictions that weaken banks, making them unnecessarily prone to failure (some of these have been corrected and others can be corrected).

1.2.1. Excessive expansion of credit followed by forced liquidation and debt deflation. Fisher (1932, 1933), and contemporary writers, such as Minsky (1972, 1977, 1991), Kindleberger (1978), and Eichengreen and Portes (1987), see financial crises as emanating from or being exacerbated by overexpansion of credit. Fisher describes business cycles as beginning with an exogenous event, such as a new invention or discovery, that encourages new investment. Output and prices increase, which encourages debt-financed additional investment and speculation in anticipation of capital gains. Banks expand loans by drawing down reserves, which increases the money supply and raises the price level. Higher prices both fuel additional optimism and reduce the real value of debt, thereby further encouraging additional borrowing. Eventually, a state of overindebtedness is reached, defined by Fisher (1932, p. 9) as "whatever degree of indebtedness multiplies unduly the chances of becoming insolvent." At this point, the economy is fragile and a crisis may be triggered by debtors' or creditors' error of judgment. Debtors may be unable to repay their debts as scheduled, and creditors may refuse to refinance performing maturing debt. This leads to distress selling and asset-price deflation. Bank capital is depleted as bad loans are written off. Depositors run on banks that appear to be or might become insolvent, creating panics and further price declines, and reductions in output and employment. The process continues until widespread bankruptcy eliminates the overindebtedness or a reflationary monetary policy is adopted.

Minsky (1972, 1977, 1991) presents a similar description. He posits that a fragile financial environment is due to an increase in debt finance, a shift from long-term to short-term debt, and shifts from debt that can be repaid fully from cash flows expected from the operation of the assets financed (hedge debt), to debt where not all the principal can be repaid without selling the assets (speculative finance), to a situation where additional debt will have to be obtained to meet expected obligations (Ponzi finance). Financial institutions' margins of safety are reduced as they finance lower-quality debt. A loss of confidence or reduced expectations can set off a refinancing crisis, business failures, runs on banks, bank failures, and economic depression. The crisis can spread internationally when banks lend internationally.

Kindleberger (1978) tells the story by means of many anecdotes from centuries of European and U.S. history. A speculative mania is fueled by bank money and increasing velocity. As euphoria takes over, interest rates increase and people shift increasingly from money to goods, resulting in "overtrading." Capital inflows from foreign purchases of goods and assets lead to inflows of specie which fuel monetary expansion and more credit. The crash comes when enough people realize that the debt cannot be repaid. For a more recent period, he concludes:

> The bank failures . . . of 1974–86 . . . were brought on by booms in real estate, farm land, oil exploration and Third World lending that went to excess before they were cut short by recessions. . . . The bank failures . . . thus seemed to arise from an historical pattern of displacement, euphoria, boom in which many bankers lost sight of conventional and conservative standards of asset management, and in some cases crossed the line into violations of the law. The relaxation of standards produced loan and investment portfolios vulnerable to recession . . . . (Kindleberger, 1985, p. 28).

21

Kindleberger does not necessarily argue that this speculative overexpansion of bank credit ignites an economic downturn, but that it worsens the problem that is started by some other force. He describes a few notable bank failures of the 1930s, from which he concludes that they "fit precisely the Minsky–Kindleberger hypothesis of credit stretched taut in a positive feedback process" (Kindleberger, 1985, p. 17).

Minsky and Kindleberger emphasize the role of the lender of last resort in preventing or mitigating financial collapse. Indeed, Minsky (1991, p. 163–164) explains why a financial collapse has not happened in recent times as follows:

> The combination of lender-of-last resort interventions, which abort the development of debt-deflation processes, the generalized increase in liquidity as the Federal Reserve reacts to an embryonic crisis, and the deficits that big government runs when income turns down explains why a serious, long-lasting and deep depression has not taken place up until now. Big government and a central bank that is willing and able to intervene explain why it has not happened yet.

Kindleberger (1978), who is more concerned with internationally transmitted financial disasters, calls for an international lender of last resort. Guttentag and Herring (1987, pp. 173–178) also conclude that an international lender of last resort would be desirable. However, they do not suggest creation of a single world central bank. Rather, they urge that each large bank with extensive international operations be "adopted" by a central bank, which would serve as its lender of last resort.

1.2.2. Asymmetric information resulting in depositors' inability to value bank assets and banks' inability to assess borrower quality.   Banks specialize in making and holding loans that are not readily marketable, in large measure because other investors cannot determine the risk posed by these loans as readily or as cheaply (Diamond, 1984). Banks can utilize economies of scale and specialization to reduce the transactions cost of determining the probability that a borrow will not repay a loan as promised, to monitor the borrower's performance and circumstances, and to take effective actions to reduce the probability and cost of defaults (Benston and Smith, 1976). Thus, banks have information about the value of loans that depositors and other outside investors do not have. This asymmetric information situation gives rise to a moral hazard that reduces the amount banks might get should they attempt to sell or securitize their loans.[3]

Several financial economists have suggested that bank panics are a consequence of information asymmetry that makes bank loans difficult for outsiders to value; when adverse economic events occur, depositors have reason to question the value of loans. Calomiris and Gorton (1991, p. 125), for example, give the following summary of this theory: "banking panics are essentially due to revision of the perceived risk of bank debt in an environment where there is asymmetric information about bank asset portfolios."[4] Mishkin (1991, p. 74) further explains: "depositors rush to make withdrawals from solvent as well as insolvent banks since they cannot distinguish between them." Indeed, some students of banking argue that many depositors want deposits redeemable on demand at par in order to exert pressure on bankers to manage their risks appropriately (Calomiris and Kahn, 1991; Flannery, 1994). Depositors expect to withdraw these funds without loss if they have reason to question the bankers' abilities or probity. This demand supplements the demand for a medium of exchange.

Thus, banking panics are seen as an inherent source of bank instability that is tipped off by economic events that are perceived to reduce asset values and endanger the value of deposits, such as the failure of large or important firms, unexpectedly large seasonal fluctuations, or major recessions (Gorton, 1988, 754–55). This theory should be distinguished from the "excessive expansion of credit" theory, which sees banks as a prime culprits or facilitators rather than victims of business collapse.

The asymmetric information hyopthesis also focuses on the inability of banks to differentiate among their potential borrowers, particularly in periods of rising uncertainty and higher interest rates. As a result, banks are likely both to charge higher quality borrowers higher rates than otherwise, encouraging them to cut back on their loan demands and reduce their investment projects, and to reduce lending to all borrowers, thereby reducing spending across the board. In this scenario, the banks transmit and possibly amplify disruptions in financial markets that adversely affect economic activity.

1.2.3. Exogenous deposit and reserve withdrawals. Deposit runs may also be started by events that may not be perceived as reducing bank asset values, such as increased demand for assets that serve as bank reserves emanating from adverse pressures on exchange rates and the balance of payments. This would result in ceteris paribus outflows of gold during a gold-standard period. Given the necessity of banks' offering depositors currency and deposits that are redeemable in specie on demand and at par, an unexpected exogenous withdrawal of specie from a country will result in a reduction in the banking system's reserves that may cause a multiple collapse of the money supply and a liquidity crisis. A similar situation can occur when central banks destroy high-powered money through their open market and other policy operations. Thus, this hypothesis posits that bank panics could occur before central banks were established (e.g., the United States in the national banking period) or when they did not neutralize an exogenous outflow of reserves from the banking system.

In a related but different approach, Diamond and Dybvig (1983) construct a self-contained model in which changes in some depositors' liquidity preferences ignite a run by encouraging other depositors to withdraw their funds rather than suffer losses should the value of the bank's illiquid assets be insufficient to repay them in full. Depositors are assumed to redeem their claims only in the sequence they are received. Thus, a run causes queuing at the bank, which is observed by other depositors who then increase their demand for liquidity in order to be more safe than sorry. Diamond and Dybvig (1983, p. 404) declare: "A bank run in our model is caused by a shift in expectations, which could depend on almost anything, consistent with the apparently irrational observed behavior of people running on banks." Such a shift may result from "a random earnings report, a commonly observed run at some other bank, a negative government forecast, or even sunspots" (1983, p. 410). They conclude that a lender of last resort can help alleviate this situation, but that government deposit insurance is the superior solution.

1.2.4. Institutional and legal restrictions that weaken banks. Because of the basic unit banking structure in the United States, banks in the pre-Federal Reserve years developed and heavily used correspondent banking arrangements to deal with both expected and unexpected withdrawals of deposits and demands for loans. In the national banking period (1863–1914), reserves were concentrated in the New York banks, and legal and cartel restrictions hindered New York banks from using interest-rate adjustments to retain those deposits during periods of heavy withdrawl demand. At the same time, the banks were (and still are) restricted from diversifying their assets and deposits.

Some of the earliest analysts of bank failures (particularly Sprague, 1910) point to restrictions on branching as the cause of the much greater number of banking panics in the United States than were experienced elsewhere. During the Great Depression, a common observation was that the United States' restrictions on branching resulted in thousands of bank failures, in comparison with Canada's nationwide branching system, which experienced no bank closures. However, Canadian banks closed many branches, and there is reason to believe that, although Canadian banks remained open, many were economically insolvent (Kryzanowski and Roberts, 1993). Thus, although branch banking can reduce failures that result from regional collapses, it cannot insulate a banking system against national or international shocks that adversely affect the entire economy or the nation's money supply.

2. Empirical research on the sources of bank failures and banking panics

A number of studies provide evidence on the four hypotheses that attempt to explain why banking and the payments system are inherently unstable. These hypotheses are: (2.1) overexpansion of credit by banks and nonbanks caused banking and economic collapse; (2.2) bank runs, suspensions, and failures were caused by asymmetric information; (2.3) exogenous deposit and reserve withdrawals are responsible for bank failures and banking panics; and (2.4) bank runs, suspensions, and failures were caused by government-instituted restrictions that weakened banks. Our review of the evidence leads us to reject the "overexpansion" hypothesis and models based on exogenous deposit withdrawals. However, we find the evidence persuasive that banks failed because of exogenous outflows of reserves. The evidence also is consistent with parts of the asymmetric information hypothesis, and with the hypothesis that government-instituted regulations weakened banks.

2.1. Overexpansion of credit by banks and nonbanks caused banking and economic collapse

There is not much evidence supporting the hypothesis that overexpansion of credit by both nonbanks and banks caused a banking collapse and then an economic collapse, although there is some reason to believe that banks fueled some local unsustainable business expansions (such as the real estate booms in Texas and New England in the 1980s and in Japan in the early 1990s).[5] There is considerable evidence, though, that business failures often preceded banking panics. Thus, it appears that banking panics or collapses did not cause economic downturns, although they did exacerbate them.

Kindleberger (1978) briefly describes (and gives references to in-depth economic studies of) dozens of events that illustrate the overexpansion theory.[6] He also presents a table listing 37 financial crises that occurred between 1720 and 1976. His text and table descriptions appear to support his thesis. He states that most of the crises were brought under control by an effective lender of last resort. Unfortunately, he does not distinguish clearly between financial expansions that were fueled by bank lending from those driven by increases in base money or by discoveries and inventions. Nor does he clearly identify crises that were caused or exacerbated by exogenous changes in the domestic gold supply, by depositor runs on solvent banks, or those that were due to institutional constraints or fraud. Nor does he contrast his narrative with examples of important business failures that were not followed by financial crises or economic contractions. Hence, although many of his examples seem plausible, they do not appear to support the case for causal relationships.

Schwartz (1986, 1988) subjects Kindleberger's theory to empirical test. First, she distinguishes between "real" and "pseudo" financial crises. A real financial crisis, she says (1986, p. 11), "is fuelled by fears that means of payment will be unobtainable at any price and, in a fractional-reserve banking system, leads to a scramble for high-powered money. . . . The essence of a financial crisis is that it is short-lived, ending with a slackening of the public's demand for additional currency." A pseudo-financial crisis, on the other hand, may involve only a loss of wealth as previously glowing expectations are replaced by uncertainty. "But a loss of wealth is not synonymous with a financial crisis" (1986, p, 23). In her 1986 article, Schwartz gives many examples to illustrate her distinction between real and pseudo crises. In her 1988 article, she catalogues the incidence of banking panics between 1890 and 1929 in 17 countries. She finds (1988, p. 39) that, "[i]n contrast to the frequency of bank failures, before 1930 banking panics—in which all depositors attempt to withdraw their deposits in currency—were uncommon." "Bank failures," she reports, "occurred in a variety of circumstances, the causes including fraud, mismanagement, banking structure, and relative price change or general price level instability. In some years of bank failures, there were runs, but no panics. Panics sometimes occurred in conditions of general price level instability, but most countries had learned by the end of the nineteenth century what actions were necessary to avert panics" (1988, pp. 35–36). She concludes: "Clearly, bank failures do not betoken either runs or the onset of panics" (1988, p. 40).

Schwartz (1988) argues that those, such as Kindleberger, who hypothesize that banks are inherently unstable because economic agents inherently act in unstable ways, fail to recognize the detrimental effect on banks of unexpected changes in price levels and of dysfunctional incentives faced by bank managers. She points out that banks' risk profiles and the stability of the banking system would be enhanced by greater macro price-level stability and by a policy of resolving bank failures before their capital turned negative.

Cagan (1965) analyzed the role of banking panics in his study of the determinants of the U.S. money supply. He associates panics with the prior failure of prominent financial institutions or railroads. However, he also finds that panics all followed peaks in economic activity, from which he concludes that they did not precipitate economic downturns. However, he finds that panics were important in reducing money supply growth, which converted mild contractions into severe contractions. But, because two severe economic downturns (1920–21 and 1937–38) and two mild downturns (1890 and 1914) were not associated with banking panics, Cagan concludes that panics were neither necessary nor sufficient for such downturns to occur.

Bordo (1986) examines evidence from six countries—the United States, Great Britain, France, Germany, Sweden, and Canada—on the relationship between the incidence of financial panics and declines in economic activity that might have resulted from overexpansion and monetary contraction. Over the period 1870–1933 in the countries studied, Bordo finds: "First, severe declines in economic activity in all countries are associated with (prior) declines in monetary growth. Second, most severe cyclical contractions in all the countries examined are associated with stock market crashes, but not, with the exception of the US, with banking crises" (1986, pp. 229–230).[7]

Finally, Eichengreen and Portes (1987) compare international financial crises in the 1930s with those in the 1980s. They are particularly interested in describing "the singular importance of linkages running from debt defaults and exchange market disturbances to the instability of banking systems" (1987, p. 18). In the prior decades, they say "foreign lending was associated with expanding trade and rosy prospects at least in the short run" (1987, p. 15). They find that "[m]acroeconomic events, rather than disturbances limited to financial markets, played a leading role in the onset of the debt crisis" of the 1930s (1987, p. 21). The defaults did not greatly affect foreign banks, as the debts were a relatively small proportion of their assets. However, domestic banks, which held proportionately more of the debt of the same borrowers, were more severely hurt. Furthermore, Eichengreen and Portes conclude that "shocks with the potential to destabilize the banking system did not lead to generalized collapse because central banks acted in lender-of-last resort capacity and simply did not permit this to happen" (1987, p. 26). The same, they state, cannot be said for the United States. (Kindleberger, 1978, and Minsky, 1991, reach a similar conclusion.)

Eichengreen and Portes (1987) describe the 1980s as characterized by a "density of international interbank relationships [that] now is incomparably greater [than the earlier period]" (1987, p. 33). Exchange rates have exhibited unexpectedly high volatility without (surprisingly, they say) exchange-market collapse or any overall drift towards controls (1987, p. 36). Foreign debt exposure has grown. But there have been no serious financial crises. Eichengreen and Portes conclude: "The main dangers lie not in disturbances originating in financial markets but in malfunctions of the real economy" (1987, p. 50).

Thus, although several studies focus on overexpansion of credit by banks and nonbanks and resulting asset bubbles as factors related to banking crises and economic collapse, none establish this causal linkage empirically and several present evidence that is inconsistent with the hypothesis.

2.2. Bank runs, suspensions, and failures were caused by asymmetric information

Studies testing the asymmetric information hypothesis provide evidence supporting the version positing that bank failures and panics are caused by business failures, rather than the reverse. Presumably, because it is difficult for depositors to value banks' assets, depositors run on banks because their experience with business collapse causes them to believe that banks also may be insolvent. However, the studies do not distinguish between bank failures caused by actual reductions in the value of banks' assets and failures caused by runs on solvent banks that were perceived to be insolvent.

Calomiris and Gorton (1991) tested the asymmetric-information and the random-withdrawal hypotheses with data from the national banking period. They examined measures of bank liquidity (reserve ratios and changes in deposits) in the weeks before the six episodes that they identify as banking panics because clearing-house certificates were issued or authorized: 1873, 1884, 1890, 1893, 1896, and 1907. They also examine the data for unusually large seasonal shocks and business failures. Adverse general economic conditions are measured by unusually large changes in stock prices. They find that the data "do not support the notion that panics were preceded by unusually large seasonal shocks or that panics resulted from tripping a threshold of bank liquidity" (1991, p. 133). They also find that "the timing of panics (with the possible exception of the Panic of 1873) places them *after* weeks of seasonal shocks associated with planting and harvesting" (1991, p. 138, emphasis in original). Thus, they reject the agricultural seasonal explanation for panics.

However, Calomiris and Gorton (1991) find that unusually adverse movements in stock prices characterized the pre-panic periods. "[L]arge withdrawals [by country banks from New York banks]", they state, "only threatened the banking system when they were accompanied by (perhaps precipitated by) real disturbances" (1991, p. 143). They find that "panics are associated with a threshold level of news receipt concerning the growth of liabilities of failed businesses, which is a leading indicator of recession" (1991, p. 148). Because the news receipt induces a sudden but rational downgrading by depositors of the financial health of their banks, Calomiris and Gorton conclude that the asymmetrical-information theory of banking panics is supported.

In addition, they examine analyses published in the annual reports of the Comptroller of the Currency of the causes of the 116 bank failures that occurred in the roughly six months around the panics. They report: "in the overwhelmingly majority of cases (91 of 116), failure was not attributed to panic-induced stringency in the money market. Furthermore, the fact that the Comptroller only attributed one failure to a bank run per se shows that the *direct* link between bank runs and bank failures during panics was not important" (1991, p. 154, emphasis in original). In addition, they find a regional pattern of failures that is "incompatible with the withdrawal risk view of panics" (1991, p. 158). Calomiris and Mason (1994) find that, even at the height of the banking panic that occurred in Chicago in June 1932, depositors were able to differentiate financially sound from financially troubled banks and that the banks that failed were both economically insolvent and had characteristics more similar to those that failed in the non-panic months of 1932 than those that survived.

Calomiris and Gorton's (1991) findings, based on tables of data, confirm Gorton's (1988) earlier econometrically based study. Gorton examined the variables associated with the deposit/currency ratio in periods characterized and not characterized by banking panics during the national banking period. Using quarterly call-date data, he finds that changes in business conditions and risk (proxied by the liabilities of failed businesses and changes in pig iron production) peak at the same time as banking panics, and concludes that "panics seem to have resulted from changes in perceived risk predictable on the basis of prior information" (1988, p. 778). Furthermore, he finds that the equations fitted with data from the nonpanic periods explain the panic periods well. He also analyzes the banking panics of 1930, 1931, and 1933, and finds that they occurred well after the business cycle peak. His analysis causes him to reject the Diamond–Dybvig "depositor instability" and Minsky–Kindleberger "loan contraction" theories: "the mechanism of causality running from depositors withdrawing currency from 'illiquid' banks and causing businesses to fail is not present, at least when all [panic] dates are examined. Second, the response of banks to panics was not to liquidate loans, but to issue circulating private money which insured depositors against the failures of individual banks" (1988, pp. 778–779).

Donaldson (1992) uses weekly data from 1867 through 1933 to test Gorton's (1988) finding that panics and nonpanics are generated by similar responses to changing perceptions of deposit risk, and the inference that changed economic conditions caused banking panics, rather than the reverse. He uses the (brokers') call-loan interest rate as the dependent variable.[8] Using a dummy variable structure to measure the effect of panics, he finds that, while call-loan interest rates increase generally when bank reserves and deposits decrease, there is a larger-than-normal increase during bank panics. Also, a stock-market index variable is not significantly related to call-loan interest rates in nonpanic weeks, but is significantly negatively related in panic weeks—lower stock prices are associated with higher interest rates during panics. Thus, Donaldson's shorter period weekly data reveal that brokers' call-loan interest rates are higher during panics, but that the relationship between panics and interest rates is played out within a quarter. We believe that his findings are consistent with Gorton's view that negative economic events as measured by stock prices caused or are associated with banking panics.

Mishkin (1991) examined banking panics over the period 1857 through 1988, primarily by charting stock prices and the spread between high-grade commercial paper and brokers' call loans monthly in periods around banking and financial panics. He also gives a narrative discussion of each panic, pointing out the specific business failures that preceded the panics. He finds (1991, p. 96) that:

1. with one exception in 1873, financial panics always occurred after the onset of recession;
2. with the same exception in 1873, stock prices declined and the spread between interest rates on low- and high-quality bonds rose before the onset of the panic;
3. many panics seem to have features of a liquidity crisis in which there are substantial increases in interest rates before the panic;
4. the onset of many panics followed a major failure of a financial institution, not necessarily a bank. Furthermore, this failure was often the result of financial difficulties experienced by a nonfinancial corporation;
5. the rise in the interest spread associated with a panic was typically soon followed by a decline . . . [followed, in 1873, 1907, and the Great Depression, by an increase] when there was deflation and a severe recession;
6. the most severe financial crises were associated with severe economic contractions; and

7. although stock market crashes often appear to be a major factor in creating a financial crisis, this was not always the case.

Mishkin (1991, p. 97) concludes that his findings are consistent with the asymmetric-information theory: "Rather than starting with bank panics, most of the financial crises began with a rise in interest rates, a stock market decline, and the widening of the interest-rate spread." He rejects the deposit-withdrawal theory of financial panics because it cannot explain why banking panics occurred when they did (1991, p. 97).[9]

Park (1991) discusses the panics of 1873, 1884, 1893, and 1907 and the nationwide bank holiday in 1993. From his narrative descriptions, he concludes that "[l]iquidity risk . . . does not by itself invite systemwide bank runs. The other necessary ingredient is a lack of bank-specific information on solvency" (1991, p. 285). He does, though, consider exogenous reductions in bank reserves as a causal factor.[10]

In sum, considerable evidence supports the hypothesis that business failures and economic downturns preceded and probably caused bank failures and panics more than bank failures caused general economic distress, although they undoubtedly exacerbated them. Banks failed because they were rendered insolvent from loan losses and fraud. Few, if any, economically solvent banks failed, because of runs where depositors may not have distinguished solvent from insolvent banks.

2.3. Exogenous deposit and reserve withdrawals

Several studies provide strong evidence leading to the conclusion that exogenous outflows of bank reserves (primarily gold before 1934) that were not attributable to actual or perceived weaknesses in bank asset values resulted in shortages of liquidity and banking panics. This situation affected primarily the United States, as it did not have an effective lender of last resort. The findings reviewed are consistent with the hypothesis that banking panics are due to actions or inactions of central banks, rather than to an inherent instability of banking.

As noted, Donaldson (1992) examined the relationship between call-loan interest rates, bank reserves, deposits, stock-market prices, and banking panics from 1914 (after the creation of the Federal Reserve) through 1934. He finds higher interest rates associated with panics but not with the other variables. Miron (1986) found that the Federal Reserve was able to reduce the magnitude of seasonal interest rate changes, compared to the national banking period before it was established. However, he also found "that the Fed accommodated the seasonal demand in financial markets to a lesser extent during the 1929–33 period that it had previously. This means that the frequency of the panics *should* have increased, as it did." (1992, p. 136, emphasis in original.) Donaldson (1992) conducted further tests showing that banking panics are characterized by the inability of the money supply to expand rapidly during economic crises. Even though panics may be "special events," he concludes that "panics can be stopped by allowing banks to turn nonliquid assets into cash by printing new banknotes during times of crisis" (1992, p. 295). These findings are consistent with the hypothesis that exogenous outflows of bank reserves or gold, or ineffective actions by the central bank, cause banking panics. (They also are consistent with the asymmetric-information hypothesis.)

Donaldson (1992) confirms Gorton's (1988) finding that the panic of 1933 would have been more serious had the Fed not (belatedly) injected new money in that year. Donaldson also reports that gold reserves at the Fed fell *prior* to the onset of the panic, which, he notes, supports Wigmore's (1987) hypotheses that the March 1933 bank holiday was caused by reductions in the money supply as people hoarded gold in anticipation of the devaluation of the dollar.

As noted above, Cagan (1965) and Bordo (1986, 1992) find that banking panics and economic downturns are associated with declines in the monetary gold stock and high-powered money. Huffman and Lothian (1984) examine the international transmission of economic fluctuations under the pre-1933 gold standard. They find that, between 1830 and 1934, gold outlfows played the most important role in reducing the domestic money stock in both the United States and Great Britain. Furthermore, because they find banking panics in but three of 12 common cycles, they conclude that panics have little importance as a means by which economic fluctuations are transmitted internationally.

Tallman and Moen (1994) investigate whether exogenous outflows of the gold stock were key in starting a banking panic during the national banking period. At that time, gold comprised the principal portion of banks' reserves that actually changed. They describe the causes of gold outflows from the United States, such as the Bank of England's raising the discount rate from 2.5 to 6.0 percent in 1882 and the European central banks raising their discount rates in 1890. The United States did not have a central bank that could neutralize these actions with offsetting increases in discount rates. Using statistical techniques, Tallman and Moen distinguish between expected and unexpected gold flows. They find that panics are due primarily to unexpected exogenous gold shocks (outflows). These outflows preceded stock market declines, interest-rate increases (spikes), and output contractions.

Wigmore (1987) provides strong evidence indicating that the banking panic of late 1932 and early 1933 was caused by a run on the dollar, rather than a loss of confidence in the solvency of banks. The run was precipitated by indications that Presiden Roosevelt would devalue the dollar once he took office (which, at the time, was not until March 4th). The prospect of substantial returns from holding gold resulted in a drain of gold from commercial banks and the Federal Reserve banks, particularly the Federal Reserve Bank of New York. Closing all banks until the reserves could be replaced (as gold was purchased by the Treasury at $35 an ounce, compared to its previous market price of $21 an ounce), as Roosevelt did in the Bank Holiday of March 1933, was an effective way to deal with this government-caused crisis.

In contrast to the implications of the empirical studies just reviewed, Diamond-Dybvig (1983) construct a model that emphasizes the role of exogenous, unpredictable deposit withdrawals as the source of bank instability. Much of the academic criticism of their model has been concerned with the restrictiveness of their assumptions. Calomiris and Gorton (1991) present an excellent review of much of this literature.[11] Some of these articles point out that panics would not occur if depositors' demands did not have to be met sequentially. Other articles attempt to make the model more consistent with reality by likening sequential panic withdrawals from a single bank to runs on individual banks that are linked by bank-held reserves of other banks, as was the situation in the national banking period where city banks held the reserves of country banks, and central reserve city banks held city banks' reserves. However, Diamond and Dybvig's model predicts that banking panics would occur at random times and in a wide variety of insitutional arrangements. Hence, its basic prediction appears to be contradicted by even a casual examination of the data.

Furthermore, by assuming a monopoly bank, Diamond and Dybvig automatically assume that a run on one bank is equivalent to a run on the banking system and do not take account of the protective arrangements banks might make in a multiple bank system. These include cooperative actions, such as correspondent banking arrangements and clearing house agreements, to mitigate bank runs.[12] At the same time, Diamond and Dybvig cannot take account of competitive actions by banks in a multiple bank system to assure depositors that they have, or can get, the funds depositors might demand. They also take no account of actions by central banks to maintain bank reserves should depositors remove their funds from the banking system (or from the monopoly bank) and keep the funds in currency or specie.

Calomiris and Gorton (1991) subjected the "random depositor-withdrawal" hypothesis to rigorous tests using data from the U.S. national banking period. These tests provide no support for the hypothesis that depositor instability was a cause of banking runs, suspensions or failures. Furthermore, Schwartz's (1988) finding that banking panics were unusual events (except in the United States) is inconsistent with the random depositor-withdrawal hypothesis. Hence, we conclude that the policy implications of the Diamond and Dybvig model are not very useful for understanding the workings of the extant banking and payments system.

2.4. Bank runs, suspensions, and failures were caused by legally instituted restrictions that weaken banks

Many empirical studies (including those discussed above) indicate that the United States experienced bank panics in large measure because of the weaknesses of the national banking system and restrictions on branching. These findings are important, because they provide reason to believe that banking panics can be reduced in frequency, if not avoided altogether, by a banking system that permits diversification through branching and in which bank reserves are controlled appropriately by a central bank.

Sprague (1910) analyzes five of the six U.S. banking panics in the national bank period associated with serious economic downturns—1873, 1884, 1890, 1893, and 1907. (The sixth occurred in 1914.) He notes that the panics occurred in either spring or fall, and that they usually were preceded by the failure of a large business or financial firm. The seasonal movement of funds between agricultural areas and financial centers put strains on banks' reserve positions, making them vulnerable to an unexpected shock, such as the failure of an important firm or an unexpectedly large harvest or a natural disaster. Without a central bank to replenish reserves, some banks had to suspend the convertibility of bank notes to specie as note holders and depositors attempted to run to what they saw as "good" money, and some banks failed.

Smith's (1991, p. 233) narrative description of banking panics during the national banking period indicates that "panic related withdrawal demands (on New York banks) came heavily from interior [country] correspondent banks. And restrictions on payments by New York (and other money center) banks fell much more heavily on correspondent banks than on non-bank depositors." This finding is consistent with the hypothesis that institutional and legal constraints caused or exacerbated banking panics.

Bordo (1986) finds that monetary contractions associated with financial contractions were more severe in the United States than in the other five countries he studied. "One explanation," he says, "is the greater instability, compared to that of the five other countries, of the US banking system—a system composed largely of unit fractional reserve banks with reserves pyramided in the New York money market. . . . In contrast with the U.S. experience, the five other countries in the same period all developed nationwide branch banking systems consolidated into a few very large banks" (Bordo, p. 230). (His second explanation is the absence of an effective lender of last resort.)

2.5. Conclusions from the empirical research on the sources of bank failures and banking panics

The empirical research reviewed leads us to reject the hypotheses that bank panics have been caused by or related to over-expansion by banks and nonbanks or to random runs by depositors. The evidence is consistent with the strand of the asymmetric-information hypothesis which posits that depositors tend to run on banks when adverse economic conditions (such as a stock market crash or the failure of well-known, important companies) leads them to doubt the value of banks' assets. The evidence supports the hypothesis that banks were rendered more likely to fail when adverse shocks were experienced because of existing government restrictions on their ability to diversify risks and institutional weaknesses of the U.S. national banking system.

Thus, bank panics frequently were caused by macro-liquidity crises that were the result of exogenous withdrawals of bank reserves. The consequent withdrawals took the form of exports of specie and depositors' runs to specie and currency. These reserve depletions can be offset by actions taken by the central bank. Moreover, at the margin depositors appear to have been able to differentiate solvent from insolvent banks. Hence, we conclude that the private banking and payments systems are not inherently unstable.

Central bankers (and others), though, often express fears that runs on banks could be contagious, spreading before the central bankers can take effective measures to neutralize reserve withdrawals. Furthermore, they are concerned that contagious bank panics could result in the failure of many banks, thereby reducing the supply of bank credit in some areas and causing considerable economic distress. Hence, we turn now to evidence on contagious runs on banks.

3. Contagion of bank runs, suspensions, and failures

Runs on banks have been a subject of fascination by finance professionals, regulators, the press, and the general public for many years. Runs, like all financial panics and doomsday scenarios, make "good press," in part because banking is not well understood, and so any perceived breakdown is frightening to the public. One of us has reviewed thoroughly the literature on bank runs in a recent article (Kaufman, 1994A). The empirical evidence on bank runs is clear: except for speed, runs on banks that lead creditors to withdraw their funding are not much different than customer and creditor responses to other industries' products that are perceived to be dangerous, e.g., contaminated soft drinks or medication, airplane crashes, and nuclear power plant accidents. The evidence suggests clearly that depositors run on particular banks for specific, well-documented reasons (e.g., large losses on LDC and real-estate loans relative to a bank's capital or fraud), and they sometimes run on other banks that appear to have similar problems because of similarities in their balance sheets, borrower characteristics, or market areas. However, depositors do not run on banks that are not so perceived. That is, runs are bank-specific and information based, not industry-wide and rumor based. This is true even in the few periods in U.S. history in which there were serious runs to currency because depositors doubted the solvency of many banks,[13] e.g., 1893 and 1929–1933 (Calomiris and Mason, 1994).

Moreover, the evidence shows that runs were not a major cause of bank failures. Runs may have caused liquidity problems, but the "fire-sale" losses were rarely great enough to render a bank insolvent. Rather, solvency problems caused by other factors led to runs that caused liquidity problems that worsened a bank's solvency problems. Thus, depositors appear capable of differentiating between solvent and insolvent banks, just as they can differentiate between tampered and untampered drug and soft drink products, and dangerous and safer modes of transportation.

The evidence suggests that bank runs and failures rarely conform to the process described in many academic models. Runs are initially ignited by specific, observable events affecting special banks rather than an exogenous shift in depositor liquidity preferences affecting all banks. Solvent banks experiencing sudden deposit withdrawals can sell assets to or borrow funds quickly from other banks to restore their deposit losses at reasonably low cost. Only banks known to other banks to be insolvent or nearly so would experience difficulties in recycling funds and face closure. Consequently, the likelihood of runs on most or all banks, which is a prerequisite for a run to currency, is small. Except for fraud, bank insolvencies are not sudden nor occur overnight. As discussed earlier, this casts doubt on the usefulness of models that assume only one bank so that a run on a bank and on the banking system are one and the same, such as the model constructed by Diamond and Dybvig (1983).

Even if there were a run to currency, the potential damage could be avoided if the central bank offset the reserve drain from banks by increasing its reserve position through open market operations or discount window lending by amounts equal to the reserve loss. In the absence of central banks, banks typically undertook cooperative actions through clearing house associations that limited reserve losses through temporary suspensions of convertibility, in early days of bank notes for specie and in later days of deposits for currency. Clearinghouses also issued loan certificates that banks used to clear checks, thereby allowing them to operate with lower levels of reserves (Dwyer and Gilbert, 1989; Tallman, 1988). Thus, as documented by Schwartz (1988), except in the United States, banking panics caused by bank runs have been rare in the last century.

3. Costs of bank failures, runs, and panics

The consequences of a bank failure and a banking panic can be severe. In section 4.1, we consider the cost of the failure of or run on a single bank, and, in section 4.2, the cost of the failure of several banks. In section 4.3, we discuss the risks to the payments system of bank failures and panics. Because derivatives have come into increasing use recently and are potentially a source of large losses, we consider the risks associated with these financial instruments in section 4.4.

3.1. The cost of the failure of a single bank

Bank customers (particularly borrowers) who made investments in bank-specific information and for whom making alternative arrangements are costly, might be hurt should their bank fail or have to reduce the extent or scope of its operations as a result of a run. However, it is important to note that other banks offer very similar services and products, and most bank customers have accounts with more than one bank.[14] Furthermore, other firms offer close substitutes to almost all of the products and services offered by banks. Many nonbank financial companies make loans, including installment loans made by consumer and sales finance companies, mortgages by mortgage bankers, and commercial loans by nonbank lenders such as General Electric Capital Corporation, and loans in the form of accounts receivable by many companies. Checking is the only important possible exception, and this service is offered, to a limited extent, by brokerage houses and money-market mutual funds, who let their customers use their bank accounts. These other financial institutions also offer employment opportunities for the employees of a closed bank. Nevertheless, some private information known only to the bank providing the loan or other financial service may be costly to transfer quickly and some bank customers are likely to suffer transition costs.

Stockholders, depositors with partially uninsured balances, nondeposit creditors, and perhaps some senior bank managers and other employees at a failed bank might suffer losses. But this possibility provides an important incentive for these parties to take actions that would avoid or mitigate losses. Moreover, except when liquidated, failed banks do not disappear. As long as there is an unmet demand for banking services in the service area, failed banks usually are acquired by or merged with an existing bank or sold to new owners. Thus, most employees are likely to keep their jobs, although not perhaps their exact positions.

Losses to uninsured depositors and other creditors depend on the magnitude of the bank's economic negative net worth when the bank is resolved. This, in turn, depends on how quickly a bank is resolved after its net worth is fully depleted. If it is resolved before that time, as is contemplated by the structured early intervention and resolution provision of the FDIC Improvement Act of 1991, little if any losses would accrue to these claimants.

Should there be runs on solvent banks that are incorrectly thought to be insolvent (perhaps because apparently similar banks failed), "innocent" bank owners, nondeposit creditors, and senior managers might be hurt. But the possibility of such runs can be negated by actions taken by banks to convince depositors that their funds are safe. Such actions include holding sufficient capital to absorb possible losses and disclosure of information about the bank's operations to obviate misperceptions. Moreover, even if such runs occur, bankers also can (and do) establish cooperative ventures, such as correspondent relationships, mutual insurance associations, and clearinghouses, to stop or reduce substantially the cost of the run. As Gorton (1985) and Gorton and Mullineaux (1987) show, these cooperative relationships were effective in mitigating the effect of banking panics on solvent banks.

Legal restrictions on branching, though, can hamper insolvent or weak banks from being acquired by other solvent banks. Even when banks can branch without restriction, laws that prohibit non-banking firms from owning banks also reduce the set of potential purchasers of weak banks. Such laws also restrict banks from diversifying optimally and from achieving economies of scope, and tend to protect ineffective bank managers from the discipline of the market for corporate control. Thus, the probability and costs of individual bank failure are increased as a result of restrictive laws.

The costs of a bank failure to stakeholders other than stockholders might be compared to the costs of the failure of other firms as an aid to assessing the relative importance of bank failures. As Horvitz (1965) observes: "The failure of the textile mill in the one-mill New England town is almost certainly a greater community disaster than the failure of the local bank in a one-bank town." The failure of a manufacturer of special purpose or unique equipment (such as milling machines and computers) would be costly to owners of that equipment who need parts and service, and to employees who had product-specific skills. In contrast, banks produce standardized products, such as checking accounts, and individualized products, such as loans, for which there are many close substitutes and alternative suppliers. Thus, there is reason to believe that bank failures are less disruptive than are business failures generally.

Benefits from bank failures and runs also should be considered. As noted above, the possibility or threat of runs gives bank managers and owners incentives to manage their banks prudently so that they can avoid and survive any run. The potential failure of banks, as with other firms, is desirable for an economic system to achieve efficiency. Actual failure also is an almost inevitable and necessary outcome of beneficial risk taking.[15]

Consequently, we conclude that there are relatively few direct costs and almost no costly externalities from individual bank failures, and there can be substantial benefits. On balance, then, individual bank failures, as such, should not be prevented. They are not a source of instability in the banking and, hence, of instability in the payments system.

3.2. The failure of several banks

Bank failures are widely perceived as more harmful than the failure of other types of firms, particularly nonfinancial firms, because they are believed to occur faster, spread more broadly throughout the industry, result in larger numbers of failures of similar firms, impose larger losses on creditors (depositors), and are more likely to affect other sectors of the economy and the macroeconomy as a whole. The evidence on each of these reasons is summarized next.[16]

Because deposits, particularly demand deposits, can be removed faster from a bank than maturity debt from other financial and nonbank firms, and faster than reduction in sales can drive firms into insolvency, the "greater speed" hypothesis is true, almost by definition. However, faster failures are not necessarily more harmful failures. Indeed, if a firm has failed because of poor management, its creditors generally benefit from its expeditious closure. Ex ante, bank managers' concerns about runs by depositors serve to motivate the managers to operate their banks so that depositors do not perceive the need to run.[17]

Bank failures are believed to affect other banks more broadly than the failures of nonbanks affect other firms in the industry, both because depositors are assumed to be less able to differentiate the products or financial health of banks than of other firms, and because banks are directly connected through interbank balances (particularly in the United States, where branching is limited), so that the failure of one bank may impose losses on other banks. But, as noted in section 3, the evidence is overwhelming that failures and runs have been bank specific and that depositors have been able, at the margin, to differentiate between good and bad banks both before and after the introduction of the FDIC in 1934. Even anecdotal descriptions focus on a few institutions during panics, although most intermediaries faced large withdrawals. Moreover, the fact that banks have credit relationships with each other does not imply that they do not act to protect themselves from this exposure. For example, although the Continental Illinois Bank had deposit or Fed funds relationships with over 2,000 banks at the time of its failure in 1984, its failure did not directly cause the failure of any other bank. Indeed, had Continental's creditors not been protected by the FDIC, only two Continental-related banks would have suffered losses as large as 50 percent of their capital when Continental failed (Staff Report, 1991).

Although bank failures generally receive greater attention than other failures, the average annual rate of bank failures has been about the same as for nonfinancial firms. This is true even before the introduction of federal deposit insurance, particularly before the establishment of the Federal Reserve in 1913, when the average rate of bank failures was actually lower than that of nonbanks. But the annual variability rate for bank failures has been greater. To a considerable extent, the relatively high failure rate for banks in the United States reflects their inability to reduce their risks effectively by freely diversifying geographically or product-wise because of legally imposed restrictions (White, 1983; Benston, 1990).

Similarly, although depositors are widely perceived to experience substantial losses in bank failures, the evidence suggests that their losses have been considerably smaller on average than those suffered by bondholders and other creditors in the bankruptcy of nonbanks (Kaufman, 1994A). The actuality is due, primarily, to the faster bank resolution process, even in the 1930s and 1980s, than the bankruptcy process applied to nonbank firms. These lower resolution costs help explain the substantially lower capital ratios maintained by banks relative to nonbanking firms, both before and after the establishment of the FDIC.

Finally, bank runs and failure are perceived to spill over beyond the banking sector to other financial sectors and the macroeconomy, primarily through runs into currency that result in a reduction in money aggregate and bank credit and through abrupt reductions in lending. But, as already discussed, with only rare exceptions, large-scale bank failures occurred after downturns in the national economy, not before. Thus, the stronger direction of causation appears to run from the real economy to banking, rather than the other way around. Loans that turned bad from bad economic conditions cause bank failures, rather than bad loans from over-expansion in a healthy economy cause bank failures and a turnabout in the economy.

3.3. Risks to the payments system

As noted earlier, bank failures are viewed particularly adversely because banks' major liabilities (demand deposits) serve as the major part of the money supply and, at least in the United States, banks operate the interbank funds clearing system. An efficient payments system, in which transferability of claims is effected in full and on time, is a prerequisite for an efficient macroeconomy. Similarly, disruptions in the payments system result in disruptions in aggregate economic activity. To some observers, instability in the payments system is more threatening than instability in deposits. This fear appears to reflect the larger dollar volume of daily payments, the speedy movement of the funds, and unfamiliarity with the clearing process.

For an individual bank, the large volume of settlements nets out within a day. However, checks and other interbank transfers through clearing houses (including the Federal Reserve) are not necessarily received and paid simultaneously during a day. Rather, within the day, banks frequently pay large claims on themselves (such as securities purchases by customers) before receiving payment from the customer. Such "daylight" overdrafts usually are settled at the close of the business day. A potential for default exists if the expected payments to the bank do not materialize in full and on a timely basis. Consequently, the paying bank may be unable to pay the receiving bank. In such a scenario, the previous payments need to be reversed or unwound. This may be complex and time-consuming and cause "gridlock" in the payments system that interrupts the smooth flow of trade. Moreover, if the losses to the paying bank from customer defaults were large enough to drive it into insolvency, the receiving banks would experience losses, which might be sufficient to drive them to insolvency if these losses exceed their capital.

However, these interruptions and losses occur because payment is not in "good funds" and daylight overdrafts are not priced correctly and, until recently in the United States, not priced at all if the transfers were conducted on the Federal Reserve's Fedwire. Indeed, to the extent the Federal Reserve guaranteed final payment on Fedwire, any losses would accrue to the Fed rather than to banks and daylight overdrafts would be implicitly encouraged. Thus, the existence of substantial amounts of daylight overdrafts on Fedwire reflects poor regulation, not an inherent weakness in the system (Flannery, 1988; Gilbert, 1989; Eisenbeis, 1995). Without a government-provided guarantee, overdrafts are a credit-risk problem, basically similar to the credit-risk problems banks incur in their daily lending activities which they have learned to evaluate, monitor, and charge for.

3.4. Banks' activities in derivative financial instruments

Recently, attention has shifted to potential instability from the activities of banks and others in derivatives. Much of this concern is due to the observation that the notional value of these instruments is much larger than either that of deposits or the payments system, that transactions and payments occur quickly, and that the design of some of these instruments is highly complex, causing them to be mysterious to and misunderstood by many. Although most of the risks are credit- and interest-rate risks that are similar to those on other securities, some other risks may be greater, as the institutional framework is newer, probably less efficient, and not yet thoroughly tested by experience. These risks include settlement, operational (control systems), valuation (pricing), and legal (netting and bankruptcy) (GAO, 1994). Nevertheless, there appears to be no evidence that derivatives involve any greater threat to the stability of banking or the payments system than do deposits or loans—which is to say, no threat if banks maintain sufficient capital (as required by the market) and if the central bank acts effectively as a lender of last resort to keep the money supply from contracting.

Furthermore, there is reason to believe that derivatives are used primarily to reduce risks to banks and their clients. Interest-rate futures, forwards, swaps, and options are effective for reducing duration gaps at banks that fund long-term assets with short-term liabilities. Foreign currency futures, forwards, swaps, and options can hedge the risks banks undertake in providing services to their customers. Those customers also benefit from banks' services in arranging interest-rate swaps and in making a market for financial derivatives. Overregulation that prevents optimal use of derivatives to reduce risk, therefore, might increase the risk and cost of bank failures, and increase costs to banks' customers. Losses from unwise use of derivatives, like losses from unwise use of other assets, may be kept from damaging the banking system by having banks maintain sufficient capital to absorb possible losses and by resolving insolvencies in a timely manner. Excessive regulation may also prevent end-users from hedging adequately. Losses and even failure of nonbank dealers or end-users is of little public policy concern. Failure of banks that use derivatives is of greater concern due to the government's provision of deposit insurance. However, the dangers of large losses and contagion is reduced by the system of prompt corrective action and least-cost resolution of seriously undercapitalized banks, as described in section 6.

4. Lender of last resort

4.1. Domestic lender of last resort

As argued above, bank panics or runs to currency should not cause bank failures in economies with central banks if the central bank performs its duties as lender of last resort to restore reserves lost to currency drains. The bank may do so either through its discount window or through open market operations. Discount window assistance has been the traditional technique used by central banks, particularly in economies in which the financial markets were not fully developed and able to transfer funds from surplus to deficit areas quickly and cheaply. In theory, banks experiencing runs could borrow from the central bank, which would lend to them as long as they believed the institution to be solvent. That is, the central bank provided liquidity assistance, not solvency assistance. To discourage banks from making unjustified use of such support, Bagehot (1873), Meltzer (1986), Schwartz (1992), and others recommended that the support be made available only at a penalty interest rate.

But recent evidence, at least in the United States, suggests that the Federal Reserve did not provide such support only at penalty rates or only to illiquid but solvent institutions (Kaufman, 1991). As a result, many banks received liquidity support at subsidized rates. A study by the House Banking Committee reported that 90 percent of the more than 400 banks that received extended credit from the Federal Reserve discount window in recent years subsequently failed (U.S. House of Representatives, 1991). It is doubtful whether most or any of the banks, including large banks such as the Continental Illinois, New England National, M Corp., and First Republic, were solvent at the time they received assistance. Although the Federal Reserve may have better information about the financial condition of banks experiencing liquidity problems than the market and other banks, past experience does not indicate that it can use this information to restrict its lending only to solvent institutions. The Fed can lend to insolvent institutions with little concern, as it requires all loans to be fully collateralized. Losses from bank insolvency are borne by others—uninsured depositors, creditors, and the FDIC.[18] To the extent that Fed discount-window lending to insolvent or near-insolvent banks resulted in their generating larger losses than otherwise, the cost of these failures to the ultimate bearers of the losses was increased.

In an economy with a well-developed financial market, the central bank need not determine the correct interest rate that it should charge or have to differentiate between solvent and insolvent illiquid banks. The bank could provide liquidity support only through open market operations, and permit the market to allocate the funds to individual banks. Market participants, whose own funds are at risk, are more likely to distinguish between banks experiencing only liquidity problems and those that are insolvent, and have incentives to determine the appropriate loan rate to charge than is a central bank, such as the Federal Reserve. Indeed, Schwartz (1988) notes that the Federal Reserve frequently confuses financial distress (individual bank problems) with financial crisis (banking system problems). Thus, the lender of last resort should provide liquidity to the banking system as a whole through open-market operations (macroliquidity), rather than directly to individual banks through the discount window (microliquidity) (Goodfriend and King, 1988; Kaufman, 1991).

4.2. International lender of last resort

Kindleberger (1978), Eichengreen and Portes (1987), and Guttentag and Herring (1987), among others, call for the establishment of an international lender of last resort, as a means of preventing banking panics from spreading country to country. However, as we discuss above, there is no reason to believe that the banking and payments systems of individual countries cannot be protected fully by these countries' domestic lenders of last resort. Furthermore, there is no international money supply. Hence, there cannot be a multiple contraction of money and credit should depositors who fear the collapse of one or more banks run to currency.

Although the failure of a bank can cause disruptions in the operations of its customers and correspondents headquartered in other countries, the costs imposed on these parties are no different than the costs imposed as a result of the failure of other firms. Nor is there any reason to believe that banks, as well as nonbanks, would not act to protect themselves from such failures. Consequently, we see no role for an international lender of last resort, although international cooperation and the prompt sharing of relevant data would be beneficial.[19]

5. Conclusions and policy recommendations

Primarily because of the short-term nature of its liabilities and low capital ratios, banking is fragile. Banks can and do fail. But so do firms in other industries. Nor is the failure rate for banks significantly greater than that for nonbanks. We delineate and examine several proposed explanations for near simultaneous multiple failures of banks that have occurred in the past, particularly in the United States. These explanations include excessive expansion of credit, runs caused by depositors' inability to value banks' assets when the economy turns down or important firms fail (asymmetric information), exogenous withdrawals of reserves that are unrelated to weaknesses in bank asset values, and institutional and legal restrictions that weaken banks. From our review of the theory and evidence, we conclude that past multiple bank failures are not inconsistent with the asymmetric information hypothesis, but were due primarily to the last two reasons— unexpected declines of aggregate bank reserves, and institutional and regulatory restrictions. We find little evidence supporting the hypothesis that banking is inherently unstable.

Indeed, banking appears no more unstable than most other industries, whose failure rate is no less than that of banks, despite the fact that, at least in the United States, banks have been prevented by regulation from reducing risk more effectively through geographic and product diversification. Bank managers, owners, creditors and the market appear to be aware of the risks faced by banks and their greater fragility. Assuming that bank owners' and creditors' investments are at risk, there is no reason to believe that bank managers will not pursue effective risk management and control procedures to maintain profitability and solvency, much as do managers of nonbanking firms. As with other fragile objects, breakage need not be greater if appropriate care is taken, and bankers appear to have taken such care in the absence of government-imposed incentives to the contrary.

Bank failures are widely perceived to be contagious to other banks. Thus, bank failures are viewed as potential economic catastrophes. But there is little, if any, empirical evidence in support of the doomsday scenario. History indicates that, at the margin, bank customers have been able to distinguish good from bad banks and almost all runs have been bank-specific. Although funding might be withdrawn quickly from insolvent banks, it is generally redeposited equally quickly at solvent banks, so that runs into currency or banking panics stemming from bank failures have been rare. When such runs have threatened, banks have been reasonably successful in taking collective action to limit the impact, both in terms of spill over to other sectors and in terms of duration. Little if any evidence suggests that bank failures, runs, and even panics ignited downturns in aggregate economic activity. Rather, the evidence strongly suggests that exogenous reductions in bank reserves that are not replaced by the central bank and serious downturns in the economy ignite banking problems. (Banking problems, though, may, worsen conditions in the rest of the economy.)

Moreover, the potential for all bank panics is reduced almost to zero when central banks act intelligently and restore aggregate reserves (not individual bank reserves) that would be reduced in runs to currency or do not prevent banks from taking their own corrective actions (both actions that the Federal Reserve failed to do in the early 1930s). Furthermore, credible deposit insurance exists on small deposits that can practically be converted into currency and large (uninsured) deposits that are withdrawn from a weak bank would certainly be redeposited in another bank. Hence, there is little reason to expect a destabilizing run to currency.

The cost of individual bank failures is relatively small and not greatly different from the failure of any nonbank firm of comparable importance in its community. In fact, on average, the societal cost of preventing insolvent banks from failing is considerably greater, as such actions make excessive risk-taking by banks more likely to occur. The simultaneous failure of large numbers of banks could be more costly if the credit and payments systems were disrupted. However, we emphasize that such failures can be prevented both by the central bank's acting as a lender of last resort that provides macroliquidity to the banking system, and by governments not offering mispriced guarantees that encourage banks to assume greater risks than otherwise. Loans to individual banks are neither necessary nor cost effective. Similarly, we see no role for an international lender of last resort.

The policy solutions for preventing potential breakdowns from becoming actual breakdowns are straightforward and clear cut. Government should remove restrictions that prevent banks from voluntary risk reduction (e.g., geographic and product restrictions for banks and appropriate use of derivatives), should reduce the risk to the payments system by providing incentives for reducing, if not eliminating, intraday overdrafts and for clearing in good funds, and be prepared to replace fully any aggregate reserves lost from currency runs. Government should be no more concerned with the failure of individual banks than with the failure of any other individual firms in any industry.

The solution for achieving greater safety is to enhance efficiency and accountability in banking and bank regulation rather than decreasing either or both. We have outlined elsewhere what we believe to be an appropriate and feasible way to accomplish these goals within the restrictions of the existing federal government deposit insurance structure (Benston and Kaufman, 1988). Evidence from both this country and nearly all other major countries suggests that, primarily for political reasons, this structure is unlikely to be scaled back dramatically. Consequently the federal government retains a direct interest in the financial well being of insured depository institutions. To minimize its potential losses, the government needs to reduce if not eliminate the now well-recognized moral hazard problem for banks and principal-agent problem for regulators. In brief, this may be achieved by requiring insured institutions to hold higher amounts of capital than they have held since the introduction of deposit insurance, amounts the market would deem in the absence of deposit insurance to be sufficient to absorb most losses that might incur. Capital should be measured in terms of the market values of banks' assets and liabilities. If capital were defined to include subordinated debentures that have a remaining maturity of at least two years and that cannot be redeemed early, this higher capital requirement would not impose higher tax or other costs on banks, except for the effective removal of a deposit-insurance subsidy. The capital requirement would be enforced by a system of structured early intervention and resolution (SEIR) by regulators to make it more effective in discouraging poor and opportunistic management.

As a bank's capital-to-assets ratio declined through pre-specified tranches or "trigger points," the banking regulatory authorities first could and then would have to impose restrictions on dividends and interest payments on subordinated debentures, expansion, fund transfers to affiliates, etc. Supervision and field examinations of banks would be conducted to ascertain that banks were reporting their capital correctly and were not engaged in extremely risky, illegal, or grossly incompetently managed activities. Banks with higher capital levels would be permitted to engage in a wider range of activities and be subject to less intense prudential regulation. Such carrots are as important as the sanction sticks. This structure is designed to mimic the sanctions the private market imposes on troubled noninsured firms and thus minimizes dead-weight losses relative to other regulatory alternatives proposed (Benston and Kaufman, 1988). Moreover, systemic risk that might result from the failure of banks would be effectively eliminated. A troubled bank that does not successfully respond to the prudential sanctions and that continues to deteriorate would be resolved through recapitalization, merger, or liquidation before its economic net worth turned negative. Hence, there would be no defaults as a result of losses to depositors and other creditors, including participants in the payments system.

A somewhat weaker version of SEIR was adopted in the prompt corrective action and least cost resolution provisions of the FDIC Improvement Act of 1991.[20] Although the capital ratio defining the tranches are lower, and regulatory discretion is broader than we would prefer, the act appears to be working well in reducing the number and cost of bank failures and in producing a healthier industry.[21] If it were enacted fully and administered rigorously, we see no reason for banks to be regulated prudentially with respect to where they can operate, the products they can afford to offer consumers, the assets they can own, or their ownership by nonbank firms.

In summary, the theory and evidence we have reviewed in this article lead us to reject Feldstein's description of economic collapse resulting from the failure of banks and the payments system that we quoted at the beginning of this paper. We also find little support for his view that there is a "public interest in avoiding the failure of banks . . . [because] the banking system as a whole is a 'public good'." We do agree, though, with his call for "the establishment of capital requirements," because these are necessary to reduce and almost eliminate the cost of government-provided deposit insurance, and permit the removal of most government-imposed restrictions on banks' activities.

Notes

1. Kindleberger (1978) describes numerous examples of all sorts, stretching over several centuries and many countries. A recent example of a Ponzi scheme (named for a 1920s Boston promoter) is what once was Russia's largest investment company, the MMM stock fund. Despite presenting no information on how it generated earnings, and repeated warnings by the government against purchasing the stock, the price of MMM shares rocketed from about a dollar in February to $50 in July, 1994, as the company drove up the price by repurchasing shares at higher and higher prices. The scheme collapsed when the government acted to close it down. (*New York Times*, July 30, 1994, pp. A1 and A4.)
2. See Benston, et al. (1986), pp. 42–45, for a more extensive discussion.
3. See Benston (1992) for an analysis of the effects of moral hazard in reducing the value to banks of securitizing commercial loans.
4. They reference eight earlier works that make this point, dating back to 1987.
5. See Horvitz (1990) for Texas and Randall (1993) for New England.
6. Minsky's (1972) extensive description of his theory, or his subsequent discussions (1977, 1991) do not provide specific examples or studies that illustrate or support his theory. He does state (1977, p. 139) that "the incipient financial crises of 1966, 1969–1970, and 1974–1975 were neither accidents nor the result of policy errors, but the result of the normal functioning of our particular economy." These dates appear to be associated with increases in credit; otherwise, he offers no explanation as to why he identifies them as "incipient financial crises." In his 1991 "clarification" he does not give examples or cite any studies. Neither does he mention the fact that the massive failure of savings and loan associations and the large number of bank failures experienced in the late 1980s did not give rise to or were associated with financial crises.
7. Bordo's paper was published before the world-wide stock market crash of 1987. That crash did not result in financial crises in any country, which is inconsistent with the international-transmission-of-financial-crises hypothesis.
8. Donaldson states (1992, note 4, p. 285) "One could use the deposit/currency ratio instead of the interest rate as the dependent variable in our tests with similar results." Presumably, he actually did this test and found similar results.
9. Mishkin calls this the "monetarist" explanation. Because he does not consider exogenous outflows of high-powered money, we prefer not to use this label.
10. For example, he concludes that "the Roosevelt administration terminated the nationwide bank panic by successfully conveying information about the soundness of individual banks" following the March 1933 bank holiday. Park does not consider Wigmore's (1987) explanation that the bank holiday was necessitated by a run on gold, which was ended when the Roosevelt administration de-monetized gold.
11. See Calomiris and Gorton (1991, pp. 121–124) for descriptions of and references to nine such articles.
12. See Gorton (1985) and Park (1991), Gorton and Calomiris (1991, section 4.3), Tallman (1988), and Dwyer and Gilbert (1989).
13. Such periods are defined as bank panics by Schwartz (1988).
14. See Benston, et al. (1986), p. 39, for references to studies.
15. See Tussig (1967) for an early explication of the benefits of bank failure, and Kaufman (1988) for a more extensive discussion.
16. The evidence is reviewed more completely in Kaufman (1994A), which includes references to the research from which the conclusions are drawn.
17. Flannery (1994) argues that banks issue demandable debt in part as a means of insuring creditors that their funds are likely to be safe from loss.

18. Under the Federal Deposit Insurance Corporation Improvement Act of 1991 (FDICIA), the Federal Reserve would lose the interest on loans it made to banks that failed.
19. See Benston (1994) for a more extensive analysis.
20. See Benston and Kaufman (1994) for a description of the provisions included in FDICIA and an analysis of the differences with SEIR as proposed by Benston and Kaufman (1988) and others.
21. Kaufman (1994B).

References

Bagehot, Walter. *Lombard Street*. New York: Scribner, Armstrong. 1873. (Reprinted with introduction by Frank Genovese. Homewood, IL: Irwin. 1962.)

Benston, George J. "The Future of Asset Securitization: The Benefits and Costs of Breaking Up the Bank." *Journal of Applied Corporate Finance* 5 (Spring 1992), 71–82.

Benston, George J. "International Harmonization of Banking Regulations and Cooperation Among National Regulators: An Assessment." *Journal of Financial Services Research* 8 (1994), 205–225.

Benston, George J., Robert A. Eisenbeis, Paul M. Horvitz, Edward J. Kane, and George G. Kaufman. *Perspectives on Safe and Sound Banking: Past Present, and Future*, Cambridge, MA: MIT Press. 1986.

Benston, George J., and George G. Kaufman. *Risk and Solvency Regulation of Depository Institutions: Past Policies and Current Options*. Monograph 1988-1. Monograph Series in Finance and Economics, New York: Salomon Center, New York University Graduate School of Business Administration. 1988. (A shortened version appears as "Regulating Bank Safety and Performance." In: William S. Haraf and Rose Marie Kushmeider, eds., *Restructuring the Financial System*. Washington, DC: American Enterprise Institute. 1988, pp. 63–99.)

Benston, George J., and George G. Kaufman. "Improving the FDIC Improvement Act: What Was Done and What Still Needs to Be Done to Fix the Deposit Insurance Problem." In: George G. Kaufman, ed., *Reforming Financial Institutions and Markets in the United States*. Boston: Kluwer Academic Publishers, 1994, pp. 99–120.

Benston, George J., and Clifford W. Smith, Jr. "A Transactions Cost Approach to the Theory of Financial Intermediation." *Journal of Finance* 31 (May 1976), 215–231.

Bernanke, Ben S. "Nonmonetary Effects of the Financial Crisis in the Propagation of the Great Depression." *American Economic Review* 73 (June 1983), 257–276.

Bordo, Michael D. "Financial Crises, Banking Crises, Stock Market Crashes and the Money Supply: Some International Evidence, 1870–1933." In: Forrest Capie and Geoffrey E. Wood, eds., *Financial Crises and the World Banking System*. London: Macmillan. 1986, pp. 190–248.

Bordo, Michael D. "The Lender of Last Resort: Some Insights from History." In: George G. Kaufman, ed., *Research in Financial Services*, Vol. 4. Greenwich, CT: JAI Press. 1992, pp. 1–20.

Bryant, John, "A Model of Reserves, Bank Runs, and Deposit Insurance." *Journal of Banking and Finance* 4 (1980), 335–344

Cagan, Philip. *Determinants and Effects of Changes in the Stock of Money*. New York: National Bureau of Economic Research. 1965.

Calomiris, Charles W., and Gary Gorton. "The Origins of Banking Panics: Models, Facts, and Bank Regulation." In: R. Glenn Hubbard, ed., *Financial Markets and Financial Crises*. Chicago: University of Chicago Press. 1991, pp. 109–173.

Calomiris, Charles W., and Charles M. Kahn. "The Role of Demandable Debt in Structuring Optimal Banking Arrangements." *American Economic Review* 81 (June 1991), 497–513.

Calomiris, Charles W., and Joseph R. Mason. "Contagion and Bank Failures During the Great Depression: The June 1932 Chicago Banking Panic." NBER Working paper, November 1994.

Corrigan, Gerald. "Challenges Facing the International Community of Bank Supervisors." *Quarterly Review* (Federal Reserve Bank of New York) (Autumn, 1992), 1–9.

Diamond, Douglas. "Financial Intermediation and Delegated Monitoring." *Review of Economic Studies* 51 (July, 1984), 393–414.

Diamond, Douglas, and Philip Dybvig. "Bank Runs, Liquidity and Deposit Insurance." *Journal of Political Economy* 91 (1983), 401–419.

Donaldson, R. Glenn. "Sources of Panics: Evidence from the Weekly Data." *Journal of Monetary Economics* (November 1992), 277–305.

Dwyer, Gerald P., Jr., and Alton Gilbert. "Bank Runs and Private Remedies." *Review* (Federal Reserve Bank of St. Louis) 71 (May/June 1989), 43–61.

Eichengreen, Barry, and Richard Portes. "The Anatomy of Financial Crises." In: Richard Portes and Alexander K. Swoboda, eds., *Threats to International Financial Stability*. Cambridge, UK: Cambridge University Press. 1987, pp. 10–58.

Eisenbeis, Robert A. "Private Sector Solutions to Payments System Fragility." *Journal of Financial Services Research* (forthcoming).

Feldstein, Martin. "The Risk of Economic Crisis: Introduction." In: Martin Feldstein, ed., *The Risk of Economic Crisis*. Chicago: University of Chicago Press. 1991, pp. 1–18.

Fisher, Irving M. *Booms and Depressions*. New York: Adelphi. 1932.

Fisher, Irving M. "The Debt Deflation Theory of Great Depressions." *Econometrica* 1 (1933), 337–57.

Flannery, Mark J. "Payments System Risk and Public Policy." In: Rose Marie Kushmeider and William S. Haraf, eds., *Restructuring Banking and Financial Services in America*. Washington, DC: American Enterprise Institute. 1988, pp. 261–287.

Flannery, Mark J. "Debt Maturity and the Deadweight Cost of Leverage: Optimally Financing Banking Firms." *American Economic Review* 84 (March 1994), 320–331.

Friedman, Milton, and Anna J. Schwartz. *A Monetary History of the United States*. Princeton, NJ: National Bureau of Economic Research, Princeton University Press. 1963.

GAO (U.S. General Accounting Office). *Financial Derivatives: Actions Needed to Protect the Financial System*. Washington, DC: U.S. General Accounting Office. May 1994.

Gilbert, Alton R. "Payments System Risk: What Is It and What Will Happen If We Try To Reduce It?" *Review* (Federal Reserve Bank of St. Louis) 71 (January/February 1989), 3–17.

Goodfriend, Marvin, and Robert G. King. "Financial Deregulation, Monetary Policy, and Central Banking." In: William S. Haraf, and Rose Marie Kushmeider, eds., *Restructuring the Financial System*. Washington, DC: American Enterprise Institute. 1988, pp. 216–253.

Gorton, Gary. "Clearing Houses and the Origin of Central Banking in the U.S." *Journal of Economics History* 45 (2) (1985), 277–283.

Gorton, Gary. "Banking Panics and Business Cycles." *Oxford Economic Papers* 40 (1988), 751–81.

Gorton, Gary, and Donald Mullineaux. "The Joint Production of Confidence: Endogenous Regulation and the 19th Century Commercial Bank Clearinghouses." *Journal of Money, Credit and Banking* 19 (4) (1987), 458–468.

Guttentag, Jack, and Richard Herring. "Emergency Liquidity Assistance for International Banks." In: Richard Portes and Alexander K. Swoboda, eds., *Threats to International Financial Stability*. Cambridge, UK: Cambridge University Press. 1987, pp. 150–186.

Horvitz, Paul M. "Stimulating Bank Competition Through Regulatory Actions." *Journal of Finance* (March 1965), 2–3.

Horvitz, Paul M. "The Collapse of the Texas Thrift Industry." In George G. Kaufman, ed., *Restructuring the American Financial System*. Boston: Kluwer Academic Publishers, 1990, 95–116.

Huffman, Wallace E., and James R. Lothian. "US–UK Business Cycle Linkages Under the Gold Standard." In Michael D. Bordo and Anna J. Schwartz, eds., *A Retrospective on the Classical Gold Standard, 1821-1931*. University of Chicago Press: Chicago. 1984, pp. 455–511.

Kaufman, George G. "Bank Runs: Causes, Benefits and Costs." *CATO Journal* (Winter 1988), 539–587.

Kaufman, George G. "Lender of Last Resort: A Contemporary Perspective." *Journal of Financial Services Research* 5 (1991), 95–110.

Kaufman, George G. "Bank Contagion: A Review of the Theory and Evidence." *Journal of Financial Services Research*. 8 (1994A), 123–150.

Kaufman, George G. "FDICIA: The Early Evidence." *Challenge Magazine*. (July/August 1994B), 53–57.

Kindleberger, Charles P. *Manias, Panics, and Crashes*. New York: Basic Books. 1978.

Kindleberger, Charles P. "Bank Failures: The 1930s and the 1980s." In: *The Search for Financial Stability: The Past Fifty Years*. San Francisco: Federal Reserve Bank of San Francisco. 1985, pp. 7–34.

Kryzanowski, Lawrence, and Gordon S. Roberts. "The Performance of the Canadian Banking System, 1922–1940." *Journal of Money, Credit and Banking* (August 1993) Pt. 1, 361–376.

Meltzer, Allan H. "Financial Failures and Financial Policies." In: George G. Kaufman and Roger C. Kormendi, eds., *Deregulating Financial Services: Public Policy in Flux*. Cambridge, MA: Ballinger Publishing Company. 1986, 79–96.

Minsky, Hyman P. "Financial Instability Revisited: The Economics of Disaster." *Reappraisal of the Federal Reserve Discount Mechanism* 3 (June 1972), 95–136.

Minsky, Hyman P. "A Theory of Systematic Financial Fragility." In: Edward J. Altman and Arnold W. Sametz, eds., *Financial Crises: Institutions and Markets in a Fragile Environment*. New York: Wiley. 1977, pp. 138–152.

Minsky, Hyman P. "The Financial Instability Hypothesis: A Clarification." In: Martin Feldstein, ed., *The Risk of Economic Crisis*. Chicago: The University of Chicago Press. 1991, 158–170.

Miron, Jeffrey A. "Financial Panics, the Seasonality of the Nominal Interest Rate, and the Founding of the Fed." *American Economic Review* 76 (March 1986), 125–140.

Mishkin, Frederic S. "Asymmetric Information and Financial Crises: A Historical Perspective." In: R. Glenn Hubbard, ed., *Financial Markets and Financial Crises*. Chicago: University of Chicago Press. 1991, 69–108.

Randall, Richard E. "Lessons from New England Bank Failures." *New England Economic Review* (Federal Reserve Bank of Boston) (May/June 1993), 13–38.

Park, Sangkyun. "Bank Failure Contagion in Historical Perspective." *Journal of Monetary Economics* 28 (1991), 271–286.

Schwartz, Anna. "Real and Pseudo-financial Crises." In: Forrest Capie and Geoffrey E. Wood, eds., *Financial Crises and the World Banking System*. London: Macmillan, 1986, pp. 11–31.

Schwartz, Anna. "Financial Stability and the Federal Safety Net." In: Rose Marie Kushmeider and William S. Haraf, eds., *Restructuring Banking and Financial Services in America*. Washington, DC: American Enterprise Institute. 1988, pp. 34–62.

Schwartz, Anna. "The Misuse of the Fed's Discount Window." *Review* (Federal Reserve Bank of St. Louis) 74 (September/October 1992), 59–69.

Smith, Bruce D. "Bank Panics, Suspensions, and Geography: Some Notes on the 'Contagion of Fear' in Banking." *Economic Inquiry* 29 (April 1991), 230–248.

Sprague, Oliver M. W. *History of Crises Under the National Banking System*. Washington, DC: U.S. Government Printing Office: National Monetary Commission. 1910.

Staff Report. *An Analysis of Federal Reserve Discount Window Loans to Failed Institutions*. Washington, DC: U.S. House of Representatives, Committee on Banking, Finance and Urban Affairs. 1991.

Tallman, Ellis. "Some Unanswered Questions about Bank Panics." *Economic Review* (Federal Reserve Bank of Atlanta), 73 (November/December 1988), 2–21.

Tallman, Ellis, and Jon Moen. "Liquidity Shocks and Financial Crises During the National Banking Era." Unpublished manuscript, Federal Reserve Bank of Atlanta, April 1994.

Tussig, Dale. "The Case for Bank Failures." *Journal of Law and Economics* (October 1967), 140–141.

White, Eugene N. *The Regulation and Reform of the American Banking System, 1900–1929*. Princeton, NJ: Princeton University Press. 1983.

Wigmore, Barrie. "Was The Bank Holiday of 1933 a Run on the Dollar Rather Than On the Banks?" *Journal of Economic History* (December 1987), 739–756.

Journal of Financial Services Research 9: 241–257 (1995)

Financial Fragility: Issues and Policy Implications

CHARLES W. CALOMIRIS
Department of Finance, University of Illinois at Urbana-Champaign, 340 Commerce West, Champaign, IL 61820

1. Introduction

This article addresses the question of how financial institutions, contracting forms, and government financial policies affect the degree of macroeconomic volatility. Models that posit such relationships are sometimes referred to as models of "financial fragility." These models explore ways in which the financial system can add to the volatility of economic activity by defining sources of financial "shocks" and financial "propagators" of other shocks. Financial shocks are defined as disturbances to the real economy that originate in financial markets. Financial propagation refers to the ways in which financial contracts, markets, and intermediaries can serve to aggravate shocks that originate elsewhere. Economists have not always been receptive to the idea that financial arrangements matter for business cycles. From the standpoint of traditional neoclassical general equilibrium theory, financial arrangements (which include financial contracting, the actions of financial intermediaries, and government policies toward the financial sector) typically are viewed as epiphenomenal—simply as a set of mechanisms for executing Arrow–Debreu contingent claims to allocate resources optimally. Mainstream macroeconomists and finance specialists of the 1960s seemed to agree.[1] Corporation financial decisions were neutral according to Modigliani and Miller (1958), with the addition of minor caveats to take account of physical bankruptcy costs and tax incentives; and firms all faced identical costs of funds adjusted for systematic risk factors according to the capital asset pricing model. Thus, there was no call to object to the standard IS-LM macroeconomic framework's assumption that all firms effectively faced the same cost of funds (summarized by "the" interest rate) and that this cost equaled the marginal product of capital.

One of the reasons that macroeconomic theorists and financial economists have changed paradigms in recent years, and have come to view financial relationships as more than epiphenomenal, is the growing evidence that financial relationships affect the volatility of economic activity. Such effects fall into two categories—namely, financial shocks to the macroeconomy, and financial propagators of disturbances that originate elsewhere.[2] Models that incorporate these financial effects imply "excessive" volatility of output from the standpoint of the neoclassical benchmark model. In an environment that allows financial arrangements to act as sources and propagators of shocks, output will vary more than in an environment in which financial arrangements are merely epiphenomenal.

In this article, I will briefly review a small subset of the theory and evidence that underlie the argument that financial factors can contribute to macroeconomic volatility. I do not provide a comprehensive review of the literature here; rather my aim is to illustrate important categories of effects and supporting evidence for those ideas.[3] In conclusion, I consider appropriate policy responses in light of theory and evidence.

2. Financial propagators

Some of the most important financial propagators include: (1) the cash-flow constraint, (2) balance-sheet (or more narrowly, leverage) constraints, (3) external supply-of-funds constraints (limitations on bank credit), and (4) financial regulations that magnify business cycles. These constraints really are not different phenomena, but different aspects of the same underlying costs of information and control attendant to corporate finance. Each acts as a financial propagator, in the sense that, relative to the benchmark of neoclassical financial neutrality, the economic activity of firms is more volatile in response to variation in exogenous disturbances as a result of these related factors.

2.1. The cash-flow constraint

The "cash-flow constraint" is simply shorthand for the statement that firms raise funds more cheaply internally than externally. Information and transaction costs account for the wedge between the cost of internal and external funds (e.g., Stiglitz and Weiss, 1981; Bernanke and Gertler, 1990; Greenwald and Stiglitz, 1990; Calomiris and Hubbard, 1990). This constraint increases the sensitivity of investment to changes in firm earnings (a "financial accelerator"), and thus makes investment more volatile that under the standard neoclassical, "flexible-accelerator" model. Empirical evidence from panel data studies emphasizes that this effect is not uniform across firms (Fazzari, Hubbard, and Petersen, 1988; Calomiris and Hubbard, 1995; Bernanke, Gertler, and Gilchrist, 1994; Calomiris, Himmelberg, and Wachtel, 1995; Kashyap, Owen, and Stein, 1993; Carpenter, Fazzari, and Petersen, 1993; Himmelberg and Petersen, 1993). Firms with identifiably higher costs of external finance display much greater cash-flow sensitivity of fixed investment and inventory accumulation, even after controlling for fundamental investment opportunities (using innovations in sales, or measures of Tobin's Q).[4]

   Calomiris and Hubbard (1995) analyze the characteristics and behavior of different classes of firms, divided according to their shadow costs of external finance. The shadow cost of external finance is derived from the firms' responses to the undistributed profits tax of 1936, which placed a progressive surtax on retained earnings. They find that firms with high external finance costs tend to be small, tend to have high debt ratios and low ratios of profits to sales, and tend to experience high profits growth. Calomiris and

Hubbard argue that these attributes can be seen as characteristics of "unseasoned" credit risks, that is, of fast growing firms, that require the discipline of short-term debt when financing themselves externally, and which have not achieved their long-run scale of operations.

Table 1 shows that firms facing high costs of external finance exhibit much greater cash-flow sensitivity of fixed investment and working capital investment than other firms,

Table 1. The cash-flow sensitivity of investment in fixed capital and working capital by firms' costs of external finance (A = Low, B = Middle, C = High)

Fixed Capital Investment Regressions, 1936				
Regression number	(1)		(2)	
Dependent variable	I_{1936}/K_{1935}		I_{1936}/K_{1935}	
Number of observations	244		244	
Adjusted R-squared	0.063		0.217	
	Coefficient	Standard error	Coefficient	Standard error
Constant	−0.019	0.022	0.015	0.021
Type B			−0.037	0.036
Type C			−0.112	0.051
Q_{1935}	0.044	0.016	0.024	0.011
$Q_{1935} \times$ Type B			0.024	0.019
$Q_{1935} \times$ Type C			0.039	0.051
$(CF_{1935} + CF_{1936})/K_{1935}$	0.018	0.016	−0.004	0.014
$[(CF_{1935} + CF_{1936})/K_{1935}] \times$ Type B			0.003	0.018
$[(CF_{1935} + CF_{1936})/K_{1935}] \times$ Type C			0.248	0.100
Change in Working Capital Regression, 1936				
Regression number	(1)		(2)	
Dependent variable	$\Delta WK_{1936}/K_{1935}$		$\Delta WK_{1936}/K_{1935}$	
Number of observations	244		244	
Adjusted R-squared	0.276		0.209	
	Coefficient	Standard error	Coefficient	Standard error
Constant	−0.016	0.047	−0.017	0.048
Type B	−0.025	0.076	−0.031	0.079
Type C	−0.211	0.385	−0.149	0.300
Q_{1935}	0.054	0.040	0.046	0.037
$Q_{1935} \times$ Type B	−0.026	0.067	0.002	0.068
$Q_{1935} \times$ Type C	0.171	0.257	0.354	0.355
$(CF_{1935} + CF_{1936})/K_{1935}$	−0.028	0.056		
$[(CF_{1935} + CF_{1936})/K_{1935}] \times$ Type B	0.214	0.061		
$[(CF_{1935} + CF_{1936})/K_{1935}] \times$ Type C	1.005	0.737		
CF_{1935}/K_{1935}			−0.023	0.093
$CF_{1935}/K_{1935} \times$ Type B			0.390	0.100
$CF_{1935}/K_{1935} \times$ Type C			0.841	1.447

Note: Heteroscedasticity-consistent standard errors are presented.
Source: Calomiris and Hubbard (1995).

after controlling for firm opportunities as measured by Tobin's Q. Moreover, the sensitivity of working capital is especially pronounced, which is consistent with the notion that firms with high finance costs self-insure against cash-flow fluctuations with working capital. They accumulate liquid assets during high earnings periods and draw them down during low earnings periods. Other firms, with lower cost access to external finance need not follow this same practice.

Calomiris, Himmelberg, and Wachtel (1995) study the characteristics of firms that differ in terms of access to credit markets. At the top of the "pecking order" are firms with access to commercial paper and rated bond markets; next are those with access to rated bond markets only; and at the bottom are firms without any rated debt. The researchers find that the size of firms, and their stocks of liquid assets, vary importantly across credit classes. Firms with limited access to credit markets tend to be smaller firms with larger stocks of liquid assets (inventories and financial working capital). As in Calomiris and Hubbard (1995), Calomiris, Himmelberg, and Wachtel show that the sensitivity of a firm's inventory accumulation or financial working capital investment decreases with the firm's access to sources of external finance.

The conclusions of these and other recent panel studies of cash-flow sensitivity are that fixed investment, R&D investment, and working capital investment are all "excessively" sensitive to cash flow (relative to the benchmark neoclassical model of investment). Sensitivity to cash flow (or "financial slack") varies systematically with the firm's costs of external finance. Liquid assets (inventories, cash, and net accounts receivable) tend to be most sensitive to cash flow, reflecting their role as a "buffer stock" to prevent fixed capital (which is costly to adjust) from fluctuating as much in response to earnings shocks. All of the above-referenced studies conclude that the "financial accelerator" is an important contributor to the macroeconomic relationship between earnings and investment.

2.2. Balance-sheet constraints

Since Keynes (1931) and Fisher (1933), economists have considered the possible role of balance sheets as "state variables" that propagate shocks. In simpler terms, firms with large amounts of debt relative to assets, or with large ratios of illiquid assets relative to liquid assets, may find it particularly difficult to attract additional external funds if sales demand falls off. Firms that increase their leverage during booms run the risk of suffering a greater response of their investment levels to any given decline in demand. This "debt-overhang effect" was invoked by several academics and chroniclers to explain the slow recovery from the recent recession in the United States and Great Britain, among other countries. Clearly, balance-sheet constraints and earnings constraints work together. "Financial slack" (as defined by Myers and Majluf, 1984) includes the firm's available internally generated funds, its liquid assets, and its capacity to float riskless debt. Thus, leverage constraints that restrict future borrowing can have a similar effect to that resulting from reductions in cash flow.

Table 2, drawn from Calomiris, Orphanides, and Sharpe (1994) provides evidence of the importance of a debt-overhang effect for employment, inventory accumulation, and

Table 2. The effect of leverage on employment, inventories, and investment

Variables	Employment	Inventories	Investment
Constant	−0.011	−0.006	−0.001
	(0.002)	(0.003)	(0.002)
Lag Dependent Variable	0.110	0.203	0.048
	(0.016)	(0.017)	(0.019)
Leverage	−0.011	−0.014	0.024
	(0.008)	(0.013)	(0.009)
Total Assets	−0.012	0.000	−0.005
	(0.010)	(0.015)	(0.010)
EXP × "Sales"	0.398	0.513	0.031
	(0.013)	(0.021)	(0.004)
REC × "Sales"	0.418	0.327	0.044
	(0.018)	(0.028)	(0.005)
EXP × LEV × "Sales"	−0.045	−0.326	−0.024
	(0.049)	(0.077)	(0.008)
REC × LEV × "Sales"	0.449	1.519	0.028
	(0.121)	(0.191)	(0.006)
EXP × Assets × "Sales"	−0.276	−0.384	0.066
	(0.071)	(0.111)	(0.015)
REC × Assets × "Sales"	0.600	1.070	0.062
	(0.163)	(0.256)	(0.018)
Adjusted R-Squared	0.191	0.118	0.045

Variable definitions: Employment and inventories are defined as log differences; investment is defined as the ratio of gross fixed investment to fixed capital. In the employment and inventories regressions, sales are defined as a log difference, while in the investment regression sales are defined as the ratio of sales to capital. Sales are defined over a two-year period (lagged plus contemporaneous years), while dependent variables are defined over one year. Sales are instrumented using firm-level and economy-wide lagged variables. EXP is an indicator variable for non-recession phases of the business cycle, and REC is an indicator variable for recession phases. LEV is an abbreviation for leverage. Standard errors are corrected for heteroskedasticity.
Source: Calomiris, Orphanides, and Sharpe (1994).

fixed capital investment, for a sample of U.S. durables manufacturers between 1959 and 1985. The table shows that the responsiveness of each of these three variables to an exogenous (instrumented) change in sales was conditioned by the lagged leverage of the firm. During times of increasing sales, higher leverage had little effect, but acted to dampen the responses of employment, inventory accumulation, and fixed capital to changes in demand; during times of decreasing sales, higher leverage magnified the decline in these variables in response to falling sales. This is consistent with the notion that debt overhang can punish firms that expand through debt during booms with greater contractions during recessions.

2.3. Supply-of-funds constraints

The recent banking/corporate finance literature has emphasized the role of intermediaries in reducing costs of external finance (for a review, see Bhattacharya and Thakor,

1994). Microeconomic studies have provided clear evidence of the importance of banks (often referred to as "delegated monitors") in reducing financing costs. For example, Slovin, Sushka, and Polonchek (1993) find that borrowers from Continental Bank suffered excess negative stock returns during its 1983 crisis, and excess positive returns during its rehabilitation. The magnitude of these returns depended on the "exclusivity" of the relationship between Continental and the borrower. Similar value-creating banking relationships were found by Petersen and Rajan (1994).

Macroeconomists have argued that shocks to the economy which reduce the net worth of banks and their borrowers, and possibly cause many bank failures, can magnify the effects of those initial shocks both by weakening borrowers' balance sheets and by reducing the supply of credit available to borrowers who depend on banks as sources of funds (Bernanke, 1983; Bernanke and Gertler, 1989; Calomiris and Hubbard, 1989; Grossman, 1993).

American macroeconomic history saw frequent episodes of banking panics or waves of bank failures, which did not always coincide.[5] Calomiris and Gorton (1991) show that historical banking panics resulted when a sufficient amount of sudden bad news about bank borrowers led depositors, who were unable to observe the precise incidence of the disturbance across banks, to doubt the solvency of their banks.[6] Banking panics during the period 1880–1913 followed moments of rapid decline in the stock market which were also associated with large (seasonally adjusted) increases in the liabilities of failed businesses. These panics occurred at business cycle peaks. While banking panics were the result of adverse macroeconomic news, they magnified the effects of that news by forcing a shrinkage of credit and disorder within the payments system. This sometimes resulted in suspension of bank convertibility (typically, for several weeks), until the uncertainty over the incidence of the disturbance within the banking system could be resolved.

Calomiris and Mason (1994) argue that the banking crises of the 1930s were different from these earlier banking panics in several respects. The collapse of the 1930s occurred in the midst of a severe depression rather than at a business cycle peak, and was associated with enormous fundamental declines in bank asset values. The transmission of bank instability was from "the bottom up"—initially bank distress was largely limited to small, rural banks, then it spread to regional financial centers, and eventually to national financial centers. Calomiris and Mason argue that existing evidence supports the view that, like bank failures during the earlier era, bank failures in the 1930s seem attributable to fundamental insolvency rather than to unwarranted closures of banks as a result of confusion or panic.

2.4. Regulatory distortions: Unit banking, credit subsidies, deposit insurance

It follows from the discussion thus far of financial "non-neutrality" that regulatory interventions by the government can affect the stability of the economy through the interventions' influences on financial contracting and financial institutions. Three illustrative examples from the U.S. experience are (1) regulations limiting bank consolidation, (2) direct and indirect credit subsidies to farming and real estate, and (3) deposit insurance.

Calomiris (1993a) reviews the history of unit banking restrictions in the United States, and argues that it was a significant contributor to American financial and economic instability. Unit banking meant greater fragility of individual banks due to less diversification and less potential for coordination among banks in response to crises. Unlike the banking systems of Britain, Canada, and Australia, the U.S. banking system was prone to large numbers of failures and to episodes of suspension of convertibility. And unlike those other systems, U.S. banks were unable to develop nationwide arrangements to coinsure risk and limit system-wide crises. Not only were individual bank failures, credit crunches, and banking panics unusually likely in the United States, but they seem to have been an especially important contributor to business cycles, as compared to other countries.

Calomiris (1995) and Calomiris and Raff (1995) argue that unit banking also inhibited the development of efficient bank-firm relationships during the pre-World War I industrial revolution. Unit banking implied a scale mismatch between the new large industrial firms and their bankers. This created a relatively high cost of external finance for American firms, and may have magnified the "financial accelerator" in the United States.

Government directed-credit programs or assistance to banks can also be destabilizing, especially when asset markets are subject to bubbles and crashes. Carey (1994) argues that subsidized financial structures that weaken or remove lenders' vigilance against the credit risk associated with asset price bubbles can magnify shocks and promote bubbles and crashes. Such structures have the effect of subsidizing and amplifying the overinvestment behavior of excessively optimistic people.

Carey draws empirical evidence from panel data on the behavior of the market for U.S. farm land and related credit markets during the period 1970–1990. Land is different from some financial assets (like stock) in that land is in fixed supply, and it is virtually impossible to sell short individual tracts of land. His model permits agents to have heterogeneous beliefs about the future, and, in the absence of short-selling, this means that optimists will set the price of land, since only those who already own land or who are interested in purchasing land will influence land's market value. If a group of agents controlling sufficient wealth becomes sufficiently overoptimistic about land values, it will push land prices away from fundamental values.

Lenders' behavior is key to the size of the distortion produced by the short-selling restriction. Lenders can dampen the price effect by refusing to loan to the optimists, as would be prudent. But if lenders are insensitive to credit risk, and willing to lend to optimists, they allow optimists to push up land prices. This, in turn, may boost further optimism and further excessive investment through the effect which inflated land values have on future borrowers' willingness to borrow, and future bankers' estimates of collateral.

Carey argues that the Farm Credit System was especially guilty of "feeding the optimists" during the agricultural boom and bust cycle of the 1970s and 1980s. Figure 1 plots the path of the real price of farm land during that period. Figure 2 plots the share of the Farm Credit System in net new farm mortgage lending. This lender's incentive structure and guaranteed funding sources made it unlikely to be vigilant or wary of a land market bubble when making loans. Unsurprisingly, its share of net new lending went to 100 percent, as prices approached the peak. A federal bailout of the Farm Credit System was ultimately the result of its imprudence, but that cost was only a fraction of the total cost of years of misdirected resources used to finance an unwarranted expansion.

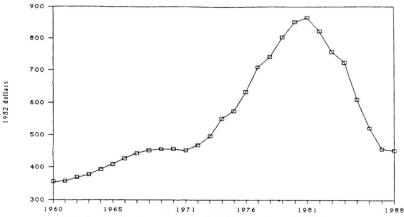

Figure 1. Average U.S. farm land price, constant dollars (Source: Carey (1994)).

The broad lessons from Carey's work are that bubbles should be taken seriously as risks when designing financial institutions or government credit programs, and that government subsidies (broadly defined) can significantly amplify macroeconomic shocks. By feeding the optimists, and promoting asset price bubbles, distortionary subsidies that the U.S. government provided to real estate investment may have played an important role in the agricultural boom and bust of the 1970s and 1980s (Calomiris, Hubbard, and Stock, 1986; Carey, 1994), in the southwestern oil and real estate boom and bust of the 1970s and 1980s (Horvitz, 1992), and in the urban real estate boom and bust of the 1980s.

Deposit insurance was part of the credit subsidy to investments in land during the recent booms, and once land and oil prices began to fall, the perverse incentives created by fixed-price deposit insurance added significantly to the subsidization of high-risk real estate investments financed through savings and loans, and in Texas, through commercial banks (Horvitz, 1992; Brewer, 1994). Boyd and Gertler (1994) also link the perverse incentives of the "too-big-to-fail" doctrine to the poor performance of large eastern banks, which undertook large amounts of high-risk lending for commercial real estate projects. The fallout of the banking and savings and loan losses and failures of the 1980s was a "capital crunch" that restricted surviving banks' abilities to lend (Baer and McElravey, 1992), and thus magnified the contractionary effects of the asset price declines.

Calomiris (1990, 1992) studies historical experiments with state-sponsored deposit insurance in several states during the 1920s. Deposit insurance acted as a credit subsidy to speculative agricultural expansion and produced a boom-and-bust cycle during the period 1914–1930 which was in many ways similar to the events of the 1970s and 1980s (Calomiris, 1990, 1992). During the years of high relative prices for agricultural products, states that had passed state-level bank deposit insurance laws—effectively subsidizing rural agricultural finance by small, vulnerable unit banks—experienced faster growth in their agricultural sectors and in bank assets than did other states. They also suffered greater losses on bank assets once the collapse came.

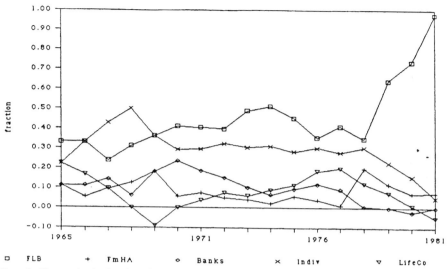

Figure 2. Changes in the fraction of new new real estate loans made by each type of lender as land prices increased during the boom (FLB = Federal Land Banks of the Farm Credit System; FmHA = Farmers Home Administration; Banks = Commercial Banks; Indiv = Non-Bank Lenders.) (Source: Carey (1994)).

The message in these regulatory examples is that financial and macroeconomic instability, manifested in waves of bank failures, banking panics, land price bubbles, and collapses in banks' abilities to lend, can be the unintended consequences of financial regulation. Ironically, the stated purposes of unit banking laws, oil, farm and real estate subsidies, and deposit insurance regulation are often at odds with the consequences of the regulations.

3. Financial shocks

Thus far I have emphasized ways in which financial arrangements can magnify disturbances that originate in "fundamentals" such as international price declines or sales demand. But financial shocks can be as important as financial propagators in contributing to macroeconomic fragility. Sometimes the distinction between financial shocks and propagators is unclear. For example, during the Great Depression, or more generally during periods of tight monetary policy, bank credit declines may have been important sources of initial shock in the economy, as well as propagators of other shocks.

Examples of shocks that unambiguously originated in the financial sector are hard to identify, particularly since asset prices respond to expectations of future shocks that have originated elsewhere, and because monetary policy (an important source of financial shock) itself responds to economic news.

One clear example of an exogenous shock coming from a financial disturbance is the commercial paper crisis of June 1970 (the Penn Central Crisis). While the collapse of Penn Central was the result of fundamental insolvency rather than a financial shock, the reverberations of its failure constituted a financial shock for other commercial paper issuers. The crisis is described in detail in Calomiris (1994). In June 1970, Penn Central, a large railroad firm with significant real estate holdings, declared bankruptcy and defaulted on its outstanding debts, including a substantial amount of commercial paper. The surprising, unprecedented failure of so prominent an issuer as Penn Central sent shock waves through the commercial paper market, and set the stage for a reevaluation of the requirements for access to this market, the method for rating issuers, and the "backup" arrangements (from banks) that were necessary for commercial paper programs. The immediate effect of the crisis was the refusal to roll over large quantities of the maturing commercial paper of other firms, that is, a "run" on commercial paper, as shown in figure 3. This forced issuers to seek emergency loans from banks en masse, a process that could have had important macroeconomic consequences for interest rates and the availability of credit. The intervention of the Fed, which encouraged banks to borrow at the discount window to finance loans to issuers, prevented the crisis from materializing, by targeting subsidized credit (indirectly through banks) to issuers with maturing paper.

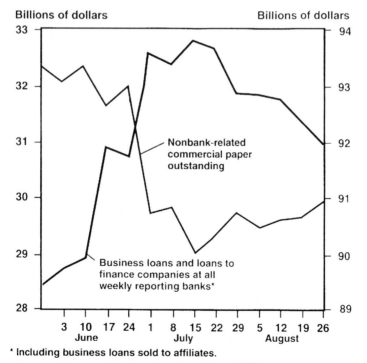

Figure 3. Commercial paper and business loans, June–August 1970.

The Penn Central example illustrates that financial disturbances are particularly likely to occur in changing financial markets, as part of the "growing pains" of financial innovation. As long as financial markets continue to change, there will be occasional episodes of painful learning about the systemic risks of new ways of managing risk and executing transactions. The potential for destabilizing financial shocks is the price we pay for a dynamic financial system. That price can be minimized, however, by an appropriately structured lender of last resort—one that provides backup protection during systemic crises, while minimizing the moral-hazard consequences of its interventions (Calomiris, 1994).

4. Policy implications

What policy implications does this summary of findings offer for reducing macroeconomic fragility? Specifically, I want to address four areas of policy. How aggressively should government protect banks, depositors, or other debt holders from insolvency? How does an awareness of financial contributors to macroeconomic instability affect monetary policy making? What improvements in fiscal policy are suggested by an emphasis on financial constraints? Can government directed-credit policies overcome costly financing constraints on firms and thus stabilize the economy?

4.1. Designing the safety net

The new literature on financial fragility emphasizes the constraints on efficient capital market allocation imposed by information and control problems in corporate finance. This new focus on the reasons for capital market "failures" defines beneficial government interventions to stabilize financial markets as those that offset the destabilizing effects of private capital market failures. Beneficial intervention requires either superior government information and control technology, or government possession of a means to offset negative externalities that come from private market failures. Most of the arguments for a financial safety net, which I define to include deposit insurance, actions by the lender of last resort, and regulation or deregulation of the activities of banks, revolve around the latter view that government interventions can offset negative externalities and thereby produce greater systemic stability.

Experience teaches that deposit insurance can be stabilizing or destabilizing, depending on the incentives that accompany the insurance. Successful, privately operated deposit insurance systems, for example, stabilized banking systems in the antebellum United States, because they were set up to encourage proper risk taking and monitoring by banks that were members of the system (Calomiris 1989, 1990; Calomiris and Schweikart, 1991). "Incentive-incompatible" deposit insurance systems destabilize banks, and can contribute to asset-price bubbles and credit crunches, all of which increase macroeconomic fragility.

Similarly, banking deregulation can provide stability or instability. Expanding banks' powers and allowing them to expand their operations can reduce risk if banks face proper incentives; alternatively, deregulation can provide greater opportunities for destabilizing risk taking by banks that face perverse regulatory incentives.

The same can be said of the lender of last resort. If the discount window is employed irresponsibly to prop up insolvent institutions, then it will promote greater macroeconomic instability. If it is structured properly to provide temporary backup protection only to "innocent victims" and only during systemic shocks, it can have a stabilizing effect. The Fed's response to the Penn Central crisis is an example of a desirable intervention. Penn Central was allowed to fail, but other commercial paper issuers were protected from the adverse temporary consequences of that failure. Government assistance came in the form of a short-term credit subsidy to commercial paper issuers, passed on through discount window lending to commercial banks. Importantly, default risk on individual loans still remained with the commercial banks that lent funds to issuers.

It is worth emphasizing the differences between the safety net policy implications of the new literature on financial fragility and those of the alternative view advocated by Minsky and Kindleberger. The new literature on financial fragility stresses the ways in which costs of information and control in corporate finance make the macroeconomy more vulnerable to shocks. Unlike the alternative view of financial fragility pioneered by Minsky and Kindleberger, the new literature views fragility as a consequence of inherent costs of corporate finance, rather than as irrational market psychology that promotes booms and busts. Consequently, the new literature leads to different perspectives on policy for dealing with financial fragility. In contrast to Minsky and Kindleberger, who call for aggressive government intervention to stabilize the financial system, advocates of the new view tend to emphasize potential costs of government intervention which were not considered before. The new literature's assumption of rational behavior (and hence the importance of private incentives) implies potentially high incentive costs of government bailouts, as rational individuals take advantage of perverse incentives created by the safety net. Furthermore, to the extent that overly optimistic (or myopic) beliefs are important driving forces in speculative booms and busts, government subsidies or government protection may fuel irrational speculation, as discussed in Carey (1994). Thus, well-intentioned government stabilization policies may actually be destabilizing.

Once one recognizes that government intervention can be destabilizing as well as stabilizing, important implications follow. First, government policy rules that presume a need for constant intervention may be falsely self-justifying—that is, the more government intervenes the more its (destabilizing) intervention seems to be necessary. Second, the costs of government intervention raise the threshold for activist policy. If there were no costs to intervention, then even a very small probability of a benefit (a trivially small probability of a financial "meltdown") can justify a very aggressive safety net. But if an aggressive safety net is costly, then advocates of such policy must do more than construct a scenario under which intervention will be helpful. They must show that the expected benefits outweigh the expected costs. Given the costs to taxpayers of the recent bailout of the savings and loan industry in the United States, and the costs of the recent Finnish bank collapse (which required a capital infusion into the banks equal to 18 percent of GDP according to Nyberg and Vihriala, 1994, p. 41), both of which reflect perverse incentives created by government intervention, advocates of a broad safety net may find it difficult to meet that challenge.

4.2. Monetary policy and financial fragility

Monetary policy is likely to be very important, and its effects may be long-lasting. Monetary policy not only affects the average level of economic activity, but the relative viability of certain firms. As Bernanke, Gertler, and Gilchrist (1994) show, small firms do poorly during recessions, and this is plausibly linked to their higher costs of credit, particularly during monetary contractions. Because unseasoned, high-growth firms (the Schumpeterian innovators of the next generation) suffer disproportionately during contractions, as Schumpeter (1939) recognized, shocks to aggregate demand (including monetary policy) can limit the growth of aggregate supply.

Monetary policy shocks will have varying effects over time, and will not be "symmetrically reversible." Because financial state variables (e.g., leverage) condition the response of investment to demand shocks, there may be no stable relationship between monetary policy and output response. In particular, it may be hard to undo a financial collapse (like the Great Depression) with stimulative, open-market operations (Calomiris, 1993b).

These considerations may have implications for monetary policy rules. In particular, they emphasize that the effects of monetary policy on firms' balance sheets and on the availability of bank credit may be important, and that these variables may be useful as indicators to guide policy. Furthermore, they suggest that there are long-term costs of extreme swings in the economy through the financial consequences of lost income during severe recessions and declines in the values of assets, which argue for making contractionary monetary policy cautious and predictable.

4.3. Fiscal policy in the presence of financing constraints

Tax policy is an important and somewhat neglected vehicle for reducing the financial accelerator. If the corporate tax were eliminated, the potential for cash-flow or balance-sheet constraints to bind for young growing firms would be reduced. As Calomiris and Hubbard (1990) argue, tax reductions that increase average after-tax corporate cash flow improve economic efficiency by reducing the frequency with which financing constraints bind. Thus a movement toward consumption taxation or personal income taxation, and away from corporate taxation, would both improve the allocation of resources on average over time and reduce volatility by weakening the financial accelerator.

4.4. Directed-credit policy

Calomiris and Himmelberg (1994a, 1994b) discuss possible benefits from directed-credit programs in relaxing financing constraints, even when government lacks any information advantage about the quality of recipients. Conceivably, such policies could reduce financial fragility by weakening firms' dependence on internal funds to finance investment. But Carey's (1994) arguments about destabilizing effects of government subsidies on asset prices provide a counterweight to that salutary effect. Furthermore, "political-economy" considerations place an important wedge between espoused justifications and likely consequences of government credit policies.

5. Conclusion

I conclude that the theory and evidence for financial fragility suggest that interventions by the government can be stabilizing or destabilizing, and that government policy should take into account the destabilizing consequences of its policies in the areas of bank regulation, taxation, credit subsidization, monetary control, and the lender of last resort.

Activist governments will not be able to rid their economies of financial fragility, and attempts to reduce fragility can backfire by producing unintended consequences (e.g., through magnifying land price bubbles). Knowing that financial factors act as sources or propagators of shocks typically does not translate into effective options for eliminating destabilizing financial effects. Financial fragility is, to a large extent, an unavoidable consequence of a dynamic capitalistic economy. Its fundamental sources—information asymmetry and learning about new systemic risks—cannot be eliminated by government intervention, and attempts to do so may create more instability than they prevent.

Notes

1. There was significant dissent against this view, as exemplified by Gurley and Shaw (1960), Kindleberger (1973), and Minsky (1975).
2. I adopt the shock and propagation view of the mechanism through which financial factors contribute to business cycles, which is consistent with rational economic behavior under asymmetric information and/or imperfect corporate control. An alternative view, espoused by Kindleberger (1973) and Minsky (1975), relies on myopia to generate endogenous boom and bust cycles in financial markets. While there is surely room for both views in understanding macroeconomic fragility—and the recent literature provides convincing evidence for waves of excessive optimism regarding stock prices (Loughran and Ritter, 1994)—the shock and propagation view is better able to explain interesting cross-sectional variation in panel data, which this article summarizes. For example, not all banking systems are equally unstable, and cross-sectional variation in instability can be linked to flaws in the regulation of banking systems and related incentive problems. Similar cross-sectional differences in the importance of cash flow constraints, leverage constraints, and bank credit constraints also argue for the "rational" view of financial fragility. The new literature on financial fragility also can explain other facts about financial-real linkages. For example, in

addition to financial influences on the volatility of output, recent research has also argued that financial constraints may lower the average level of economic activity, or limit the ability of the economy to grow as quickly as it otherwise might over long periods of time (Calomiris, 1993a, 1995; Calomiris and Raff, 1995).

3. For the sake of coherence, I emphasize "corporate-finance" examples, and neglect interesting examples from the literatures on consumption and agricultural investment. For discussion of evidence for agricultural investment, see Calomiris, Hubbard, and Stock (1986), and Calomiris and Himmelberg (1994a).

4. In most studies, firm-level differences in the costs of external finance are identified on a priori grounds by firm size, dividend payout, or access to public debt markets. In Calomiris and Hubbard (1995), cost differences are measured directly, using firms' responses to a special tax experiment in 1936.

5. Waves of large numbers of bank failures and suspensions of convertibility did not generally coincide. For example, the Panic of 1907 saw a protracted suspension of convertibility but few bank failures. Similarly, the 1920s witnessed thousands of bank failures among rural banks without suspensions of convertibility.

6. For useful reviews of the literature on information externalities among banks, see Kaufman (1994), and Bhattacharya and Thakor (1994).

References

Baer, Herbert L., and John N. McElravey. "Capital Shocks and Bank Growth." *Economic Perspectives* (Federal Reserve Bank of Chicago) (July/August 1993).

Bernanke, Ben S. "Non-Monetary Effects of the Financial Crisis in the Propagation of the Great Depression." *American Economic Review* 73 (June 1983), 257–276.

Bernanke, Ben S., and Mark Gertler. "Banking in General Equilibrium." In: William Barnett and Kenneth Singleton, eds., *New Approaches to Monetary Economics*. Cambridge: Cambridge University Press. 1989.

Bernanke, Ben S., and Mark Gertler. "Financial Fragility and Economic Performance." *Quarterly Journal of Economics* 104 (February 1990), 87–114.

Bernanke, Ben S., Mark Gertler, and Simon Gilchrist. "The Financial Accelerator and the Flight to Quality." NBER Working Paper No. 4789, July 1994.

Bhattacharya, Sudipto, and Anjan V. Thakor. "Contemporary Banking Theory." *Journal of Financial Intermediation* 3 (1994), 2–50.

Boyd, John, and Mark Gertler. "The Role of Large Banks in the Recent U.S. Banking Crisis." *Federal Reserve Bank of Minneapolis Quarterly Review* (Winter 1994), 2–21.

Brewer, Elijah, III. "The Impact of the Current Deposit Insurance System on S&L Shareholders' Risk/Return Trade-offs." *Journal of Financial Services Research* 9 (1995), 65–69.

Calomiris, Charles W. "Deposit Insurance: Lessons from the Record." *Economic Perspectives* (Federal Reserve Bank of Chicago) (May/June 1989), 10–30.

Calomiris, Charles W. "Is Deposit Insurance Necessary?" *Journal of Economic History* 50 (1990), 283–95.

Calomiris, Charles W. "Do Vulnerable Economies Need Deposit Insurance: Lessons from U.S. Agriculture in the 1920s." In: Philip L. Brock, ed., *If Texas Were Chile: A Primer on Banking Reform*. San Francisco: ICS Press. 1992, pp. 237–350.

Calomiris, Charles W. "Regulation, Industrial Structure, and Instability in U.S. Banking: An Historical Perspective." In: Michael Klausner and Lawrence J. White, eds., *Structural Change in Banking*. Homewood, IL: Business One Irwin. 1993a, pp. 19–116.

Calomiris, Charles W. "Financial Factors and the Great Depression." *Journal of Economic Perspectives* (Spring 1993b), 61–85.

Calomiris, Charles W. "The Costs of Rejecting Universal Banking: American Finance in the German Mirror, 1870–1914." In: Naomi Lamoreaux and Daniel Raff, eds., *Coordination Within and Between Firms*. Chicago: University of Chicago Press. 1995, pp. 257–321.

Calomiris, Charles W. "Is the Discount Window Necessary? A Penn-Central Perspective." *Review* (Federal Reserve Bank of St. Louis) (May/June 1994), 31–56.

Calomiris, Charles W., and Gary Gorton. "The Origins of Banking Panics: Models, Facts, and Bank Regulation." In: R. Glenn Hubbard, ed., *Financial Markets and Financial Crises*. Chicago: University of Chicago
Press. 1991, 109–173.

Calomiris, Charles W., and Charles P. Himmelberg. "Directed Credit Programs for Agriculture and Industry:
Arguments from Theory and Fact." In: *Proceedings of the World Bank Annual Conference on Development
Economics 1993*. 1994a, pp. 113–137.

Calomiris, Charles W., and Charles P. Himmelberg. "Government Credit Policy and Industrial Performance:
Japanese Machine Tool Producers, 1963–1991." Working Paper, University of Illinois, December 1994b.

Calomiris, Charles W., Charles P. Himmelberg, and Paul Wachtel. "Commercial Paper, Corporate Finance,
and the Business Cycle: A Microeconomic Perspective." *Carnegie-Rochester Series on Public Policy*. 1995.

Calomiris, Charles W., and R. Glenn Hubbard. "Price Flexibility, Credit Availability, and Economic Fluctuations." *Quarterly Journal of Economics* 103 (August 1989), 429–452.

Calomiris, Charles W., and R. Glenn Hubbard. "Firm Heterogeneity, Internal Finance, and Credit Rationing."
Economic Journal 100 (March 1990), 90–104.

Calomiris, Charles W., and R. Glenn Hubbard. "Internal Finance and Investment: Evidence from the Undistributed Profits Tax of 1936–1937." *Journal of Business*, 1995.

Calomiris, Charles W., R. Glenn Hubbard, and James Stock. "The Farm Debt Crisis and Public Policy."
Brookings Papers on Economic Activity 2 (1986), 441–485.

Calomiris, Charles W., and Joseph P. Mason. "Contagion and Bank Failures During the Great Depression: The
June 1932 Chicago Banking Panic." NBER Working Paper No. 4934, November, 1994.

Calomiris, Charles W., Athanasios Orphanides, and Steven Sharpe. "Leverage as a State Variable for Employment, Inventory Accumulation, and Fixed Investment." NBER Working Paper No. 4800, July 1994.

Calomiris, Charles W., and Daniel M.G. Raff. "The Evolution of Market Structure, Information, and Spreads
in American Investment Banking." In: Michael Bordo and Richard Sylla, eds., *Anglo-American Finance*.
Homewood, IL: Irwin. 1994.

Calomiris, Charles W., and Larry Schweikart. "The Panic of 1857: Origins, Transmission, and Containment."
Journal of Economic History 51 (December 1991), 807–834.

Carey, Mark S. "Feeding the Fad: The Federal Land Banks, Land Market Efficiency, and the Farm Credit
Crisis." Working paper, Federal Reserve Board of Governors, 1994.

Carpenter, Robert E., Steven M. Fazzari, and Bruce C. Petersen. "Inventory (Dis)Investment, Internal Finance
Fluctuations, and the Business Cycle." Working paper, Washington University in St. Louis, 1993.

Fazzari, Steven, R. Glenn Hubbard, and Bruce C. Petersen. "Financing Constraints and Corporate Investment," *Brookings Papers on Economic Activity* (1989), 1141–195.

Fisher, Irving. "The Debt-Deflation Theory of Great Depressions." *Econometrica* 1 (1993), 337–357.

Greenwald, Bruce, and Joseph E. Stiglitz. "Macroeconomic Models with Equity and Credit Rationing." In:
R. Glenn Hubbard, ed., *Asymmetric Information, Corporate Finance, and Investment*. Chicago: University of
Chicago Press, 1990, pp. 15–42.

Grossman, Richard. "The Macroeconomic Consequences of Bank Failures under the National Banking System." *Explorations in Economic History* 30 (July 1993), 294–320.

Gurley, John G., and Edward S. Shaw. *Money in a Theory of Finance*. Washington, DC: Brookings Institution.
1960.

Himmelberg, Charles P., and Bruce Petersen. "R&D and Internal Finance: A Panel Study of Small Firms in
High-Tech Industries." Working paper, New York University, 1993.

Horvitz, Paul. "The Causes of Texas Bank and Thrift Failures." In: Philip L. Brock, ed., *If Texas Were Chile: A
Primer on Banking Reform*. San Francisco: ICS Press. 1992, pp. 131–193.

Kashyap, Anil, Owen Lamont, and Jeremy Stein. "Credit Conditions and the Cyclical Behavior of Inventories:
A Case Study of the 1981–82 Recession." Working paper WP-93-7, Federal Reserve Bank of Chicago, 1993.

Kaufman, George G. "Bank Contagion: A Review of the Theory and Evidence." *Journal of Financial Services
Research* (1994) 123–150.

Keynes, John M. "The Consequences to the Banks of the Collapse of Money Values." In: *Essays in Persuasion*.
New York: W.W. Norton and Company. 1963 (1931).

Kindleberger, Charles P. *The World in Depression, 1929-1939*. Berkeley: University of California Press. 1973.

Loughran, Tim, and Jay R. Ritter. "The New Issues Puzzle." Working paper, University of Illinois, 1994.

Minsky, Hyman P. *John Maynard Keynes*. New York: Columbia University Press. 1975.

Modigliani, Franco, and Merton Miller. "The Cost of Capital, Corporation Finance and the Theory of Investment." *American Economic Review* 48 (1958), 261–275.

Myers, Stewart C., and Nicholas N. Majluf. "Corporate Financing Decisions When Firms Have Investment Information that Investors Do Not." *Journal of Financial Economics* 13 (June 1984), 187–220.

Nyberg, Peter, and Vesa Vihriala. "The Finnish Banking Crisis and Its Handling." Bank of Finland Discussion Paper 7/94, 1994.

Petersen, Mitchell A., and Raghuram G. Rajan. "The Benefits of Lending Relationships: Evidence from Small Business Data." *Journal of Finance* 49 (March 1994), 3–38.

Schumpeter, Joseph. *Business Cycles: A Theoretical, Historical and Statistical Analysis of the Capitalistic Process*. New York: McGraw-Hill. 1939.

Slovin, Myron B., Marie E. Sushka, and John A. Polonchek. "The Value of Bank Durability: Borrowers as Stakeholders." *Journal of Finance* 48 (1993), 247–266.

Stiglitz, Joseph E., and Andrew Weiss. "Credit Rationing in Markets with Imperfect Information," *American Economic Review* 71 (June 1981) 393–410.

Journal of Financial Services Research 9: 259–290 (1995)
© 1995 Kluwer Academic Publishers

Off-Exchange Derivatives Markets and Financial Fragility

FRANKLIN R. EDWARDS
Arthur F. Burns Professor, Graduate School of Business, Columbia University, New York, NY 10027 U.S.A.,
Visiting Scholar, American Enterprise Institute, Washington, D.C., and member of the shadow Financial
Regulatory Committee

1. Introduction

Huge losses suffered by users of off-exchange (or OTC) derivatives have created wide-spread concern that derivatives may be undermining the stability of financial markets. During the last 12 months alone companies have reported losing more than $10 billion on derivatives investments. A prime example is Metallgesellschaft A.G. (MG), Germany's 14th largest industrial firm corporation, which reported losses of almost $1.5 billion as a result of a hedging strategy gone sour.[1] Only a massive $1.9 billion rescue operation by 150 German and international banks kept MG from going into bankruptcy. While MG did not default on its futures or swap obligations, had it done so the ramifications for some major international banks and for OTC derivatives markets in general may have been far-reaching. Substantial losses also have been reported by other large firms and investment funds: Orange County California ($1.5 billion), Showa Shell Sekiyu ($1.5 billion), Kashima Oil ($1.4 billion), Pacific Horizon Funds of Bank of America ($167.9 million), Procter & Gamble ($157 million), Air Products and Chemicals ($113 million), and Gibson Greetings ($19.7 million), to name just a few.[2] These incidents have left the clear impression that even sophisticated firms may not appreciate the potential risks associated with using derivatives, and that derivatives-related losses can be large enough to impair the solvency of even sizeable firms.

Concern about the potential effects of defaults on OTC derivatives also has resulted in nearly a dozen studies of the OTC derivatives market. Prominent among these studies are those by the Bank for International Settlements (the "Promisel" report), the Bank of England, the Group of Thirty, the Office of the U.S. Comptroller of the Currency, the Commodity Futures Trading Commission, and the U.S. Government Accounting Office (GAO). The GAO report, the most recent study, concludes that OTC derivatives pose a systemic risk to financial markets, and that additional government regulation is needed to

The author wishes to thank participants at the conference on "Coping with Financial Fragility: A Global Perspective" in Maastricht, and both Robert Eisenbeis and Michael Canter for helpful comments.

safeguard the financial system.[3] The report raises the prospect that a default by a major OTC derivatives dealer could result in spillover effects that "close down" all OTC derivatives markets, with potentially serious ramifications for derivatives users and the entire financial system.

The GAO report makes a number of recommendations aimed at strengthening the regulation and supervision of OTC derivative markets. Most importantly, it recommends bringing "unregulated" OTC dealers, such as those affiliated with securities and insurance firms, under federal supervision, and imposing on these dealers "safety and soundness" regulations similar to the capital adequacy requirements imposed on bank OTC derivatives dealers. In addition, it recommends that the Securities and Exchange Commission (SEC) be given enlarged powers to oversee the use of derivatives by *all* major end-users, and calls for improved accounting and disclosure principles for both dealers and end-users of OTC derivatives. The report proposes that market-value accounting be implemented for all financial instruments, but stops short of spelling out exactly how such a system would work.

In response to the GAO report, Congressman Edward Markey (D-Massachusetts) has introduced legislation (the "Derivative Dealers Act") that would require unregulated derivatives dealers (such as those affiliated with securities and insurance companies) to register with the SEC and be subject to SEC regulation. Among other things, this legislation would subject these dealers to SEC sales practices and standards and to anti-fraud and anti-manipulation regulations, and would establish minimum capital requirements for these dealers, conduct on-site inspections or examinations of dealers, and require periodic financial reports from dealers.

Earlier, Congressman Henry B. Gonzales (D-Tex.) and Congressman Jim Leach (R-Iowa), respectively the former chairman and the ranking Republican of the House Banking Committee, introduced the "Derivatives Safety and Soundness Act of 1994." This bill directs the Federal banking agencies and other regulatory agencies to work together to establish common principles applicable to capital, accounting, disclosure, and examination standards for financial institutions using derivatives. The bill also would require the Federal Reserve and the Comptroller of the Currency to work with other central banks to develop comparable international supervisory standards for financial institutions using derivatives. In discussing the need for this legislation, Congressman Leach said: "one of the ironies of the development [of derivative markets] is that while [individual firm] risk can be reduced . . . systematic risk can be increased." A second problem, Leach said, is that in many cases derivative instruments " . . . are too sophisticated for financial managers."[4]

Other pending derivatives bills are the "Derivatives Limitations Act of 1994," introduced by Senator Brian Drogran (D-SD) and Senator Barbara Mikulski (D-Maryland), and the "Derivatives Supervision Act of 1994," introduced by Senator Donald Riegle (D-Mich.). In general, these bills are aimed at eliminating proprietary trading by federally insured depository institutions and by federal agencies, such as the Federal National Mortgage Association (FNMA). Senator Riegle's bill also contains a section pertaining to systemic risk: it requires regulators to "promulgate appropriate regulations to require regulated entities and major dealers to increase use of clearinghouses and multilateral netting agreements; to reduce intraday debit positions; shorten intervals between delivery of and payment for financial products; and otherwise to reduce payments and settlement risk."

The objective of this article is to evaluate the arguments and the evidence that have been advanced in support of the view that OTC derivatives markets pose a systemic risk to financial markets. Because many of these arguments can be found in the recent GAO report, much of this article is directed toward evaluating the arguments and evidence presented by that report. While it is obvious that the possibility of a systemic crisis occurring in any financial market can never by completely ruled out, I find that OTC derivatives markets are in general working well and do not pose an unacceptable risk to the financial system.

2. A derivatives-induced systemic crisis: What is it and how will it occur?

A confusing aspect of the debate about the possibility of a derivatives-induced systemic collapse is that there is never a clear articulation of the sequence of events that might trigger such a collapse. While critics of derivatives markets frequently allege that derivatives trading has increased "systemic risk," and that if such trading is not reined in by additional regulation, it may result in a "systemic crisis," they seldom attempt to spell out the precise sequence of events (and the implicit assumptions) that they envision as causing such a crisis.

A common definition of the term "systemic crisis" is the following:

A disturbance that severely impairs the working of the financial system and, at the extreme, causes a complete breakdown in it. Systemic risks are those risks that have the potential to cause such a crisis. Systemic crises can originate in a variety of ways, but ultimately they will impair at least one of these key functions of the financial system: credit allocation, payments, and pricing of financial assets.[5]

What kind of "disturbance" do critics envision as occurring in OTC derivatives markets? And why should we expect this disturbance to spread to other firms and markets, causing a complete breakdown in the financial system? Without a clear articulation of the sequence of events that might trigger a systemic collapse, it is difficult to evaluate concerns about systemic risk in OTC derivatives markets.

In reciting the concerns of regulators, the GAO report identifies several factors which it argues could make OTC derivatives markets particularly vulnerable to a systemic collapse. It reports that

Concerned regulators and market participants said that the size and concentration of derivatives activity, combined with derivatives-related linkages, could cause any financial disruption to spread faster and be harder to contain. Because the same relatively few major OTC derivatives dealers accounted for a large portion of trading in a number of markets, regulators and market participants feared that the abrupt failure or withdrawal from trading of one of these dealers could undermine stability in several markets simultaneously. This could lead to a chain of market withdrawals, or possibly firm failures, and a systemic crisis.[6]

Based on these concerns, therefore, we can infer that both the GAO and regulators believe that a systemic collapse might occur because of the following hypothetical sequence of events:

1. *An initial shock due to the failure of a large end-user.* Because of mismanagement or an operations control failure, a large derivatives end-user fails to meet its counterparty obligations to one or more derivatives dealer. (Metallgesellschaft, for example, defaults on its swap obligations to banks.) Such a failure could be due to the misuse of derivatives by the end-user, or could be due to factors totally unrelated to derivatives (such as general business problems).
2. *The failure of a large derivatives dealer.* As a result, one or more derivatives dealers experience substantial losses, resulting in the insolvency of one or more of these dealers, some of which may be major financial institutions.
3. *Counterparty spillover effects.* Spillover effects occur when the defaulting dealers fail to meet their counterparty obligations to other derivatives dealers, as well as to end-users and possibly clearing associations. As counterparty defaults spread throughout the system, other dealers also experience losses and have difficulty meeting their counterparty obligations. Finally, since some of these dealers will almost certainly be financial institutions, confidence in the solvency of financial institutions in general is undermined.
4. *Price effects in other derivatives markets.* Because of the customized nature of OTC derivatives and their general opaqueness, uncertainty caused by actual or potential dealer defaults can result in dealers refusing to trade with each other or with other end-users until conditions improve, or until the risk of counterparty defaults diminishes. Thus, a general lack of liquidity (or a "freeze-up" of the OTC derivatives market) forces dealers and end-users to turn to the more liquid exchange-traded derivatives (such as futures and options) in an effort to hedge or "liquidate" their positions, putting these markets under intense liquidity pressures. The result is a "price break" on exchange-traded derivatives markets.
5. *Market linkages spread the "price break."* Because of extensive links between derivatives markets and other financial markets, the "price break" in derivatives markets quickly spreads to other markets, creating widespread uncertainty about asset values in general. This, in turn, sets off a general wave of precautionary selling, sending asset prices plummeting in financial markets in all major countries.
6. *Credit disruptions and real economic effects.* Finally, sharply falling asset prices and heightened uncertainty disrupt normal credit relationships, making it more difficult and more costly for firms to obtain credit. As a result, there is a general curtailment of business activity, causing widespread adverse economic effects.

3. Analysis of the sources of systemic risk in OTC derivatives markets

In discussions of the vulnerability of OTC derivatives markets to a systemic crisis, four characteristics of OTC markets have been singled out as particularly troublesome: the magnitude of dealer counterparty risk that exists in OTC derivatives markets, the concentration of OTC derivatives activity among a few large OTC dealers, the extensive linkages among derivative dealers and between dealers and financial markets generally, and the "regulatory gap" that exists because of "unregulated" (or nonbank) OTC derivatives-dealers.[7] Further, there has been some concern that since many large derivatives dealers are banks, counterparty derivatives losses could threaten the solvency of some of our principal banks, with potentially serious consequences for the entire banking system. These concerns are analyzed in the remainder of this section and in section 4.

3.1. Dealer risk in OTC derivatives markets

OTC dealers are exposed primarily to two kinds of risk—namely, market risk and credit (or counterparty) risk. Market risk refers to changes in the value of derivatives contracts that can occur because of changes in market conditions, especially prices. Just as bonds and currencies change in value when interest rates and exchange rates change, derivatives change in value when relevant prices change. The sensitivity of a particular derivative's value to a price change depends on the characteristics of that derivative: some are more sensitive than others to price changes. Market risk, of course, is not unique to derivatives—all financial instruments expose holders to market risk.

Credit risk arises because of the possibility that a party to a derivatives contract will renege on his or her contractual obligations. Credit exposure on a derivatives contract, however, exists only for parties holding "in-the-money" contracts. Assume that A enters into a forward contract with B to buy Mexican pesos from B in one month at a peso/dollar exchange rate of 10. Further, assume that the exchange rate remains constant for the indefinite future. Under these conditions, neither party has a credit exposure to the other, because nonperformance by either party will not impose costs on the other party. Alternatively stated, in the event of nonperformance, the non-defaulting party can replace the forward contract on exactly the same terms—at a peso/dollar exchange rate of 10. There is, therefore, no "replacement cost" associated with nonperformance.

Assume, instead, that before A can purchase the pesos from B, the exchange rate falls to 5. If A now reneges on his or her obligation to purchase pesos from B at an exchange rate of 10, B will be injured. Party B can only replace this contract at a substantial cost—by agreeing to sell pesos (or buy dollars) at a peso/dollar exchange rate of 5 rather than 10. The value of this forward contract can be said to be "in-the-money" for B but "out-of-money" for A. Thus, derivatives pose a counterparty credit exposure only to parties holding in-the-money contracts. Losing counterparties (those holding out-of-the-money derivatives) do not have a credit exposure.[8]

Losing counterparties may default on their obligations for a number of reasons. Sharp price changes may result in such large changes in the value of a firm's derivatives contracts that they bankrupt the firm. (Examples are the bankruptcy of Orange County, California, and the near-bankruptcy of Metallgesellschaft.) Alternatively, a firm holding out-of-the-money derivatives may default for reasons unrelated to derivatives: general business reversals, operational errors, fraud, etc. Thus, the credit exposure of a party holding in-the-money derivatives is similar to that of a party who loans a sum of money equivalent to the amount that the derivatives contracts are in-the-money. Managing derivatives-related credit risk, therefore, is similar to managing credit exposure generally.

With respect to systemic risk, the predominant concern appears to center on the possibility that major counterparty defaults could trigger a "domino effect" among OTC dealers, resulting in a market meltdown. A critical issue, therefore, is the size of dealers' counterparty credit exposures and whether dealers are managing these exposures prudently. It is important to recognize that OTC dealers will have a credit exposure even if they have completely and correctly hedged their entire derivatives portfolios against all market risks (or changes in prices). Even a dealer that is simply "making a market," as opposed to taking positions, can have a substantial credit exposure.

3.2. The relationship between credit exposure and notional size

A factor driving the concern about credit risk in OTC derivatives markets is the apparent size of these markets. Outstanding contractual amounts in OTC derivatives markets are in the trillions of dollars. Further, if these contracts are held by only a handful of OTC derivatives dealers, is not the potential derivatives-related credit exposure of these dealers enormous? This fear, however, stems more from a misunderstanding of derivatives instruments than from concrete evidence of significant credit risk.

Reported measures of the size of OTC derivatives markets are impressive. The most common measure is based on outstanding "notional" (or contractual) amounts. Some estimates for 1994 have put the notional outstandings of OTC forwards, options, and swaps at around $40 trillion.[9] This figure represents a substantial increase from the 1992 figures reported in the GAO report, which estimates outstanding OTC derivatives to be about $12 trillion.[10]

Most of the concern about systemic risk in the OTC derivatives market seems to center on the swap market. Current estimates put the notional value of all swap contracts at about $7 trillion[11] (see table 1). Interest rate swaps constitute the bulk of this amount, with currency swaps making up the remaining contracts. For the seven-year period 1987–1993, interest rate swaps accounted for 88 percent of all swaps written (see table 2). Although detailed information about the nature of these swap agreements is not available, it is likely that most were "plain-vanilla" swaps—an exchange of fixed for floating rates. As such, they are similar to strips of forward or futures interest rate contracts (such as Eurodollar strips). The attractiveness of swap contracts, in comparison to futures contracts, lies in their customized features, low cost, and potentially longer maturity. Finally, the GAO reports that about 22 percent of the total swaps outstanding at year-end

Table 1. National contract amounts for derivatives worldwide by individual product type as of the end of fiscal years 1989 through 1993 (billions of dollars)

Type of Derivative	1989	1990	1991	1992	1993	Percentage of Total 1993	Percentage Increase from 1989 to 1993
Forwards							
Forward Rate Agreements*	$ 770	$ 1,156	$ 1,533	$ 1,807	$ 2,522		
Foreign Exchange Forwards**	$2,264	$ 3,277	$ 4,531	$ 5,510	$ 6,232		
Total Forwards	$3,034	$ 4,433	$ 6,064	$ 7,317	$ 8,754	35%	189%
Futures							
Interest Rate Futures	$1,201	$ 1,454	$ 2,157	$ 2,902	$ 4,960		
Currency Futures	$ 16	$ 16	$ 18	$ 25	$ 30		
Equity Index Futures	$ 42	$ 70	$ 77	$ 81	$ 119		
Total Futures	$1,259	$ 1,540	$ 2,252	$ 3,008	$ 5,109	20%	306%
Options							
Exchange-Traded Interest Rate Options	$ 387	$ 600	$ 1,073	$ 1,385	$ 2,362		
OTC Interest Rate Options	$ 450	$ 561	$ 577	$ 634	$ 1,398		
Exchange-Traded Currency Options	$ 50	$ 56	$ 61	$ 80	$ 81		
Exchange-Traded Equity Index Options	$ 66	$ 96	$ 137	$ 168	$ 286		
Total Options	$ 953	$ 1,313	$ 1,848	$ 2,267	$ 4,127	16%	333%
Swaps							
Interest Rate Swaps	$1,503	$ 2,312	$ 3,065	$ 3,851	$ 6,177		
Currency Swaps	$ 449	$ 578	$ 807	$ 860	$ 900		
Total Swaps	$1,952	$ 2,890	$ 3,872	$ 4,711	$ 7,077	28%	263%
Total Derivatives +	$7,198	$10,176	$14,036	$17,303	$25,067	100%	248%
Total Derivatives#	$4,934	$ 6,899	$ 9,505	$11,793	$18,835		

* GAO estimated forward rate agreements as of the end of fiscal year 1992 on the basis of methodology the New York Federal Reserve used in computing estimates for year-ends 1989, 1990, and 1991.
**GAO estimates for foreign exchange forward contracts are from GAO Report, Table IV.5. These also include an unknown amount of OTC foreign exchange options.
+ Does not include complete data on physical commodity derivatives and equity options on the common stock of individual companies. Table IV.2, of the GAO Report, shows that seven of the databases contain equity and commodity derivatives that ranged from 1.1 to 3.4 percent of total derivatives notional/contract amounts.
# Before including GAO estimates for foreign exchange forwards and OTC options.
Source: Bank for International Settlements, GAO Report, ISDA, and the Federal Reserve Bank of New York.

1991 were between dealers, as opposed to between dealers and end-users, such as financial institutions and corporations.

The notional size of outstanding OTC derivatives contracts does not provide an accurate indication of the magnitude of potential counterparty credit exposure. Derivatives transactions do not involve exchanges of principal amounts. The role of notional amounts in transactions like swaps is to determine the magnitude of the periodic cash payments made by the parties to the contract. A default by a party to a swap contract puts his or her counterparty

Table 2. Interest rate and currency swaps written annually by underlying and outstanding (notional principal in billions of U.S. dollars: 1987-93)

Type of Swap	1987	1988	1989	1990	1991	1992	1993
Interest Rate Swaps							
US$	287	366	545	676	926	1336	1546
DM	22	33	41	106	103	237	399
Yen	32	43	62	137	194	428	789
Others	47	126	185	345	397	821	1370
Subtotal	388	568	833	1264	1620	2822	4104
Currency Swaps							
Dollar	38	70	93	65	122	106	109
Non-Dollar	48	54	86	148	206	196	186
Subtotal	86	124	179	213	328	302	295
Total Swaps Written	474	692	1012	1477	1948	3124	4399
Total Swaps Outstanding (at year-end)	867	1328	1952	2890	3872	4711	7077

Source: International Swaps and Derivatives Association.

at risk only for the cash payments owed now or in the future (or the "replacement cost" of the contract). Neither party risks losing the notional amount of the contract, unlike a loan or a bond. Thus, counterparty credit exposures in OTC derivatives markets are far less than suggested by the enormous notional value associated with derivatives contracts.

A survey of 14 major OTC derivatives dealers by the GAO report indicates that, as of year-end 1992, the *gross* credit exposure of these dealers was only 1.8 percent of the $6.5 trillion of their notional outstandings (or $114 billion).[12] This figure, however, does not take into account the various risk-management devices that dealers commonly use to reduce their counterparty credit exposures. In particular, bilateral contractual netting provisions allow dealers to offset losses on some contracts with gains on other contracts outstanding with a defaulting party or its corporate affiliates. In addition, when swaps are undertaken with lower quality parties, such counterparties are often required to post collateral on a mark-to-market basis. After taking these risk-reducing mechanisms into account, the GAO reported that the *net* credit exposure of the 14 dealers was less than 1 percent of the notional value of their outstanding derivative contracts (about $68 billion).

OTC dealers manage their credit exposures in a variety of ways. Internal credit limits are commonly used to diversify credit risk and to restrict the size of exposures to individual counterparties, industries, and countries. Most counterparties in swap transactions are required to have investment grade ratings,[13] and credit "triggers" frequently require the automatic termination of a swap agreement if the credit rating of either party falls below a prespecified threshold (such as a single A rating), requiring losing counterparties to make immediate payments.

To put total credit exposures in the swap market in the perspective of other credit markets, at fiscal-year-end 1992 the notional value of swaps outstanding was $4.7 trillion. Thus, the net counterparty credit exposure in the swap market would have been about $47 billion (1 percent of the notional amount). In comparison, at that time the credit exposure in the bond market was about $14.4 trillion.[14]

The derivatives exposures of bank-derivatives dealers also can be compared to the credit exposures that the same banks had in their loan portfolios.[15] For the twenty-five largest U.S. bank derivatives-users, derivatives-related exposures, as a percentage of bank equity, were generally much less than their loan exposures (see table 3). Although the derivatives exposure exceeds 100 percent of the equity for many of these banks, a bank's capital would be wiped out by derivatives losses only if *all* counterparties were to default, there were no offsetting netting agreements or other risk-reduction mechanisms in force, and actual counterparty losses were identical to total credit exposures. Such assumptions are extreme, for loan defaults as well as for derivatives-related exposures.

Thus, while derivatives-related exposures are not insignificant, the oft-cited notional value of outstanding OTC derivatives greatly exaggerates the magnitude of this exposure. Properly measured, exposures are a small fraction of reported notional amounts, and do not seem to be out of proportion to exposures in other financial markets. Finally, there is no evidence that derivatives-dealers are not managing their derivative-related exposures as well as their other exposures. (The GAO reports that, in the past, actual losses incurred by derivatives dealers as a result of counterparty defaults have been quite small: 0.2 percent of their combined gross credit exposure.[16])

3.3. Concentration among dealers

High concentration among OTC derivatives dealers has been cited as an important source of systemic risk. Relying on the Group of Thirty study, the GAO report emphasizes the high level of dealer concentration that exists and the potential spillover effects that could flow from a default by one of these dealers. The Group of Thirty study reports that the largest eight U.S. or foreign bank OTC derivatives dealers account for 56 percent of the total worldwide notional outstandings of interest rate and currency swaps.[17] There are only five U.S. securities-affiliate dealers of any size[18] (see table 4).

Data in the GAO report, however, suggest a lower level of dealer concentration than the 56 percent reported by the Group of Thirty study. Using the GAO's list of the 15 largest U.S. OTC dealers in 1992 (table 4), the top eight U.S. dealers (seven banks and one securities firm dealer) together held outstanding derivatives contracts totalling $8.7 trillion.[19] The GAO report (table 4.1) also indicates that in 1992 the largest 50 dealers held $25.9 billion of derivatives. (This figure, like the figure for the eight dealers, includes some double-counting.) Thus, the largest eight U.S. dealers appear to account for only about 33 percent of the worldwide notional amounts held by these dealers. Further, the largest U.S. derivatives dealer holds only 6 percent of the total. This estimate may overstate dealer concentration because it does not take into account all of the reported 150 OTC derivatives dealers that exist worldwide; however, it may also understate dealer

Table 3. Credit equivalent exposure of the 25 commercial banks and trust companies with the most off balance sheet derivatives contracts March 31, 1995, $ millions, ratios in percent

Rank	Bankname	State	Total Assets	Total Derivatives	Bilaterally Netted Current Exposure	Future Exposure (RBC add on)	Credit Exposure From all Contracts	Credit Exposure to Capital Ratio
								(%)
1	Chemical Bk	NY	$149,034	$3,633,994	$30,100	$14,455	$44,555	375.0
2	Citibank NA	NY	$228,437	$2,872,943	$33,838	$16,030	$49,868	222.9
3	Morgan Guaranty TC	NY	$143,348	$2,833,956	$37,096	$16,484	$53,580	570.5
4	Bankers TC	NY	$ 82,119	$2,082,579	$20,287	$11,994	$32,281	588.7
5	Bank of Amer NT & SA	CA	$159,010	$1,603,803	$13,479	$ 9,442	$22,921	152.2
6	Chase Manhattan Bk NA	NY	$ 99,349	$1,547,905	$13,859	$ 9,484	$23,343	230.3
7	First NB of Chicago	IL	$ 47,679	$ 677,786	$ 8,808	$ 4,041	$12,849	295.0
8	Nationsbank NA Carolinas	NC	$ 51,144	$ 627,018	$ 3,813	$ 1,565	$ 5,378	175.2
9	Republic NB of NY	NY	$ 33,461	$ 284,236	$ 4,509	$ 1,684	$ 6,193	195.7
10	First NB of Boston	MA	$ 36,872	$ 88,831	$ 771	$ 229	$ 1,000	27.2
11	Bank of NY	NY	$ 41,703	$ 77,673	$ 1,697	$ 488	$ 2,185	46.8
12	Natwest Bk NA	NJ	$ 29,131	$ 73,148	$ 183	$ 92	$ 275	10.9
13	First Union NB NC	NC	$ 24,190	$ 54,951	$ 145	$ 120	$ 265	12.5
14	State Street B & TC	MA	$ 22,778	$ 52,164	$ 1,306	$ 516	$ 1,821	136.2
15	Bank of Amer IL	IL	$ 16,902	$ 44,331	$ 840	$ 128	$ 968	35.1
16	Mellon Bk NA	PA	$ 33,399	$ 39,275	$ 487	$ 167	$ 654	18.0
17	Seattle-First NB	WA	$ 15,775	$ 33,876	$ 87	$ 53	$ 140	8.0
18	PNC Bk NA	PA	$ 43,817	$ 31,513	$ 94	$ 102	$ 196	5.6
19	Wells Fargo Bk NA	CA	$ 51,175	$ 29,125	$ 122	$ 101	$ 224	4.6
20	Bank One Columbus NA	OH	$ 6,467	$ 27,476	$ 264	$ 59	$ 323	39.2
21	Boston Safe Deposit &TC	MA	$ 6,188	$ 20,688	$ 451	$ 105	$ 556	106.6
22	Harris T&SB	IL	$ 11,690	$ 19,186	$ 2,337	$ 15	$ 2,352	214.3
23	Marine Midland Bk	NY	$ 18,558	$ 18,680	$ 136	$ 43	$ 179	9.4

								Average %
24	National City Bk	OH	$ 9,628	$ 16,947	$ 218	$ 68	$ 286	33.3
25	Corestates Bk NA	PA	$ 21,067	$ 16,191	$ 106	$ 51	$ 158	8.2

						Average %
Top 25 commercial banks & TCs with derivatives	$1,382,923	$16,808,276	$175,034	$87,516	$262,550	140.9
Other 596 commercial banks & TCs with derivatives	$1,727,718	$ 515,211	$ 4,231	$ 1,647	$ 5,878	N/A
Total amounts for all bks & TCs with derivatives	$3,110,640	$17,323,486	$179,265	$89,163	$268,428	8.5

Note: The bilaterally netted current credit exposure is the current credit exposure across all off-balance sheet derivative contracts, after considering bilateral netting arrangements

Note: Future exposure is calculated in the following manner: [Notional amounts of short term (i.e. less than one year) contracts from foreign exchange. gold, other precious metals, other commodity, and equity derivative contracts) · 01] + [Notional amounts of long term (i.e. one year through five years of the above contracts) • .05] + [Notional amount of long-term interest rate contracts • 005] Short term interest rate contracts get a "0" risk weight, and therefore, do not factor into the summation.

Note: Credit exposure is the sum of the bilaterally netted current credit exposure and future exposure.

Note: The credit exposure to capital ratio is calculated using risk based capital (tier one plus tier two capital).

Commercial banks also hold on-balance sheet assets in volumes that are multiples of bank capital. For example:

Exposures from other assets	Exposure to risk based capital:	Average % of the top 25 credit
All commercial banks	All banks	exposure ratios in each category
1-4 family mortgages	153%	1342%
C&I loans	163%	862%
Securities not in trading account	213%	1291%

Note: In previous quarters, total derivative included spot foreign exchange. The first quarter 1995 reports spot foreign exchange separately
Source: Call Report Schedule RC = R, Office of the Comptroller of the Currency

Table 4. 15 Major U.S. OTC derivatives dealers and their notional/contract derivatives amounts

Dollars in millions	1994	1992
Banks		
Chemical Banking Corporation	$ 3,177,600	$ 1,620,819
Citicorp	$ 2,664,600	$ 1,521,400
J.P. Morgan & Co., Inc.	$ 2,472,500	$ 1,251,700
Bankers Trust New York Corporation	$ 2,025,736	$ 1,165,872
BankAmerica Corporation	$ 1,400,707	$ 886,300
The Chase Manhattan Corporation	$ 1,360,000	$ 787,891
First Chicago Corporation	$ 622,100	$ 391,400
Securities Firms		
Salomon, Inc.	$ 1,509,000	$ 752,041
Merrill Lynch & Co., Inc.	$ 1,326,000	$ 729,000
Lehman Brothers, Inc.	$ 1,143,091	$ 724,000
The Goldman Sachs Group, L.P.	$ 995,275	$ 424,937
Morgan Stanley Group, Inc.	$ 843,000	$ 337,007
Insurance Companies		
American International Group, Inc.	$ 376,869	$ 198,200
General Re Corporation	$ 306,159	$ 121,515
The Prudential Insurance Co. of America	$ 102,102	$ 82,729
Total	**$20,324,739**	**$10,994,811**

Source: Annual reports for 1994
Annual reports from Shearson Lehman for 1992; and GAO Report, p. 188.

concentration by failing to account for a foreign dealer large enough to rank among the top eight dealers worldwide.[20]

It is not obvious that high dealer concentration increases systemic risk. It may, on the contrary, be a source of stability. Dealer concentration in OTC derivatives markets, as in many OTC markets, arises out of a need for large dealers. There are economies of scale associated with managing risk, raising capital, and developing and maintaining in-house expertise and operational systems. Large dealers also are better able to diversify risk than are small dealers. Probably for these reasons dealer concentration in derivatives and other OTC markets—such as U.S. Government bonds—is generally high. Would an OTC derivatives market populated by many small financial institutions acting as dealers be less susceptible to a systemic crisis? Are large financial institutions more susceptible to bankruptcy than small institutions? Probably not.

3.4. Linkages among dealers and financial markets

The GAO report argues that the growth of derivatives has increased systemic risk by expanding linkages among markets and financial institutions. As a result, a liquidity problem in one market can quickly spread to other markets.[21]

While it is true that linkages among financial markets have never been greater, it is not clear whether such linkages increase or decrease the likelihood of a systemic crisis. As markets become more interlinked, market participation widens, which should result in greater and not less overall market liquidity. The more substitution there is among assets, the more elastic the demand for these assets, so that a demand or supply shock should result in smaller price changes. By increasing market linkages, derivatives should cushion financial disturbances by spreading market shocks widely among many markets. If we have learned anything in recent years it is that financial risks can be better managed when markets are not segmented. The collapse of the thrift industry in the United States is testimony to the instability that can result from segmented financial markets (in that case, government-mandated segmentation).

Concern about expanded market linkages appears to stem from experience with the October 1987 stock market crash, where price declines in the U.S. stock market seemingly were quickly transmitted to equity markets around the world. But there is another side to this story: in October 1987 one of the most serious collapses in equity prices to ever occur took place *without* precipitating a systemic crisis. Whether this outcome was the result of increased market linkages which diffused the financial shocks, or timely central bank intervention, or just plain good luck, we have no way of knowing. However, evidence from another market collapse—namely, the September 1992 EMS currency crisis—suggests that links between the underlying currency markets and related derivatives markets helped to diffuse price shocks and prevent a systemic crisis from developing.[22] Thus, greater market linkages may be a source of systemic strength rather than weakness.

3.5. Unregulated derivatives dealers

The GAO report contends that "unregulated" OTC derivatives dealers create a regulatory gap, because regulators do not have the authority to intervene if a problem were to occur.[23] Although most major derivatives dealers are banks, five large U.S. securities firms and three U.S. insurance companies have affiliates dealing in derivatives. Together, these unregulated (or nonbank) dealers account for about 30 percent of total U.S. OTC derivatives-dealers' outstandings.[24] Nonbank dealers are subject to SEC or state reporting requirements, but are not subject to federally imposed capital standards or to examination by federal regulators, as are bank derivatives dealers (see table 5 for a summary of the current regulatory oversight of different kinds of OTC derivatives dealers).

It is not clear that additional regulation of nonbank derivatives dealers is necessary. Unlike banks, affiliates of nonbanks are not beneficiaries of government deposit insurance, and taxpayers are not at risk for losses incurred by failed nonbank dealers. GAO interviews with five securities firms with major OTC derivatives-dealers indicate that these dealers are all well managed and well capitalized. The dealers also reported that rating agencies and counterparties insist that they voluntarily set aside sufficient capital, based on calculations of their risk exposures.[25] In general, nonbank derivatives dealers had relatively large amounts of capital as compared to banks. Thus, both pressures from rating agencies and self-preservation incentives impose management and capital discipline on nonbank derivatives-dealers.[26]

Table 5. U.S. Regulatory Oversight of OTC Derivatives Activities of Financial Institutions and Financial Institution Affiliates as of April 1994

Type of Institution	Examination Requirements	Capital Requirements	Reporting Requirements
Banks	Banks are subject to annual examinations. Those major OTC derivatives dealers regulated by the Office of the Comptroller of the Currency are subject to continuous on-site examinations.	For credit risk, banks are to hold capital against their derivatives' positions equal to 8 percent of the adjusted value of their positions. The adjustments serve to reduce required capital, depending on the type of counterparty and the maturity of the contract. Since March 1994, these firms also must hold at least 3 percent of the unadjusted replacement cost of certain contracts.	Banks are to report quarterly their total derivatives notional amounts by product type. They also are to report the total gross replacement cost of these positions. Reporting on individual counterparty credit exposures is not required, but the exposures may be reviewed by regulatory staff during periodic examinations.
Securities firm affiliates	None.	None.	Since October 1992, securities firm affiliates have been required to report quarterly their total derivates notional amounts by product type. They also were to report the total gross replacement cost of those positions. Information on individual counterparty credit exposures is to be reported only when exposures are above a certain threshold.
Insurance firm affiliates	None.	None.	Insurance firm affiliates' financial information is consolidated with parent company reports.

Source: GAO

Finally, with respect to the "domino effect" that the GAO envisions, the key regulatory objective should be to maintain the stability of the banking system. This can be accomplished by directly regulating banks; it is not necessary to regulate institutions that deal with banks. A central regulatory issue, therefore, is whether current regulation of bank derivatives dealers is sufficient to ensure the safety of banks and the stability of the banking system.

4. Banks as derivatives dealers

Despite the existence of comprehensive U.S. federal government regulation of banks' derivatives activities,[27] the GAO suggests that there may be an intrinsic regulatory problem associated with banks' dealings in OTC derivatives.

The regulation of banks is essential, because they have deposit insurance and direct access to the Federal Reserve's discount window. At the same time, however, this combination of deposit insurance and access also can result in potential problems because it may induce the banks and their customers to inappropriately rely on such backing. Therefore, banks may be willing to run greater risks in their trading activities—in relation to their capital—than otherwise would be the case. In addition, market participants may prefer using banks for derivatives and related trading activities simply because banks are perceived to be safer counterparties. In the past, similar concerns caused us to recommend that nontraditional banking activities, such as those associated with underwriting and dealing in corporate debt and equity securities, be conducted only by well-managed and well-capitalized banks in separate subsidiaries of the bank holding company. Whether derivatives should be placed in this category depends on regulators' determinations on how they are being used by individual banks.[28]

The issue, therefore, is whether prudential regulation of banks' derivatives activities can adequately protect the federal deposit insurance fund and taxpayers, or whether there is something special about derivatives that makes this difficult or impossible to achieve. A key element of this issue is whether regulators can establish and monitor minimum capital requirements that can successfully protect the federal deposit insurance fund. If not, there may be an argument for segregating banks' derivatives activities into separately capitalized affiliates, or even for prohibiting these activities entirely.[29]

Existing U.S. capital requirements for banks, as well as those under the Basle Accord, apply to banks' derivatives activities. U.S. banks are required to comply with two different types of capital requirements—a risk-based requirement and a leverage ratio requirement. The risk-based requirement applies to the credit risk associated with derivatives contracts or activities. The leverage ratio requires banks to hold capital as a cushion against losses arising from other risks associated with derivative positions. While there is disagreement about whether current capital requirements are too low or too high, there is little doubt that risks associated with derivatives can be measured as well as other risk exposures. Further, these risks are no different from those that banks commonly take in many of their other activities, such as in making loans or trading fixed-income securities. Thus, there is no apparent reason why prudential regulation cannot be applied to banks' derivatives activities just as effectively as to many other activities that banks now engage in.

5. Metallgesellschaft: A case study in what can go wrong

The staggering derivatives losses suffered by MG Refining and Marketing, Inc. (MGRM), the American affiliate of Germany's 14th largest industrial firm Metallgesellschaft AG (MG), provide a good case study of how derivatives users can go wrong and what needs to be done to make derivatives markets safer. MGRM's losses, resulting from its positions in energy swaps and futures, reportedly could exceed $1.3 billion, about half of the total capital of DM3.672 reported by MG on September 30, 1994.[30] Only a massive $1.9 billion rescue operation by 150 German and international banks kept MG from going into bankruptcy, an event which would undoubtedly have had far-reaching consequences for MG's the creditors, suppliers, and some 58,000 employees of MG.[31] Had MG defaulted on its enormous derivatives and debt obligations, substantial losses could have been taken by a number of major derivatives dealers and international banks, the ramifications of which we will never know.

What went wrong at MG, and what can be learned about the dangers of using derivatives? How could a large, sophisticated, worldwide energy conglomerate like MG have been so inept as to incur derivatives-related losses that all but destroyed the firm?

5.1. Was MGRM hedging or speculating?

Initial press reports of MGRM's losses suggested that MGRM incurred these losses as a result of massive speculative positions in energy futures and over-the-counter (OTC) energy swaps. During the latter half of 1993, MGRM purportedly established long energy futures and swap positions equivalent to nearly 160 million barrels of oil, positions that would benefit handsomely if energy prices rose. Instead, energy prices (crude oil, heating oil, and gasoline) fell sharply during the latter part of 1993, causing MGRM to incur huge unrealized losses and margin calls on its derivatives positions.

Subsequent press reports, however, suggest that MGRM was not speculating but was in fact using derivatives to *reduce* the exposure it had to rising energy prices. In particular, MGRM was said to be engaged in a complex hedging operation using both futures and swap contracts as a hedge against a large volume of fixed-price, forward-supply contracts for gasoline and heating oil that it had written.[32]

MGRM's forward-supply contracts committed it to supplying at fixed prices some 160 million barrels of energy products over the next ten years to end-users of gasoline and heating oil. The fixed supply prices were agreed to when the contracts were entered into, and were typically three to five dollars a barrel higher than were the prevailing spot prices at the time the contracts were negotiated (this was MGRM's profit margin or markup). Most of these contracts were negotiated during the summer of 1993, when energy prices were falling and end-users saw an attractive opportunity to lock in low energy prices for the future. MGRM's counterparties in these forward contracts consisted of retail gasoline suppliers, large manufacturing firms, and even government entities. Although many of the end-users were small firms, some were substantial—namely, Chrysler Corporation, Browning-Ferris Industries Corporation, and Comcar Industries, which has annual diesel fuel use of some 60 million gallons a year.[33]

These forward-supply contracts exposed MGRM to rising energy prices. If energy prices were to rise in the future, MGRM could find itself in the unprofitable position of having to supply energy products to its customers at prices below prevailing spot prices. If prices rose high enough, MGRM's profit margin could be eroded and it could even have ended up with substantial losses for years to come. Thus, MGRM reportedly sought to hedge this price risk with long futures and OTC swaps. Not to have hedged this risk would have put MGRM (and therefore MG) in the position of making a substantial bet that energy prices either would fall or at least not rise in the future, a bet that was too large for MG to have prudently made.[34]

5.2. MGRM's hedging strategy

MGRM sought to hedge the risk of rising energy prices by acquiring long energy futures positions on the New York Mercantile Exchange (NYMEX) and by entering into OTC energy swap agreements to receive floating and pay fixed energy prices.[35] MGRM's swap counterparties were large OTC swap dealers, such as major banks. During the latter part of 1993, MGRM held long futures positions on the NYMEX equivalent to 55 million barrels of gasoline and heating oil (55,000 futures contracts), and had swap positions amounting to some 100 to 110 million barrels, substantial positions by any measure.[36] Thus, MGRM was hedging its forward-supply contracts on a one-to-one basis with energy derivatives.

An important aspect of MGRM's hedging strategy was that its derivatives positions were concentrated (or "stacked") in short-dated futures and swaps that had to be "rolled" forward continuously to maintain the hedge.[37] In general, MGRM's futures and swap positions were in contracts with maturities of at most a few months from the current date, so that it had to roll these contracts forward periodically (perhaps even monthly) to maintain its hedge against the forward-supply contracts. This short-dated, stack, hedging strategy clearly exposed MGRM to the basis risk associated with its having to roll its futures and swap positions forward through time.[38] MGRM apparently believed this to be an acceptable risk.

Indeed, MGRM believed that a short-dated, stack, hedging strategy was the most attractive hedging strategy for two reasons.[39] First, because its forward delivery contracts contained an "early liquidation" option for end-users if energy prices were to rise, MGRM believed that the actual duration of its forward-supply contracts would likely be far shorter than the periods stated in the contracts.[40] If end-users were to exercise their options, presumably because the options had value to them, MGRM would have to make substantial up-front, lump-sum, payments to them at the time of exercise. These lump-sum payments would be based on changes in spot (or near-month) energy prices. Specifically, they would be based on the difference between the prevailing near-month futures price at the time of exercise and the contractually fixed supply price times the quantity yet to be supplied over the term of the contract. MGRM believed that a stack hedge, which would increase in value substantially as spot and near-term energy prices rose, could be relied on to provide the needed funds for MGRM to meet these potential early-payment obligations.

Second, MGRM saw the necessity of having to roll its positions forward constantly as a benefit and not as a risk. MGRM believed that it could earn a positive return by rolling its positions forward.[41] More specifically, its rolling-forward strategy was designed to take advantage of a common characteristic of energy futures markets; that is, backwardation. In backwardation markets, oil for immediate delivery (nearby-oil) gets a higher price than does deferred-delivery oil such as three-month oil. Thus, a strategy of purchasing deferred-delivery contracts and continually rolling these positions forward yields profits (or "roll gains"). MGRM strategy, therefore, sought to exploit the backwardation that is common in energy futures markets. MGRM's implicit assumption was that energy futures markets would continue to be in backwardation much of the time, and that the roll gains it made when markets were in backwardation would more than offset the roll losses that it would incur when markets were in contango.[42]

While it is clear that under certain conditions a short-dated, stack, hedging strategy such as MGRM used can be an effective way to hedge long-dated forward commitments, there are, nevertheless, risks associated with this strategy.[43] First, as with any hedging strategy, there is "operational" risk: hedge positions must be correctly implemented and managed (and, in particular, the "hedge ratio" must be correct) for the hedge effectively to reduce price exposure. Second, there is "basis risk" associated with all hedging strategies. MGRM's hedging strategy exposed it to "intertemporal basis risk" because it required MGRM continually to roll its derivatives positions forward through time.[44] Under certain conditions, rolling positions forward can result in substantial losses. Third, MGRM was potentially subject to a "funding risk," because its derivatives positions were subject to mark-to-market valuation and to variation margin payments, while its forward-supply contracts were not. Under some circumstances this marking-to-market asymmetry could result in MGRM's needing sizeable amounts of funding to meet margin calls. Fourth, MGRM's forward-supply contracts exposed it to "credit risk." MGRM's ability to profit on its forward-supply contracts depended on its customers honoring their contractual obligations to purchase oil for many years into the future. Finally, MGRM was subject to "reporting risks." As we shall see, the application of inappropriate accounting and disclosure conventions to MGRM's hedging activities resulted in misleading financial statements that threatened to undermine public confidence in the firm.[45]

5.3. What went wrong?

MGRM's problems surfaced in late 1993 when energy spot prices tumbled (instead of rising, as MGRM had expected and feared). As a result, MGRM experienced large unrealized losses on its stacked long futures and swap positions and incurred huge margin calls.[46] Adhering to German accounting and disclosure principles, MG disclosed these unrealized losses publicly, sending shock waves through the financial community. In addition, because of an unusual forward pricing curve in energy futures markets during 1993, MGRM sustained substantial "rolling losses" when it rolled its large stacked futures positions forward through time. In 1993, energy futures markets were in "contanto" for almost the entire year, causing MGRM to incur losses each time it rolled its derivatives positions forward.

If, instead, energy prices had risen rather than fallen, there would have been no problem. MGRM would have had unrealized gains on its derivatives positions and positive margin flows (or cash inflows). In addition, when prices are rising energy markets are often in backwardation, rather than contango, so that MGRM might have had rollover gains rather than losses. The fact that MGRM also would have had unrealized losses on its forward-delivery obligations would not have mattered. No one would have cared. But energy prices did fall, from around $19 a barrel of crude oil in June of 1993 to less than $15 a barrel in December of 1993, causing MGRM to have to come up with enormous amounts of money to fund margin calls and rollover losses so that its hedge positions could be maintained. In response to these reversals, MG's supervisory board brought in new management, which quickly made the decision to liquidate the bulk of MGRM's derivatives positions and forward-supply contracts.

While complete information about all aspects of MGRM's energy and hedging strategies is not yet available, some key implications can already be drawn from the MG experience. First, conflicting and inappropriate accounting and disclosure conventions can undermine a firm's hedging strategy by causing confusion among its creditors and investors about what the firm is doing and about its financial position. Confusion of just this kind undermined public confidence in MG and may have weakened its ability to cope with MGRM's problems. Second, short-term funding requirements, such as MG experienced, if not anticipated and properly managed, can undermine a hedging strategy. Finally, a lack of understanding at the level of the supervisory board (or board of directors) about how a firm is using derivatives can ultimately undermine a firm's hedging strategy.

5.4. Conflicting and misleading accounting conventions

MGRM's problems were compounded by widespread confusion about its financial position caused by conflicting and inappropriate accounting conventions. Under German accounting principles, unrealized *losses* on open forward positions have to be recognized at the end of the financial year, but unrealized *gains* on open forward positions are not allowed to be recognized.[47] Applied to MGRM, this meant that, when energy prices fell in late 1993, MG had to recognize MGRM's unrealized losses on its derivatives positions (futures and swaps) but was unable to recognize any unrealized gains that MGRM may have had on its forward-supply contracts. Thus, MG reported huge derivatives-related losses, leaving the impression that these losses were incurred by inappropriate and possibly speculative trading in derivatives by MGRM, and that MG's financial solvency was itself in jeopardy.

Not recognizing the gains on MGRM's forward-supply contracts resulting from the fall in energy prices distorted the true picture of MGRM's financial position. Falling energy prices would have made MGRM's forward-supply contracts more valuable because these contracts gave MGRM the right to sell oil at higher fixed prices. Hypothetically, it is possible that MGRM's unrealized derivatives losses could have been almost entirely offset by unrealized gains on in its forward-supply contracts.[48] In any case, MGRM would certainly have had some amount of unrealized gains on its forward-supply contracts, which would have offset some of its derivatives losses. Thus, had MGRM's unrealized gains on its forward-supply contracts been recognized as well as the unrealized losses on its derivatives positions, MGRM (and therefore MG) would have been able to report smaller losses than it did.[49]

In contrast to German accounting conventions, U.S. hedge accounting principles recognize this reporting asymmetry and impose different disclosure requirements on hedgers. U.S. "hedge-deferral" accounting principles do not require that either unrealized gains or unrealized losses on hedged positions be recognized. Thus, had MGRM adhered to U.S. accounting principles, it would not have had to report its unrealized derivatives losses at all. It would not have had to report these losses until realized, which would presumably have occurred at the time that MGRM also recognized the gains on its forward-supply contracts. Alternatively, U.S. accounting conventions allow a firm with a hedged position to mark both sides (or positions) to market. In particular, MGRM could

have marked-to-market both its forward-supply contracts and its derivatives positions, permitting the immediate recognition of the respective gains and losses on both
positions.

The application of both German and U.S. accounting principals to MGRM clearly
created confusion among MG's creditors and investors. In particular, MG's U.S. and
German auditors issued conflicting reports on MG's condition at different times. On
November 19, 1993, just before the supervisory board meeting at which MG's then
chairman's contract was extended for another five years, MG's U.S. auditor, Arthur
Andersen, disclosed that MGRM had a $61 million profit before taxes for the fiscal year
ending September 30, 1993. Further, it reported that MGRM's U.S. parent, MG Corporation, had a profit of $30 million for the fiscal year.[50] Just a short time later, however,
MG's German auditor, KPMG, apparently applying German accounting principles, reported a loss of hundreds of millions of dollars for MG's U.S. operations for the same
fiscal year ending September 30, 1993.[51] Which set of figures gave the most accurate
picture of MG's financial health? One indicated that MG was profitable and doing nicely;
the other that MG's losses were so large that they threatened the solvency of the firm.
Thus, conflicting and inappropriate accounting conventions contributed importantly to
the confusion which existed about MG's true financial state and undoubtedly weakened
the firm's ability to deal with its problems.

5.5. Funding problems

Because of falling energy prices, MG was forced to fund sizeable margin calls on
MGRM's derivatives positions. According to press reports, MG's creditors balked at
providing the necessary funds for MGRM to meet these margin calls.[52] It is not clear,
however, why MG's creditors refused to make this credit available. If, for example,
MGRM had unrealized gains on its forward-supply contracts (due to falling energy
prices) that were equal and offsetting to the unrealized losses on its derivatives positions,
it is not clear why MG's creditors would have refused to make loans against the
collateral of these forward-supply contracts. The market value of the firm, after all,
would not have changed.

MG's creditors may have been reluctant to lend against the collateral of MGRM's
forward-supply contracts for two reasons. First, these contracts may have lacked sufficient
transparency. In particular, although falling energy prices, everything else being equal,
should have increased the net present value of MGRM's forward-supply contracts, MG's
creditors may have been concerned about the continued creditworthiness of MGRM's
contractual counterparties over the long time period covered by these contracts (as much
as 10 years). For MGRM to realize its full profits on these contracts, its counterparties
would have to make good on their future obligations to purchase oil from MGRM at the
fixed contractual prices, which could have been considerably higher than prevailing spot
prices at the time of the required purchases. Thus, if MG's creditors believed that they did
not have sufficient information to make an independent evaluation of MGRM's credit
risk, they may have responded by heavily discounting the potential increase in MGRM's

cash flows on its forward-supply contracts. This would have made it difficult for MG either to sell (or liquidate) its forward-supply contracts or to borrow against them to meet margin calls.

Notwithstanding this possible non-transparency, it has been reported that, on December 7, 1993, Chemical Bank (and possibly other banks) offered financing to MGRM on the basis of MGRM's securitizing its forward-supply contracts.[53] Of course, we do not know the terms that the banks were offering, or how big the "haircut" would have been. In addition, it is worth noting that MG had available a DM 1.5 billion Euro-credit line with 48 banks that it could have used to fund margin calls.[54]

The second reason that MG's creditors may have refused to make the necessary funds available is that MGRM may have been "overhedged." MGRM has reported using a one-to-one hedge ratio, which may have resulted in its derivatives position being greater than required to match (or to offset) changes in the net present value of its forward-supply contracts due to price changes.[55] If this were the case, when energy prices fell, MGRM would have incurred greater losses on its long derivatives positions than it would have had gains on its forward-supply contracts. Thus, the value of MGRM's forward-supply contracts would not have been sufficient to collateralize the loans it needed, forcing MG to borrow by increasing its general debt obligations. The prospect of such a large increase in MG's debt may have alarmed its creditors, especially since MG's conflicting financial disclosures about MGRM's activities were creating an atmosphere of uncertainty and confusion about the continued viability of the firm.

MG's funding needs also were aggravated by actions taken by the New York Mercantile Exchange (NYMEX) at the end of December of 1993. Just when MGRM's funding needs were the greatest, the New York Mercantile Exchange (NYMEX) demanded "supermargin"—margin in excess of twice normal levels—from MGRM, placing an even greater strain on MG's resources. In addition, the NYMEX revoked MGRM's "hedger exemption" from exchange speculative position limits, forcing MGRM to liquidate part of its futures positions and to realize some of its unrealized losses.[56] It is not clear why the NYMEX took these drastic "regulatory" actions, but it appears to have acted only after the entire management board of MG was fired on December 17 by MG's supervisory board. Also, the new management's decision to force MG's commercial counterparties to draw down on the standby letters of credit issued to MG by various banks may have convinced the NYMEX that MG was caught in a liquidity squeeze.[57]

Thus, in retrospect, it is clear that MGRM's hedging strategy did expose it to "funding risk" associated with having to meet margin calls on its short-dated derivatives positions, and the MGRM was not adequately prepared to meet these funding needs. Further, MGRM's funding problems appear to have been exacerbated by conflicting and misleading accounting and disclosure conventions and by a lack of understanding on the part of its creditors and the financial community about exactly what it was doing.

5.6. Lack of understanding at the supervisory board level

On November 19, 1993, the supervisory board of Metallgesellschaft extended the contract of its management board chairman, Heinz Schimmelbusch, for another five years. Exactly four weeks later, the same supervisory board fired Schimmelbusch.[58] Further, MG's new management quickly decided to liquidate the bulk of both MGRM's derivatives positions and its forward-supply contracts, a strategy which proved to be immensely costly for MG.

Between December 20 and December 31 of 1993, when prices for crude oil, heating oil, and gasoline were at their lowest in many years, MGRM liquidated most of MGRM's futures and swap positions, resulting in substantial realized losses on its derivatives positions.[59] Judging from daily closing prices for that period, MGRM probably liquidated these positions at an average price of about $14 a barrel.[60] Assuming that MGRM had acquired these derivatives positions at an average price of $18 a barrel, an average liquidation price of $14 a barrel would have meant a loss of $640 million on its 160-million-barrel derivatives position.[62] In addition, in order to eliminate its exposure on its forward-supply contracts if prices rose, MGRM liquidated these contracts as well, apparently waiving cancellation penalties on the contracts, thereby giving up unrealized gains that could have offset at least some of MGRM's derivatives losses.[62]

Had MG's new management not ordered the liquidation of MGRM's position, the situation would be far different today. From December 17, 1993, when the new management took control, to August 8, 1994, crude oil prices increased from $13.91 to $19.42 a barrel, heating oil prices increased from $18.51 to $20.94 a barrel, and gasoline prices increased from $16.88 to $24.54 a barrel.[63] Given these price increases, MGRM would have had substantial unrealized gains in its derivatives positions and a huge inflow of margin funds.

What inferences can be drawn from MG's supervisory board's decision to liquidate MGRM's forward-supply contracts and its derivatives position? We know that during the summer of 1993, when energy prices decreased sharply, MGRM substantially expanded its strategy of providing its customers with fixed-price, long-term, forward-supply contracts and then hedging its price risk with derivatives. Thus, prior to its extending Schimmelbusch's contract on November 19, MG's supervisory board must have known (or, if it did not, it should have known) about MG's forward-contracting strategy and its use of derivatives.

The supervisory board's liquidation decision in December, therefore, suggests three interpretations. One is that the board was informed about MG's forward-contracting strategy but did not fully understand the potential risks and funding requirements that the strategy entailed. Another is that the board understood the risks that were involved but later changed its collective mind about the magnitude of these risks in the face of the huge margin calls that occurred. Still another possibility is that the strategy that the board approved was sound, but the board panicked in the face of huge margin calls when it ordered the liquidation of MGRM's positions. Under all three scenarios, one thing seems clear: at some point MG's supervisory board either failed to understand fully MGRM's forward-contracting and associated hedging strategies or seriously misjudged the risks that MGRM's strategy entailed.[64]

6. What are the lessons from Metallgesellschaft?

Metallgesellschaft's near-collapse and experience with derivatives suggests the following lessons for firms using derivatives and for policy makers:[65]

1. Conflicting and inappropriate accounting and disclosure conventions can create uncertainty about a firm's hedging program and can make it difficult for the firm to raise
   money when it needs to. Accounting and disclosure requirements for firms using
   derivatives to hedge can be informative *if they are appropriate and provide meaningful
   information.* Otherwise, they can result in misleading financial statements that can
   wreak havoc on firms and markets. Particularly in rapidly developing markets like
   OTC derivatives, accounting and disclosure conventions developed to meet past needs
   may be inappropriate for reporting new activities.

   The MG case clearly demonstrates the dangers of treating derivatives positions
   differently from the assets or liabilities that the derivatives are being used to hedge. There
   should not be accounting recognition of gains and losses on derivatives positions used for
   hedging unless the gains and losses on the positions that are being hedged also are
   recognized. In MG's disclosures based on German accounting principles, it recognized
   losses on its derivatives positions but did not recognize any gains on the forward-energy
   contracts that it was hedging. Thus, accounting and disclosure conventions which treat
   derivatives positions in an asymmetrical fashion with respect to the positions that are
   being hedged are misleading and can result in unwarranted market responses to firms'
   disclosures.

   Two accounting alternatives seem preferable to the one used by MG's German
   auditor. One is to mark-to-market both sides—the derivatives positions and the positions being hedged. The other is to adopt "hedge-deferral" principles.[66] The first,
   marking both positions to market, requires an ability to determine reasonably accurate
   and unambiguous values for all positions. In some cases, this may be difficult, and may
   give the firm wide latitude in determining values. MG may be a case in point. MGRM's
   forward-supply energy contracts were for durations as long as ten years. To determine
   the net present value of these contracts, therefore, it would be necessary to select a
   forward pricing curve for the various energy products on which the forward contracts
   were written.[67] No choice is clearly correct, and any choice could subject MG to
   criticism, since MG would be able to exercise considerable discretion in making its
   choice. In particular, MG could have chosen to value the contracts on the assumption
   that current spot energy prices would exist for the next ten years. Alternatively, it could
   have used the forward pricing curve that existed at the time of its report, but reliable
   forward prices for energy products are available for only a short period of time into the
   future. MG would have had to select a methodology for extrapolating existing forward
   prices out to ten years. Thus, whatever method MG used to estimate the present value
   of its forward-supply contracts could subject it to criticism.

   The valuation of MGRM's forward-supply contracts was made even more difficult
   by the existence of two additional factors—namely, that the contracts contained
   "early-liquidation" customer options, and that there was considerable uncertainty
   about MGRM's counterparty credit risk. With respect to its customer options, if
   energy prices were to rise such that MGRM's forward-supply contracts went "into-
   the-money" for its customers, MGRM's customers had an option to "cash-out" of
   these contracts, requiring MGRM to make substantial up-front payments. Further,
   the exercise of these options would substantially shorten the duration of the forward-
   supply contracts. Thus, to value the forward-supply contracts, it would have been

necessary to estimate the likelihood of the embedded options being exercised (which was dependent on the likelihood of an increase in energy prices and on changes in the forward pricing curve), and the likely costs to MGRM if the options were exercised. Considerable discretion exists in the procedures that MGRM could have used to value these options. Finally, the options were asymmetrical: MG's customers had no option in the event of falling energy prices (which is what actually occurred).

The value of MGRM's forward-supply contracts was also dependent on how the credit risk associated with these contracts was evaluated. Although these contracts would become more valuable to MGRM if energy prices fell, MGRM's ability to reap the full value of these contracts was dependent on the willingness and ability of its customers to meet their contractual obligations over a period of time as long as ten years. To value the forward-supply contracts, therefore, it would be necessary to estimate probable default rates over many years and to place a concrete number on the likely distribution of MGRM's default losses.[68] Once again, MGRM would have had considerable discretion as to how it determined its likely default losses.[69]

The second alternative accounting convention is the "hedge-deferral" principle, under which neither gains nor losses on derivatives positions used for hedging are recognized until the gains and losses on the positions being hedged are realized. While this procedure has the virtue of treating both sides symmetrically, it may not provide adequate disclosure of the risks that firms are taking. In particular, application of deferral-hedge accounting principles to MGRM's hedging strategy would not have made clear the risks that this strategy entailed. It would not, for example, have made clear the implications of MGRM's not having a hedge position that balanced changes in the net present value of its forward-supply contracts, or the implications of its using short-dated derivatives to hedge long-term commitments. At minimum, therefore, adoption of deferral-hedge accounting conventions should be accompanied by foot-notes explaining the nature and purpose of the firm's derivatives positions and the potential risks to which the firm is exposed.[70] There remains, of course, the issue of how complete a firm's disclosures can be before they become unacceptable because they require revealing proprietary information.

2. It is critical that both senior managers and the board of directors of a firm understand how a firm is using derivatives, and, if the firm is using derivatives as part of a hedging strategy, that they understand and approve of the potential ramifications and risks associated with this strategy. In general, the board should formally ratify this strategy before it is implemented.[71] In addition, senior managers should understand the firm's exposure to changes in prices and to basis changes, and should be informed about potential funding needs. The facts of the MG case suggest that MG's supervisory board either did not fully understand the risks associated with MGRM's forward-contracting and associated hedging strategy or did not correctly evaluate these risks when it approved this strategy.

3. It is important for hedgers to anticipate and to manage funding needs.[72] A critical need is to have the backing of financial institutions that understand and approve of the firm's use of derivatives, and are willing to advance credit to fund margin outflows on derivatives positions. MG apparently did not have such an understanding with its creditor banks.

4. Managers of firms using complex derivatives strategies must be cognizant of the possibility of unanticipated "regulatory" actions (by either government regulators or exchange officials), and of the potential consequences of these actions for the firm's position. The actions taken by MYMEX in raising MGRM's margins and revoking its hedger exemption clearly exacerbated MG's problems.

5. The MG case suggests that both organized futures markets and OTC derivatives markets may be more liquid than commonly believed.[73] The forced liquidation of MGRM's massive derivatives positions was accomplished quickly with very little market impact. Almost all of this liquidation was done, either directly or indirectly, on the NYMEX. MGRM sold its long futures positions directly, and, in liquidating its swap positions, it undoubtedly forced its swap counterparties (or dealers) to liquidate the long futures positions on NYMEX that they were almost surely using to hedge their swap positions with MGRM. During the period of MGRM's massive liquidation late in December of 1993, energy prices were largely unchanged and even rose a bit. Apparently, there were ample buyers readily available to absorb MGRM's forced sales.

6. The MG debacle raises an obvious question about the efficacy of the German system of corporate governance. This system relies on large stakeholders in a company acting as directors and managers of the company. As I have argued elsewhere, directors with a large stake in a company's performance should be better informed about the company's activities and should be more vigilant monitors of the company's mangaement.[74]

MG is a classic example of a German firm: seven institutional investors held just over 65 percent of the company's stock. The Emir of Kuwait held 20 percent; Dresdner Bank, Germany's second largest commercial bank, held 12.6 percent; a holding company jointly owned by Deutsche Bank (Germany's largest commercial bank) and Allianz (a major insurance company) held 13.2 percent; Daimler–Benz, the giant automaker, held 10 percent; the Australian Mutual Provident Society held 6 percent; and M.I.M. Holdings Ltd. of Australia held 3.5 percent[75] In addition, German banks typically control large amounts of stock through proxies given to them by their clients. The chairman of MG's supervisory board was and still is Ronaldo Schmitz, who also is a prominent member of the management board of Deutsche Bank. Despite this high-powered board, a lack of understanding at the supervisory board level appears to have contributed substantially to the MG debacle.[76] The MG experience, therefore, clearly brings into question the effectiveness of the German system of corporate governance and, in particular, of large banks as corporate monitors.[77]

7. Conclusion

The possibility of a systemic crisis occurring in financial markets obviously can never be ruled out. No amount of regulation can completely eliminate this possibility. However, the notion that the expansion of OTC derivatives markets has somehow increased the likelihood of a systemic crisis has no obvious factual basis. There is nothing in the GAO report to indicate that counterparty risk exposures in OTC derivatives markets are dangerously high, or to support the view that concentration among OTC dealers and expanded market linkages are destabilizing factors. Indeed, the use of derivatives may *reduce* systemic risk by diffusing market shocks. In providing a superior mechanism for the sharing risks, derivatives may cushion financial shocks by distributing the losses among a greater number of market participants. Finally, more regulation can have negative consequences. It can create institutional and market rigidities that exacerbate market stresses by impeding the flow of funds and preventing financial institutions from adjusting to changing market conditions.

It is instructive to remember that the worst U.S. financial crisis since the Great Depression occurred in a highly regulated industry—the thrift industry. Restrictive regulations and inept regulatory management were primary culprits in that incident. Similarly, the genesis of the Eurocurrency crisis in October 1992, was not destabilizing speculation but rather the Bank of England attempting to peg the exchange rate at an unrealistic level, giving speculators a "heads-you-win/tails-I-lose" opportunity which they could hardly be expected to pass up.

The best preventative against a systemic crisis in any market is to foster an environment in which all participants have an incentive to manage their risks prudently and can respond quickly and innovatively to changing market conditions. To a large extent, these conditions already exist in OTC derivatives markets. An area where improvements can be made, however, is with respect to accounting and disclosure practices for derivatives dealers and users. The experience of Metallgesellschaft clearly demonstrates the harm that can come from inappropriate accounting and disclosure practices. Better public disclosure of the risks incurred by derivatives users can improve market transparency and increase both market efficiency and market discipline by enabling investors and creditors to better monitor the use of derivatives.

A concerted effort is now underway to improve accounting and disclosure practices for derivatives users. The Financial Accounting Standards Board (FASB) recently issued an exposure draft addressing such issues as disclosure of fair values for derivatives transactions, the value of derivatives over an entire reporting period, and the purpose for which derivatives transactions are entered.[78] In addition, in September 1994, the Bank for International Settlements and the Central Banks of the Group Ten countries released a discussion paper entitled "Public Disclosure of Market and Credit Risks by Financial Intermediaries."[79] This paper proposes that quantitative public disclosures be made about the market and counterparty risks to which financial institutions are exposed when using derivatives, and about how effective institutions have been in the past in managing these risks. However, at present no consensus on best practice exists for how risk should be measured and disclosed.

Notes

1. See J. Eckhardt and T. Knipp, "Metallgesellschaft: Neue Probleme in den USA," *Handelsblatt,* November 4, 1994; and F. Protzman, "When German Safeguards Fail," *New York Times,* February 28, 1994, p. D1.
2. "Fill That Gap!" *Euromoney,* August, 1994, pp. 28–32, 29.
3. United States General Accounting Office, "Financial Derivatives: Actions Needed to Protect the Financial System," Report to Congressional Requestors, GAO/GGD-94-133, May, 1994, (hereafter referred to as the "GAO Report").

4. Mark Kollar, "Congressman Sees Need for Safety Net," *Knight-Ridder Financial Products & News,* July/ August, 1994, p. 1, col. 2.
5. *Recent Developments in International Interbank Relations,* Report prepared by a Working Group established by the Central Banks of the Group of Ten Countries, Bank for International Settlements, Bfasle, October, 1992.
6. GAO Report, *op. cit.,* p. 39.
7. Other risks are legal and operational. Legal risks occur because of the possibility that a contract will not be enforceable. Operational risks occur because of inadequate systems and controls, inadequate disaster or contingency planning, human error, or management failure.
8. An example of credit exposure arising from an interest rate swap is the following. Assume that, under an interest rate swap agreement, a firm receives fixed-interest payments and pays floating rates. At the inception of this swap, the market value of the firm's position in the swap is zero. If, subsequently, interest rates decline, the firm will receive more than it will pay, so the firm will have a valuable or profitable position in the swap. This value, created by the change in interest rates, is the firm's credit exposure, or the loss to the firm if its counterparty defaults. Alternatively, this credit exposure can be measured by what it would cost the firm to replace the swap on the same favorable terms if its counterparty defaulted on its future payments.
9. Forwards and swaps, along with exchange-traded futures and options, are the fundamental building blocks for other derivatives-related instruments. For example, "structured debt," or "hybrid" debt, are instruments that effectively combine straight debt instruments with one or more attached derivatives to create payoff features different from either of the component parts. Reported OTC derivatives, therefore, are often components of other derivatives instruments.
10. GAO Report, *op. cit.,* p. 34.
11. See Swaps Monitor Publications, Inc., *The World's Major Swap Dealers,* various issues. The GAO Report estimated that at year-end 1992 the notional value of all swap contracts outstanding was $4.7 trillion. See GAO Report, *op. cit.,* p. 34.
12. These include both their swaps and forward contracts.
13. GAO Report, *op. cit.,* p. 59, Table 3.1.
14. Group of Thirty Report, *op. cit.,* p. 58, Table 6.
15. GAO Report, *op. cit.,* pp. 54–55.
16. GAO Report, *op. cit.,* p. 55.
17. Cited in the GAO Report, *op. cit.,* p. 36. The GAO Report references *Derivatives: Practices and Principles,* Working Paper of the Systemic Issues Subcommittee, The Group of Thirty, Washington, D.C., July, 1993, pp. 131–132. The Group of Thirty study, in turn, relies on a survey referenced in *The World's Major Swap Dealers,* Swaps Monitor Publications, Inc., November, 1992. In its cite of the Group of Thirty study, the GAO Report incorrectly refers to the largest worldwide dealers (U.S. or foreign) as being only U.S. bank dealers (see p. 36).
18. GAO Report, *op. cit.,* p. 188, Table Appendix V.
19. This figure is not comparable to the $17.6 trillion which the GAO reports as being the total size of the derivatives market in 1992. The $8.7 trillion figure for the eight dealers includes some double-counting, which is eliminated in arriving at the total market figure of $17.6 trillion. Specifically, a $100 million notional swap between Citicorp and J.P. Morgan & Co., Inc., for example, would be counted in the total for the two dealers as $200 million because it appears in the accounts of both dealers. In contrast, in the GAO's $17.6 trillion estimate for the size of the total derivatives market, the same swap would be counted as only a $100 million swap.
20. It is noteworthy that, on average, only 10.97 percent of dealers' total net derivatives-related credit exposures were with other derivatives-dealers. See GAO Report, *op. cit.,* Appendix III, p. 157 and p. 167.
21. GAO Report, *op. cit.,* p. 37.
22. See U.S. Board of Governors of the Federal Reserve System, Federal Deposit Insurance Corporation, and Office of the Comptroller of the Currency, *Derivatives Product Activities of Commercial Banks,* Joint Study Conducted in Response to Questions Posed by Senator Riegle on Derivatives Products, Washington: Board of Governors of the Federal Reserve System, January 27, 1993.
23. GAO Report, *op. cit.,* pp. 8, 11–12, and 85–91.
24. GAO Report, *op. cit.,* p. 11.
25. GAO Report, *op. cit.,* p. 89.
26. A possible danger of imposing regulatory-mandated capital requirements is that over time these requirements can turn out to be *lower* than the market would demand in the absence of regulation. In other words,

counterparties may come to rely more on government regulation and the associated implicit government guarantees than on the firm's capital and internal management.

27. For a review of this regulation, see GAO Report, *op. cit.,* pp. 69–84.

28. GAO Report, *op. cit.,* p. 125.

29. Alternatively, there may be an argument for some form of "narrow banking," where the deposit-taking function of the bank is separated from other activities of banks, such as their derivative activities.

30. See Ferdinand Protzman, "When German Safeguards Fail," *New York Times,* February 28, 1994, p. D1; and Jens Eckhardt and Thomas Knipp, "Metallgesellschaft: Neue Probleme in den USA," *Handelsblatt,* November 4, 1994.

31. Karen Lowry Miller, "I Came, I Saw, I Conquered," *Business Week,* 58, July 4, 1994.

32. See Affidavit of W. Arthur Benson, W. Arthur Benson vs. Metallgesellschaft Corp. et. al., U.S.D.C. Maryland, Civil Action No. JFM-94-484, filed October 13, 1994.

33. See "New Shadows Hang Over the Crisis Management," Handelsbatt, October 22/23, 1994.

34. For a description of MGRM's business and hedging activities, see W. Arthur Benson vs. Metallgesellschaft Corp. et. al., Civ. Act. No. JFM-94-484, U.S.D.C.D. Md. 1994.

35. Jeffrey Taylor and Kenneth Bacon, "How the NYMEX Cooled MG's Oil Crisis," *The Wall Street Journal,* April 5, 1994.

36. Jeffrey Taylor and Allanna Sullivan, "German Firm Finds Hedges Can Be Thorny," *The Wall Street Journal,* January 10, 1994.

37. A "stack" hedge refers to a futures position being "stacked" or concentrated in a particular delivery month (or months) rather than being spread over many delivery months. In MGRM's case, it placed the entire 160 million barrel hedge in short-dated delivery months, rather than spreading this amount over many, longer-dated, delivery months. "Rolling over" this stacked position refers to the process of rolling it forward: selling contract months which will soon expire and purchasing (or replacing these contracts with) deferred-month contracts. Common reasons for using short-dated stack hedges are that liquidity is much better in near-month contracts, that longer-dated derivatives are simply not available on reasonable terms, and that hedgers may hold certain expectations about how the term structure of forward prices will change in the future. In a recent article, MGRM's short-dated, stack, hedging strategy is referred to as a "textbook" strategy. See Culp and Miller (1994a).

38. The "basis" is the difference between the price of the instrument that is being used to hedge (in the case of MGRM, near-month futures and swaps) and the price of the instrument or commitment that is being hedged (forward sales in the case of MGRM). "Basis risk" is the volatility of the basis. All hedgers, by definition, choose to assume basis risk as a trade-off for eliminating the price risk they would have if they did not hedge, presumably because the basis risk is less than the price risk. The risk that MGRM assumed in continually rolling its positions forward can be viewed as a particular type of intertemporal basis risk. See Edwards and Ma (1992), Chapter 5.

39. See W. Arthur Benson vs. Metallgesellschaft Corp. et. al., Civ. Act. No. JFM-94-484, U.S.D.C.D. Md. 1994.

40. See William Falloon, "Triple Whammy," *Energy Risk,* 1:4 (May, 1994).

41. Jeffrey Taylor and Kenneth Bacon, *op. cit.*

42. Markets in which nearby prices are below deferred-month prices are commonly referred to as "contango" markets. In contango markets MGRM's rolling-forward strategy would produce losses.

43. For a discussion of the pros and cons of stack hedging strategies, see Franklin R. Edwards and Cindy W. Ma, *Futures and Options* (McGraw-Hill, Inc.: New York), 1992, pp. 305–307. In addition, for a discussion of using a short-dated, stack, hedging strategy to hedge long-dated forward obligations, see Christopher L. Culp and Merton H. Miller, "Hedging a Flow of Commodity Deliveries with Futures: Lessons from Metallgesellschaft," *Derivatives Quarterly,* Vol. 1, No. 1 (1994).

44. MGRM may also have been exposed to basis risk if it "cross-hedged"—hedged, say, heating oil with crude oil futures. The full details about MGRM's hedging positions have not been made public—which futures, what amounts, on which dates, and so forth.

45. In another paper I analyze these risks in greater detail. See Edwards and Canter (1995).

46. Futures contracts are marked-to-market daily by exchanges, and traders are required to post with the exchange any losses they occur. In addition, while swap contracts usually are not formally marked-to-market, it is not

uncommon for counterparties in swap agreements to call for additional collateral from losing counterparties as losses mount. Such collateral can often be posted in the form of bank letters of credit.

47. One reason for these accounting principles may be that in Germany financial statements are used for tax purposes as well. Thus, if the objective is to maximize "tax losses," recognizing only unrealized losses accomplishes this.

48. This would have been true, for example, if MGRM had successfully used a "minimum-variance" hedge ratio.

49. Even if MGRM had used a minimum-variance hedging strategy, it would still have experienced losses due to rolling costs during 1993. However, these losses would have been less than the losses it incurred.

50. See Jens Eckhardt and Thomas Knipp, *op. cit.*

51. See Knight-Ridder Money Center, "Benson's Billion Dollar Lawsuit vs. MG Seen Hinging on Accounting," News No. 14149 (March 11, 1994).

52. Christopher Parkes, "Metallgesellschaft Stuns Banks with Loss Near DM 2bn," *Financial Times,* January 6, 1994; and David Waller, "German Group Hastens Talks with Bankers," *Financial Times,* December 31, 1993.

53. See Jens Eckhardt and Thomas Knipp, "Metallgesellschaft: New Problems in the United States?" *Handelsblatt,* November 4, 1994.

54. See Jens Eckhart and Thomas Knipp, "Metallgesellschaft: Neue Probleme in den U.S.A.?" *Handelsblatt,* November 4, 1994; and W. Arthur Benson vs. Metallgesellschaft Corp. et. al., Civ. Act. No. JFM-94-484, U.S.D.C.D. Md. 1994.

55. See Affidavit of W. Arthur Benson, W. Arthur Benson vs. Metallgesellschaft Corp. et. al., U.S.D.C. Maryland, Civil Action No. JFM-94-484, filed October 13, 1994.

56. Christopher Culp and Steve Hanke, "Derivative Dingbats," *International Economy,* 8:4 (July/August, 1994).

57. See Jens Eckhart and Thomas Knipp, *op. cit.*

58. See Jens Eckhardt and Thomas Knipp, *op. cit.*

59. MRC Oil Division Retainer Fax, Ref. 43/93, December 30, 1993.

60. MGRM had long futures positions in crude oil, heating oil, and gasoline.

61. MG did not finish liquidating its positions until sometime early in 1994.

62. W. Arthur Benson vs. Metallgesellschaft Corp. et. al., Civ. Act. No. JFM-94-484, U.S.D.C.D. Md. 1994.

63. I assume liquidation began when the new management took control on December 17, 1993. See MRC Oil Division Retainer Fax, Ref. 43/93, December 30, 1993; "CEO Schimmelbusch to Leave MG," Reuter, nFJ1700047; and "MG Fires Top Management After Loss, nL17313480, Reuter, Dec. 17, 1993.

64. The fact that MG's Supervisory Board in December rejected alternative actions that could have protected MG against further margin outflows is evidence that it did not believe that MGRM's forward-contracting strategy was fundamentally sound. For example, MG could have protected itself against further margin outflows due to price declines by purchasing put options on energy products, which were available in December, 1993. This strategy would have neutralized further margin outflows on MGRM's long futures and swap positions and may have been able to lock-in the net gains MGRM had.

65. The lessons I discuss below can be drawn from the MG experience independent of what one might conclude about whether MG's strategy exposed it to unreasonable risk.

66. See "Recommendation 19: Accounting Practices," of the Group of Thirty Study, *op. cit.,* p. 19, which states:
    —"End users should account for derivatives used to manage risks so as to achieve a consistency of income recognition treatment between those instruments and the risks being managed. Thus, if the risk being managed is accounted for at cost (or, in the case of an anticipatory hedge, not yet recognized), changes in the value of a qualifying risk management instrument should be deferred until a gain or loss is recognized on the risk being managed. Or, if the risk being managed is marked to market with changes in value taken to income, a qualifying risk management instrument should be treated in a comparable fashion.
    —End-users should account for derivatives not qualifying for risk management treatment on a mark-to-market basis."

67. For alternative views about how to determine the net present value of forward energy contracts, see Culp and Miller (1994b) and Gibson and Schwartz (1990).

68. There is evidence that "cumulative" default rates rise sharply with time. See Jerome S. Fons, "Using Default Rates to Model the Term Structure of Credit Risk," *Financial Analysts Journal,* September-October, 1994, pp. 25–32.

69. See "Recommendation 10: Measuring Credit Exposure," the Group of Thirty Study, *op. cit.,* p. 13, which proposes that end-users and dealers measure credit exposure in two ways:

    —"Current exposure, which is the replacement cost of derivatives transactions, that is, their market value.

    —Potential exposure, which is an estimate of the future replacement cost of derivatives transactions. It should be calculated using probability analysis based upon broad confidence intervals (e.g., two standard deviations) over the remaining terms of the transactions."

    In addition, on managing credit risk, see "Recommendation 12: Independent Credit Risk Management," *op. cit.,* p. 15.

70. See "Recommendation 20: Disclosures," of the Group of Thirty Study, *op. cit.,* p. 21, which recommends disclosure of:

    —"Information about management's attitude to financial risks, how instruments are used, and how risks are monitored and controlled;

    —Accounting policies;

    —Analysis of positions at the balance sheet date;

    —Analysis of the credit risk inherent in those positions;

    —For dealers only, additional information about the extent of their activities in financial instruments."

    See also "Public Disclosure of Risks Related to Market Activity," Federal Reserve Bank of New York, Discussion Paper, September, 1994.

71. See "Recommendation 1: The Role of Senior Management," of the Group of Thirty study, *op. cit.,* p. 9, which states:

    —"Dealers and end-users should use derivatives in a manner consistent with the overall risk management and capital policies approved by their boards of directors. These policies should be reviewed as business and market circumstances change. Policies governing derivatives use should be clearly defined, including the purposes for which these transactions are to be undertaken. Senior management should approve procedures and controls to implement these policies, and management at all levels should enforce them."

72. See "Recommendation 9: Practices of End-Users," of the Group of Thirty study, *op. cit.,* p. 13, which states:

    —"As appropriate to the nature, size, and complexity of their derivatives activities, end-users should adopt the same valuation and market risk management practices that are recommended for dealers. Specifically, they should consider regularly marking-to-market their derivatives transactions for risk management purposes; periodically forecasting the cash investing and funding requirements arising from their derivatives transactions; and establishing a clearly independent and authoritative function to design and assure adherence to prudent risk limits."

73. See, for example, United States General Accounting Office, "Financial Derivatives: Actions Needed to Protect the Financial System," GAO/GGD-94-133, May, 1994, p. 37.

74. See Franklin R. Edwards, "Financial Markets and Managerial Myopia: Making America More Competitive," in *Reforming Financial Markets and Institutions in the United States,* ed. by George Kaufman (Kluwer Academic Publishers: Boston, Mass.) 1993, pp. 141–172; and Mark J. Roe, "Some Differences in Corporate Structure in Germany, Japan, and the United States, *The Yale Law Journal,* Vol. 102, 1993, pp. 1927–2003.

75. See Ferdinand Protzman, "When German Safeguards Fail," *New York Times,* February 28, 1994, p. D1; and "Metallgesellschaft Woes Put Spotlight on Two-tier Boards," *Director's Monthly,* Boardroom News, August 27, 1994, p. 14.

76. Ferdinand Protzman, "When German Safeguards Fail," *N.Y. Times,* February 28, 1994, p. D1.

77. Recent press articles have indicated that leading politicians in all parties in Germany have introduced legislation to limit the stakes that banks can hold in industrial companies. They also report that Deutsche Bank has threatened to challenge in court any law that would force it to reduce its equity stakes in industrial companies, and has even threatened to move some of its operations from Frankfurt to London. See Alan Friedman, "Deutsche Bank Fights Back to Save Reputation," *Herald Tribune,* December 5, 1994, P. C1. For a discussion of the pros and cons of large ownership by financial institutions, see Bernard S. Black, "The Value of Institutional Investor Monitoring: The Empirical Evidence," *UCLA Law Review,* Vol. 39, 1992, pp. 896–933; and Mark J. Roe, "Some Differences in Corporate Structure in Germany, Japan, and the United States," *The Yale Law Review,* Vol 102, 1993, pp. 1928–1998

78. See FASB's "Proposed Statement of Financial Accounting Standards: Disclosure of Derivative Financial Instruments and Fair Value of Financial Instruments," Financial Accounting Series No. 136-B, April, 1994.
79. Central Banks of the Group of Ten Countries, "Publijc Disclosure of Markets and Credit Risks by Financial Intermediaries," Euro-currency Standing Committee Discussion Paper, September, 1994.

References

Affidavit of W. Arthur Benson. *W. Arthur Benson v. Metallgesellschaft Corp. et al.* U.S.D.C. Maryland, Civil Action No. JFM-94-484, filed October 13, 1994.

Bank for International Settlements. *Recent Developments in International Interbank Relations.* Working Paper of Central Banks for the Group of Ten Countries, October, 1992.

Black, Bernard S. "The Value of Institutional Investor Monitoring: The Empirical Evidence." *UCLA Law Review* 39(1992), 896–933

Central Banks of the Group of Ten Countries. "Public Disclosure of Markets and Credit Risks by Financial Intermediaries." Euro-currency Standing Committee Discussion Paper, September, 1994.

Culp, Christopher, and Steve Hanke. "Derivative Dingbats." *International Economy* 8(4)(July/August 1994).

Culp, Christopher L., and Merton H. Miller. "Hedging a Flow of Commodity Deliveries with Futures: Lessons from Metallgesellschaft." *Derivatives Quarterly* 1(1)(1994a).

Culp, Christopher L., and Merton H. Miller. "Metallgesellschaft and the Economics of Synthetic Storage." Mimeo, December 13, 1994b; *Journal of Applied Corporate Finance* (forthcoming).

Eckhardt, Jens, and Thomas Knipp. "Metallgesellschaft: Neue Probleme in den USA." *Handelsblatt,* November 4, 1994.

Edwards, Franklin R. "Financial Markets and Managerial Myopia: Making America More Competitive." In: George Kaufman, ed., *Reforming Financial Markets and Institutions in the United States.* Boston, MA: Kluwer Academic Publishers. 1993.

Edwards, Franklin R., and Michael Canter. "The Collapse of Metallgesellschaft: Unhedgeable Risks, Poor Hedging Strategy, or Just Bad Luck?" *The Journal of Futures Markets* 15(3)(May 1995).

Edwards, Franklin R., and Cindy W. Ma. *Futures and Options* New York: McGraw-Hill, Inc. 1992.

Euromoney. "Fill That Gap!" August 1994.

Falloon, William. "Triple Whammy." *Energy Risk* 1(4)(May 1994).

Financial Accounting Standards Board. "Proposed Statement of Financial Accounting Standards: Disclosure of Derivative Financial Instruments and Fair Value of Financial Instruments." Financial Accounting Series No. 136-B, April 1994.

Fons, Jerome S. "Using Default Rates to Model the Term Structure of Credit Risk." *Financial Analysts Journal* (September/October 1994).

Friedman, Alan. "Deutsche Bank Fights Back to Save Reputation." *Herald Tribune*, December 5, 1994.

Gibson, R., and E.S, Schwartz. "Stochastic Convenience Yield and the Pricing of Oil Contingent Claims." *The Journal of Finance* 45(1990), 959–976.

Group of Thirty. "Derivatives: Practices and Principles." Overview of Derivatives Activity, July 1993, Washington, DC.

"How a Former Banker Took a German Giant to the Cleaners." *Global Finance*, November 1994.

Kollar, Mark. "Congressman Sees Need for Safety Net." *Knight-Ridder Financial Products & News*, July/August 1994.

Knight-Ridder Money Center. "Benson's Billion Dollar Lawsuit vs. MG Seen Hinging on Accounting." News No. 14149, March 11, 1994.

"Metallgesellschaft Woes Put Spotlight on Two-tier Boards." *Director's Monthly*, Boardroom News, August 27, 1994.

Miller, Karen Lowry. "I Came, I Saw, I Conquered." *Business Week* 58, July 4.

MRC Oil Division Retainer Fax. Ref. 43/93, December 30, 1993.

"New Shadows Hang Over the Crisis Management." Handelsbatt, October 22/23, 1994.

Parkes, Christopher. "Metallgesellschaft Stuns Banks with Loss Near DM 2bn." *Financial Times*, January 6, 1994.

Protzman, Ferdinand. "When German Safeguards Fail." *New York Times*, February 28, 1994.

Roe, Mark J. "Some Differences in Corporate Structure in Germany, Japan, and the United States." *The Yale Law Journal* 102(1993).

Swaps Monitor Publications, Inc. *The World's Major Swap Dealers*, November 1992.

Taylor, Jeffrey, and Kenneth Bacon. "How the NYMEX Cooled MG's Oil Crisis." *The Wall Street Journal*, April 5, 1994.

Taylor, Jeffrey, and Allanna Sullivan. "German Firm Finds Hedges Can be Thorny." *The Wall Street Journal*, January 10, 1994.

U.S. Board of Governors of the Federal Reserve System, Federal Deposit Insurance Corporation, and Comptroller of the Currency. *Derivative Product Activities od Commerical Banks* (Joint study conducted in response to questions posed by Senator Riegle on derivative products). Washington, DC: Board of Governors of the Federal Reserve System, January 27, 1993.

U.S. General Accounting Office. "Financial Derivatives: Actions Needed to Protect the Financial System." GAO/GGD-94-133, May 1994.

Waller, David. "German Group Hastens Talks with Bankers." *Financial Times*, December 31, 1993.

W. Arthur Benson v. Metallgesellschaft Corp. et al. Civ. Act. No. JFM-94-484, U.S.D.C.D. Md. 1994.

Journal of Financial Services Research 9: 291–297 (1995)
© 1995 Kluwer Academic Publishers

Comment

JACQUES J. SIJBEN
Tilburg University, Tilburg, 5000 LE Tilburg, The Netherlands

The articles by Minsky and Calomiris in this volume deal with the mechanisms through which financial factors contribute to business cycles, emphasizing the sources of the increased macroeconomic fragility and what public policies should be adopted in response.

1. A new competitive financial environment

After the second world war, the dominant macroeconomic view was one that assumed a frictionless neoclassical world with perfect or symmetric information on markets; this view was based on the idea of the efficiency of a decentralized competitive market system. For half a century, the role of financial markets and financial institutions has been subordinated to a secondary place by economic theorists, and, in macroeconomics, the whole of financial analysis has been subsumed under the control of the money supply. If the Modigliani–Miller analysis applies, the financial structure of the firm is irrelevant to both its value and its operating decisions and, therefore, has no influence on the real economic process. Also, in macroeconomic theory, it was postulated that the course of real economic development would be accompanied by a smooth working of the financial system. So, analogously to the classical view about the neutrality of money and the associated idea that "money is a veil," in the context of the role of financial markets, it was assumed that "the financial system is a veil."

However, with regard to the link between the financial system and macroeconomic performance, which is emphasized in these articles, it can be pointed out that recent research in macroeconomics has resurrected the idea that capital market imperfections may be significant factors both for business volatility and the ultimate outcome of the macroeconomic process. Imperfections in capital markets have allocative effects which can involve interactions between disruptions in financial markets and economic activity.

During the last decade, financial markets have become more integrated domestically and internationally, and have undergone profound changes. Driven by deregulation processes, increased monetary uncertainties, internationalization and advances in information technology, a wave of financial innovations has brought about quite a new competitive international financial environment. Also, in the 1980s, a change in attitude toward debt can be observed, reflecting the declining influence of those who experienced the Great Depression in the 1930s. Moreover, changes in the tax structure have encouraged the use of debt rather than equity, thereby, increasing the leveraging of business corporations. By the substitution of debt for equity financing as a result of leveraged buyouts, mergers, and acquisitions, and by the use of capital markets instead of bank credit (disintermediation), the business sector has made itself strongly dependent on current cash flows for meeting debt-servicing obligations. Finally, the availability of both official safety-net deposit insurance and the lender-of-last-resort functions of the central bank has further reduced the perceived risk of borrowing (moral hazard) and has encouraged risk taking by banks and other financial intermediaries. This means that market forces are no longer allowed to exercise their full discipline over financial institutions. There is one common thread running through many recent banking crises. In my view, that thread is the recognition that the competitive pressures unleased by financial liberalization do not merely increase efficiency; they also carry risks, as banks and other financial institutions have increased their tolerance for risk.

Summarizing, financial innovation processes played an important role in fueling the leveraging in the 1980s, increasing access to debt and overshooting some asset values. Then, when the process collapsed, consumers, firms, and financial institutions were left with excess debt and impaired net worth, causing them to restructure their balance sheets.

2. Implications for financial stability

The question now arises as to whether this new financial world in which banks meet the market place has increased or decreased the stability of the financial system. In my view, the answer to this question is by no means clear. Therefore, it has been a good idea to organize this conference to explore the implications of the new competitive financial environment for the stability of the system.

Professor Minsky's article deals with the general sources of financial fragility. The main point in his study is based on his earlier work on the "financial instability hypothesis," which builds upon an interpretation of Keynes and is centered on the interaction process between capitalist firms and financial intermediaries during the accumulation process. His main thesis is that in good times there is a change in the financial structure of modern capitalist economies, which are by their nature unstable, from being robust to being fragile; this position is not only validated by the experience of history but also by the recent events in the 1980s.

According to Minsky's view, the finance needed for the investment process is largely obtained through (mostly short-term) debt, and therefore firms commit themselves to future cash outflows in order to service the debt. He assumes a closed economy with a Keynesian–Kaleckian framework, in which gross profits are determined by the level of aggregate investments and the government deficit. Professor Minsky emphasizes the meaning of uncertainty, the business cycle, and finance.

In his article, Professor Minsky stresses that the capitalist system is characterized by a "financial instability bias," manifested by rapid and accelerating changes in prices of real and financial assets in relation to prices of production. The so-called "boom-bust cycle," in which endogenous cyclical forces may lead to financial instability, goes along the following line of reasoning. During the upswing in economic activity, firms and households behave in such a way that they don't bother about the development of their financial structure. Owing to a short memory, economic agents have less aversion to building up debts and to an increasing ratio of debts to liquid assets. However, this behavior makes the financial system rather vulnerable to possible disturbances in the real economy. In this context, he distinguishes three types of financial structures, namely, hedge, speculative, and Ponzi finance. In Ponzi financing, income flows are not sufficient even to cover interest on outstanding debt, so the refinancing necessarily entails an increase in indebtedness. The proliferation of speculative and Ponzi financing arrangements generates a fragile financial structure in which any sharp rise in interest rates will generate present value reversals, thereby impairing the ability of firms to refinance investment projects in process and their willingness to undertake new investment. The fragility of the financial system is determined by the relative weights of the different types of financial structures, the degree of liquidity of the financial system, and the reliance on debt to finance the investment projects. The larger the relative share of Ponzi units with respect to hedge and speculative units, the more fragile is the financial structure of the economy.

The fragility of the financial system increases when relatively small changes in cash flows, the discount rate, and contractual repayments influence negatively the fulfilment of the debt service commitments. In a situation of increasing debt financing, it will be more difficult to meet these debt-service requirements with existing income flows if there is a downturn in the economic cycle. Therefore, "hedge finance units" will become "speculative finance units," and these agents will have difficulty in refinancing their debts. Moreover, the rate of interest will rise because of a higher demand for credit, thus increasing the riskiness of credit extension. Next, the rise of the rate of interest will increase the reproduction costs of new capital goods, and, according to Tobin's q-mechanism, will further reduce investment activity. On the other hand, the rise of the rate of interest will result in a fall in the price of existing capital goods (equities), or in a higher required rate of return, also reducing investment activity. Feedback effects from rising interest rates at the peak of the cycle lead both to financial distress in the business sector and to a reluctance to lend on the part of the banks, which may trigger a Fisher debt-deflation process. Corporations try to reduce the increased leverage built up during the expansion stage, and banks refuse to continue to finance investment spending. There also exists a forced selling of assets to raise cash, sharpening the asset-deflation process, which will further reduce investments.

In sum, it can be stated that Minsky's financial instability hypothesis describes a theory of how a capitalist economy endogenously generates a financial structure of economic agents which is susceptible to a financial crisis. Moreover, it shows how the normal functioning of financial markets in the resulting speculative investment boom will trigger a financial crisis.

3. Implications for monetary policy

Minsky's analysis can be linked up with the anti-inflation strategy of monetary policy makers and may face them with a new trade-off problem, namely, that of financial robustness versus price stability. In his earlier publications, he pointed out that during periods of a restrictive monetary policy in the United States since the 1960s, the U.S.

economy was brought to the brink of a debt-deflation process. If, in these circumstances, a financial crisis threatens, the central bank as lender of last resort can help to avoid the debt-deflation spiral. Through a large addition of liquidity to financial markets and the induced reduction of interest rates, a further fall in the price of equities and thus of investment activity can be averted. However, he argued that since the 1960s, a downturn in economic activity and the associated income flows have been prevented by a discretionary expansive fiscal policy at the price of higher inflation. In the *Journal of Economic Issues* (1980, p. 519), Minsky expressed this view as follows: "Stagflation is truly a result of big government, but so is the absence of a deep depression in the years since 1966. There is no free lunch: we have eliminated deep depressions but the price has been first chronic and now accelerating inflation." The intervention of the central bank to manage a threatening financial dislocation will reduce the fear of a further fall of profits and prevent the loss of confidence by economic agents. Subsequently, he concludes: "Both the Great Depression and the great inflation and intermittent stagnation of 1966–1979 are symptoms of the underlying instability of capitalism. A great stagflation is the outcome when government is big and the central bank intervenes forcefully." In this context, I will put the following remarks.

From a monetary-policy perspective, the increased indebtedness of U.S. corporations, via the substitution of debt for equity financing during the last decade, has increased the risk that sluggish growth could lead to a recession, thus generating widespread and potentially cumulative debt defaults. The increased likelihood of debtor distress during a business downturn could reduce the central bank's tolerance for allowing a recession, and thereby accept a higher average rate of inflation. The increased financial fragility could force policy makers to choose between financial stability and price stability as the primary goal of monetary policy. This would mean that, in these circumstances, monetary authorities might be less aggressive in sticking to their anti-inflationary policies to prevent a cumulative crisis in the financial system, thus worsening a current recession.

This implies that if enlarged business indebtedness raises the likely costs of economic downturns and the risks associated with them, policy authorities may be less likely to accept such periods of economic weakness, and it therefore also imparts a systemic inflationary bias. This bias is likely to meet less resistance than would have been the case some years ago.

I hold the view that if the financial system has become too fragile to withstand any but the shortest recession, it is unlikely to be able to support a genuine attack on inflation. This also implies that the issue of moral hazard (too-big-to-fail doctrine) and the associated phenomenon of financial stability have to be included in the modern analysis both of the rules-versus-discretion debate in a game-theoretic framework, and the independency of central banks.

In his concluding remarks Professor Minsky stresses that big government can stabilize aggregate profit flows, which are the driving forces of the economic activity, and can prevent financial fragility from leading to great depressions.

I fully agree with him that government intervention cannot simply entail a recourse to extraordinary inflationary measures. However, I am afraid that his strong assumption that government can validate its debt by its income flows and high taxation will not hold in practice, thereby shifting the problems to the near future. In my view, the final outcome of this policy will be increasing budget deficits, with the concomitant crowding-out effects, resulting in a reduction of investment activity in the private sector and in a less beneficial macroeconomic performance in the long run.

4. Financial shocks and propagators

Let me begin by saying that I agree with almost everything that Professor Calomiris states in his clearly written article. He summarizes the key issues with regard to the growing evidence that financial relationships affect the volatility of macroeconomic performance. He makes mention of financial shocks to the economy, such as the Penn-Central crisis on the commercial paper market in 1970, on the one hand, and of financial propagators of financial disturbances, on the other hand.

Starting in section 2, with an analysis of the financial propagators, Calomiris puts forward the "cash-flow constraint." This propagation mechanism emphasizes the fact that procyclical movements in borrowers' financial positions lead to countercyclical movements of the premium for external funds. In an asymmetric information context, this means that investment activity will be more volatile than in the neoclassical, frictionless, Modigliani–Miller world. So there exists an endogenous interaction between the financial structure of firms, defined as net worth in relation to the debt service, and real economic activity. The difference between the cost of capital in the case of external and that of internal finance is negatively correlated with the business cycle. This means that during booms it becomes easier to borrow, agency costs are relatively low, and the rise in internal net worth will reduce the premium attached to external finance. Conversely, in recessions, the "lemon's premium" rises, and the cost of external finance will increase.

He shows that firms with high external finance costs tend to be small, bank-dependent, firms with high debt ratios and low ratios of profits to sales, exhibiting a great cash-flow sensitivity of fixed investment and working capital. I fully agree with him that this financial accelerator mechanism is an important contributor to the macroeconomic relation between profits and investment. This relation is also one of the central issues in Professor Minsky's financial instability hypothesis.

The second financial propagation mechanism refers to the operation of the "debt-overhang effect," which dates from the debt-deflation spiral in the 1930s and what academic economists have called the "credit view" of monetary economies. I hold the view that the sluggishness of the recovery in the early 1990s in the U.S. and the U.K., which currently persists in Japan, came about by the need for a restructuring of the balance sheet of firms, households, and the banking industry, owing to the asset-price deflation process. This process is one of balance-sheet adjustment, which is fundamentally different from a traditional cyclical episode characterized by an inventory-adjustment process.

This point is linked with Calomiris's third financial propagator, namely, the relation between a deterioration of the quality of the borrowers' balance sheets and the reduction of credit available to small, less established, bank-dependent borrowers. This means that, because of asymmetric information problems, financial markets may be important sources and propagators of a decline in economic activity.

Calomiris also puts forward the important issue that regulatory distortions in the financial industry may have magnified the working of the financial accelerator in the U.S., thereby affecting macroeconomic stability. In this context, regulatory interventions by the government may give rise to less diversification of banking activities and to less potential for coordination among banks, thus increasing fragility of individual banks. He also refers to the influence of the Farm Credit System in the U.S., which was guilty of "feeding the optimists" during the agricultural boom-and-bust cycle of the 1970s and the 1980s.

Without doubt, the availability of a safety net for avoiding a possible crisis and for calming market fears by supplying liquidity to the market may also give rise to moral-hazard problems by the lenders. These problems are reflected in the lenders' acceptance of higher risk investment projects and in their willingness to lend to optimists, thereby allowing the latter to push up land prices.

The same boom-bust cycle also came about in the last decade in the oil and the real-estate sector, driven by the perverse incentives of the "too-big-to-fail" doctrine. At that time, many banks responded to the new competitive financial environment by increasing the riskiness of their portfolios. This strategy was also encouraged by the existence of a net of explicit and implicit government guarantees, which both protected depositors and made failure a less credible deterrent of excessive risk taking.

In section 3 of his article, Calomiris is talking about financial shocks which can also contribute to macroeconomic fragility. In this context, he argues that monetary policy itself can be an important source of a financial shock. I think that this statement is only true under circumstances in which the central bank attempts to use monetary policy to reduce unemployment, reacting to bad news about the unemployment figures and thereby causing long-term financial instability.

I hold the view that, in a game-theoretic framework, a policy of using interest rates to lower unemployment will only fuel inflationary expectations, thereby pushing up bond yields and wage contracts, with counterproductive long-term macroeconomic results. In my opinion, a stable and preannounced target zone for an appropriately chosen monetary aggregate would help to prevent inflation and prevent inflationary expectations from being mistaken, and would make the monetary authorities more predictable and credible. Without doubt, such a design of a rule-based monetary policy will increase macroeconomic and financial stability. This policy framework can contribute to a more stable financial and economic environment with less volatility in inflation, interest rates, and exchange rates, resulting in a reduction of capital-market innovation processes. The higher the credibility and reputation of monetary policy makers with regard to reducing monetary uncertainties, the lower the variability and uncertainty in inflation and the higher the level and efficiency of investment. Both factors would result in a more stable macroeconomic environment in the long run, with a concomitant stabilizing effect on the financial sector.

I agree with Calomiris's remark that the potential for destabilizing financial shocks is the price that we have to pay for a dynamic financial system. He points out that this price can be minimized by an appropriately structured lender of last resort, while simultaneously minimizing the moral-hazard consequences of its interventions.

In my view, it is also possible to accept the reality that certain troubled institutions have no remaining value, and that liquidating them before they can do more harm is the most sensible long-term solution to the problem. It is obvious that this approach is subject to the judgmental problem of distinguising a permanent from a transitory or cyclical weakness.

5. Implications for supervisors

Finally, in the context of the central issue of this conference, I will comment on the role of bank supervisors in ensuring financial stability. Some analysts believe that supervision reduces the efficiency of the banking system and weakens market discipline. Other analysts hold the view that the benefits outweigh the costs of re-regulation.

Some years ago, the Bank for International Settlements (BIS) took the initiative to stimulate central banks to consult and cooperate internationally, aiming at a sharpening of the control of banking institutions to safeguard the stability of the financial system. In 1988, The Committee on Banking Regulations and Supervisory Practices (Cooke Committee) designed internationally comparable, risk-based, capital-adequacy ratios (8 percent) to be imposed on banks beginning in 1993. In April 1993, the Basle committee of central bankers released proposals to extend its existing capital standards for credit risk to cover two other big new risks faced by international banks, namely, market risk (price changes of securities) and interest-rate risk (the risk of a mismatch).

It will soon be clear whether the supervisors will succeed in controlling the consequences of the revolution in financial markets in the 1980s by their coordinated design of a new framework of supervision which is aimed at a stronger banking industry in an era of more freedom. It will be a great challenge for central banks to realize a balance between the stability and efficiency of the financial system. In the context of an overall tendency to make greater room for market discipline alongside official prudential supervision, I fully agree with BIS's conclusion as stated in its Annual Report (1991, p. 221): "Above all, reducing incentives to excessive risk-taking will depend on the credibility of the authorities' commitment to limiting intervention to the necessary minimum in the event of turmoil. In much the same way as the monetary authorities' anti-inflation commitment, it needs to be demonstrated in consistent action." The primary danger for financial stability is that a downturn of the business cycle will interrupt the cash flows of households and firms, giving rise to an inability to service the accumulated level of debt. Such a process can lead to a crisis in the financial system with negative spillover effects upon the real economy. I am convinced that the robustness of the financial system can be maintained both by stable, consistent, and predictable government policies, and an institutional environment that encourages sufficient diversification of risks, thereby reducing the risk of future economic and financial crises.

I hope that this conference can help us to understand the implications of the new competitive financial world and to anticipate the challenges that innovations provide, toward the goal of achieving a reduction of fragility in the global financial system.

Journal of Financial Services Research 9: 299–302 (1995)
© 1995 Kluwer Academic Publishers

Sources of Financial Fragility:

Comment

STUART I. GREENBAUM
Olin School of Business, Washington University, St. Louis, MO 63130-4899, U.S.A.

The following comments are directed at two articles: "Is The Banking and Payments System Fragile?" by George J. Benston and George G. Kaufman (hereafter B–K), and "Systemic Risk in OTC Derivatives Markets: Much Ado About Not Too Much" by Franklin R. Edwards. The discussion of B–K is more extensive and comes first.

B–K insinuate a potpourri of beliefs and public policy prescriptions relating to financial system regulation, suffusing them in a selective review of the voluminous academic literature on bank runs, panics, and the interface between the financial and real sectors of the economy. For effect, the authors stress their disagreement with Irving Fisher, Charles Kindleberger, Martin Feldstein, Diamond-Dybvig, Adam Smith, Joseph Schumpeter, and Walter Bagehot, among others.

The flavor of the B–K findings is conveyed by the following:

> The cost of individual bank failures is relatively small and not greatly different from the failure of any non-bank firm of comparable importance in its community. In fact, the societal cost of preventing insolvent banks from failing is greater . . .

Further, B–K aver:

- The widely observed proclivity of banks to fail—"inherent instability"—is mistaken.
- The alleged contagion of bank failures is likewise mistaken.
- The lender-of-last-resort (LLR) function of central banks is distorting and readily disposable.
- Bank capital requirements should be further elevated, to some unspecified level, to mitigate moral hazard problems.
- Sanctions for noncompliance with capital requirements should be swift, sure, and severe—"structured early intervention and resolution (SEIR)."
- Market-value accounting (MVA) should replace generally accepted accounting principles (GAAP).
- Virtually all geographical, functional, and ownership restrictions on banks should be eliminated.

These and other positions are legitimized as inferences, suggestions, or even implications of the surveyed literature. Some are comfortably familiar. For example, the argument for replacing regulatory discretion with swift, sure, and severe sanctions for noncompliance with capital requirements was advanced at least a decade ago (Greenbaum, 1985).

105

Nevertheless, these criticisms leap to mind:

- Although B–K's findings are presented as if they follow from the literature reviewed, the linkages are not always transparent. For example, the "inherent instability" (undefined by B–K) of banks is debunked by marshalling evidence that recessionary shocks from the real sector of the economy often precede banking distress. Does such evidence obviate bank runs of the Diamond–Dybvig (1983) or Chari and Jagannathan (1988) variety? Would such bank runs constitute inherent instability? Not clear!
- It is too easy, even niggling, to criticize a literature review for selectivity. But in light of the prescriptions advanced, important contributions are ignored. For example, Mailath and Mester (1994) on forbearance, O'Hara (1993) on MVA, Boyd and Gertler (1993) on too-big-to-fail (TBTF), and Chari and Jagannathan (1988) on bank runs, are widely cited on the questions at issue in B–K. Likewise, to dismiss the LLR in two double-spaced pages strikes me as heroic, at best.
- At least one key point in B–K is contradicted internally. On the one hand, "the evidence is overwhelming . . . that depositors have been able, at the margin, to differentiate between good and bad banks. . . . " On the other, " . . . past multiple bank failures are consistent with the asymmetric information hypothesis. . . . "
- Given our messy world of second best, in order to be persuaded of the merits of B–K's proposals I would want to see them evaluated against alternative reform proposals. In this regard, I found it surprising that neither the U.S. Treasury's (1991) recommendations nor the more recent FIRREA Commission Report (1993) were mentioned. Also ignored were the Ely (1986) proposals for privatizing deposit insurance, the aforementioned Boyd–Gertler proposals regarding TBTF, and the pristine proposals to scale back, or even eliminate, deposit insurance. All of these have been seriously advanced with the same motivation as the authors', namely, to reduce moral hazards and other distortions of the safety net and to reduce subsidies flowing from taxpayers to bank owners and managers. The appropriate context for advocating the B–K reforms is that they in some compelling sense dominate these alternatives.

Having chided B–K, in the spirit of candor, let me offer my own perspective. I think we know the following:

- Fractional reserve banks evolve naturally from goldsmiths as warehouse receipts become more widely accepted as payments media.
- Even apart from asset quality problems, individual banks suffer periodic withdrawal crises owing to their production of liquidity (Edgeworth, 1888).
- The probability that individual bank's distress will develop into panic increases with the opaqueness of banks.
- Even very small probabilities of banking panics can imply large expected value losses to the community. (This is not to say that nonbank failures are incapable of generating important externalities. They are!)

- The liquidity problems of fractional reserve banks are readily addressed with a credible LLR. (This is not to say that a Federal Funds market can't effectively redistribute reserves under ordinary circumstances. But markets for liquidity occasionally gridlock, and credit rationing is reasonably well documented.)
- However, the introduction of a central bank LLR immediately creates a moral hazard in that banks respond by reducing their cash–asset reserves; this is true at any finite discount rate. The dissipation of banks' cash assets transfers seigniorage from taxpayers to the banks. (Publicly provided and most-of-the-time idle fire-fighting capability is often found to be worthwhile despite a robust private market in fire extinguishers, sprinkler systems, and inexpensive and readily available water. Moreover, the public provision of fire-fighting services results in a moral hazard too.)
- This is the most basic argument for prudential regulation. (Of course, if you could safely dispose of the LLR, the moral hazard disappears and along with it the rationale for regulation.)
- But deposit insurance, TBTF, guarantee of the payments system and other safety-net features produce their own moral hazards.

It would seem to follow that the discussion of bank regulation appropriately begins with how much safety net is needed—here I believe B–K and most of the academic profession would join hands as minimalists—and how much regulation would be required to sustain the public protection of banks and the payments system.

At the next level lies the issue of regulatory design ("the devil is in the details"), and the most interesting cut here is one originating in the literature on macroeconomic stabilization policy, from Simons (1936) and Friedman (1948) to Kydland and Prescott (1977). That is, how much *discretion* ought public officials have, and how much can be accomplished with *rules*.

Whereas Simons and Friedman questioned the motives and judgment of central bankers, and Kydland and Prescott introduced the issue of time consistency, the point here is different. Discretionary prudential regulation adds uncertainty from the bank investor's standpoint, what Gerald Corrigan (1990) called "constructive ambiguity." This ambiguity may ameliorate some moral hazards (Boot and Thakor, 1993), but it also inflates the bank's cost of capital, and this cost typically is not internalized by the public regulator. Hence, if the regulatory problem can be addressed with rules that limit regulatory discretion, in the spirit of SEIR, the deadweight costs of regulation can be reduced. This, it seems to me, is the broader context within which to evaluate alternative banking reform proposals.

Franklin Edwards' paper makes the plausible point that the systemic risk (however defined) posed by the recent explosive growth of over-the-counter (OTC) derivatives is very likely exaggerated, and that largely overlooked are the benefits of more cost-effective hedging opportunities. The author then proceeds to an interpretation of the Metallgesellschaft (MG) affair that brought one of Europe's great companies perilously close to the abyss owing to the (ab)use of derivatives. Edwards explains the loss of $1.5 billion in terms of inept management at the highest levels in MG, and the market's naive response to misguided accounting conventions.

The lessons drawn include:

- Inappropriate accounting conventions can cause great harm.
- Managers should understand their firm's use of derivatives.
- Managers should understand the risk of regulator caprice.
- The market smoothly absorbed the precipitous liquidation of MG's massive open position in derivatives.
- European corporate governance may require re-examination.

Here, I fault the author for timidity. What are the lessons for public regulation of OTC derivatives, if any? What about public policy regarding disclosure? One possible interpretation is that since market participants can be confused by accounting conventions, some form of public regulation is warranted. Moreover, since the New York Mercantile Exchange inappropriately elevated MG's margin requirements precipitating a liquidity crisis, should the self-regulating exchanges be brought under greater public sector scrutiny as well?

The author's interpretation of the MG disaster suggests a host of fascinating questions, but these are left largely unaddressed. He tantalizes, but ultimately frustrates the reader.

References

Boot, Arnoud W. and Anjan V. Thakor. "Ambiguity and Moral Hazard." Working paper, Indiana University, 1993.

Boyd, John H., and Mark Gertler. "U.S. Commercial Banking: Trends, Cycles, and Policy." *NBER Macroeconomics Annual* (1993), 319–68.

Chari, V.V., and Ravi Jagannathan. "Banking Panics, Information, and Rational Expectations Equilibrium." *Journal of Finance* 43 (1988), 749–61.

Corrigan, E. Gerald. "Reforming the U.S. Financial System: An International Perspective." *Quarterly Review of the Federal Reserve Bank of New York* 15 (1990), 1–14.

Diamond, Douglas W., and Phillip H. Dybvig. "Bank Runs, Deposit Insurance, and Liquidity." *Journal of Political Economy* 91 (1983), 401–19.

Ely, Bert. *Bailing Out the Federal Savings and Loan Insurance Corporation.* Alexandria, VA: Ely and Company. 1986.

Ely, Bert. *The FSLIC Recap Plan is Bad Medicine for Healthy Thrifts and for the American Taxpayer.* Alexandria, VA: Ely and Company. 1987.

Friedman, Milton. "A Monetary and Fiscal Framework for Economic Stabilization." *American Economic Review* 38 (1948), 246–64.

Greenbaum, Stuart I. "Deregulation of the Thrift Industry: A Prologue to Transitional Problems and Risks." In: *Financial Stability of the Thrift Industry: Proceedings of the Eleventh Annual Conference*, Federal Home Loan Bank of San Francisco. 1985, pp. 15–39, 41–45.

Kydland, Finn E., and Edward C. Prescott. "Rules Rather than Discretion: The Inconsistency of Optimal Plans." *Journal of Political Economy* 85 (1977), 473–91.

Mailath, George J., and Loretta J. Mester. "A Positive Analysis of Bank Closure." *Journal of Financial Intermediation* 3 (1994), 272–99.

"Modernizing The Federal System: Recommendations For Safer, More Competitive Banks." Washington, DC: Department of The Treasury. 1991.

National Commission on Financial Institution Reform, Recovery, and Enforcement. "Origins and Causes of the S&L Debacle: A Blueprint for Reform." A report to the President and Congress of the United States, Washington, DC, 1993.

O'Hara, Maureen. "Real Bills Revisited: Market Value Accounting and Loan Maturity." *Journal of Financial Intermediation* 3 (1993), 51–76.

Simons, Henry C. "Rules versus Authorities in Monetary Policy." *Journal of Political Economy* 44 (1936), 1–30.

Journal of Financial Services Research 9: 303–325 (1995)
© 1995 Kluwer Academic Publishers

Market Discipline of Banks' Riskiness:
A Study of Selected Issues

FRANCO BRUNI
"Paolo Baffi" Centre for Monetary and Financial Economics, Università Bocconi, 20136 Milano, Italy.

FRANCESCO PATERNÒ
"Paolo Baffi" Centre for Monetary and Financial Economics, Università Bocconi, Milano, Italy.

Introduction

Market discipline "means that markets provide signals that lead borrowers to behave in a manner consistent with their solvency" (Lane, 1993, p. 55). It is a crucial element in "private sector solutions" to the problem of financial fragility. A different category of solutions are "regulatory solutions." But the two categories are deeply connected, and market discipline towards financial safety cannot be separated from regulation. It is true that, to some extent, market discipline can *replace* government supervision and regulation. But, in the authors' view, the main influence of market forces is to *complement* the efforts of supervisors and regulators (Gilbert, 1990, p. 3; Lane, 1993, p. 63). An adequate regulatory setting is needed for market disciplining mechanisms to be effective.

A useful classification of conditions for the effectiveness of market discipline is provided by Lane (1993). Four classes of conditions are necessary: (1) capital markets must be open; (2) information on the borrowers' existing liabilities must be readily available; (3) no bailout must be anticipated; and (4) the borrower must respond to market signals. It is immediately evident that all these conditions are heavily dependent on regulation.

In some sense one could state that "private sector solutions" to financial instability coincide with those "regulatory solutions" that rest on the working of market discipline and favor the structural conditions for its effectiveness. The only exception is probably the

The authors, keeping full responsibility for their paper and for all possible errors, are grateful to Erio Castagnoli, Laura Mollame, Fausto Panunzi, Alessandro Sbueltz, Alberto Zorzi, for precious help and suggestions. They also thank for their comments Stuart Greenbaum, George Kaufman, and the other participants in the September 1994 Maastricht Conference on "Coping with Financial Fragility: A Global Perspective," for which the paper was prepared, as well as the discussants of previous versions of parts of this paper that were presented at a Bocconi workshop on "Ricerche di base" and at the Rockefeller Foundation Bellagio Conference in May 1994. The Research Department of Credito Italiano and the IGIER Institute of Mirasole were so kind as to make available their data banks. Partial financial support from CNR (project n. 87.01109.10–115.20972) is gratefully acknowledged. The authors have worked together, but Franco Bruni has special responsibility for section 2, Francesco Paternò for section 1.

microeconomic organization of financial operators, which can be shaped in different ways under a given set of regulations, and that should be such as to provide the internal incentives and controls for the reactivity indicated above as condition (4).

Everybody is well aware of the rapidly shifting frontiers between banks and the rest of the financial sector (Borio and Filosa, 1994). A discussion of market discipline cannot neglect this fact. The separateness of banks' financial fragility from the problems of safety of other financial operators and markets is quickly decreasing. The risk of nonbank markets becoming suddenly illiquid and "crashing" shows growing analogies with the classical risk of bank runs (Davis, 1994).

This paper considers two issues involving the potential role of market discipline in financial markets, trying to offer, for each of them, a specific empirical or theoretical contribution. Section 1 deals with a topic connected to points (1) and (2) of Lane's classification: we conduct some empirical tests of market information on banks' risk exposure and try to assess how much of this information gets incorporated into banks' funding costs and stock prices. We therefore test both market information and market efficiency as conditions for market discipline. As a by-product of our testing procedure we discuss two special topics: the role of the rating agencies, and the level of deposit insurance premia.

Section 2 is about point (3) of Lane's classification: a simple theory of optimal bailout policy is sketched, mostly with the aim of proposing an analytical framework for discussing the *credibility* of no-bailout announcements, which is "probably the most important reason for the failure of discipline" (Lane, 1993, p. 64).

Section 3 contains some concluding comments.

1. Market assessment of banks' risk: some empirical tests

1.1. Two approaches for testing market information on banks' risk

An informed market is crucial for exerting a disciplinary effect on banks' risk taking. But how can we measure the degree and accuracy of information possessed by the market? Complete, symmetric information can be excluded a priori, "opaqueness" is a characteristic of the intermediaries' operations, essential for the process with which the financial industry produces value-added. But some information on risks taken by banks undoubtedly reaches the markets where they collect savings and can influence the costs and the availability of their funding.

Bank funding takes place on various markets. The typical funding market is the *deposit* market; however, testing the degree of information concerning depositors is quite difficult. The rate-setting mechanism on many types of deposits is very imperfect, and both explicit and implicit deposit insurance is widespread. The informative content of banks' funding costs seems much more promising if we look at *bond* and *stock* financing.

In the next subsection (1.2) we will concentrate on the yield of bonds issued by banks in the international market. In the following one (1.3) we will look at banks' stock prices. In both cases the tests, designed to see how much the providers of funds take into account the risks of the intermediaries' assets, are organized in special ways, in order to obtain interesting by-products from the analysis.

As far as the bond market is concerned, we will make use of the information propagated by the rating agencies, thus jointly testing these agencies' ability to keep the market informed. Our discussion will start from capital ratios, that are often considered both the simplest index of banks' riskiness and the most natural instrument for a direct control of risk exposures. Our tests will then involve the relationship between capital ratios and ratings.

When dealing with the stock market we will construct our test using stock prices to calculate theoretical insurance premia for individual banks. This will connect our discussion to the issue of the correct pricing of deposit insurance.

1.2. Ratios and ratings

Capital ratios, as instruments for controlling bank risk, have well-known weaknesses. In particular, simple unweighted ratios are often criticized, on various grounds. Perhaps the most important groundbreaking criticism was raised by Kahane (1977) and by Koehn and Santomero (1980) (further developed in Kim and Santomero, 1988), using a portfolio approach for a utility-maximizing risk-averter bank. In such a context, limiting a bank's leverage doesn't prevent the bank from running very high risks: it simply constrains the intermediary on a worse than expected return / risk trade-off.

Different, well-known counterarguments have been proposed (Furlong and Keeley, 1989; Keeley and Furlong, 1990) to this criticism of capital ratios for banks with and without deposit insurance. For an insured bank, a higher capital ratio decreases the value of the Merton put-option, thus raising the effective cost of its funding and keeping it from expanding towards riskier portfolios.

But for our discussion of market discipline the case of an hypothetical *non-insured* bank is more relevant. In this case the counterargument runs as follows: the bank will be restrained from reaching high risk points on the trade-off associated with an imposed capital ratio, because "the deposit rate demanded by uninsured depositors will [positively] depend on the risk of the bank's portfolio" (Keeley and Furlong, 1990, p. 77).

We would therefore have a nice complementarity between (capital) regulation and market discipline, while, in absence of the latter, the former could be counterproductive. The problem is to prove that the market mechanism, making banks' interest costs sensible to the risk of their portfolio of assets, *does* work in reality.

Testing this hypothesis is a very difficult task, because of the necessity of controlling the effect of the explicit and implicit insurance. Moreover, the hypothesis can look somewhat unrealistic, if one takes into account the asymmetry of information. In fact the hypothesis implies that the lenders of funds to banks have some substantial information even on the covariances between the intermediaries' asset returns.

This empricial problem seems to lend itself to the introduction of the *rating agencies* in the picture. For our purposes the agencies can be useful in two ways: by issuing ratings, they, first, reduce the asymmetry in information between the bankers and the market, enhancing the plausibility of the market discipline hypothesis we want to test; and second, they provide objective indicators of estimated bank risk. To be sure, their ability to produce a net enrichment in the information set of the market is, by itself, an hypothesis that should be subjected to test.

Based on this reasoning we performed a set of estimations, the results of which are summarized in table 1.

The interest-cost variable that we chose to consider is the yield to maturity of dollar-denominated fixed interest bonds issued by European banks. We think our choice minimizes the problem of explicit and implicit insurance: the former is obviously present when dealing with *deposits*; the latter is present when considering *foreign-currency denominated* securities: a bail-out of the issuer will probably treat them as subordinated to domestic-currency denominated debentures. An implicit insurance effect could in part explain, for instance, the weak correlation between ratings and yields found by Avery and Belton (1988) for U.S. banks' subordinated debt. We also think our choice of data

Table 1. Regressing the yield to maturity of dollar denominated fixed interest bonds issued by European banks (data: June 29, 1993)

Regressor	equation 1		equation 2		equation 3		equation 4	
	coeff	t-ratio	coeff	t-ratio	coeff	t-ratio	coeff	t-ratio
constant			7.14	8.01				
amount	−0.011	−4.15	−0.012	−4.27	−0.010	−3.75	−0.011	−4.03
AAA	7.13	9.33			6.85	9.08	6.85	7.29
AA1					6.97	7.90		
AA2					7.98	10.99		
AA3					7.94	10.66		
AA	7.94	12.38					7.44	8.40
A1					8.45	6.28		
A2					10.96	11.74		
A	10.30	12.26					8.84	6.50
ROA			−1.76	−3.06			−1.11	−1.68
Cap. Ratio			0.26	1.84			0.14	0.91
n observations	28		28		28		28	
R-squared	0.638		0.633		0.702		0.683	
Adj. *R*-squared	0.593		0.587		0.617		0.611	
S.E.	1.266		1.275		1.227		1.237	
Log likelihood	−44.170		−44.369		−41.440		−42.316	
Durbin–Watson	2.205		1.967		2.575		2.135	
Mean dep. var.	5.525		5.525		5.525		5.525	
S.D. dep. var.	1.984		1.984		1.984		1.984	
Sum sq. resid.	38.448		38.999		31.638		33.680	
F-statistic	14.11678		13.80473		8.259000		9.486580	
Prob (*F*-stat)	0.000016		0.000019		0.000114		0.000062	

Legends: *amount*: dollar amount of the bonds floated; *AAA, AA1, etc.*: dummy variables equal to 1 when the bond has the corresponding Moody's ratio, and zero otherwise; *ROA*: return of assets of the issuing bank; *Capital ratio*: simple, unweighted ratio of the issuing bank. Databanks: *Datastream, IBCA*, and *Moody's*.

maximizes the homogeneity of the sample, which is all taken from the Eurodollar market. But this choice has a high cost in terms of sample size: we deal with only 28 observations, taken from the same day (June 29, 1993, from Datastream).

In the first equation shown in the table, the yield has been regressed on Moody's first three rating classes of the issuing banks: no bonds in the sample is rated lower than A. A 0–1 dummy variable has been used for each rating class. The regression has no constant term: thus the coefficients of the dummies represent the absolute influence of the rating on the dependent variable. The amount of the bonds floated has been added as an explanatory variable to control for the negotiability/liquidity factor, which should have a crucial impact on the price of the bond.

The results of the regression seem very good. All the regressors have significant coefficients with expected signs. The coefficients of the rating classes have a nice inverse correlation with the class level, even if the difference between the coefficients of the double and triple A's is insignificantly different from zero. The amount of variance explained is considerable. On the basis of this estimation, the joint hypothesis that the ratings are informative and that interest costs, by incorporating a risk factor, convey a market-disciplining effect to bank management, cannot be rejected.

The second equation in table 1 casts some doubts, to be sure, on the net informative value of ratings, because it explains approximately the same amount of variance in the yields, using as regressors only publicly available data on the issuing banks' accounts: the return on assets and the unweighted capital ratio. But the third equation in the table, using rating subclasses, marginally improves the R^2 values; and the fourth equation, where both the ratings and the banks' accounts data are included in the regressors, doesn't seem to allow the rejection of the hypothesis of an autonomous informative content of the ratings, which could depend on an informational or analytical advantage of the rating agencies in examining the banks' situation. The dimension of the coefficient of ROA shows sufficient stability, but its significance is soaked up by the ratings, which obviously reflect, among other things, the agencies' knowledge of banks' returns. To be sure, our judgment on the *autonomy* (which does not mean *dominance*) of the informative content of the ratings (shown also by Ederington et al., 1984) is conditional on the choice of the set of publicly available banks' accounts data used in the regressions. We tried to use other variables, with no success. In particular, "total assets" were considered as regressors, but their contribution was insignificant.

One might suspect that the results of the fourth equation can be affected by multicollinearity between the rating dummies and the two variables taken from bank accounts. No clear-cut test is available to exclude this possibility, and the small sample at our disposal prevents us from drawing any strong conclusion. To argue against a possible distorsion from multicollinearity we can only cite the following evidence: (1) The standard errors of both the ROA and the capital ratio variables in the fourth equation are insignificantly different from those resulting from the second equation; moreover, all the estimated parameters have the same sign in both regressions. (2) From the covariance matrix of the coefficients, the correlation between each of the rating regressors and the ROA variable appears low (< 1.2, with the exception of the correlation between A and ROA, which reaches 0.4); somewhat higher correlations ($-0.5 - -0.65$) result between the capital ratio variable and the rating regressors, while the correlation between ROA and the capital ratio is insignificantly different from zero. The overall picture of cross correlations does not seem sufficient for justifying a serious multicollinearity problem. (3) While multicollinearity would tend to cause instabiity in the parameters' estimated values when the regression is run on different subsets of the original sample, we failed to observe this result when performing a "dropping observations" exercise. When the fourth equation is estimated on different subsets of the entire sample (excluding in various ways three observations out of 28) the estimated parameter values show a high degree of stability. (4) Regressing ROA and/or the capital ratio on the three rating dummies (which yields R^2 values < 0.3) and using the residuals, instead of the original series of ROA and/or of the capital ratio, in the fourth equation, yields nearly identical values for all estimated coefficients and for their standard errors. This seems to us the most significant symptom against multicollinearity.

We are therefore inclined to deny that a substantial multicollinearity problem might be distorting the coefficients of the fourth equation in table 1 and might be the cause of the fact that the explanatory power of the ratings looks clearly autonomous with respect to the contribution of the ROA and of the capital ratio variables.

It must be noted that the coefficient of the capital ratio is always insignificant, and with the wrong sign. The informative content of that variable seems to be negligible (in support of Santomero's type of criticisms), perhaps also because it reflects book value rather than market value. We have also tried with weighted Cooke ratios, but is does not make any difference. Moreover, table 2 seems to tell us that capital ratios are not very important even to rating agencies, as there is an inverse relationship between capital and ratings.

But the fact that capital ratios cannot be considered, per se, good indicators of banks' portfolio risk does not prevent bank capital from serving an important role in providing a cushion against losses. Nor does it exclude the fact that capital regulation can be an effective constraint for risk exposure, when combined with a market-disciplining effect of bank-funding costs based on other independent pieces of information, among which those conveyed to the market by rating agencies appear to play a considerable role.

1.3. Foreseeing banks' problems on the basis of theoretical insurance premia

The "fair premium" that should be paid for insuring banks' deposits reflects the riskiness of banks as assessed by the premium-setting mechanism. Merton (1977) has devised a well-known approach for calculating this premium, based on the price of put-options (Flood, 1990, is an updated primer on this subject.).

Table 2. Moody's ratings versus simple and Cooke capital ratios

Ratings	Simple capital ratios	Cooke-Weighted ratios
AAA	3.59	13.13
AA	4.34	10.21
A	6.09	11.00

Average ratios of the banks issuing the bonds with different ratings, in the sample of table 1

Provided that the assessment of risk is rational, theoretical risk premia should, on average, anticipate the future performance of banks: a bank, which may become a problem-bank at time $t + 1$, should have correspondingly higher theoretical premium at time t; the more serious the oncoming problem, the higher the current premium.

On the basis of this argument, we have tried to test how much banks' problems and crises are forseeable. The procedure we use is a more restricted test: a test of the ability of the *market for bank stocks* to foresee banks' problems.

In our exercise we encountered two main difficulties. The first is a well-known limit of the Merton's approach. His formula for the insurance premium contains two variables that are, in some sense, unobservable, or that at least cannot be found in publicly available statistical sources: the market value of banks' assets, and the standard deviation of their yield.

Our second difficulty has been the lack of a formal model relating the level of calculated premia to expected banks' performance. We made no theoretical effort to overcome this problem, and we proceeded with casual observation, by using a case-by-case method to search for the existence of some relationship between the level and ranking of the premia at a certain date and the subsequent behavior of a small set of indicators of bank performance.

As far as the first difficulty is concerned, we made use of the Ronn and Verma (1986) method for estimating the "unobservable variables." Their solution can be summarized as follows.

Merton's put-option Black–Scholes-type formula for the theoretical fair insurance premium (P) relates it to the value of insured liabilities (D, the strike price of the option), the current market value of bank assets (A), the standard deviation of the assets' yield (Sa), the riskless rate of interest (r), and the time "to the next audit of the insurer" (T):

$$P = P(D, A, Sa, r, T). \tag{1}$$

Ronn and Verma apply a call-option formula to the valuation of bank equity (E). In fact, because of limited liability, a bank is worth, for its shareholders, $\mathrm{Max}\,(A - D, 0)$, as a call-option with strike price D on an underlying with market price A:

$$E = E(D, A, Sa, T'), \tag{2}$$

where the riskless rate does not appear if (and only if) bank liabilities are (explicitly or implicitly) fully insured (as we assume), and where T' differs from T and should measure the time to maturity of bank liabilities.

A third equation is then added, taken from option theory, according to which the standard deviation of the yield of a call is equal to the standard deviation of the yield of the underlying times the elasticity of the price of the call with respect to the price of the underlying:

$$Se = (\partial E / \partial A)\,(A/E)\,Sa \tag{3}$$

Taking D from banks' balance sheets and Se and E from stock market data, making using of the somewhat arbitrary simplification $T = T' = 1$ (arguments in favor of it can be found in Ronn and Verma, 1986, pp. 884–887), (2) and (3) can be solved for Sa and A, and the solutions used in (1) to compute P.

Having thus solved the "marking-to-market" problem in Merton's formula, we compare the level, the ranking, and the changes of the theoretical premia of individual banks, calculated in each year from 1990–1993, with the behavior, in the years that follow, of three indicators of banks' performance: net income, the ratio of nonperforming loans to total assets, and the return on assets. For obvious reasons of homogeneity we conduct a separate analysis for each country. Some of our results are shown in tables 3 and 4 and in figure 1. Before commenting on them, two observations are in order.

First, it should be noted that what we are really performing is a joint test of two different hypotheses: that banks' problems can be foreseen on the basis of theoretical insurance premia, and that the market for banks' stocks is adequately efficient. Thus, our test can fail for at least three reasons, and we cannot tell which is the true cause of its failure: banks' problems might be unforeseeable on the basis of theoretical premia; the market could lack the information to calculate the premia; and the market for banks' stocks might be inefficient in incorporating that information in stock prices.

It has to be stressed that the last of the three motives could also depend on the expectation that the authority, in case of banks' difficulties, would also bail out the

Table 3. Theoretical insurance premia of U.S. banks (per $10,000 of deposits)

Bank	premium 1990	premium 1991	premium 1992	premium 1993
Midlantic	50	10	3	0.3
Shawmut	50	7.3	0.2	0.78
State Street Boston	40	0.001	0.003	0.02
Bank of Boston	20	4.1	0.1	0.23
Bank of New York	20	5.8	0.001	0.0005
First Bank System	20	0.09	0.002	0.003
Crestar Financial Corporation	10	2.1	0.6	0.002
Citicorp	10	1.8	0.4	0.08
BankAmerica	10	4.4	0.01	0.0005
Continental	8.4	0.3	0.03	0.08
Chase	7.5	0.8	0.03	0.003
Baybanks	5.9	0.2	0.2	0.002
National City	5.0	0.03	0.0000..	0.006
Northern Trust	2.7	0.0002	0.0000..	0.001
J.P. Morgan	2.7	0.04	0.0000..	0.0000..
Boatmen's Bankshares	0.5	0.00003	2.0	0.01
First Commerce	0.3	0.4	0.00005	0.57
Commerce Bankshares	0.1	0.00006	0.0003	0.04
Marshall & Ilsley Corp.	0.1	0.1	0.0000..	0.0008
Wachovia Corporation	0.08	10	0.0000..	0.001
Firstar Corporation	0.007	0.01	0.05	0.009
Chemical	n.a.	0.5	0.002	0.01
Median	7.5	0.29	0.01	0.009
Legal	8.33	8.33	8.33	8.33

Table 4. Performance and forecasting power of theoretical insurance premia in the sample of U.S. banks of Table 3

Forecast	efficient	weakly efficient	inefficient	nonrankable	total
Performance					
good	5	3	2	0	10
bad	4	1	0	1	6
ambiguous	1	2	1	2	6
total	10	6	3	3	22

The performance of the banks has been judged on the basis of nonperforming loans, income, and the ROA. Databanks: IBCA and Datastream. For definitions see the text, subsection 1.3.

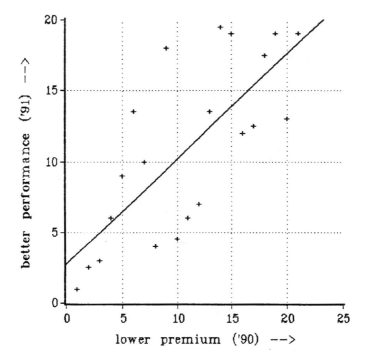

Figure 1. Current theoretical insurance premia and future banks' performance: the rank correlation (U.S., 1990 and 1991). Performances are ranked with the average of the ranks in nonperforming loans to total assets and in the ROA. Premia are from table 3. The equation of the regression line (where only one outlier has been dropped) is as follows:

$$Y = 2.75 + 0.74*X$$
$$(1.93) (0.15),$$

with standard errors in parenthesis, and $R^2 = 0.55$.

shareholders, at least in part and indirectly, by not resolving the insolvent institutions. In fact our model of theoretical insurance premia assumes total bailout of depositors, but no bailout of shareholders.

The second observation has to do with the relation of our test to the market discipline of banks' behavior. To the extent that theoretical insurance premia are reflected in banks' stock prices, they influence the cost of capital. This should tend to discipline the decision of bankers about their risk-taking. We are therefore really testing for the existence of a mechanism of market discipline.

To summarize the results, we think it is fair to say that our testing procedure has been successful in the case of U.S. bank-holding companies (BHC). A set of 22 BHCs has been selected from the 80 institutions covered by the IBCA data bank for 1990–1991. The selection has been done trying to maximize the number of institutions clearly belonging to one of two groups: a group of "good" and a group of "bad" performers. Ambiguous cases (where, for instance nonperforming loans and the return on assets had contrasting behaviors) were kept to a minimum. Six of the 22 sampled banks were considered bad performers, having had nonperforming loans higher than 1.5% of their total assets for at least two consecutive years *and* a negative return for at least one year. Ten were good performers, with nonperforming loans always lower than 1% of total assets and ROA never significantly lower than 1. Only the remaining 6 were ambiguous cases.

Stockmarket data were obtained from Datastream. Calculations, according to Black–Scholes formulas indicated by (1), (2) and (3), were performed with Mathcad 3.0. The following results seem to emerge from tables 3 and 4 and from figure 1:

- The average and aggregate behavior of the premia correctly anticipate the crisis of U.S. banks and the following recovery. Nearly half of the 1990 premia were above the charged ½ of 1% = 0.083%, showing substantial cross-subsidies with a strong redistributive effect (as in the Ronn and Verma results for 1983). From 1991 on, there was a sharp decrease in the premia, which in 1992 and 1993 were all smaller than 0.083%. A much longer cycle is needed in order to judge the actuarial equilibrium of this fixed premium.
- A case-by-case inspection of the correlation between each bank's premium and subsequent performance (classified as "bad" or "good," as explained above, on the basis of nonperforming loans and ROA) shows that the former is a strongly or weakly efficient forecaster of the latter in 16 of 22 cases. We classified the forecast "weakly" efficient (in 6 of 16 cases) when the premia appeared to behave in an adapting fashion, reflecting the current, more than the future performance.
- Figure 1 shows an impressive order correlation between the rank of the 1990 premium and the rank of the performance in 1991.

We also tried to test European banks in France, Spain, and Austria. Data availability was much scarcer and our samples very small. Calculated premia often looked unexplainable as far as either the dimension and/or the time profile were concerned. From this failure of our test for Europe, we tend to conclude that stock market forecasts are inefficient. More research effort has to be made, but we are inclined to think that a combination of general imperfection of European stock markets, peculiar governance structures of European bank corporations, and widely held expectations of shareholders bailouts do not allow the functioning of the market-disciplining mechanism that we have been considering.

2. The credibility of bailout policies

2.1. The problem

"Market discipline is only effective if market participants do not believe that the borrower would be bailed out in the case of an actual or impending default. This condition for market discipline is crucial. . . . And what makes it so difficult to achieve is the essential role of credibility: . . . market participants must believe that the (no bailout) promise will be kept. . . . The source of the credibility problem is *time inconsistency*" (Lane, 1993, p. 64; our italics).

Theoretically, at least, the social preference function can be such that, ex post, bailouts turn out to be beneficial, even when, ex ante, it was optimal to announce that no bailout will take place. Like monetary policies that try to reach both price stability and low unemployment, prudential policies derive their time inconsistency problem from the multiplicity of their objectives, which include both stability and efficiency of the financial system (Bruni, 1992 and 1993). Thus, the ex ante optimal point on the trade-off between the two targets is different from the ex post optimal; therefore the former is not credible. But, while the monetary policy problem can be solved by assigning the full-employment objective to other policies, prudential authorities cannot but live with their trade-off. The assignment to different agencies of different, well-defined prudential tasks and instruments (like entry controls, lending of last resort, management of bank crises, etc.) can help (see below, subsection 2.4, and Bruni, 1992, 1993). But given that both stability and efficiency are always involved in their objectives, no simple and clear-cut solution to their credibility problem is available.

We think that in order to offer a contribution towards a precise formalization of this problem, it is better to start with a very simple model and a very general approach. In fact, bailouts are relevant not only for the discipline of *borrowers*. The government can bailout any economic activity, and the expected bailout policy will affect the attitude towards risk of any investor or entrepreneur. In all cases an issue of credibility will arise.

In the next subsection (2.2., drawing upon Bruni, 1994) we propose a model where investment activities, in general, can be bailed out when they have unfavorable outcomes. We derive optimal bailout policies and study the conditions for their credibility. In the following subsection (2.3) we comment on our results and the possible extension of the analysis to the specific case of the bailout of a bank and/or of bank depositors. But a more robust and complete development of this extension is left for further research. Finally, subsection 2.4 contains some thoughts on how to enhance the credibility of bailout policies.

2.2. A theory of bailout policy

Consider a financial sector with two investment opportunities: a risk-free asset with zero yield, and a risky asset. $x\%$ of the portfolio is invested in the latter, and the yield is $+1$ in the favorable (F) state of nature, -1 in the unfavorable (U) state. Let $f > 1/2$ indicate the probability of F.

Investors have unlimited liability, i.e., there is no limit to their potential loss. If $\underline{b}\%$ of the loss (in case of U) is "bailed out," the negative yield becomes: $-1 + \underline{b}$. Let b indicate the expected value of $\underline{b}$. All of this is summarized in the payout matrix (I) of table 5.

Note that bailouts are here directed towards generally defined "investors" or, better, towards their investments. The model could perhaps have a more immediate application to the bailout of unsuccessful "projects" financed by (indebted) investors with unlimited liability, than to the bailout of bank deposits.

Let the expected *utility of the private financial market* be the following function:

$$E(U) = E(R) - \frac{a}{2}[x(1 - b)]^2 \tag{4}$$

where

$$E(R) = x[f - (1 - f)(1 - b)] \tag{5}$$

and a is a risk-aversion parameter multiplying the square of the maximum possible loss.

Maximizing $E(U)$ over x yields the optimum portfolio for a given b:

$$x_0 = \frac{2f-1+(1-f)b}{a(1-b)^2} \tag{6}$$

which monotonically increases with $0 \le b \le 1$, has a positive minimum value $\frac{2f-1}{a}$ and, for $b \to 1$, can grow larger than 1, towards infinity, implying leveraged investment (with borrowing costs equal to the zero riskless rate). On the contrary, the constraint $f < 1/2$ does not allow for shorting in the risky asset.

Let us now consider the *social loss function* taken into account by the authority. We assume its expected value to be the sum of three components:

$$E(L) = -E(R) + E(D) + E(S) \tag{7}$$

Table 5. Payout matrix (I)

	States probability	F f	U 1−f
Assets risk free risky	% of wealth 1 − x x	Expected Yields 0 +1	0 −1+b

Payout matrix (II)

	States probability	F f	U 1 − f
Assets risk free risky	% of wealth 1 − x x	Expected Yields 0 g − zx	0 −1

The first component has a negative sign and coincides with the above-defined *private expected return* from investment. For simplicity, the risk-aversion term in $E(U)$ is not included in $E(L)$. The effect of the bailout on this term can be thought to be, at least in part, included in the second term $E(D)$. This is the *net* expected *social cost of bailout*, consisting in its distortionary effect plus the cost to the taxpayer, less the benefit for the bailed investor. The third component of $E(L)$ includes the expected *welfare costs of the systemic consequences of the private loss*, or, more generally, all the expected social costs of the loss not accounted for by private investors.

The cost of a bailout can be expressed as the amount involved, bx, times a parameter d measuring the net social value of the distorsion caused by the transfer of one unit of money for bailout purposes. Calculating the expected value and considering the expected behavior of the private investors, i.e., setting $x = x_0$ according to (6), we have:

$$E(D) = (1 - f)dbx_0 = (1 - f)db\frac{2f - 1 + (1-f)^b}{a(1-b)^2}. \tag{8}$$

We assume the welfare cost of the systemic consequences of the private loss to be proportional to the *square* of the loss and to a scale parameter s:

$$E(S) = (1 - f)s[(1 - b)x_0]^2 = (1 - f)s\frac{[2f - 1 + (1-f)b]^2}{a^2(1-b)^2} \tag{9}$$

Substituting (6) into (5) and then (5), (8) and (9) into (7), taking the first derivative with respect to b, one obtains:

$$E'_b = [2f - 1 + (1 - f)b]\frac{2f(1-f)s - 2fa}{a^2(1-b)^3} + [2f - 1 + b]\frac{ad(1 - f)}{a^2(1-b)^3} \tag{10}$$

By equating (10) to zero and solving for b, the optimal bailout rate can be derived:

$$b_0 = \frac{(2f - 1)[(2fa - (ad + 2fs)1 - f)]}{(1-f)[2f(1-f)s - a(2f - d)]} \tag{11}$$

The second derivative of $E(L)$ with respect to b, evaluated at b_0, is positive iff $0 \le b_0 \le 1$: therefore b_0, in the interval 0–1, minimizes the expected social loss. It represents the *ex ante optimal bailout policy with commitment*: the authority preannounces that it will bail out, in the unfavorable state U, at a rate b_0 and this is taken into account by the private sector in its portfolio choice.

The expression in (11) has to be analyzed to find the constraints on the parameters that guarantee $0 \le b_0 \le 1$. This is done in the Appendix 1, with the following results:

$$s \le \frac{a}{1-f}; \tag{12}$$

$$\frac{f}{a(1-f)}[a - s(1 - f)] \le d \le \frac{2f}{a(1-f)}[a - s(1 - f)]. \tag{13}$$

Geometrically the constraints can be represented as in figure 2. The admissible triangle $D_2D_3S_1$ has an upper border along and beyond which the ex ante optimal non-negative bailout rate b_0 is zero, and a lower border along and beyond which the optimal $b_0 \le 1$ is 1. In the region $D_2D_1S_1$, $b_0 = 1$ is a corner optimum: the second derivative of $E(L)$ with

121

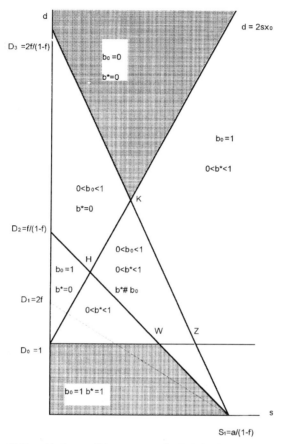

Figure 2. The credibility of bailout policies: an example. Only in the shadowed regions the ex ante optimal bailout policy with commitment (b_0) is equal to the ex post optimal (b^*), i.e., it is time-consistent and credible. For the definition of symbols see the model in subsection 2.2 and Appendix 1.

respect to b, calculated with $b = 1$, is negative in that region: the loss will thus increase with the lowering of the bailout ratio. In the region below D_1S_1 the unconstrained b_0 would be negative, but the second derivative of $E(L)$ is also negative: Therefore b_0 maximizes the loss, and the minimum of $E(L)$ over $0 \leq b_0 \leq 1$ is at 1.

The intuitive economic interpretation of the constraints can be explained as follows. With the exception of a relatively "small" set of parameter values, the optimal prean-nounced bailout policy is a *never-bailout-policy*. The reason is that, when b grows larger than zero, the *moral hazard* effect causes an increase in the risk exposure of financial operators and of their possible loss. The increase is so quick (see (6)) that the bailout will not compensate for the increase in the social cost of the systemic consequences of the loss and will produce a much larger distortion from the required transfer of resources. The validity of this result is dependent upon the hypothesis of a strong moral hazard effect, like the one produced by maximizing (4). On the other hand, if s and d are sufficiently small (with respect to f, or if f is sufficiently large for given s and d), the increase in $E(R)$ caused by a larger b will dominate the increase in $E(D)$ and $E(S)$. Therefore it will pay to set $b > 0$. The smaller d and/or s, the larger the optimal bailout rate; the larger d, the smaller must be s to get a given optimum $0 \leq b_0 \leq 1$. (This also explains the negative slope of D_3S_1.) For very small s and d (think of the case $d = s = 0$), the optimal bailout policy requires $b = 1$. Note, again, that the intuition according to which for s tending to infinity the optimal b tends to 1 is wrong, because of moral hazard and the fact that $x_0 \to \infty$.

Suppose now that $0 \leq b_0 \leq 1$ has been announced, and x_0 chosen. Suppose also that the state U prevails. The *ex post bailout policy* of the authority can be obtained by minimizing over b the following loss:

$$x_0(1 - b) + x_0 db + s[x_0(1 - b)]^2 \tag{14}$$

where $0 \leq b \leq 1$ can differ from b_0. Actually, the value of b^* that minimizes (14) is

$$b^* = \frac{1-d}{2sx_0} + 1 \tag{15}$$

so that for $d < 1$ we have a corner solution $b^* = 1$, while, if $d > 1 + 2sx_0$ it must be $b^* = 0$. In figure 1 we have shaded the regions where the ex post b^* coincides with the ex ante b_0. In the rest of the quadrant, *the optimal bailout policy with commitment is time inconsistent*, with the social loss larger than expected.

It has to be noted that time inconsistency can work in both directions: the ex post bailout can be larger or smaller than the ex ante. When it is larger, like in the nonshaded region above S_1K, there is overinvestment in risky assets, and *the positively sloped line tends to rotate towards the vertical axis*, with x (and the socialized losses) converging towards infinity. The case of underinvestment is also possible, in the other nonshaded regions, with *an opposite rotation of the line*.

Examples of intuitive explanations of why there are regions of time consistency, i.e., where the ex ante optimal bailout policy is credible, can run as follows. *A no-bailout policy* can be credible (in the shaded angle above K), for a given s, if d is sufficiently large; the ex post cost of the bailout will then be sufficient to keep the commitment. For a given d, the credibility of the no-bailout policy requires s to be neither too small nor too large. With too small systemic consequences, the authority will prefer to promise some bailout, while when the consequences would be too serious, bailing out will turn out to be ex post optimal. *An always-bailout policy* will be credible (in the region OD_0WS_1), for a given s, provided that the unit cost of bailing out, d, is small enough, and for a given d, provided that s is not too large (because with large potential systemic consequences the moral hazard effect pressures the authorities towards obtaining a lower risk exposure of investors by limiting their expectations of bailout).

2.3. Commenting on the model

2.3.1. "Ad hoc" structure.
The choice of a somewhat *arbitrary analytical structure* of the model obviously causes a loss of generality. However, it allows us to make more clear how certain type of parameters can be relevant and to show that certain sets of parameter

values can be crucial in determining credibility. Alternative specification structures can be adopted, sometimes producing untractable algebraic problems. An example is the substitution of the maximum possible loss in (4) with the variance of the probability distribution of the yield. In this case the optimal portfolio, for a given b, becomes:

$$x_0 = \frac{f - (1-f)(1-b)}{af(1-f)(2-b)^2},$$

which looks similar to and has the same properties as (6), with the advantage of exhibiting a more gradual moral hazard effect. However, the algebra for completing the model becomes less neat.

Using very general and implicit formulations is also possible, and could probably allow to prove some useful but highly abstract theorems.

2.3.2. Limited liability.

An important modification of the model could be obtained by introducing the hypothesis of *limited liability*. In this case x can be thought as the inverse of the capital ratio, i.e., measured in units equal to the net worth of the investors. Our model would thus be valid only as long as the maximum loss does not exceed 1, that is

iff $x_0 \leq \dfrac{1}{1-b}$, requiring, according to (6), $a \geq \dfrac{f}{1-b} - (1-f)$.

Outside of these parameter values, i.e., for

$$\frac{a + 1 - 2f}{a + 1 - f} < b \leq 1,$$

the optimal amount of (leveraged) investment becomes infinity. This has many consequences, including that the case of a credible always-bailout policy is no longer possible. Note that, even with $b = 0$, if the risk aversion a is smaller than $2f - 1$, the risky investment tends to infinity. This shows that *the presence of limited liability is an important source of moral hazard, quite independently of the bailout problem*. The reason is, obviously, the asymmetric information structure that allows the bank to borrow at a constate risk-free rate against a growing risk of its portfolio. We will show below how a transparent setting can result in a disciplined behavior of the risk-neutral banker with limited liability.

2.3.3. Capital ratios for time consistency.

We might note that, if x is interpreted as the inverse of the capital ratio, we can think of the authority setting it at a binding level and using it as a policy instrument.

In this case the ex ante and ex post values of b will always coincide, and preannounced bailout policies will always be credible. This is a possible rationalization for the imposition of capital ratios.

Suppose the values of d and s are located in a dangerously time-inconsistent region of figure 2. By limiting x, the authority will be out of the problem (forcing the positively sloped D_0K line to rotate rightwards). This will probably have costs in terms of allocative efficiency, but a higher social welfare could result than from the consequences of time-inconsistency.

As we are thinking in terms of the previously exposed highly simplified model, we are obviously abstracting here from portfolio effects whereby the risk exposure of the investor cannot be limited with capital ratios.

2.3.4. The bailout of bank depositors.   The hypothesis of limited liability is particularly interesting when it is introduced in a model where the *bailout is not in favor of the investor but of its creditors*. This could allow the discussion of the specific case of banks and deposit insurance.

If, however, the bailout does not benefit the banker (shareholder), there is in our model no channel through which it will affect the amount invested in risky assets. A channel can be introduced, to be sure, which is important both in reality and in the literature (see, for instance, Gilbert, 1990): *the expected bailout will affect the interest rate paid by the banks to the depositors*.

Let us see how the analytical framework of our model could be modified to study the impact of this channel. Setting the bankers' net worth equal to 1 (which makes x the inverse of the capital ratio), the amount of deposits will be $x - 1$. Let us suppose that depositors are risk neutral: they want an expected yield equal to the riskless rate, which by hypothesis has been set at zero (also for the banker, as in table 5). Let us also suppose that the information is symmetric, i.e., the depositors' estimate of f is the same as the bankers'. To compensate for the loss in the U state, the depositors will require a *risk premium* (r) that can be calculated from the following equation:

$$f(x - 1)(1 + r) + (1 - f)(x - 1)b = x - 1$$

where, to simplify the algebra, the hypothesis is made that the accrued interests on deposits will not be bailed out. The solution for r is:

$$r = (1 - f)(1 - b)/f, \tag{16}$$

obviously decreasing with b. Let us now assume also that the bank is risk neutral, and that it has limited liability, i.e., it cannot lose more than its net worth, which is equal to 1. Note that, in our previous model, *the risk aversion of the investor was the basis of market discipline*. Now the discipline, even with limited liability of the banker, will rest on the working of the risk premium required by depositors.

With risk neutrality, in order to obtain a positive, limited optimal size of the risky investment, we assume decreasing returns. With probability f the yield of the risky asset will be ($g - zx$), while in state U all x will be lost (i.e., the yield will be -1; see the payout matrix (II) in table 5). Expected bank profits will therefore be:

$$E(P) = f[gx - zx^2 - (x - 1)r] - (1 - f) \tag{17}$$

Maximizing (17) with respect to x and substituting (16) in the solution, the optimal portfolio, for a given b, will be:

$$x_0 = \frac{fg - (1-f)(1-b)}{2fz}. \tag{18}$$

An optimal ex ante bailout policy can now be obtained, based on (18), minimizing a social loss function. An example is sketched in Appendix 2, together with the calculation of the ex post optimal policy, giving rise to the situation pictured in figure 3. In this case the set of parameters for which the optimal bailout policy is time-inconsistent turns out to be much smaller. We tend to conclude that the credibility of prudential policies depends heavily on the precise specification of the theoretical model with which it is studied.

2.4. Enhancing credibility

Which institutional arrangements can increase the credibility of policies towards financial and banking crises? Some elements of a possible answer are listed in what follows:

1. The commitment to follow a preannounced bailout policy is more credible if it is explicit and based upon *rules as opposed to discretion*. In terms of the model of the preceeding paragraph, the authority would be prevented "by law" from following the ex post optimal policy, if it implied $b \neq b_0$, with a few, very well-specified exceptions. "Early intervention" schemes (like in the recent U.S. reform or, better, in the original Benston–Kaufman, 1988, proposal) would help in this direction. Opposed to this idea

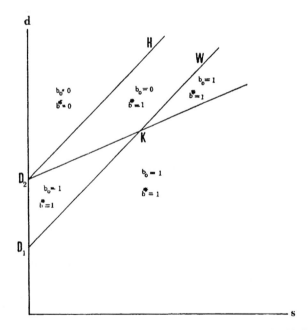

Figure 3. The credibility of bailout policies: a different example. The ex ante optimal bailout policy with commitment (b_0) is always equal to the ex post optimum (b*), except in the region HD_2KW, where it is not credible and time-inconsistent. For the definition of symbols and the specification of the model, see subsection 2.3 and Appendix 2.

are the advocates of "constructive ambiguity," deliberately creating uncertainty about the scope of a possible bailout (Leipold et al., 1991) according to what is sometimes called the "art" of central banking (Lamfalussy, 1992, p. 14). Contrary to the insistence on rules is also the approach that relies on the building of *reputation* by the prudential authority (Boot and Greenbaum, 1993). With the right set of incentives, reputational benefits can undoubtably be very good substitutes for explicit rules. We cannot enter here into any depth on this crucial topic. Let us only observe that, with sufficiently flexible rules, the two approaches do not look incompatible, but the frequency of potential financial crises could turn out to be insufficient for building a reputation in bailout policy.

2. The credibility of prudential policies increases with the *international harmonization* of prudential schemes and of the rules of intervention in case of financial crises, provided that the risk of converging towards the weakest regulations is avoided. Repeated deviation from preannounced policies would be considered less probable if the same policies were established in many countries. This argument has special relevance for Europe, where credibility would also be enhanced with some *centralization* of prudential authorities (Bruni, 1993), increasing the "political distance" between the bailout agency and the origin of a given financial crisis.

3. A clear *separation between the authority that decides bailouts* and manages insolvency crises *and the central bank* (Goodhart and Schoenmaker, 1993; Bruni, ed., 1993), would increase the credibility of a commitment to limit bailouts. The financing of bailouts should be an explicit political decision, clearly distinct from the ordinary lending of last resort.

3. Conclusions

In the first part of this article we performed two tests in order to see how much the holders of claims on banks are informed on the risks taken by the intermediaries. We were able to find that the yields on dollar-denominated bonds issued by European banks are sufficiently sensitive to the information incorporated in bank ratings. We also found that the rating agencies seem to produce net information for the market, beyond what can be derived by publicly available data on bank accounts. Among these data, capital ratios did not appear from our tests as good indicators of bank risks.

Using data on bank stock prices we tested the hypothesis that theoretical insurance premia are efficient forecasters of banks' performance in terms of both return on assets and nonperforming loans. The test was successful for the United States, while, when we tried it with some European banks' stocks, their market appeared inefficient to the point of preventing meaningful calculations of theoretical premia.

In the second part of the article we discussed the topic of bailout policy in financial markets. We constructed a model of optimal bailout policy commitments and analyzed its credibility. The problem of the time-inconsistency of prudential policies has been often confined to footnotes in the literature (see Merton and Bodie, 1993, p. 6; Flannery, 1993, p. 37), but is beginning to be studied with more care (Mailath and Mester, 1994).

Our contribution was a theoretical analysis of how credibility depends on the structure and on the parameter values of the system with which the behavior of investors, banks, depositors, and prudential authorities are described. Our main conclusion was that it is not true that the no-bailout clause is always time-inconsistent. We also suggested lines of action for enhancing the credibility of prudential policies.

To the extent that "market discipline" of financial risk-taking rests on a sufficient degree of market information and on the credibility of the no-bailout clause, our article would like to appear somehow encouraging about the potential role of such discipline.

Appendix 1

The following note derives the conditions for expression (11) in the text to be comprised in the interval 0–1. The numerator is positive iff:

$$d < \frac{2f}{a(1-f)}[a - (1 - f)s]; \tag{A1.1}$$

the denominator is positive iff:

$$d > \frac{2f}{a}[a - (1 - f)s]. \tag{A1.2}$$

Consider first the case where the term in square brackets in (A1.1) and (A1.2) is negative. With $d \geq 0$ condition (A1.1) could not be satisfied. A positive b_0 could also result if both the numerator and the denominator in (11) were negative, i.e., if neither (A1.1) nor (A1.2) were satisfied. But from (A1.2) we understand that a negative denominator would require d being lower than a negative number.

We must therefore impose $[a - (1 - f)s]$ to be positive, i.e., condition (12) in the text. With f between 0 and 1, the right-hand side of (A1.1) is larger than the right hand side of (A1.2), and the two conditions define the set of values of d guaranteeing $b_0 > 0$. To secure $b_0 < 1$ the numerator must be lower than the denominator, which can be shown to happen iff:

$$d > \frac{f}{a(1-f)}[a - s(1 - f)]. \tag{A1.3}$$

The right-hand side of (A1.3) can be shown (taking into account that the probability f has been required to be no smaller than 1/2) to be inside the set of values of d defined by (A1.1) and (A1.2). This proves that the subset where b_0 is between zero and 1 is the one defined by (13) in the text.

Appendix 2

Let the expected social loss function be: $E(L) = E(D) + E(S) - E(P)$. $E(P)$ is (17) in the text with the interest rate defined in (16). $E(D)$ is the expected net social cost of the distortion caused by the bailout; it is specified as in (8), but taking into account that *only deposits* ($x_0 - 1$) *are bailed out*: $E(D) = (1 - f)db(x_0 - 1)$. $E(S)$ is the expected systemic damage. Wherease in (9) it was assumed to be proportional to the square of the loss, to simplify our algrebra we now assume it to be linear in the depositors' loss: $E(S) = (1 - f)s(x_0 - 1)(1 - b)$. Substituting (18) in the three components of $E(L)$, the latter becomes a parabola whose first derivative with respect to b is zero where:

$$b = \frac{(1-f)(d-2s-1)-f(g-2z)(d-s-1)}{(1-f)(2d-2s-1)}. \qquad (A2.1)$$

When (A2.1) holds we can have either a minimum or a maximum of the expected social loss function, depending on the sign of its second derivative, which is positive iff:

$$d > s + \frac{1}{2}. \qquad (A2.2)$$

(A2.2) is also the condition for the denominator of the expression in (A2.1) to be positive, while the numerator is positive iff:

$$d < Qs + 1, \text{ where } Q = \frac{f(g-2z)-2(1-f)}{f(g-2z)-(1-f)}. \qquad (A2.3)$$

Using (A2.1), (A2.2), and (A2.3) and adding the hypothesis $g > 2z + 2(1 - f)/f$, we can find the value of b that minimizes $E(L)$ over the closed interval $0 \le b \le 1$. Let us indicate it with b_0, i.e., the *optimal ex ante bailout policy with commitment*. The value of b_0 depends on the parameters d and s, but it turns out that it is always a "corner" optimum, i.e., it equals either zero or one. The results are shown in figure 3 using the four regions of the (d,s) space obtained by crossing the two lines D_1K and D_2K, which correspond, respectively, to (A2.2) and (A2.3).

Let us now consider the *ex post decision of the bailout authority*. We can suppose that in the unfavorable state U the bailout policy b^* will be chosen to minimize the following loss:

$$db^* (x_0 - 1) + s(x_0 - 1)(1 - b^*) + 1 + (x_0 - 1)(1 - b^*), \qquad (A2.4)$$

where x_0 is given by (18) with $b = b_0$, independent of the ex post b^*. (A2.4) is analogous to (14). It accounts for the ex post social costs due to the distorsionary effect of the bailout and to the systemic damages of the non-bailed out losses, as well as for the net losses of the banker (its capital: 1) and of the depositors (the last addend). Minimizing (A2.4) over the closed interval $0 \le b^* \le 1$ yields $b^* = 0$ iff d is above the line (D_2H in figure 3)

$$d = s + 1, \qquad (A2.5)$$

and $b^* = 1$ if d is below (A2.5).

From figure 3 one can see that only in the region HD_2KW is $b^* \ne b_0$, i.e., only in that region is the ex ante optimal bailout policy time inconsistent. Everywhere else the bailout policy is credible and, for a very wide set of parameter values, an "always bailout" policy is optimal both ex ante and ex post.

References

Avery, R.B., and T.M. Belton. "Market Discipline in Regulating Bank Risk: New Evidence from the Capital Markets." *Journal of Money, Credit and Banking* 20 (1988).

Benston, George J., and George G. Kaufman. *Risk and Solvency Regulation of Depository Institutions: Past Policies and Current Options.* Monograph 1, Monograph Series on Finance and Economics, Salomon Brothers Center, New York University, 1988.

Boot, Arnoud W.A., and Stuart I. Greenbaum. "Bank Regulation, Reputation and Rents: Theory and Policy Implications." In: Mayer C. and Vives X., eds., *Capital Markets and Financial Intermediation.* London: CEPR. 1993, pp. 262-285.

Borio, Claudio E.V., and Renato Filosa. *The Changing Borders of Banking: Trends and Implications.* BIS Working Paper No. 23, Basle, October 1994.

Bruni, Franco. "Sui rapporti fra politica monetaria, regolamentazione finanziaria e vigilanza." *Giornale degli Economisti e Annali de Economia* (Gennaio/Aprile, 1992), 27-75.

Bruni, Franco. *Monetary and Prudential Issues in the Planned European Monetary Union* (Proceedings of the Hitotsubashi International Symposium on "Financial Markets in a Changing World"). Tokyo: Josui-Kaikan, 1993.

Bruni, Franco, ed. *Prudential Regulation, Supervision and Monetary Policy: Theory, International Comparisons and the ESCB Role* (Proceedings of the Conference organized by the "Paolo Baffi" Centre for Monetary and Financial Economics), Bocconi University, Milan, February 1993.

Bruni, Franco. "A Model of Financial Bailout: Implications for European Prudential Policies." Mimeo, Rockefeller Foundation Bellagio Conference on "Global and Comparative Analysis of Financial Institutions," May 1994.

Davis, Philip E. "Market Liquidity Risk." Mimeo, SUERF Colloquium on "The Competitiveness of Financial Institutions and Centres in Europe," Dublin, Ireland, May 1994.

Ederington, Louis H., Jess B. Yawitz, and Brian E. Roberts. "The Informational Content of Bond Ratings." NBER Working Paper No. 1323, April 1984.

Flannery, Mark J. "Deposit Insurance Reform: A Functional Approach. A Comment." *Carnegie-Rochester Series on Public Policy* 38 (1993), 35-40.

Flood, Mark D. "On the Use of Option Pricing Models to Analyze Deposit Insurance", *Federal Reserve Bank of St. Louis Review*, (January/February 1990), 19-35.

Furlong, Frederick T., and Michael C. Keeley. "Capital Regulation and Bank Risk-Taking: a Note." *Journal of Banking and Finance* 13 (1989), 883-891.

Gilbert, Alton R. "Market Discipline of Bank Risk: Theory and Evidence." *The Federal Bank of St. Louis Review* 72 (1) (January/February 1990), 3-18.

Goodhart, Charles, and Dirk Shoenmaker. "Institutional Separation Between Supervisory and Monetary Agencies." In: Franco Bruni, ed., *Prudential Regulation, Supervision and Monetary Policy: Theory, International Comparisons and the ESCB Role.* Milan: Bocconi University. 1993.

Kahane, Yehuda. "Capital Adequacy and the Regulation of Financial Intermediaries." *Journal of Banking and Finance* 2 (1977), 207-217.

Keeley, Michael C., and Frederick T. Furlong. "A Reexamination of Mean-Variance Analysis of Bank Capital Regulation." *Journal of Banking and Finance* 14 (1990), 69-84.

Kim, Daesik, and Anthony M. Santomero. "Risk in Banking and Capital Regulation." *Journal of Finance* 43 (5) (December 1988), 1219-33.

Koehn, Michael, and Anthony M. Santomero. "Regulation of Bank Capital and Portfolio Risk." *Journal of Finance* 35 (December 1980), 1235-44.

Lamfalussy, Alexandre. "The Restructuring of the Financial Industry: A Central Bank Perspective." *SUERF Papers on Monetary and Financial Systems* 12 (1992).

Lane, Timothy D. "Market Discipline." *IMF Staff Papers* 40 (1) (March 1993), 53-88.

Leipold, Alessandro et al. *International Capital Markets: Developments and Prospects.* Washington, DC: IMF, World Economic and Financial Surveys, 1991.

Mailath, George J., and Loretta J. Mester. "A Positive Analysis of Bank Closure." *Journal of Financial Intermediation* 3 (1994), 272-299.

Merton, Robert C. "An Analytic Derivation of the Cost of Deposit Insurance and Loan Guarantees: An Application of Modern Option Pricing Theory." *Journal of Banking and Finance* 2 (June 1977), 3–11.

Merton, Robert C., and Zvi Bodie. "Deposit Insurance Reform: A Functional Approach." *Carnegie Rochester Series on Public Policy* 38 (1993), 1–34.

Ronn, Ehud I., and Avinash K. Verma. "Pricing Risk-Adjusted Deposit Insurance: An Option-Based Model." *Journal of Finance* 41 (4) (September 1986), 871–953.

Journal of Financial Services Research 9: 327–349 (1995)
© 1995 Kluwer Academic Publishers

Private Sector Solutions to Payments System Fragility

ROBERT A. EISENBEIS
Wachovia Professor of Banking, Kenan-Flagler Business School, University of North Carolina at Chapel Hill, Chapel Hill, NC 27599-3490, U.S.A., and member of the Shadow Financial Regulatory Committee

1. Introduction

The 1974 failure of Herstatt Bank and the disruptions which hit financial markets ushered in an era of heightened concern about the potential vulnerability of payments systems, especially the wholesale large-value systems, to systemic risk and other problems. Systemic risk—the likelihood that a problem in one institution will cause the insolvency of healthy institutions—through runs, the creation of liquidity problems, or other forces, has been a major policy focus.[1]

This concern has grown with the stock market crashes during 1987 and 1989, the problems in unwinding some of the contracts in the failure of Bank of New England and for several other important reasons. First, the sheer growth in large volume payments has heightened the potential financial stakes, should a financial meltdown occur.[2] Second, technology and technological change have had a major impacts on the kinds of transactions taking place, both increasing the speed and lowering the costs with which they may be completed. Third, technology has also permitted the unbundling and restructuring of transactions whose risk characteristics and cross institutional linkages are just now being understood. Complicated derivative transactions with notional values in the trillions did not exist as recently as five or six years ago. A recent *Wall Street Journal* article placed the amounts at more than $35 trillion.[3] These new instruments and markets have introduced new and complex linkages across securities markets and domestic and world payments systems. Fourth, the globalization of financial markets has tied economies and markets together in ways that introduce new risks and concerns into the mechanisms by which traditional clearing and settlement take place. Fifth, recent private sector and public sector developments in the way large-volume payments are cleared and settled, and more specifically, the introduction of bilateral and multilateral settlements procedures may affect systemic risks in important ways. Finally, the above developments have served simply to heighten both private and public sector concerns about the need to understand and control system vulnerability to systemic risks. Fortunately, private sector and public sector entities have paid a great deal of attention to these issues at both the domestic and international levels. The payment system risks and uncertainties are affected by the nature of the market infrastructure (e.g., the type of computer systems, software, backups,

The author is grateful to Paul M. Horvitz and David B. Humphrey for comments that greatly aided the completion of this article.

audit and control procedures that are in place), the legal structure governing asset own-ership and settlement of claims in default, and market conventions (such as netting arrangements, the timing of the provision of good funds, by collateral and reserve provi-sions, by delivery conventions, and by time and distance). Both governments and private markets have sought to curtail payments system risks, and these risks are the focus of the remainder of this article. All have received intensive consideration and review by both regulators and market participants. The key types of risks are listed in table 1 (fraud risk and technology, e.g., hardware and software risk, seem to be self-evident and will not be examined further).

Great strides have been made in understanding the risks created by the rapid evolution of financial markets. Well-structured analyses of the risks and related problems have been underway for some time, and the outline, if not the details, of the public policy issues have been well delineated. In this context, it is difficult to carve out a contribution that might make a difference in this debate. What this article seeks to do is a bit more modest. It reviews recent concerns about risks in financial markets and attempts to synthesize what is known about the policy issues. Finally, it seeks to explain why the recent evolution of more and more payments, clearing, and settlement systems, toward real-time gross settlement systems (RTGS) is taking place in the face of evidence and analysis that alternative systems employing bilateral netting and multilateral netting can, in the ab-sence of uncertainty about the status of claims in bankruptcy, both reduce risk and be more efficient.

The central thesis of this article is that despite the theoretical advantages of payments systems which incorporate various netting schemes and credit provisions, the movement towards real-time gross settlement systems is being driven by three main considerations which increasingly are reducing the advantages of netting-type clearing and settlement systems.[4] The first is the problem of resolving uncertainties in the way defaults will be handled in payments systems at a fast enough rate to keep pace with the evolution of new instruments and markets. The second is the rapid decline in computing costs and in-creases in processing speed which are reducing the efficiency gains from netting arrange-ments. The third is the movement towards 24-hour trading which will make netting arrangements difficult to implement.[5]

The rest of this article first lays out the nature of the systems that have evolved to clear and settle payments and asset transfers in very generic terms. It then discusses the risks associated with these systems. Finally, the evolutionary path that systems have taken are described and perhaps explained, with emphasis on the private-sector responses that have emerged to deal with risk control and financial system fragility.

Table 1. Risks in payments system relationships

A.	Legal risks
B.	Supervisory risks
C.	Settlement/credit risks
D.	Settlement/Liquidity risk
E.	Herstatt risk
F.	Fraud risk
G.	Technology risk

2. Asset and payment transfer systems

The potential for fragility in the payments system has long been the source of public policy concern. In the U.S., an early source of instability was due to the fact that bank notes were issued with the promise to redeem their face amount in specie (gold and/or silver). Runs occurred when demands for note conversion exceeded the available supply of specie, creating both liquidity and solvency problems if, given sufficient time, enough good assets were not available to convert to specie to meet the demand.

Early private sector responses resulted in extensions of credit and liquidity to the affected banks by other banks or through local clearing houses which had been organized to clear and return notes to the issuing banks within a region. Alternatively, banks experiencing runs either suspended convertibility or went out of business. Suspension of convertibility prevented the spread of the demand for money to other institutions whose reserves would not be depleted to meet the demand for converting assets into specie by the institution(s) experiencing the run.[6] Suspension did however result in loss of purchasing power by the holders of the nonconvertible notes, which were often only accepted at deep discounts in exchange for goods or services or at redeeming banks.[7] Since note holders ultimately bore much of the costs of nonconvertibility, they had incentives to worry about bank solvency. Indeed, the evidence is that they did; the result was that banks during this period typically had significantly higher capital ratios than in the post deposit-insurance era.[8] The first public sector regulatory actions to ensure convertibility were to establish maximum ratios of notes to specie.

With the growth of deposits and importance of checks as a medium of exchange, liquidity concerns changed from focusing on specie convertibility to the ability to meet demands for withdrawal of currency or payments of checks to other banks. This was accomplished by maintaining sufficient volumes of reserve balances, demand notes (which could be recalled at any time), government securities, or other marketable assets. Again, clearing houses often required maintenance of reserve assets as collateral to meet check-clearing demands, and the clearing houses also were sources of emergency funds from time to time. Many states also imposed minimum reserve requirements as a condition for being granted a charter.

Not all regulatory responses, however, were stabilizing; in fact, some even proved to be an important source of systemic risk. An important example of this in the U.S. was the reserve requirement feature of the National Banking Act of 1864.[9] Under this act, legal reserves to meet liquidity needs included not only cash in vault but also deposits held at Reserve City and Central Reserve City Banks. This feature proved to be a source of structural systemic risk. A run or unforseen demand for funds from a country bank was essentially a run to currency, which reduced the currency portion of National Bank reserves and could trigger one or more of the following events: a call of deposit/currency reserves from a Reserve City or Central Reserve City Bank, a call in of loans, or liquidation of assets at fire-sale values. This in turn might precipitate a liquidity crisis and force closure of an otherwise healthy institution. The result was a potential cumulative collapse in bank reserves and the money supply, if the crisis was transmitted from one bank to another within the system. Thus, this structural design defect sometimes had system-wide effects and can be properly viewed as structural systemic risk.[10]

During this early period of U.S. history, most payments were made by checks drawn on demand deposits with the remainder being made in currency. Demand deposits were the dominant form of bank liability to fund loans. There were not close substitutes for bank liabilities or the transactions functions they performed, nor were financial markets sufficiently deep that there were ready markets for the assets on bank balance sheets. Within that structure, protecting the payments mechanism meant preventing the cumulative collapse of the money supply when runs to currency occurred and the supply of demand deposits contracted cumulatively.[11] Since the money supply consisted chiefly of currency and demand deposits, protecting the payments system meant that eliminating bank failures and ensuring bank soundness would prevent the destruction of demand deposits. This key feature of the U.S. banking system was largely true of systems in other countries as well. Currency and demand deposits were the prime mediums of exchange.

Today, payment systems are larger, inherently more complex, have many more components—both private and public—and are subject to different risks than in the past. The check/demand deposit system, which most country regulatory systems and central banks sought to protect, is relatively small in terms of the value of payments and financial transactions made.[12] In the U.S., for example, cash payments account for less than .5% of the value of dollar payments.[13] Table 2 shows how variable, but generally small, checks are for different countries. The disparity between Canada and the U.S. or U.K. is quite striking.

Corrigan (1990), Junker, Summers and Young (1991), and Mengle (1992) have detailed the complexity of modern-day payments systems. They lay out the relationships among the various types of financial-asset transfer, clearing, and settlement systems within the U.S., concentrating on large dollar or wholesale payments. In characterizing the U.S. system, Corrigan (1990) describes an inverted pyramid set of relationships with over-the-counter and pit-trading dealer and parties at the top. In these markets, trades are negotiated, and then delivery takes place at agreed upon times. Payment and settlement take place in different markets altogether. The next layer are those markets with netting relationships as part of their trading, such as securities, futures, and options-clearing corporations. Here, buy-and-sell transactions are cumulated through the course of the day and are netted to determine the amount to be settled, usually at the end of the

Table 2. Relative importance of noncash payments instruments (1992). (Percent of total value of cashless transactions)

Group of 10 Countries	Checks	Payment by card	Credit transfers	Direct debits
Belgium	6.2	0.16	93.4	0.2
Canada	98.8	0.3	0.7	0.2
France	6.4	0.2	91.2	0.6
Germany	2.4	0.02	95.5	2.1
Italy	7.1	0.04	91.1	0.2
Netherlands	.02	0.0	98.6	1.2
Sweden	10.0	1.0	86.0	3.0
Switzerland	0.1	*	99.9	*
United Kingdom	12.0	0.2	87.0	1.1
United States	13.0	0.1	85.7	1.1

*Small

business day. These systems settle through other financial institutions, which in turn clear and settle through clearing houses, private settlement systems such as U.S. CHIPS or U.K. CHAPS, which in turn ultimate settle through (in the case of the U.S.) Fedwire. At the foundation, or bottom, of Corrigan's inverted pyramid is the central-bank clearing and settlement system. In the U.S., this is Fedwire, where interbank clearings are settled, and ownership of book entry securities are exchanged. With a little modification, their discussions apply to how the systems most countries operate today.

With few exceptions throughout the world, private sector arrangements handle all aspects of payments transactions, except perhaps for final settlement (or payment), which usually requires exchange of ownership on an agent basis of central-bank money. Hence the system for exchanging ownership of central bank deposits—the so-called wholesale market—underpins the clearing and settlement activities in other markets. It is the potential for disruptions in these other markets to suddenly impact each other and ultimately and unwittingly transmit problems to the large-value payments markets that has become a major source of concern.

In nearly every one of these markets, each part of the transaction process is often broken into several parts, with different intermediaries often interjecting themselves in the middle between the transacting parties. For example, in the case of the sale of book-entry Treasury securities, the buying agent instructs his bank or broker to purchase a security. The receiving institution's bank takes possession of the security and transfers that ownership to the buyer. Time delays and clearing arrangements may dictate exactly when the selling institution's bank and the seller receive and are given use of funds and when the buyer and its agent bank ultimately settle. For example, the two intermediary banks may have several securities transactions with each other during the course of the day, with only the net difference owed actually being transferred at the end of the day.

There are several ways to categorize these payments systems in terms of the types of customers they serve, the types of transactions involved, the size of typically transactions that are exchanged, the frequency of transactions, the types of participants, etc. For example, retail checks and European gyro systems handle large volumes of relatively small paper and electronic transactions as individuals engage in day-to-day exchange. Paper check systems in the US have traditionally been the focus of regulatory and supervisory concerns and provided the rational for much of the financial regulatory and infrastructure in place today. Large-value payment systems are largely electronic inter-bank markets and account for the vast majority of the value of payments in developed economies. Such systems tend to be the entry point for central bank implementation of monetary policy. They also generally involve urgent intraday transfers of claims which may be reused several times during the course of the day before they are settled. Participants in these markets may be direct, indirect, or customers. Table 3 (from BIS [1993]) provides a categorization of participants in interbank funds transfer systems and their responsibilities. Direct participants usually own the systems or are specifically authorized members who settle accounts directly with the system or its other direct participants. Indirect participants clear and settle through the accounts of the direct participant who act as their agents. Finally, customers usually are the initiators and ultimate recipients of value resulting from the purchase and sale of assets. They work through agents who may be either direct participants in the payments system—and who are

Table 3. Classification of participants in IFTS

	Responsibilities					
	Identified by IFTS					
Participants	Identified with a system or SWIFT address and permitted to send payment orders	Exchange of payment instruments	Responsibility for intra-system settlement	Responsibility for fulfillment of standards and laws	Shares expenses	Power of decision
Direct	Yes	Yes	Yes	Yes for its own operations	Yes	Yes or No
Indirect	Yes or No	Yes or No	No	Yes or No	Yes or No	Yes or No
Customers	No	No	No	No	No	No

Source: BIS (1993), pg. 10.

ultimately responsible for settlement—or through indirect participants who settle with the direct participants.

Literally hundreds of different markets exist to facilitate the exchange of financial assets (not to mention real assets), such as government securities, mortgage-backed securities, stocks and bonds, options and futures, short-term debt instruments such as commercial paper, and foreign exchange contracts. Transactions in these assets often take place on organized exchanges while others do not. Some of the exchanges are privately owned while others are publicly owned. Regardless, the transaction has several aspects which need to be managed for it to be completed. These include notification of the intent for two parties to enter a transaction and the terms of that transaction, the delivery of the asset to the ultimate purchaser, and finally the payment and settlement of the transaction in an acceptable medium.

The simplest of these markets is the cash market, where currency (government fiat money) is exchanged for goods and services. Notification, clearing, and settlement takes place simultaneously. No major markets, however, use currency to accomplish trades; transportation costs, security concerns, and the sheer volume of currency required make settlement in currency impractical.[14]

Once a transaction ceases to be a spot transaction, with instantaneous delivery and settlement in cash government fiat money, it is either paid for using a paper check or some other method of transferring value, such as an electronic transfer of funds. Any such transaction has two main components that must be discharged: clearing and settlement. During clearing, which can be done by any number of different parties (both banks and nonbanks alike), information is transferred from the payor to payee concerning the transaction which establishes the terms and parties to the transaction. The final transfer of value, or settlement, however, is almost always done through banks. Thus, banks and interbank payments systems are at the heart of all these markets.

Value can be transferred in several ways. If the payor and payee both have accounts at the same institution, then the payor's account can be debited and the payee's account credited. Clearing and settlement take place through the exchange of bank debt, with no governmental involvement. If the contracting parties have accounts at different institutions, then similar transfers can be made by debiting and crediting clearing house accounts. Alternatively, value can be conveyed by settling through the central bank by exchanging ownership of central bank deposits.

The institutional arrangements for completing the clearing and settlement functions have grown extremely complex. Most clearing is done in the private sector, while settlement takes place in both the private sector and through central banks. The specifics of the settlement arrangements differ widely across the various systems, both within the United States and across and banking systems throughout the rest of the world.[15] These range from gross settlement systems, such as Fedwire in the US, through which each transaction results in a debt or credit to a settlement account, to various types bilateral and multilateral netting arrangements. Table 4 details some of the netting and related features of both retail and large value payments systems in G-10 countries. They include both government and privately owned systems. Most are netting systems, but several are real-time gross settlement systems. Some have open membership; others are restricted.

Under bilateral netting arrangements, which occur in many derivative, foreign exchange, securities, and equity markets, two institutions mutually agree to cumulate transactions during a specified period of time, with only the net amount being settled for value, usually through the banking system, at the end of the business day or several days thereafter. Under multilateral netting, an institution agrees to cumulate transactions involving several parties, and settle the amount either owed or to be received collectively from the other parties to the agreement through a single agent, usually a clearing house. Examples of multilateral netting systems are CHIPS (Clearing House Interbank Payments System) through which most of the world dollar payments are settled or CHAPS (Clearing House Automated Payment System) in the U.K. Interestingly, CHAPS has recently indicated its intention to move to 100 percent collateralization and real-time gross settlement.[16]

Netting arrangements can drastically reduce the number of payments that have to be settled, can reduce the need for liquidity, and also have significant implications for risk exposure of the parties involved.[17] The orders of magnitude of the payments reductions can be dramatic. If for example, if an institution has 100 transactions with each of 10 institutions, then 1000 individual transactions have to be settled under a real-time gross settlement system. The institution must maintain sufficient liquidity to be able to settle each transaction as it flows through the payments system. In contrast, under bilateral netting $\frac{10 \times 9}{2}$ or only 45 transactions need to be settled. Under multilateral netting, a maximum of only 1 transaction per institution in the netting arrangement has to be settled. In general, if m is the number of transactions and k is the number of institutions, then the limits on the number of transactions to be processed are:

m for gross settlement systems,
$n(n-1)/2$ for bilateral netting systems, and
Max(n) for multilateral netting systems with n participants.

For $m > n$, the potential reductions in transactions are

$$m > n(n-1)/2 > \max(n) > = 0$$

Table 4. Attributes of G10-retail and large value payments systems (1992)

Country System	Type	Owner/ manager	No. of partici- pants	No. of direct partici- pants	Settlement
Belgium					
Clearing House of Belgium(CH)	Large value + retail	Banks	147	71	Multilateral netting
Centre for Exchange of Operations to be Cleared(CEC)	Retail	Central banks	129		Multilateral netting
Canada					
Interbank International Payment System (IIPS)	Large value	Banks and payment as	67	23	
France					
SAGITTAIRE[1]	Large value	Central banks	62	62	Multilateral netting
Paris Clearing House (CH Paris)	Large value + retail	Banks	421	40	Multilateral netting
Clearing House of Provinces (CH Provinces)	Retail	Central banks	10	10	Multilateral netting
Systeme Interbancarie de Telecom- pensation(SIT)	Retail	Banks	204	25	Bilateral netting
Clearing Computer	Retail	Central banks	597	18	Multilateral netting
Centres Regionaux d'Echanges d'Imags-Cheques (CREIC)	Retail	Central banks	16	16	Multilateral netting
Card Payments	Retail	Banks	207	11	Multilateral netting
Transferts Banque d France (TBF)	Large value	Central banks			Real time gross settlement
Germany					
Maschinell optische Beleglesung (MAOBE)	Retail	Central banks	5703		Other gross settlement
belegloser Datentrageraustausch (DTA)	Retail	Central banks	5703		Other gross settlement
Eiliger Zahlungsverkehr (EIL-ZV)	Large value	Central banks	5703		Real time gross
Platzuberweisungsverkehr (Platz)	Large value + retail	Central banks	5703		settlement Other gross settlement
Konv. Abrechnung	Large value + retail	Central banks	1783		Multilateral netting
Elektronische Abrechnung mit Filetransfer(EAF)	Large value	Central banks	39		Multilateral netting Multilateral netting
Italy					
Local clearing	Large value + retail	Central banks	574	274	Multilateral netting
Retail	Retail	Central banks	948	148	Multilateral netting
Electronic Memoranda(ME)	Large value	Central banks	106	106	Multilateral netting
Interbank Society for Automation (SIPS)	Large value	Central banks	292	292	Multilateral netting
Banca d'Italia continuous Settlement System (BISS)	Large value	Central banks	379	379	Real time gross settlement
Japan					
Foreign Exchange Yen Clearing System (FEYCS)	Large value	Banks	371	371	Multilateral netting
Bank of Japan Financial Network System (BOJ-NET)	Large value	Central banks	175	175	Real time gross settlement
Netherlands					
(Bank-GiroCentre(BGC-CH)	Retail	Banks	67	67	Multilateral netting
8007-SWIFT	Large value	Banks	58	58	Multilateral netting
Central bank current account system(FA)	Large value	Central banks	132	132	Multilateral net.-Real time
Sweden					
Clearing and Interbank System (RIX)	Large value + retail	Central banks	111	20	Real time gross setl. + Other
Data-Clearing	Retail	Banks	109	19	
Switzerland					
Swiss Interbank Clearing(SIC)	Large value + retail	Central bank and banks	162	162	Real time gross settlement
DTA/LSV	Retail	Banks	162	162	Multilateral netting
United Kingdom					
Clearing House Automated Payment System(CHAPS)	Large value	Banks	434	14	Multilateral netting
TOWN Clearing	Large value	Banks	12	12	Multilateral netting
BACS	Retail	Banks	35000	19	Multilateral netting
Check Clearing and Credit Clearing(Cheque/credit)	Retail	Banks	625	12	Multilateral netting
United States					
Fedwire	Large value	Central banks	11200	11200	Real time gross settlement
Clearing House Interbank Payment System(CHIPS)	Large value	Banks	122	122	Multilateral netting

Source: BIS(1993c), Table 10a.
1. Systeme Automatique de Gestion Integree par Teletransmission de transactions avec Imputation de reglemen Etranger

Table 4. continued

Membership	Degree of concentration	Processing	Pricing	Closing time for same-day settlement	Number of transactions (thousands)	Value of transactions (USD billions)	Ratio of trans-actions value to GDP (at annual rate)
Open	Decentralized	Manual	Variable C	16.30	24666	6322.13	28.9
Open	Centralized	ACH(off line)	Full costs	13.45	695200	496	2.7
Restricted	Decentralized		No costs	16.00	1560	8359	14.7
Restricted	Centralized	Real time trans.	Full costs	13.00	3300	10981	8.5
Restricted	Centralized	Manual	Full costs	15.00	761969	22294	17.2
Open	Decentralized	Manual	No costs	11.00	3121268	1537	1.2
Restricted	Decentralized	Real time trans.	Full costs	13.30	301800	44	0.03
Restricted	Decentralized	ACH(off line)	Full costs	11.00	1811000	1421	1.1
Open	Decentralized	ACH(off line)	Variable C	No Same day	231000	24	0.02
Restricted	Decentralized	ACH(off line)	Full costs	10.30	1609000	106	0.08
Open		Real time trans.	Full costs	17.00	11000	40423	31.2
Open	Decentralized	ACH(off line)	Variable C	No same day	588472	2019	1.13
Open	Decentralized	ACH(off line)	Variable C	No same day	2061044	1089	0.61
Open	Decentralized	Real time trans.	Full costs	14.30	2649	8728	4.87
Open	Decentralized	Manual	No costs	12.00	71865	5406	3.02
Open	Decentralized	Manual	No costs	12.00	381159	35510	19.82
Restricted	Centralized	Real time trans.	Variable C	12.30	7774	53237	29.71
Open	Decentralized	Manual	Variable C	9.30	292129	5157	4.2
Open	Centralized	ACH(off line)	Full costs	No same day	361783	213	0.2
Open	Centralized	Real time trans.	Variable C	16.00	1804	8480	6.9
Open	Centralized	Real time trans.	Full costs	14.00	2780	9733	8
Open	Centralized	Real time trans.	Variable C	17.00	20	80	0.1
Restricted	Decentralized	Real time trans.	Variable C	13.45	6119	49029	13.4
Restricted	Decentralized	Real time trans.	Variable C	17.00	3710	283462	77.2
Open	Decentralized	ACH(off line)	Full costs	12.45	1043.7	1942	3.4
Open	Centralized	ACH + real time	Full costs	12.45	1.8	8055	14.3
Open	Centralized	Manual + real ti	Variable C	15.30			
Restricted	Centralized	Real time trans.	Full costs	16.30	79	7660	31
Open	Centralized	ACH(off line)	Full costs	11.00	141436	3083	12.5
Restricted	Centralized	Real time trans.	Full costs	16.15	64279	23774	98.6
Restricted	Centralized	ACH(off line)	Full costs	No same day	56704		
Restricted	Decentralized	Real time trans.	Full costs	15.30	9000	36969	35.2
Restricted	Centralized	Manual	Full costs	15.30	100	2576	2.3
Restricted	Centralized	ACH(off line)	Full costs	No same day	1820000	1459	1.3
Restricted	Decentralized	Manual	Full costs	No same day	2577000	2270	2.2
Open	Decentralized	Real time trans.	Full costs	18.30	67600	199175	33
Restricted	Centralized	Real time trans.	Full costs	16.30	39073	238255	39.5

The benefits of netting to liquidity management are also clear. Netting arrangements obviate the need to assure that funds are available to settle each transaction.[18] The risk implications of the various systems are discussed in the next section.

The breaking up of the clearing/settlement process into component parts results in a tiering of markets. Securities, futures and options, derivatives and other markets clear under one arrangement, but largely settle in the interbank market. Moreover, as a result of this separation, seemingly unrelated markets and institutions are linked together in ways that both create and may transfer risks in one market to participants in other markets. There are four generally accepted generic types of risks that have been identified and have been the focus of much attention. These are discussed in the next section.

3. Payment system risks[19]

Payments system risks have been well explored in the literature. They include operational, legal, credit, and liquidity risks.[20] Conceptually, it is easy to identify these risks separately, but in reality they tend to be interrelated, and the realization of one can lead to occurrences of the others.

Operation risks arise from possible breakdowns in the computer systems or problems with accounting, physical delivery, internal controls, or other process elements associated with clearing and settling transactions. Numerous examples of such process risks have occurred and have been the source of both considerable embarrassment and consternation. One of the most glaring was the overloading of the government securities clearing system of the Bank of New York in 1985. When the processing capacity of the computer program was exceeded, instead of stopping the system or sending an error message, the system simply continued to accept delivery of securities with the corresponding debiting of the bank's reserve account through Fedwire at the Federal Reserve Bank of New York. But the system did not then complete the rest of the transaction by forwarding the securities to the ultimate purchaser and receiving payment. The deficit in the bank's reserve account exceeded $22 billion by the close of the business day. This created a liquidity risk—that is, a temporary inability to settle transactions at the agreed upon date. Bank of New York clearly was not insolvent, but was neither able to liquidate assets to meet the demand for funds nor to obtain needed funds by completing the delivery of the securities, thus replenishing its funds from the delivery proceeds. In this case, the problem was solved when the central bank provided an overnight loan from the discount window. Given the amount of funds needed, it is doubtful that the other historic way that solvent but illiquid institutions met the demand for funds, that is, by borrowing from a clearing house or other banks, could have been accomplished. This example illustrates that the four categories of risk are not independent, and that a settlement or operational risk can create credit risk, or, in this case, lead to a liquidity crisis which could expose system participants to large, unanticipated losses. Whether the system exposure to Bank of New York would have caused liquidity or solvency problems at other institutions is unclear, and no scenarios have been put forth to indicate how problems might have spread. Nevertheless, it is this uncertainty which creates the spector of financial fragility (the realization of large risks in certain states of the world).

Similarly, during the 1987 crash of the stock market, transactions ran far ahead of the ability of the electronic clearing system to process transactions. The breakdown disrupted the orderly flow of prices to the market place. Limit, stop, and other order flows were disrupted by the sheer volume of transactions and the inability of existing computer systems to handle them.[21] As a result, many trades were either not made or were made at prices that participants would not have accepted had they had full information. The market responses to such problems have been (1) to expand capacity, which generates an interesting side issue of how much idle capacity a market should maintain to deal with an infrequent peak load problem, (2) to build in redundancy by providing backup computer and other systems, not unlike the arrangements made by public utilities to reroute electricity or telephone calls, (3) to perform process audits, and finally (4) to engage in disaster scenario planning and simulations in order to identify risks and build in appropriate protections. But unanticipated circumstances, such as the disruptions caused by the World Trade Center bombing, show that even unlikely events can both occur and have significant ripple effects through markets.

The difference between a liquidity problem and credit risk, as it relates to settlement, is largely one of degree rather than kind. Credit risk arises when an institution defaults by failing to settle on any or all of its obligations. It arises as a logical by-product of separating the clearing and settlement functions. Credit risk can occur at any step of the payments process, affecting customers, direct and indirect market participants. For example, if a customer initiates a transaction ordering a bank to purchase an asset, but then cannot accept delivery, the institution is faced with several alternatives. Credit can be provided to the customer until funds are received. Alternatively, the transaction can either be canceled, or it can be completed by the bank, which then takes possession of the asset (or the customer's available collateral) and proceeds to unwind it. Finally, in the extreme, the bank can default on its own obligation to settle if settlement time has not yet occurred. If the buyer has good collateral and a sound credit rating, then extension of credit may be the best alternative. Canceling the transaction may not be an option, especially if delivery has already taken place.

Settlement failure in the above example can be controlled if the bank puts a hold on the buyer's funds at the time the transaction was ordered, effectively collateralizing the transaction.[22] For good customers, however, this may not be necessary, practical or efficient, especially if both the probability of default and the expected loss are small relative to the bank's resources. This suggests that diversification, control of credit concentrations, and maintenance of adequate capital are key management tools in limiting settlement/credit risk exposure.

The lack of a hold-policy illustrates that an institution's vulnerability to credit risk often results from the underlying conventions and structure of the markets involved, rather than from the realization of performance risks associated with the underlying projects and investments. For example, under Fedwire, which is a gross settlement system in which an institution's reserve account is debited or credited on a transactions-by-transactions basis, the Fed has chosen not to prohibit transactions when an institution does not have good funds in its reserve account. Subject to limits, the Fed permits an institution to make and accept transfers continuously throughout the day, but only requires that the institution close out its account at the end of the day, either by transferring in good funds or by borrowing from the discount window. Since delivery conventions on various securities transactions, federal funds, and commercial paper vary considerably across markets, it is not uncommon for major dealer and correspondent banks to be in net deficit reserve positions for a large portion of the business day.[23] When this happens, the Federal Reserve becomes a lender, providing credit to the institution with the daylight overdraft. Not only is the Federal Reserve, and hence the US taxpayer, a creditor, but also, until April of 1994, this credit was provided free of charge, which had implications for risk-management incentives within the payments system and individual institutions.[24]

The historical roots of this convention lie partly in the Federal Reserves' technical inability to monitor continuously the flows of funds into and out of all banks' reserve accounts, and hence to prevent overdrafts from arising.[25] Also, this free credit helped offset the other burdens of Federal Reserve membership, which was, up until the Monetary Control Act of 1980 mandated holding of reserves against transactions accounts, eroding at a rate sufficient to cause the Federal Reserve to believe that it might be losing its ability to implement monetary policy.

Another structural feature of the Fedwire system—the fact that the system provides finality—increases the likelihood that credit will be extended. That is, once a Fedwire transaction is initiated and accepted by the Federal Reserve into the system for electronic processing, the receiving bank is granted immediate use, and an irrevocable claim, on the funds (regardless of whether the sender ultimately defaults). In this respect the Fed interposes itself between the two parties to the transaction, as do many other clearing and settlement institutions such as futures and options exchanges, increasing its exposure to credit risk.

Not all payments systems have finality; some of those that do, do not necessarily have absolute credible finality.[26] Again, a useful example can be taken from the United States. The other major wholesale dollar clearing system in the U.S. is CHIPS, the large-dollar clearing and settlement system owned by major New York money center banks and operated by the New York Clearing House Association. Until recently, CHIPS did not provide finality. Failure to settle on the part of a system member meant that transactions involving the defaulting party would have to be unwound, and in the extreme, potentially all transactions would have to be unwound. Because of the extreme number and volume of transactions which flow through CHIPS every day, unwinding the failure of a participant to settle could put other institutions in extreme deficit positions which might not easily or quickly be settled. The result could unwittingly transmit a problem in one institution to others in the system, resulting in a systemic risk problem. The only recourse to affected institutions would be to seek emergency loans or to discount assets with the Federal Reserve. This makes the Federal Reserve the backup source of liquidity and lender of last resort to CHIPS, even though it does not run or is not directly involved with CHIPS, except to allow settlement through a reserve account at the Federal Reserve Bank of New York.

Concern for the systemic risks inherent in the structure of CHIPS lead participants to institute payments finality. To provide the necessary resources to make the promise of finality credible, loss-sharing arrangements among members were instituted in the form of posting of collateral sufficient to cover an institution's maximum net debt exposure. On the one hand, the result is to use finality to avoid the need to unwind transactions in the event of a settlement failure, but it also ties the fate of all member institutions to the overall health of the system, and potentially increases the member institutions' exposure to catastrophic systemic risk, to the extent that posted collateral may not be sufficient to cover actual losses. The effects of this change on member incentives to limit risk or to engage in moral hazard behavior to shift even greater burdens to the Federal Reserve remains to be seen.

Whether CHIPS finality is credible, is open to question; it is inconceivable that the member institutions would, in the extreme, all go out of business to meet their commitments. Rather, the more likely scenario is that institutions facing default would turn to the Federal Reserve as lender of last resort. It is this problem that makes central banks the lenders of last resort to all payments systems, and raises the issue of whether and to what degree they are subject to moral hazard and adverse selection behavior during times of crisis and fragility.

As markets have become increasingly global, timing differences and differences in clearing and settlement conventions can add temporal and other dimensions to credit risks not always found in domestic markets. This was clearly demonstrated in 1974, when Herstatt bank failed and was closed by German authorities. The bank had entered into agreements to exchange marks for dollars. The mark leg of the transactions were settled, but the dollar portions were not settled in New York at the time Herstatt was closed, since the deadline on CHIPS for final settlement was about 4:30 PM Eastern Standard time. This left the counterparties to the foreign exchange transaction thinking that they had more funds than they did. When the dollar transactions failed to settle, large losses to counterparties resulted. This temporal dimension to credit/systemic risk has come to be known as "Herstatt risk" and can be very large. A more recent example is provided when BCCI (Bank of Credit and Commerce International) was closed in 1991. The Industrial Bank of Japan had paid 44 billion yen into BCCI's branch in Tokyo, for which payment was to be received in New York from BCCI's New York Branch. When BCCI was closed, the dollar portion of the transaction was never completed, and Industrial Bank of Japan became a creditor for $30 million. To some, this may look like ordinary credit risk, which indeed it is. But its incidence is determined by the intervention policies pursued by the regulatory authorities, whose actions cannot be easily predicted or priced. Summers (1991) indicates that settlement of foreign exchange transactions originating in the Far East may be delayed in settlement through CHIPS by as much as 14 hours and amount to as much as $425 billion dollars.

The losses to dollar counterparties in the Herstatt case were the consequence of the German authorities' timing of the closure of the institution rather than to the realization of estimable default risk. Had the authorities waited until the U.S. dollar markets had settled, then the losses to those expecting dollar transfers would not have occurred.[27,28] Such exposure is better characterized as settlement uncertainty rather than settlement risk, since it is not possible to reliably estimate and cost out the implications of regulatory actions and policies.

Herstatt-type risk can also be involved in solely dollar clearing systems. In Asia, through its Tokyo branch, the Chase Manhattan Bank operates a dollar clearing and settlement service which offers finality and limited overdrafts and is guaranteed by Chase. Participants are permitted to settle these overdrafts in New York across the Tokyo/New York

business day. Furthermore, Tokyo balances at the end of the day may be transferred to
New York, either through the New York offices of Chase or Tokyo banks or through
CHIPS. In this case, problems in this satellite settlement and clearing system, quickly have
the potential to transmit liquidity and credit risk from Asia to New York, and ultimately
to the Federal Reserve, if it affects either CHIPS, Chase, or significant New York correspondents. A failure to settle in New York on payments guaranteed in Japan by Chase
would create a form of Herstatt risk that would end up having to be resolved in New York.
How problems in this system might be handled is uncertain. Moreover, there has been
little discussion of how the problem of the failure of one institution to settle would cause
a ripple effect across many institutions. At present, concern flows from the sheer size of
the potential losses rather than from an understanding of well-articulated scenarios.
Furthermore, regulatory agencies have sometimes played on the fears that these potential losses represent in seeking to increase their regulatory scope.

Many other significant sources of uncertainty can also be identified in the clearing and
settlement processes in modern financial markets. For example, when clearing and settlement of financial assets are separated, a given country's rules usually establish the exact
point in time that a transaction has been completed. The issue centers around transaction
finality and the legal criteria for when debts are discharged and who bears the losses in the
event of default. Finality usually occurs when the party selling the asset actually has "good
funds," and may or may not correspond to the time that the sender has actually settled.
For example, because Fedwire provides finality, acceptance of a payment order "guarantees" the receiver "good funds" and discharges the debt, since the sender's reserve
account is debited and the receiver's bank's account is credited, even though the sender's
bank may default on the settlement of its reserve account with the Fed at the end of the
day.[29] When the institutions are located in two separate countries, then transactions can
sometimes be governed by the laws of two separate countries, and, if transactions involve
clearing houses, the laws where they are located.

The issue can quickly become murky, however, when one starts to examine the problems involved in settlement failures in bilateral and multilateral netting arrangements—
especially those involving forward dated contracts, such as foreign exchange, derivatives
and other cross-border markets. Final disposition of the liability depends critically on the
legal rules governing the disposition of debts and transactions in the event of a default or
bankruptcy.[30] For example, if two institutions have entered into a bilateral netting arrangement, then completion of all the transactions subject to the arrangement depends
upon settlement of the net position. If one of the parties fails to settle because of a
bankruptcy, then all the gross transactions subject to netting may have to be undone,
depending upon the legal rules affecting the markets in which the transaction was settled.
Since the legal rules may differ depending upon where settlement takes place, and this
may be beyond the receiver's control, significant settlement uncertainty may exist.

The exact status of these transactions, therefore, depends upon several sets of laws:
those governing bilateral netting arrangements, those governing the particular settlement
market involved, and the bankruptcy provisions and other related laws of the country of
the failed institution (and/or the laws of the resident country if the transaction is recorded
on the books of a branch of the failed bank). For example, netted transactions may, or may
not be regarded as discharged. Thus, the bankruptcy court may decide to unbundle netted

transactions, demanding payment for debts owed and disavowing liabilities to creditors. In addition, country bankruptcy law may give creditors the right to offset their liabilities to a failed entity against their claims on that entity. Thus, debts owed on foreign exchange may be discharged with debts on securities, loans, or any other assets. Not only do these bankruptcy laws affect the losses, but also how the losses may be apportioned across various creditors. The legal situation in multilateral netting arrangements introduce complexities several orders of magnitude greater than those affecting bilateral arrangements.[31]

There is considerable variation across countries in the treatment of transactions; and thus uncertainty exists about how particular bankruptcies will be treated. This uncertainty undermines the risk-reducing potential of bilateral and multilateral netting arrangements, and creates the very real possibility that systemic risks could be heightened rather than reduced when the laws governing netting are uniform across countries.[32] The uncertainties associated with their resolution make it virtually impossible in today's environment to reliably assess the likely outcome of a default scenario for many transactions.[33]

4. Private sector responses to risk and uncertainty

Private sector entities have responded to the increased uncertainties, market risks and evolving market technologies in many interesting ways. The responses involve (1) contract design, (2) the micro market structure of exchanges and their rules governing transactions, (3) private proposals to change laws governing transactions, and (4) suggestions to increase governmental cross-border cooperation in financial rules, regulation and supervision.[34]

Given the complexity of financial transactions and their interrelationships, there are significant problems in measuring, monitoring and pricing what institutions' true risk exposures are to each other and how risks flow directly and indirectly though relationships with related customer groups. For example, customer X may have several relationships with its primary bank (bank A). This might include a loan, a swap, a deposit account, and several foreign exchange transactions, etc. Customer X may also have similar relationships and transactions outstanding with bank B. In addition, bank A may also have made loans in the form of advancing fed Funds to bank B. If customer X fails, the entirety of its net position with bank A across all the relationships and transactions represent its net direct risk exposure. Bank A may also be indirectly exposed through bank B, if the customer's default causes bank B to default on its Federal Funds obligations to A's primary bank. Measuring and monitoring these interrelated exposures across the world and across different markets is truly a daunting modeling and monitoring problem, made even more so by the dynamic and continual evolution of new instruments and markets.

The private sector responses to these risk measurements and monitoring of payments risk-exposure have attempted to substitute rules and other mechanisms to control customer risk-taking incentives. Actions have involved cooperatively owned clearing and settlement systems and responses by individual participants as well. Control mechanisms include maintenance of adequate capitalization, reliance upon contract design to allocate risk and losses, collateralization of transactions, use of outside guarantees and bonding, pricing, imposition of system membership requirements, and self-imposed (and system-mandated) caps and other limits on risk exposure to individual and related parties. These responses may be viewed as attempts to limit uncertainty and to provide incentives for member institutions to control their own risks exposures.

For example, a great deal of attention has been paid to the process concerning the structure of payment orders and to contract design as methods of reducing payment system uncertainty regarding the legal status of various transactions in the event of default. In netting arrangements, especially when dealing with customers with large numbers of transactions and different types of credit and other relationships with a bank or other payment system participant, institutions have employed rules to define rights of setoff, defining collateral in the case of collateralized transactions. Netting by novation, for example, is one contract feature that explicitly specifies that parties discharge all their obligations to each other by transferring only the net amount due. Netting by novation replaces two existing contracts for delivery of an asset on the same day with a single net contract for that date.[35] Similarly, another contract provision that has evolved is a close-out provision. A closeout provision becomes effective in bankruptcy and defines a formula which will convert outstanding transactions into an immediately payable amount. This would include all future date futures, options, forwards, and other future liabilities. So important are these contract provisions and their design for netting arrangements, that Gilbert (1992) notes that in the U.S., a private sector firm provides legal advice and communications specifically addressing netting arrangements. (Of course, many private law firms provide similar services as well.) While attention to contract design is necessary, without defaults and continual testing of contract features in the courts, reliance upon contract design to provide needed risk control and protection may tend only to mask the true uncertainties and losses for which members are potentially liable.

Second, private sector contracting activities also focus on apportioning risks, defining performance, and allocating losses among participants in a payments system or exchange in the event that a default occurs. These provisions can take many forms. For example, in CHIPS, unwinding was a way of apportioning losses ex post on other participants in the system. Agreements are also executed, however, that make system participants liable for portions of losses if problems arise.[36] CHIPS has abandoned unwinding as a loss apportionment mechanism and has substituted apportioning losses through collateralization of exposures. Such collateralization provides incentives for member to control and monitor their own exposure to other clearing house members so as to protect their collateral.

Third, because of the difficulties in continuously measuring and monitoring total risk exposure to individual system members, private system members often impose caps on the amount of exposure they will take with any member, and the system imposes a similar total cap across all system members. Caps are a gross attempt to put outer bounds on exposures to individual institutions in lieu of developing pricing algorithms designed to price these exposures.

Fourth, private sector entities also impose various types of membership and participation requirements. In futures exchanges, for example, members are required to post collateral in the form of maintenance margins and initial margins. Additional constraints include membership requirements, minimum capital requirements, and collateralization and backup lines of credit. All of these rules impose costs on members which attempt to internalize the costs of risk to the system and its members.

Fifth, recognized accounting rules can impact the ease of information transfer and reduce monitoring costs. Most futures exchanges require that transactions be marked to market and that any deficiencies in coverage as the result of price or interest rate movements be made up with immediately available funds. Again, for systems which operate continuously, this is equivalent to requiring that good funds be posted continuously. Uniform accounting, and especially market-value reporting, increasingly have become recognized as an important component of effective risk controls systems.

5. Conclusions: Responses to risk and uncertainty

Perhaps one of the more interesting developments in this evolution of regional and globalized payments markets in both the public and private sectors has been the push towards real-time gross settlement systems with collateralization. This applies to both private systems and publicly run systems. Nowhere are these efforts more apparent than in Europe where the struggle to create a single financial market place has focused attention and generated analyses of the underlying issues, with the BIS (1990, 1993a, 1993b), the Group of Ten, and EC central banks spearheading much of this work.

At the market level, the process of financial integration suggests that as the barriers to real production within Europe break down and as financial institutions operate branches throughout Europe, more and more of the domestic payment and financial markets will have cross-border attributes. Hence, the EC central banks have paid particular attention to the structure and operations of cross-border and multicurrency netting and settlement schemes. In an attempt to limit risks resulting from cross-border payments activities and from differences in intracompany payments systems, the BIS and central banks have proposed a set of minimum features that domestic payments and cross-border netting systems should have. Table 5 lists the key attributes that the EC committee have put forth. It is interesting that the Committee gives heavy weight to getting the "legal situation" right. Given that public sector responses are the prime focus of other papers at this conference, the legal issues and governmental responses will only briefly be discussed. However, the evidence and analysis suggests that infrastructure differences from different legal environments are of paramount importance in introducing uncertainty in payments system operations. Also, most of the private sector responses take place in a world of second best, where the "legal situation" isn't right, and thus they may be viewed as market responses to uncertainty. Interestingly, the public sector recommendations have tended to mirror the private sector responses, implying that the elimination of uncertainty may be outweighing efficiency and risk considerations.

Casual empiricism suggests several reasons why the systems are evolving in this direction, despite considerable analysis suggesting that netting arrangements are both more efficient and involve less potential risk. The first reason is that systems, instruments, and markets are evolving faster than the political entities can harmonize or bring their various

Table 5. Minimum standards for the design and operation of cross-border and multi-currency netting and settlement schemes

Attributes	Special features or considerations
I. Netting schemes should have well-founded legal basis under all relevant jurisdictions.	For risk exposure in a multilateral netting schemes to be the net amount requires recognition by (a) the law of the country in which the counter party is chartered (and if a branch of a foreign bank), then under the law of the jurisdiction in which the branch is located, (b) the law governing the individual transactions subject to the netting scheme, and (c) the law governing any contract or agreement necessary to effect the netting. This test is cumulative.
II. Netting scheme participants should have a clear understanding of the impact of the particular scheme on each of the financial risks affected by the netting process.	(a) Netting may not cause a default but may convert a hedged position into an unhedged position, such as in the case of a default on a swap agreement. (b) Replacement costs of contracts depend upon both the volatility of interest rates and exchange rates. (c) Forward replacement-cost risks increase with the maturity of the contract. (d) Reciprocal payments under financial contracts involve possible losses when markets settle at different times.
III. Multilateral netting systems should have clearly defined procedures for management of credit and liquidity risks which specify respective responsibilities of the netting provider and participants. These procedures should also ensure that all parties have both the incentives and capabilities to manage and contain each of the risks borne, and that limits are placed on the maximum level of credit exposure with the largest single net-debit position.	Risk control requires clear responsibility for identifying, quantifying, and allocating risks. Critical to this is the division of responsibility between the central counterpart or clearing house and the participants. There needs also to be a clear link between the ability to control risk and the incentives to do so. Decentralized systems are more vulnerable to problems here than centralized systems. In forward claims markets, the exchange should be modeled after futures and options exchanges, with participants required to post collateral equal to the full extent of the central counterparty's exposure to that participant. This suggests marking to market with margin requirements.
IV. Multilateral netting schemes should, at the minimum, be capable of ensuring the timely completion of daily settlements in the event of an inability to settle by the participant with the largest single net-debit position.	Systems should provide for prompt settlement and apportion loss to system members, but not provide for unwinding of transactions or delay until the next day for settlement. Systems with centralized, collateralized risk management systems can apply the same principles to liquidity management.
V. Multilateral netting schemes should have objective and publicly disclosed criteria for admission which permit fair and open access.	System membership criteria should be based upon financial strength, managerial capacity and effectiveness of supervision.
VI. All netting schemes should ensure the operational reliability of technical systems and the availability of backup facilities capable of completing daily processing requirements.	Contingency plans and backup systems to deal with system failures should be in place.

rules and regulations into harmony.[37] This is certainly true within the EC. The difficulties become even greater when it comes to attempts to harmonize the world legal structure governing financial transactions. Issues of jurisdiction and sovereignty have essentially brought the EC movement toward a single currency to a halt. This regulatory lag introduces a significant source of uncertainty into the functioning of regulated markets. Real-time gross settlement systems significantly reduce these problems. Transaction-by-transaction clearing and settlement avoid disputes over when debts are discharged, and they reduce credit risk exposure to the extent that overdrafts are not involved.

Second, harmonizing systems to control effectively the systemic risks (such as Herstatt risks) inherent in non-synchronized clearing and settlement systems, such as foreign exchange markets, even if all the legal rules are in place requires, requires complete international coordination and cooperation when payment system principals enter bankruptcy. That is, unless all markets are open 24 hours, Herstatt risk will still be an important consideration.[38] Such coordination and cooperation is far from certain, and is clearly not in place.

Third, central banks realize that regardless of the explicit rules governing exchanges, they still may be thrust into the role of the "lender of last resort," should major participants get into financial difficulties which threaten to bring down settlement and clearing systems. This potential exposure is not only large, but also often outside of central bank jurisdiction and control. For example, in the U.S., despite all the cross guarantees, etc., the Federal Reserve is the residual bearer of risk for CHIPS participants. Interestingly, while the Federal Reserve can examine domestic banks (or obtain supervisory help from the Comptroller of the Currency and FDIC) many of the CHIPS members and indirect participants are foreign institutions, over which the Fed has no authority or jurisdiction. These institutions can potentially, through default, shift CHIPS system problems to the Fed. This potentiality exists across all major markets in which U.S. banks participate, and carries the same types of implications for the Fed and U.S. taxpayer. In the face of this growing potential problem, system net debit caps and other risk-limiting features are the only feasible option. For this reason, regulatory constraints on cross-market risk exposures are also key features of the EC recommendations. Ultimately, the Federal Reserve will be forced to give up providing free daylight overdrafts (pricing of daylight overdrafts has been the subject of debate in both the Congress and within the System for several years). When institutions believe that the costs of extreme market fluctuations will be absorbed by the central bank because of either implicit or explicit guarantees, this introduces potential moral hazard into the system.

Finally, the movement towards expanding the overlapping hours that exchanges are open will increasingly make the operation of net settlement systems more difficult. For example, in the extreme, as markets evolve towards 24-hour operations, agreement upon the exact number of times and when net settlements will be posted becomes an arbitrary, and essentially unnecessary, complication vis-à-vis real-time gross settlement systems. In addition, as the pace of technology continues to expand computer storage and processing capacities, the cost benefits to netting become less and less. With billions of transactions being moved at virtually the speed of light, the marginal benefits of netting seem to be declining at an exponential rate.

In light of the problems and uncertainties in the existing operations of payments systems, the EC central banks' proposals for modeling payments systems after futures exchanges— which only clear against good funds—radically simplifies the central bank risk- management and control concerns. For those central banks with active payment system roles, such as the Federal Reserve, however, elimination of overdrafts reduces the need for direct central bank involvement in operating payments systems.

Notes

1. See Kaufman (1994) for a recent discussion of contagion and systemic risk. He defines contagion as the "spillover effects of shocks from one or more firms to others." A more refined definition is contained in Bank for International Settlements (1990) which defines systemic risk as "the risk that the inability of one institution within a payments system, as in the financial markets generally, to meet its obligations when due will cause other participants or financial firms to be unable to meet their obligations when due." Cohen and Roberds (1993) attempt to sharpen this concept further when they propose that because of lender of last resort intervention and "too-big-to-fail" policies, a better view of systemic risk is that it can be approximated by the "expected costs incurred by such intervention. . . . "
2. It is now estimated that transactions in large dollar payments are in the neighborhood of $1.4 trillion per day. Similarly, foreign exchange transactions are clearly over $750 billion, and derivative transactions clearly are in that range as well. Finally, private sector securities transactions that settle through large dollar settlement systems probably involve gross transactions more than equal the above amounts.
3. See Smith and Lipin (1994).
4. Kane (1991, 1988) also attributes the regulators' preference for RTGS systems as the response to market forces.
5. This third factor is more prospective and has had little direct impact to date.
6. See Kaufman (1986), Bryant (1980), or Kaufman (1994) for discussions of runs.
7. See Eisenbeis (1987).
8. See Kaufman (1986).
9. National banks were permitted to redeem their holdings of government securities with National bank notes, and thereby to make loans at yields higher than those paid on the federal debt. The intent of the Union was to replace bank notes with federal bank notes and thereby to finance the Civil War through inflating the money supply.
10. The creation of the Federal Reserve in 1913 dealt with this structural systemic risk in two important ways. It eliminated the use of interbank deposits as legal reserves and substituted default-free, high powered money in the form of deposits held at Federal Reserve Banks held as legal reserves. This broke the reserve pyramid and severed the ability of a reserve deficiency at one bank from snowballing into reserve deficien- cies at other banks. Finally, it provided that the central bank was to serve as a temporary source of liquidity through the provision of emergency credit through the discounting of eligible assets and provision of emergency loans. This gave the central bank the power to provide instant liquidity, since it had the ability to create an infinite supply of the riskless reserve asset.
11. The cumulative collapse could only result when, after 1913, the Federal Reserve did not offset any decline in currency reserves through discount window and lender of last resort activities. It is widely accepted that the Fed did not provide this liquidity during the Great Depression. There is little evidence that runs, as compared with macro- and other causes, have ever been as great as conventional wisdom suggests (Kaufman, 1994). Studies by Calomiris and Gorton (1991) and Saunders and Wilson (1993) suggest that bank deposit flows during the 1930–32 period of contagion during the Great Depression are consistent with the view that depositors did distinguish between healthy and less healthy banks.
12. See BIS (1993c) for detailed descriptions and statistics on small volume payments by country.
13. See Furash and Company (1994).

14. See Mengle (1992).
15. See Table 10a of BIS (1993c) for a the details of these differences.
16. See Bank of England and APACS (1994).
17. For detailed discussions see Gilbert (1992), BIS (1989, 1990, 1993a), and Mengle (1990, 1992).
18. If the system provides for daylight overdrafts, as Fedwire did for many years, then liquidity considerations go away.
19. This initial discussion follows Mengle (1992).
20. See Flannery (1988), Gilbert (1992), Mengle (1990, 1992), BIS (1989, 1990, 1993a,b,c) for a few examples.
21. Not only did the technical systems break down, but the specialist system ceased to function.
22. This leaves aside the issue of whether collateral is perfected or not.
23. Limits were imposed by the Fed on daylight overdrafts when it was discovered in the early 1980s that institutions, such as Continental Illinois Bank, were relying extensively on this source of credit to fund daily operations, running overdraft positions several times an institution's capital.
24. The Federal Reserve has begun to measure daylight overdrafts on a minute-by-minute basis.
25. The Federal Reserve still lacks the ability to monitor all participants positions on a real-time basis, but can and does monitor certain, more risky institutions continuously. See Juncker, Summers, and Young (1991).
26. Because only central banks can create riskless money assets in unlimited amounts, only central-bank lending can provide truly riskless guarantees of finality.
27. If CHIPS had finality, then the losses would have been born by CHIPS (and distributed across the membership according to agreed upon loss sharing arrangements) rather than by the counter-parties to the transactions.
28. Of course, the losses would have then been born by a different set of creditors.
29. In effect the Fed interposes itself between the parties of the transaction similar to the way that futures exchanges do.
30. For complete discussions see Mengle (1990) or BIS (1990).
31. Juncker, Summers, and Young (1991) report that the Federal Reserve provides settlement services to over 160 small-value, netting arrangements involving checks, automated clearing house transactions, and automatic teller systems. It also provides net settlement services to Participants Trust Company, which clears and settles mortgage-backed securities, and to Depository Trust Company, which clears and settles new issue instruments such as commercial paper.
32. For a discussion of this see BIS (1990) and Cohen and Roberds (1993).
33. The uncertainties referred to are in the spirit of the classic sense of Frank H. Knight (1921, 1971). Knight described uncertainty as involving situations where the probability distributions of events are unknown; hence there is no easy way to ascertain expected payoffs across possible states of the world. This contrasts with risky events, for which the probability distribution of outcomes is known, and hence expected payoffs across different states of the world can be calculated.
34. Governmental efforts have pushed forward on (3) and (4) as well.
35. This is like a swap contract. Position netting nets payment obligations but neither satisfies nor discharges the original obligations that were netted.
36. In Fedwire, given that the Fed provides finality, this effectively makes the defaulting entity liable to the Fed and relieves other participants of any obligation to replace funds.
37. Kane (1991) has devoted substantial attention to regulatory lags to financial innovation and change.
38. The Federal Reserve has proposed extending Fedwire operating hours in 1997 to 12:30 am to 6:30 PM.

References

Bank of England and APACS. "The Development of Real-Time Gross Settlement (RTGS) in the United Kingdom." Information release, April 1994.

BIS. "Report on Netting Schemes." prepared by the Group of Experts on Payments Systems of central banks of the Group of 10 Countries, February 1989.

BIS. "Report of the Committee on Interbank Netting Schemes of the Central Banks of the Group of Ten Countries." November 1990.

BIS. "Central Bank Payment and Settlement Services with Respect to Cross-Border and Multi-Currency Transactions." Report prepared by the Committee on Payment and Settlement Systems of the central banks of the Group of Ten countries, September 1993a.

BIS. "Minimum Common Features for Domestic Payments Systems." Report of the Committee of Governors of the Central Banks of the Member States of the European Economic Community: Action 2 of the Report on issues of common concern to EC central banks in the field of payments systems, by the Working Group on EC Payment Systems, November 1993b.

BIS. *Payment Systems in The Group of Ten Countries*. Prepared by the Committee on Payment and Settlement Systems of the central banks of the Group of Ten countries, Basle, December 1993c.

Bryant, John. "A Model of Reserves, Bank Runs, and Deposit Insurance." *Journal of Banking and Finance* 4 (1990).

Calomiris, Charles W., and Gary Gorton. "The Origins of Banking Panics: Models, Facts, and Bank Regulation." In: R. Glenn Hubbard, ed., *Financial Markets and Financial Crises*. Chicago: University of Chicago Press. 1991, pp. 109–173.

Cohen, Hugh, and William Roberds. "Towards the Systematic Measurement of Systemic Risk." Working Paper 93-14, Federal Reserve Bank of Atlanta, October 1993.

Corrigan, E. Gerald. "Perspectives on Payment System Risk Reduction." In: David B. Humphrey, ed., *The U.S. Payment System: Efficiency, Risk and the Role of the Federal Reserve* (Proceedings of a Symposium on the U.S. Payment System Sponsored by the Federal Reserve Bank of Richmond). Boston, MA: Kluwer Academic Publishers. 1990.

Eisenbeis, Robert A. "Eroding Market Imperfections: Implications for Financial Intermediaries, the Payments System, and Regulatory Reform." In: *Restructuring the Financial System* (A Symposium Sponsored by the Federal Reserve Bank of Kansas City), Jackson Hole, Wyoming, 1987.

Flannery, Mark J. "Payments System Risk and Public Policy." In: William S. Hararf and Rose Marie Kushmeider, eds., *Restructuring Banking and Financial Services in America*. Washington, DC: American Enterprise Institute, 1988.

Furash and Company. *Banking's Role in Tomorrow's Payments System: Ensuring A Role for Banks*, Vol. 1. (A Study Prepared for the Banking Research Fund on Behalf of the Payments System Committee of the Bankers Roundtable), June 1994.

Gilbert, R. Alton. "Implications of Netting Arrangements for Bank Risk in Foreign Exchange Transactions." *Economic Review* (Federal Reserve Bank of St. Louis.) (January/February 1992).

Juncker, George R., Bruce J. Summers, and Florence M. Young. "A Primer on the Settlement of Payments in the United States." Federal Reserve *Bulletin* (November 1991).

Kane, Edward J. "Incentive Conflict in the International Regulatory Agreement on Risk-based Capital." In: R.P. Chang and S. G. Rhee, eds., *Pacific Basin Capital Markets Research*, Vol. 2. Amsterdam: Elsevier. 1991, pp. 3–21.

Kane, Edward J. "How Market Forces Influence the Structure of Financial Regulation." In: W. Haraf and R. M. Kushmeider eds., *Restructuring Banking and Financial Services in America*. Washington, DC: American Enterprise Institute for Public Policy Research. 1988.

Kaufman, George G. "Banking Risk in Historical Perspective." Proceedings of a Conference on Bank Structure and Competition, Federal Reserve Bank of Chicago, May 1986.

Kaufman, George G. "Bank Contagion: A Review of the Theory and Evidence." Journal of Financial Services Research 8 (2) (April 1994).

Knight, Frank H. *Risk, Uncertainty, and Profit*. Chicago: University of Chicago Press. 1971 (1921).

Mengle, David L. "Behind the Money Market: Clearing and Settling Money Market Instruments." *Economic Review* (Federal Reserve Bank of Richmond) (September/October 1992).

Mengle, David L. "Legal and Regulatory Reform in Electronic Payments: An Evaluation of Payment Finality Rules." In: David B. Humphrey, ed., *The U.S. Payment System: Efficiency, Risk and the Role of the Federal Reserve* (Proceedings of a Symposium on the U.S. Payments System Sponsored by the Federal Reserve Bank of Richmond). Boston: Kluwer Academic Publishers. 1990.

Saunders, Anthony, and Steven Wilson. "Contagious Bank Runs: Evidence from the 1929–1933 Period." Stern School of Business, New York University, March 1993.

Smith, Randall, and Steven Lipin. "Beleaguered Giant: As Derivatives Losses Rise, Industry Fights to Avert Regulation." *Wall Street Journal*, Thursday, August 25, 1994.

Summers, Bruce J. "Clearing and Payments Systems: The Role of the Central Bank." Federal Reserve *Bulletin* (February 1991).

G-28 U.S.
G-24
G-10

15 7- 68

Journal of Financial Services Research 9: 351–362 (1995)
© 1995 Kluwer Academic Publishers

Derivatives and Stock Market Volatility: Is Additional Government Regulation Necessary?

SEHA M. TINIÇ
Koc University, Istinye 80860, Istanbul, Turkey

Financial institutions and markets occupy a pivotal position in the economy through their role in allocating funds and as the core of the payment systems. Moreover, financial intermediaries are in a unique position of trust in managing funds belonging to the general public. These considerations have led governments to legislate a plethora of regulations that are designed to enhance or maintain public confidence in financial markets. To a large degree, this regulatory emphasis reflects the worry that failure of financial intermediaries and chaotic episodes in securities markets can impair public confidence in the financial system, which may lead to a massive withdrawal of funds from financial intermediaries. Obviously, such a crisis would cause a serious breakdown of the financial system in which not only investors would lose, but the entire economy would suffer. However, government regulation of the securities markets also reflects the concern for the protection of investors whose savings are invested either directly in the securities markets or entrusted to profesionally managed financial intermediaries.

To promote public confidence in the securities markets, the governments have instituted far-reaching regulations that affect both the structure of the financial services industry and the conduct of financial transations. Briefly, governments have promulgated extensive regulations that (1) mandate disclosure of information, (2) discourage trading on privileged information, (3) restrict the scope of financial transactions which different types of financial institutions can pursue, (4) specify capital requirements, (5) prescribe standards of prudence and business conduct, (6) guide the rules for operation of organized securities exchanges and the over-the-counter markets, and facilitate governmental supervision of the same.

Although some of the regulations that deal with the securities markets and various financial institutions have been modified, abandoned, or totally revamped over the course of 60 years, most regulations that are presently in effect in the U.S. were enacted as a reaction to the alleged fraudulent activities and the market failure associated with the stock market crash of 1929 and the banking crises of 1930–1932. Similarly, the 1987 stock market crash and the financial demise of a large number of savings and loan institutions in late 1980s and early 1990s refueled the interest in increased public regulation of financial intermediaries, margin requirements, and trading procedures.

More recently, concerns about possible adverse consequences of the rapidly growing use of over-the-counter, customized derivative securities on the stability of financial markets have initiated calls for additional regulations that are specifically tailored for dealers

and end-users of derivative securities.[1] While investor protection and solvency of financial institutions are paramount concerns underlying public regulation of securities markets, it is also evident that the regulatory framework is to a considerable extent based on
the premise that unregulated securities markets are fragile and prone to inefficiencies
and systemic crises. The literature abounds with theoretical arguments and lively academic exchanges about the role of public regulation in improving the operational and
informational efficiency of the securities market. However, empirical analyses of the data
could identify only minor differences in the behavior of securities prices before and after
the advent of public regulation in the U.S.[2]

The purpose of this article is not to review these studies. Instead, I examine two
intertwined issues that have important ramifications for formulating the nature and
extent of regulatory intervention in the securities market. The first issue deals with the
fragility of the securities markets. Are unregulated markets inherently prone to systemic
crises, and does growing use of derivative securities increase the risk of a serious crisis in
the securities markets? The second deals with the availability of nonregulatory (private)
arrangements that enhance the efficiency of the securities markets and control the systemic risk in the industry.

1. Volatility of securities markets

Over the past 30 years, we have accumulated voluminous evidence that shows that
unanticipated information material to valuation of securities causes their prices to
change. For example, the sudden appearance of unfavorable news about a firm or the
market as a whole typically induces a precipitous drop in the prices of the securities. This
is what would be expected in a well functioning, rational market. Like those of nonfinancial corporations, fortunes of financial intermediaries that operate in the securities markets are also susceptible to major changes. Indeed, history is replete with securities firms
that have experienced financial distress, reorganization, or bankruptcy. Although they
make interesting news stories in the financial press, the occasional collapse of an individual financial institution and the accompanying losses incurred by its owners, creditors,
and clients are a natural consequence of risk taking and say very little about the fragility
of the securities markets.

Fragility connotes the susceptibility of the securities markets to an industry-wide financial crash, the accompanying liquidity crisis, and their adverse impact on real economic
activity. Although fragility of a market is virtually impossible to measure ex ante, typically,
thin securities markets with high price volatility and low liquidity are likely to be more
fragile. Indeed, many observers of the markets, including regulators, seem to consider
unusually high price volatility as a sign of instability in the securities markets.[3] The
empirical evidence supports this view. Brown, Harlow, and Tinic (1988) show that return
volatilities of common stocks tend to rise around unusually large price innovations. The
return variance on the day preceding an unusually large drop in common stock prices is,
on average, 58 percent greater than the normal daily variance. Similarly, the variance
before a major price rise is, on average, 91 percent larger than its normal level. Nelson

(1989) also shows that volatility of securities prices tends to be exceptionally high during financial crises. Using a simple exponential Auto Regressive Conditional Heteroscedasticity Model, he demonstrates that the high volatility associated with stock market crashes could have been predicted. Nelson's results imply that high volatility is caused by forces that are not unique to a particular time period. Thus, unusually large increases in the volatility of the securities markets may serve as a useful proxy measure of a potential fragility in the securities markets.

Schwert (1989, 1990) presents the longest data series on volatility of U.S. stock returns. His data on the monthly and daily volatility span the 1802–1989 and 1885–1989 periods, respectively. Although the volatility of securities prices changes randomly over time, the data show that, with the exception of the unusually large jumps in volatility associated with the Great Depression, the banking crises of 1932–1933, and the October 19, 1987 crash of the stock market, the level of return volatility in the U.S. stock market has been remarkably stationary. Table 1 summarizes the standard deviation of monthly returns on the U.S. stock market from 1802 to 1993.

As Schwert observes: "The estimates . . . and the plots of volatility . . . show remarkable homogeneity for these series through time. Moreover, the seasonal patterns of monthly and daily stock returns are similar in the nineteenth and twentieth centuries. This is surprising because of the large changes in the U.S. economy over this period, the growth of wealth represented by traded common stocks, and the changes in the market microstructure for stock trading."[4] What is also interesting is the fact that, when the period of the Great Depression is excluded from the data, the volatility of the securities markets in the pre- (1802–1928) and post-regulatory (1933–1987) eras appears virtually identical. Stock market volatility measured with daily returns leads to the same conclusion. Thus, if one is willing to accept volatility as a proxy for the potential fragility of the securities markets, there is no compelling evidence that the public regulation of the securities markets in the U.S. had made the market less fragile.

Table 1. Standard Deviation of Monthly Stock Returns in the U.S. (1802–1993)

Time Period	Standard Deviation
1802–1820	0.0152
1821–1840	0.0276
1841–1860	0.0479
1861–1880	0.0414
1881–1900	0.0458
1901–1920	0.0414
1921–1940	0.0797
1941–1960	0.0364
1961–1980	0.0433
1981–1987	0.0500
1987–1993*	0.0448

Source: Schwert (1990, pp. 416–417).
*Standard deviation of the Center for Research in Security Prices (CRSP) value-weighted index of New York Stock Exchange stocks.

How about the impact of derivative securities on the volatility of the stock market? Did the advent of exchange traded stock and index options and index futures contribute to an increase in the volatility of the securities markets? There is quite a large body of empirical research that has addressed these questions. For example, Skinner's (1989) results show that the volatility of individual stock returns experienced a small but detectable decrease after commencement of options trading on the stocks. Edwards (1988) has documented the fact that the advent of futures and options contracts on stock indices did not increase the volatility of stock returns except on the futures' expiration days. On futures' expiration days, volatility increased for a short time period towards the end of the trading day. Similar findings were reported by Stoll and Whaley (1987). Broad, Goodhart, and Sutcliffe (1992) also found that the advent of futures trading did not increase the volatility of the spot market in London. Taken as a whole, the available empirical evidence does not support the proposition that exchange-traded, derivative securities contribute to higher volatility in the securities markets.

On the contrary, as Smith, Smithson, and Wilford (1990) document, the advent of trading in derivative securities and major innovations in financial instruments were spawned as a response to increased uncertainty (volatility) in financial markets. To illustrate, figure 1 presents the monthly percentage changes in the German mark/U.S. dollar exchange rates from 1960 to August 1994. Although not reported here, the U.S. dollar/Japanese yen exchange rate exhibits a similar pattern. After the breakdown of the fixed exchange-rate system of Bretton Woods, the volatility of the foreign exchange markets increased dramatically. Futures contracts in foreign exchange began trading soon thereafter in 1972 as a response to increased uncertainty in the foreign exchange markets. Similarly, the explosion in the volatility of U.S. interest rates in 1979 stimulated trading in options on treasury securities and on treasury futures in 1982, as a vehicle for managing interest rate risk. The evidence clearly indicates that the impetus for derivative securities and the rapid growth of OTC-traded, complex derivative contracts was provided by the enormous increase in volatility of foreign exchange, interest rates, and commodity prices. On the other hand, there is no compelling evidence that the growth of trading in derivative securities by itself has contributed to higher volatility in the securities markets.

Nevertheless, computerized portfolio trading strategies that are based on taking simultaneous positions in stocks, options, or futures contracts quickly became a principal suspect as a potential culprit in inducing the stock market crash in October 1987. However, in an interesting study, Roll (1988, 1989) compared the severity of the crash in 23 major stock markets of the world and concluded that computerized trading based on derivative securities could not have been the principal (or even a major) driving force in causing the crash. Stock markets in 13 countries where either computer-directed trading or options and/or futures contracts were available experienced an average return of -26.65 percent in October 1987. The average return of ten stock markets that neither had derivatives trading nor computerized order transmission systems was -26.18 percent. By comparison, the U.S. stock market, which probably experienced the largest volume of derivatives and computer-based trading, dropped by 21.6 percent. Roll's results cast serious doubt upon the importance of the role played by derivatives-based trading in the market crash of 1987.[5]

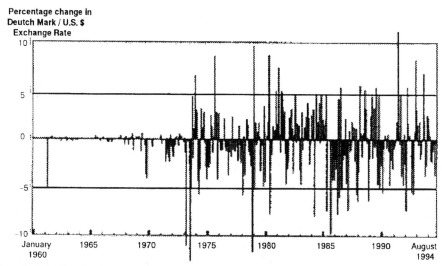

Figure 1. Volatility of exchange rates.
(Source: *Business Week*, October 3, 1994, p. 48)

What is also interesting is the fact that there were significant differences in the organization, margin requirements, trading systems, and regulatory structures of these markets. None of the institutional features of the markets that Roll examined, however, could explain the differences in the severity of the crash across these 23 countries. Roll's analysis did not uncover a statistically significant relationship between the magnitude of the October 1987 returns and the specific institutional features of the markets, after controlling for the sensitivities of the 23 countries' stock markets to the random movements in the world stock index. Markets where trading was organized as a continuous auction system seemed to perform marginally worse than others.

The results of volatility analyses and numerous examinations of the data on stock, futures, and options contracts around the October 1987 crash did not produce persuasive evidence that exchange-traded, derivative securities was the cause of the crash in the securities markets. However, the present concern about growing use of derivative securities is focused on the fast evolving over-the-counter market for customized contracts. Currency and interest rate swaps and derivatives constitute the bulk of the derivative products traded in the over-the-counter markets.[6] In its recent report, *Financial Derivatives*, the U.S. General Accounting Office (GAO) warned that derivatives pose a serious risk to the financial system and called for increased regulatory measures to supervise the derivative dealers—securities firms, insurance companies, and banks—to reduce the probability that the U.S. government would have to step in and bail out these institutions in the case of a serious market breakdown. The report claims that over-the-counter derivatives contribute to higher systemic risk in the financial markets. That is, financial difficulties or failure of a large dealer or problems in a segment of the derivatives market may produce serious liquidity disruptions in the industry or the financial markets as a whole.

Needless to say, systemic risk is not peculiar to derivative securities. It is inherent in many sectors of the financial system. What is special about the over-the-counter market for derivative securities that kindles this concern about systemic risk? Although the GAO report and other studies identify several features of the off-exchange derivatives markets that allegedly make these markets more susceptible to a systemic crisis than other segments of the securities markets, in reality, the primary reasons behind regulators' concerns appear to be (1) the rapidly growing size of the market, (2) the complexity of some of the derivative contracts that are being custom tailored in the market, and (3) the absence of specialized regulatory supervision over the activities of OTC derivative dealers.

The size of the derivatives market is measured by the aggregate notional principal of the contracts outstanding. While most observers of the securities markets recognize that the notional values of such OTC derivatives contracts as foreign exchange and interest rate swaps grossly exaggerate the magnitudes of risk exposure that exist in the market, the scenarios for major systemic crises are often based on the notional principals of contracts outstanding.[7] Unlike bank loans or ordinary bonds, notional amounts do not constitute an obligation. They are used to determine the magnitudes of the periodic cash flows of the derivatives contracts. For example, when one of the parties to a swap contract fails to meet its cash flow obligation, the loss to the counterparty is limited to the replacement cost of the contract (or its market value).

Replacement costs of the contracts constitute only a very small fraction of their notional amounts. To wit, while in June 1994 the notional amount of interest rate and foreign-currency swap contracts outstanding was $13.9 trillion, the replacement cost exposure in counterparty default was $15.5 billion, or 0.11 percent of the notional principal. Of these contracts $24.3 million were in default and the total replacement value of the delinquent contracts was $8.7 million.[8] It is particularly important to note that these data pertain to a time period when interest rates and foreign exchange rates were highly volatile.

Even if the magnitudes of the risk exposure are large enough to cause financial distress for some individual derivatives dealers, they do not appear to be large enough to fuel a serious systemic crisis in the securities markets. In fact, the survey results presented by the GAO confirm this view. The data show that 14 major derivatives dealers in the U.S. experienced a total loss of $250 million as a result of counterparty defaults on derivative securities in 1992, without a detectable influence on the securities markets as a whole.[9]

Many of the customized derivative contracts are indeed complex securities, because they are created to manage multidimensional risks. It is also true that unlike the prices of standardized contracts that trade on organized exchanges, market values of customized securities are not observable. They are priced according to sophisticated theoretical financial models, which rely heavily on the ability to decompose complex contracts into such simpler components as options, futures, forwards, etc., for which the information necessary for valuation is widely available in the prices observed in the organized securities markets. In fact, as pointed out in the report prepared by the Group of Thirty (1993), derivatives dealers manage the market risks associated with complex securities either by matching their positions or by constructing hedges between their individual components and traded options, futures, or forward contracts.

Moreover, most major derivatives dealers report that they mark their portfolios to market daily (in some cases, in real time) and have instituted well-defined limits on their exposures to market risk. Availability of a large variety of traded derivative securities also enables dealers to provide liquidity to esoteric securities for which the component risks can be hedged. Needless to say, the liquidity of the derivatives market could be challenged by a major random shock to the financial system if many major dealers were caught using the same dynamic hedging strategies. However, instead of channeling the disturbance into a small number of contracts, availability of a large variety of derivatives securities may help in diffusing the liquidity demand created by the shock across different segments of the securities markets.

The third reason behind the concern about the over-the-counter derivatives markets rests on the premise that the institutions functioning in this market are subject to minimal regulation.[10] While it is true that some financial institutions, such as the affiliates of insurance companies that participate in the derivatives markets, may not be subject to the same degree of regulatory oversight as other participants, commercial banks and securities firms, which account for the largest share of the derivatives market, are in fact regulated. More importantly, there is no compelling evidence that shows that public regulation actually reduces the risk of a systemic crisis in the securities markets. Preoccupation with regulatory solutions to potential crises in the securities markets stems to an important degree from the beliefs that during the past decade financial innovation has outpaced regulatory changes and that private initiatives in the market do not provide sufficient safeguards for sound and efficient functioning of the system.

2. Private sector arrangements

For purposes of maintaining public confidence in the securities markets and to prevent disruptions in the financial system, public regulations of the markets have emphasized information disclosure, fairness, transparency, and investor protection. Far too often, however, these goals are pursued without regard to the costs imposed on firms and investors. Moreover, the adverse consequences of regulation on competition, innovation, and efficiency do not receive adequate consideration. The dramatic rise of institutional investors, advances in computer and communications technologies, increased mobility of funds across national boundaries, and globalization of capital markets and financial innovation pose serious challenges to regulations that were designed to protect the interests of small individual investors.

In light of these changes, many observers argue that government regulations should incorporate and foster private market mechanisms (including self-regulatory initiatives by the securities industry) to achieve the desired public-policy objectives to the maximum extent possible. However, one can question whether there are general conditions under which private sector arrangements might not be sufficient to control systemic risk in the securities markets? Clearly, if there is a "contagion effect" among financial intermediaries, the risk of a systemic crisis would be high, and this risk is magnified if the intermediaries are highly leveraged, have inadequate internal risk-management systems, carry unhedged positions, or use the same dynamic hedging techniques. Under such conditions, it may be foolhardy to rely primarily on nonregulatory arrangements to curb systemic risk, particularly if the market lacks transparency. But it is highly questionable that these conditions actually characterize the securities markets.

Public confidence in the soundness and efficiency of the markets is in the best long-run interest of corporations, securities firms, exchanges, and the OTC market. It is important to keep in mind that technological advances have enlarged the variety of trading venues and increased the level of competition among securities markets around the globe. Self-regulatory organizations like the National Association of Securities Dealers (NASD) and the International Swaps and Derivatives Association (ISDA), securities exchanges, and other participants in the securities markets have strong economic incentives to innovate and devise private mechanisms that enhance the financial soundness and efficiency of their operations. Private market solutions to many thorny issues that confront securities regulators have two very important advantages: first, private market solutions are more likely to balance private costs and benefits; second, they would be quicker to respond to changes in the competitive environment.

There are numerous examples of how securities markets generate private solutions through market forces and self-regulatory organizations, without any governmental compulsion. To illustrate a few, I briefly discuss (1) information disclosure, (2) market transparency, and (3) management of default risk in securities transactions.

1. *Disclosure.* Corporations that depend on the securities markets to raise debt and equity capital have a natural incentive to disclose information which has value to investors in excess of the marginal cost of producing and disseminating that information. Firms compete for investors' funds in the market, and those firms that disclose information useful for assessing the prospective risks and rewards to be gained from holding the securities stand to benefit from higher prices for their securities. Higher security prices, of course, translate into a cheaper cost of capital for the disclosing firms. In fact, long before the advent of mandated disclosure requirements, numerous publicly traded corporations voluntarily disclosed financial information.[11]

Recent evidence on Rule-144A, private placements confirms that disclosure has economic value to firms issuing securities. Smith and Armstrong (1992) report that private placements of equity by firms that have publicly traded common stock outstanding are sold at an average discount of 20 percent relative to the public market price after the issue. Since the discounts associated with Rule-144A offerings are observed for both restricted shares and shares registered at or shortly after the date of issue, they cannot be attributed solely to the illiquidity of the shares. Instead, the discounts appear to be a compensation required for the expected information costs that would be incurred by investors to determine the value of the securities. It is also reported that the discounts on Rule-144A securities that are rated by private rating agencies have all but disappeared. This evidence is consistent with the claim that firms would garner a measurable economic benefit from disclosing credible information to investors, which they would disclose unless the costs (including the cost of informing competitors) exceeded the expected benefits.

In the event that some firms misjudge the economic calculus of disclosing information demanded by investors, there would be opportunities for private organizations to specialize in production of financial information for sale on an exclusionary basis. The fact that myriad private information services, market letters, financial publications, and non-brokerage investment research firms have survived and prospered in the securities markets suggests that financial information which has value is likely to be produced without mandated disclosure.

Beyond these, securities exchanges also have an economic incentive to require disclosure from firms whose securities they list and trade. Securities exchanges are essentially firms that are competing for business. To the extent that disclosure of financial information by the listed corporations contributes to the overall economic welfare of the exchange, it will be required as a condition for listing. Indeed, the New York Stock Exchange had instituted disclosure requirements for listed firms long before disclosure was mandated by public regulation of the securities markets in the U.S. in 1934.

2. *Market transparency*. Transparency refers to the degree of informativeness of a securities market. In a perfectly transparent market, all relevant information about transaction prices, order sizes and flows, trading volume, identity of the traders, all bids and asks, etc., are transmitted instantaneously in real time, and the customers of securities firms would have information about the financial conditions of the intermediaries with whom they are likely to deal. It is true that transparent markets facilitate greater competition and monitoring. However, in a world where information has costs, perfect transparency is unattainable. Moreover, some investors and dealers exhibit a strong preference for anonymity, and efforts to enforce full transparency in a market may force those investors to take their trades to other markets where they can maintain their anonymity. In fact, in some cases, full transparency may have adverse consequences for the liquidity of the market. For example, in the London Stock Exchange, transaction prices and information on trading volume is purposely released with a considerable time lag. The rationale for this intended opaqueness is to enhance the liquidity of the market. The London Stock Exchange is a dealer market where competing jobbers supply liquidity to the securities by standing ready to trade as principals and taking large positions. The willingness of the dealers to take large positions diminishes considerably if they are not given an opportunity to unwind these inventories before information about their transactions is revealed to the market. That is, greater transparency in the case of London may end up reducing the liquidity of the market. Thus, the level of transparency which a securities market has to provide must be a private decision that boils down to delicately balancing the benefits of facilitating rapid price discovery and the costs associated with migration of some transactions to other venues and the resulting fragmentation in trading and possible reduction in liquidity.

When markets with different levels of transparency compete for the same business, serious problems of externalities arise. For example, the price discovery facilitated by the transparency of the NYSE may be exploited by less transparent exchanges and off-exchange proprietary trading systems for attracting investors who value opaqueness. In other words, other markets may free ride off the costly information produced by the transparent market. Even these externality problems are more likely to be resolved through private arrangements and contracting. For example, the NYSE's decision to organize one of its after-hours trading sessions as deliberately more opaque for large traders is viewed as a response to the loss of order flow to the third market and the London Stock Exchange. Similarly, the Exchange's Rule 390, which prevents NYSE member firms from consummating transactions in listed stocks in the over-the-counter market or on foreign exchanges during the NYSE's trading hours is intended to mitigate the free-rider problems associated with transparency.

3. *Management of default risk.* A clearinghouse serves as an effective insurance mechanism against random idiosyncratic defaults on securities exchanges. In the over-the-counter derivatives market, there is no such arrangement. Absence of a clearinghouse and the associated prudential regulation appears to be a major source of concern for the regulators. However, the over-the-counter market for derivative securities has developed alternative safeguards against default risk. Instead of the certification provided by the clearinghouse system, the market relies on the credit quality of the dealers who are monitored by credit-rating agencies. Virtually all major institutions in the derivatives business carry AAA ratings. The demand for the highest credit rating is so strong that firms with lower ratings have been forced to organize well capitalized subsidiaries to raise their ratings to the top bracket.[12]

Of course, credit ratings do not fully protect against systemic risk. But neither can the clearinghouse system. In general, insurance arrangements are not able to cope completely with systemic crises. The clearinghouse system was severely strained in October 1987, and, without the liquidity provided by the Federal Reserve, it may not have been able to withstand the crisis.

In addition, dealers have instituted a variety of other safeguards that reduce their exposures to default risk. Dealers typically limit their transactions with individual counterparties to relatively small fractions of their overall derivatives business. That is, they diversify credit risk. The data contained in the GAO Report also show that over 97 percent of the swap contracts outstanding were consummated with counterparties that had at least an investment-grade credit rating. Lower quality counterparties to swap transactions were typically required to provide collateral and mark it to market. Bilateral netting arrangements are also frequently used to offset losses on a defaulting contract with gains that may have accrued from other outstanding derivatives contracts with the defaulting party.

Despite the high volatility of interest rates and foreign exchange rates in recent years, the institutional structure and the private arrangements that were in place in the over-the-counter market for derivative securities did not experience any serious system-wide strains.

3. Conclusions

An examination of the evidence shows that the volatility of the securities markets has not changed significantly over long periods of time. The advent of public regulation of the markets did not have a material impact on the fragility of the securities markets. Random systemic crises have occurred both before and after the securities regulations. It seems that the resilience of the market is to a large degree based on natural competitive forces and a variety of private institutional arrangements that foster stability and encourage efficiency.

The evidence also does not support the proposition that financial innovation in derivative securities has increased the volatility of the securities markets. Although a systemic crisis caused by a random shock to the financial system can never be totally ruled out, there is no indication that the markets are more susceptible to crises now than they were before the growth of institutional investors, globalization, and the rapid financial innovation of the past decade.

To be sure, to the extent that derivative securities facilitate increased leverage, heavy use (misuse!) of derivative instruments may increase the probability of financial distress for individual end-users and/or derivative dealers. But for a systemic crisis to develop, bankruptcy of one or more firms would have to induce equally serious financial distress for other firms in the securities markets. However, as Miller (1990) noted in his Nobel Memorial Prize lecture: "Neither economics generally nor finance in particular . . . offers much support for [the] notion of a leverage-induced 'bankruptcy multiplier' or a contagion effect."[13]

Notes

1. See United States General Accounting Office (GAO), *Financial Derivatives: Actions Needed to Protect the Financial System*, May 1994.
2. See e.g., Benston (1973) and Simon (1989).
3. See e.g., Nelson (1989) and Schwert (1990).
4. Schwert (1990) pp. 423–424.
5. King and Wadhwani (1988) claim that pricing errors in one market can be transmitted to other markets if investors in one market rationally view price changes in another market as "news" that can only be observed in the foreign market. Roll does not rule out the international "contagion effect" as a possible explanation for the crash. However, he raises serious questions about the original source of the pricing error and the time sequence of the price declines in different stock markets. King and Wadhwani claim that trading induced by portfolio insurance in the U.S. was not the source of pricing error.
6. GAO (1994), p. 35.
7. See e.g., *Wall Street Journal*, May 19, 1994, p. 9.
8. *Veribanc News Release*, June 27, 1994.
9. GAO (1994), p. 55.
10. See e.g., GAO (1994), p. 87.
11. Benston (1973), p. 133.
12. GAO (1994), p. 59.
13. Miller (1990), p. 485.

References

Bank of England. *Derivatives: Report of an Internal Working Group*. London. April 1993.
Benston, G. "Required Disclosure and the Stock Market: An Evaluation of the Securities Exchange Act of 1934." *American Economic Review* 63 (March 1973) 132–155.
Broad, J., Charles Goodhart, and Charles Sutcliffe. "Inter-Market Volatility Linkages: The London Stock Exchange and London International Financial Futures Exchange." Working paper, London School of Economics, 1992.
Brown, K.C., W. Van Harlow, and Seha M. Tinic. "Risk Aversion, Uncertain Information, and Market Efficiency." *Journal of Financial Economics* 22 (December 1988) 355–385.

Edwards, F. R. "Does Futures Trading Increase Stock Volatility?" *Financial Analysts' Journal* 44 (January/February 1988), 63–69.

Flood, R.P. and Robert J. Hodrick, "On Testing Speculative Bubbles," *Journal of Economic Perspectives*, 4 Spring 1990, 85–101.

Group of Thirty. *Derivatives Practices and Principles*. Washington, D.C. July 1993.

King, Mervyn, and Sushil Wadhwani. "Transmission of Volatility Between Stock Markets." Discussion paper, London School of Economics, 1988.

Magnusson, Paul. "The IMF Should Look Forward, Not Back." *Business Week*, October 3, 1994 p. 48.

Miller, Merton H. "Leverage." *Journal of Finance* 46 (June 1991) 479–488.

Nelson, D. B. "Commentary: Price Volatility, International Market Links, and their Implications for Regulatory Policies." *Journal of Financial Services Research* 3 (1989) 247–254.

Recent Developments in International Interbank Relations. Report Prepared by a Working Group of the Central Banks of the Group of Ten Countries BIS, Basle, Switzerland, October 1992.

Roll, R. "The International Crash of October 1987." *Financial Analysts' Journal* 44 (September 1988), 19–35.

Roll, R. "Price Volatility, International Market Links, and Their Implications for Regulatory Policies." *Journal of Financial Services Research* 3 (1989) 113–148.

Schwert, G. W. "Stock Market Volatility." Working paper, New York Stock Exchange, December 1989.

Schwert, G. W. "Indexes of U.S. Stock Prices from 1802 to 1987." *Journal of Business* 63 (July 1990) 399–426.

Shiller, R.J., *Market Volatility*, Cambridge, Massachusetts: MIT Press, 1989.

Simon, C. J. "The Effects of the 1933 Securities Act on Investor Information and the Performance of New Issues." *American Economic Review* 79 (June 1989), 295–318.

Skinner, D.J. "Options Markets and Stock Return Volatility." *Journal of Financial Economics* 23 (June 1989), 61–78.

Smith, C.W., Jr., C.W. Smithson, and D.S. Wilford. *Managing Financial Risk*. New York: Harper & Row, Publishers. 1990.

Smith, R.L., and Vaugn S. Armstrong. "Misperceptions About Private Placement Discounts: Why Market Reaction to Rule 144A Has Been Lukewarm." In: K. Lehn and R. Kamphuis, eds., *Modernizing U.S. Securities Regulation: Economic and Legal Perspectives*. Pittsburgh, PA: Joseph M. Katz Graduate School of Business, University of Pittsburgh, December 1992, pp. 153–170.

Stoll, H. and R.E. Whaley. "Program Trading and Expiration-day Effects." *Financial Analysts' Journal* 43 (March/April 1987), 16–28.

Sylla, W. "Financial Market Panics and Volatility in the Long Run, 1830–1988." In: E.N. White, ed., *Crises and Panics: The Lessons of History*. Homewood, IL: Dow Jones Irwin. 1990.

U.S. General Accounting Office. *Financial Derivatives: Actions Needed to Protect the Financial System*. Washington, DC. May 1994.

"U.S. Report Issues Warning on Derivatives." *Wall Street Journal*, May 19, 1994, p. 19.

Veribanc News Release, June 27, 1994.

Journal of Financial Services Research 9: 363–368 (1995)
© 1995 Kluwer Academic Publishers

Global Financial Fragility and the Private Sector

CHARLES R. TAYLOR
Executive Director, The Group of Thirty, 1990 M Street, N.W., Washington, D.C. 20036

1. Introduction

We do not, in any real sense, have an integrated, truly global financial system. There are many financial institutions in the industrial countries, such as the majority of S&Ls in the United States, whose involvement with the global economy is minimal and indirect. There are countries, many in the developing world, for example, which have no indigenous international institutions of any global systemic significance, even though some of their local institutions are very large in terms of deposits or assets or some other measure. What is true, however, is that the dividing line between global and national (or regional) financial institutions has grown more vague and there are many more institutions that have some kind of international presence, or involvement, than in the past.

If there is this grayness about the edges of what is the global financial system, there is little doubt about what kind of firms lie at its core. These are the major wholesale financial institutions, numbering perhaps two or three dozen, which are active in all the major financial centers of the world and in all major markets and activities. They are, from the global point of view, the only systemically signficant institutions. They include investment banks and securities houses as well as commercial banks. It is they, and only they, with which we should be concerned, if we are considering the subject of global financial fragility and the role of the private sector in containing it.

This exclusion of many more local or smaller institutions may not strike some as legitimate. After all, it was Herstatt (Berry, 1991), a relatively small provincial German bank that brought the foreign exchange markets and the many larger firms who dealt with it, to the edge of ruin a mere 20 years ago. But, I would contend, that it was only because these larger firms were so threatened that we had the makings of a global systemic crisis in 1974. In addition, I believe that it was sloppy management of settlement and counterparty risk concentration on the part of those larger banks which was as much responsible for the crisis as the collapse of Herstatt itself. Today, with much better standards of risk management in the globally significant core firms, I believe that the chances of a major crisis developing outside the core and creating a systemic threat are, in fact, very small. We, therefore, should concentrate on the core firms and the way in which they interact to discern what types of financial fragility the international financial system may face as it approaches the 21st century.

First, however, we should pause in our consideration of the core firms to reflect for a moment on what we mean by "financial fragility" itself.

2. Global financial fragility defined

No long ago, we might have thought of financial fragility as market volatility. The Bretton Woods system of fixed but adjustable exchange rates ended, not as a result of any financial institutional failure as such, but because of the pressures of exchange rates to change by what today look like ludicrously small amounts. That system proved to be decidedly fragile. But today we have developed considerable tolerance for volatility, not just of exchange rates but also of most other financial-asset prices. At least in international financial markets, the range of hedging instruments now available to both financial and nonfinancial firms alike makes it relatively easy for them to manage in such a volatile environment. Market volatility is not associated in a one-to-one correspondence with financial fragility any more.

Nevertheless, extreme market volatility may still be associated with financial fragility at the global level. Presumably, a large move in any major price or index, especially if it was correlated with large movements in other markets, might cause the collapse of some systemically significant core institution or market; or, the failure of such an institution might precipitate changes in market prices that were large by historic standards. But we should note that even the very large price movements in recent times have not had that effect: the movements in exchange rates in 1992 and 1993 in the European Exchange Rate Mechanism exceeded six times the standard deviation of past volatility; and the crash of 1987 saw the market capitalization of the world's stock markets fall by 20 percent in less than a day without the collapse of a single systemically significant firm.

There are, of course, problems that may flow from market turbulence, even of a nonsystemically threatening scale, such as some inefficiency in price signalling. But, markets can be quite inefficient without being fragile in the sense of market arrangements breaking down.

This leads toward the idea that financial fragility on the global level is not very usefully thought about, in the first instance, in terms of market volatility, but can best be defined as the collapse of one or more systemically significant core firms in such a way as to shake confidence in the financial system as a whole. A firm can collapse without a systemic threat if the collapse is contained by the market, by the authorities, and by the counterparties of the firm in question. But there cannot be a systemic collapse without the collapse of at least one core firm.

3. Coping with global financial fragility

Thus, there are two lines of defense against global financial fragility, namely, the internal defenses of the individual core firms, and, where that fails, the prevention of contagion from one firm to another.

3.1. Internal defense: risk management

In the past 20 years, the core firms have begun to look upon the risks which they face as the subject of a separate discipline within financial management. This risk-management discipline has grown and developed at different speeds in different countries and within different functions inside financial institutions. To some extent, the investment and security houses were in the forefront of managing market risk—the risks of volatility in asset and liability values, with which they are traditionally more familiar. The related risk of illiquidity is also something that they, without de jure access to central-bank discount facilities to manage liquidity in extremis, may also have had the lead. In addition, the commercial banks, which traditionally dealt with credit risk, made the greatest headway in systematizing their understanding, measurement, and management of credit risk and related payments risks. But, in recent years, these two traditions within risk management have begun to coalesce, especially in the area of derivatives dealing (Corrigan, 1994).

The reason for this is not difficult to see. In the absence of a market, many over-the-counter derivatives can only be valued by taking volatility directly into account. Market as well as credit risk is inherently important in most derivative transactions. Moreover, these risks change over the life of a derivatives transaction, so that some sophistication is required to manage them. Concern over these risks[1] led senior management in most derivatives-dealing firms to require that methods of risk management and analysis be developed alongside the phenomenal growth in the trading of these instruments (The Institute of International Finance, Inc., 1993). When it comes to risk management, the need, and the ability, was greatest in the area of over-the-counter derivatives (Corrigan, 1994; U.S. House of Representatives Banking Committee, 1993).

One parenthetic insight which I can offer is that very few losses in the past have in fact been the result of over-the-counter derivatives trading, despite what the papers have to say. Earnings from over-the-counter derivatives trading—meaning swaps and options in currencies, interest rates, equities, and commodities, and combinations of these—have been among the steadiest as well as the highest for most derivatives dealers. The majority of the publicly cited losses of the past 12 months that have been attributed to derivatives have been associated with mortgage-backed securities and other securitized instruments that are traded out of bond desks. These desks have a tradition of thinking in terms of short-term risks and returns, and generally lack the sophistication of the over-the-counter derivatives desk. They often seem to have taken on risks without fully appreciating their extent, and they seem to have sold risks to end-users without fully appreciating how unsuitable the instruments in question might be.

What is required here would seem to be a transfusion into other trading areas of the kind of risk management and product understanding developed in the over-the-counter activity. In fact, it also seems to be the case that, at many derivatives dealers, the art of risk management is seeping out from the derivatives area. In banks, I expect that it will in time move out to the nontrading, traditional banking activities where, for example, considerable market risks are sometimes still taken with very little idea of their scale. How many mortgage departments, for example, stop to price their loans for the risks inherent in the option feature of a traditional household mortgage? To end this parenthetic observation, I think we are close to seeing derivatives as part of the solution rather than the problem, not only because of their usefulness in managing financial risk, but also because of the rigor which they bring to the art of risk management.

This is not the place to attempt a definitive taxonomy of the risk that financial institutions face. The taxonomy used in the Group of Thirty study "Derivatives: Practices and Principles," which divides financial risks into market, credit, legal, and systems risk, suffices fairly well—provided market risks are assumed to include liquidity risks (including clearance and settlement risks), and credit risks to include concentration and political risks.

To varying degrees, these different types of risk are amenable to mathematical analysis, albeit with the assumptions regarding the parameters of the probability distributions and the covariances between them still being subject to a good deal of judgement. Increasingly, too, firms are allocating their capital to their businesses in accordance with more precise measures of the risks involved, which means more accurate pricing of risk, to ensure a decent return across activities, and a greater sufficiency of capital against more risky activities, which should redound to the strength of the institution and, ultimately, to the system itself.

However, there are some risks that still seem to be very difficult to analyze and anticipate properly, namely, some types of settlement risk; the risk that covariances change, either because of drift through time, or in a sudden fashion in stress situations; and the risk of correlation through time in abnormal market conditions, that is, that bad times persist.

In addition, in the dynamic of the process of increasing refinement in the measurement of risk and allocation of capital against it, there is one cause for systemic concern. And that is that competitive conditions may eventually lead all systemically significant core firms to operate without any margin of safety so far as capital is concerned. In principle, this is handled by carefully examining a wide range of stress scenarios (McDonough, 1994) and ensuring that there is enough capital to handle them all. But, in practice, the design and use of stress scenarios is one of the weaker areas of risk management, even in the more sophisticated firms.

3.1. External defenses

At the beginning, I stated that there were two lines of defence against global financial fragility; they are the internal defensive systems of the core firms; and, where that fails, the prevention of contagion from one firm to another. On that second score, disclosure plays a key role (McDonough, 1994), because it is only when there is adequate disclosure that counterparties can make well-founded judgements about the risks of doing business with a particular firm.

This is an area in which many regulators are pushing for improvements in private practice. Some strengthening of regulatory disclosure, especially for credit risk, is in the works in the United States; the Institute for International Finance has just published guidelines for credit-rated-exposures disclosure. And the U.K., U.S., and international accounting authorities are all developing guidelines for credit-exposure disclosure for derivatives, at least in the management section of annual reports (Global Derivatives Study Group, Appendix 2, 1993).

The problems with these disclosures initiatives are, generally, that they are narrow in scope. This comes from their concentration on derivatives instruments and the associated credit risks. Market risks and risks from nonderivatives instruments are not covered, despite the fact that these are as often as not the major sources of loss.

In addition, many of these efforts are guidelines of a exhortatory kind. This seems odd when one stops to think of the private gains and losses associated with disclosure. A firm wants, of course, its counterparties to disclose as much as possible and might well, in principle, prefer to operate in a world where everyone, including itself, is forced to disclose a great deal more information. It may be that they themselves would want to disclose more information anyway, since more complete disclosure should lead to greater confidence (and therefore better terms) from counterparties and the capital markets. But counterparties and markets can be asymmetric in this regard: it is generally true that firms will be penalized for disclosing less than the current norm; but Bank One, for example, was penalized in 1994, for disclosing a good deal more information about its derivatives activities than was typical at that time, because market analysts chose to interpret increased disclosure as evidence of increased emphasis within the bank's operations in an area that the analysts generally (and erroneously) considered risky. Moreover, assuming that the management of banks and other financial institutions can educate their outside stakeholders about the meaning of their increased derivatives disclosures, they still have to weigh the benefits of increasing confidence outside against the loss of discretion that may result in the future. For, once a new kind of disclosure is made, it is very difficult to stop making it, for whatever reason. So exhortation to greater disclosure in this area may at best take a while to work.

Finally, a general shortcoming with current disclosure practice is that it is too infrequent. This is not being addressed by any initiative of which I am aware. If it is possible for a firm to change its risk exposures within a matter of hours, how can counterparties put any faith in annual, or even quarterly reports of activity which are published with a considerable delay? As a matter of some urgency, work needs to proceed on how to develop much more frequent and up-to-date financial information.[2]

Obviously, effective disclosure does not guarantee that crises will be contained. In some circumstances, some might argue that it could contribute to a crisis. However, my impression is that, first, rumors play a far more corrosive role in relation to confidence than facts ever do. In early 1994, for example, Banker's Trust was the subject of a rumor, traced to two young traders in the London markets, that the Bank was in grave difficulty as a result of its overdependence on derivatives activities. The New York Federal Reserve Bank was obliged to go into the market to quell the rumors, pointing to Banker's considerable capital. Moreover, good disclosure should help everyone concerned to anticipate risks better, rather than to be taken by surprise when the extent and force of such risks can no longer be disguised.

4. Conclusion: facing global financial fragility, a private and public responsibility

From a private sector viewpoint, global financial fragility is a concern with relatively few major financial firms. These firms manage their risks increasingly well. This is a source of comfort, but only to a degree. Their increasingly sophisticated methods of risk management and analysis do not absolve management from making judgments about parameters used in their analysis, as well as about those areas of risk that are not subject to mathematical analysis. There are dynamics at work that are not yet fully understood regarding the adequacy of capital in the long term in a competitive environment. In addition, if the marketplace is to encourage better risk management by the core firms, then disclosure has to improve greatly, and it will take time for the development, agreement, and implementation of appropriate standards.

The global financial system seems to have survived recent upheavals well, and there are grounds for cautious optimism regarding the increasing sophistication of risk management in the major firms. But there are no grounds for complacency. Further improvements in risk-management practice are needed at the firm level. But the private sector can only do so much. I strongly suspect that there continues to be a vital role for the public sector in containing financial fragility, but exactly what that role should be and how it should be executed is a subject for another day.

Notes

1. Global Derivatives Study Group, "Derivatives: Practices and Principles, Appendix 3: Survey of Industry Practice," The Group of Thirty, March 1994, p. 9. A representative group of 80 dealers and 72 end-users responded to this survey.
2. Global Derivatives Study Group, "Derivatives: Practices and Principles, Appendix I: Working Papers," The Group of Thirty, July 1993, p. 77. On the basis of the survey, it was concluded that "a majority of dealers are concerned about the inadequate financial reporting of off-balance sheet exposures of counterparties."

References

Berry, John. "Can We Do About The To Doctrine?" *Financier* (April 1991), 6–7.
Corrigan, Gerald. "A Framework for Financial Stability." *Financial Times*, June 3, 1994.
McDonough, William J. "Financial Market Innovations: Practical Concerns." Remarks before the Money Marketers of New York, June 16, 1994.
Global Derivatives Study Group. "Derivatives: Practices and Principles." The Group of Thirty, July 1993; Appendix 1, July 1993, p. 88; Appendix 3, March 1994, p 9.
The Institute of International Finance, Inc. "Banking Law and Regulation Report." The Institute of International Finance, Inc., March 1993, pp. 4–6.
U.S. House of Representatives. *Financial Derivatives, Part I: Market Overview and Supervisory Concerns.* Report prepared by House Banking Committee, Minority Staff, November, 1993, pp. 7–8.

175-86

Journal of Financial Services Research 9: 369–380 (1995)
© 1995 Kluwer Academic Publishers

Banking Regulation as a Solution to Financial Fragility

PAUL M. HORVITZ
*Judge James Elkins Professor of Banking and Finance, University of Houston, Houston, TX, 77204-6282
U.S.A., and member of the Shadow Financial Regulatory Committee*

The purpose of this article is to evaluate the role of government regulation dealing with the risk that fragility of the financial structure may lead to a collapse of the system. Other papers presented at this conference deal with the possible sources of such a collapse—the payments system, international connections, or derivative securities—and with the likelihood that the system is fragile, and the extent to which private solutions may be adequate to deal with the problem.

The Federal Deposit Insurance Act of 1991 (FDICIA) represents a political consensus on the major components of the regulatory framework, which includes federal deposit insurance, a supervisory system which emphasizes capital adequacy, and provides for early intervention to resolve failing banks. Despite this consensus, there are critics of all these elements. A key issue in the debate over the role of government regulation is the extent to which the supervisory authorities should be able to exercise discretionary judgement in handling weakened banks, or should be constrained by explicit rules.

We do not know how fragile the financial system is. Our knowledge of financial fragility is based on a history that covers a very small fraction of the possible states of the world. There has been intensive review of financial instability in the U.S., and much has been learned from that review (Benston et al., 1986; Kaufman, 1994). We now know that irrational, contagious bank runs were not a common occurrence in the U.S., even before federal deposit insurance. We know that it is possible to design a financial system that will be prone to systemic weakness. The National Banking System involved a pyramiding of reserve requirements based on actual currency held by a relatively small number of banks in a few cities. This could lead to periodic stress as seasonal or other pressures on country banks became concentrated on reserve city or central reserve city banks. That system had no central bank or other means of creating additional liquidity in times of need.

This experience demonstrates that financial systems are not inherently stable. Since it is possible to create a system which is fragile, it is a legitimate question to ask whether our present system is fragile. The fact that the system has operated for many years without collapsing does not prove that it is structurally sound.

In fact, the National Banking System, despite its structural weaknesses, operated rather smoothly most of the time. Even when crises arose (as they undeniably did), the bankers were usually able to limit their spread through joint action within local clearing houses, frequently by temporary suspension of payments. Moreover, in these crisis situations, the clearing houses offered a payments device that allowed the economy to continue to function through the period of suspension. And even though the law required that banks maintain their currency reserves at all time, in practice, as Haines (1961, p. 148) pointed out, "some banks did attempt to meet a crisis by reducing reserves below the legal requirements, and in most cases the Comptroller of the Currency tacitly ignored such violations."

Suspension of payments by all members of a clearing house could be viewed as a collapse of the banking system (at least the local banking system). However, modern reviews of this history (Gorton, 1985) tend to treat such suspensions favorably—as a means of limiting the spread of financial panics. Suspension avoided the need for banks to liquidate assets at "fire sale" prices. Such sales could convert a liquidity problem into a solvency problem, and could affect the valuation of similar assets held by other banks. I think that the key to these discussions is that what we really mean by systemic failure, or collapse of the financial system, is a breakdown that spreads to the real sector of the economy (Bernanke and Gertler, 1989). The experience of the 1930s is viewed as an example of systemic collapse, because the real economy also collapsed.[1] Note that we do not have to resolve the debate over causality. That is, regardless of whether financial crises cause nonfinancial businesses to fail, or whether business failures cause bank failures, as Kaufman (1994, p. 142) stresses, "bank failures, for whatever reason, clearly amplify macroeconomic downturns" (cf. also Cagan, 1965; Dwyer and Gilbert, 1989).

There was enough experience with crises under the National Banking Act to conclude that it was a poorly designed system that was fragile. The experience of the 1930s may be viewed as an aberration, but some see the potential for this instability as inherent in the private enterprise financing system (Minsky, 1982). It is plausible to argue that the Federal Reserve learned from the experience of the 1930s, and that could not be repeated, but that argument has not been accepted by Congress, which has mandated additional regulation of the financial system to assure stability.

Since we cannot know whether a robust financial system has been created since the legislation of the 1930s, we must discuss this problem in the context of possibilities, rather than knowledge of the extent of fragility. Even if one is convinced that the legislation of the 1930s, and improved understanding of its responsibilities by the Federal Reserve, preclude a repetition of the experience of the 1930s, it is possible that the stresses on the system are greater now than in the 1930s. Two possible sources of increased stress are discussed in this conference: the greater interconnections among the economies of different countries, and changes in the payments system. The consequences of a real financial collapse—one that spreads to the real economy—are so serious that we must consider the possibility that the financial system is fragile, and attempt to minimize even small probabilities that a shock could trigger a systemic collapse.

This does not mean that all expressed concerns about financial fragility are equally valid, or that any cry of "systemic instability" deserves to be treated seriously. It is appropriate to demand that those who do the crying be able to demonstrate the mechanism by which the shock they fear can cause financial collapse. That is, if someone claims that a failure in the payments system, or an increase in derivatives trading, or a spontaneous run on banks can lead to collapse of the system, they must be able to produce a model in which a systemic problem in the financial system spreads to the real side of the economy, and they must be able to show why that is a reasonable depiction of the real world.

The National Banking Act system involved a very small role for government regulation. Government involvement in and responsibility for the stability of the financial system took great leaps forward (or backward) with the creaton of the Federal Reserve System and the FDIC. Other papers at this conference consider the possibilities for private solutions to the problem of financial fragility. The issue explored in this article is the extent to which government regulation can or should contribute to the solution, and what the form of that regulation should be. The article focuses on the extent to which government policy should be formulated in written rules or should, alternatively, rely on the discretion of the supervisory authorities.

In discussions of this issue there are differences in the views of bankers, regulators, psychologists, theologians, and economists. The economists, like the theologians, seem split between those who believe that the end of the world is coming, and those who believe in a beneficent god who will make sure that all comes out well. The "invisible hand" that most economists believe in is not inconsistent with financial fragility.

Economists do have a strong preference for market solutions, though attitudes differ. The extreme view would be a belief in market efficiency and stability to the extent that we need do nothing more to deal with the potential problem of financial fragility than rely on market forces. Even if that view is rejected, the preference among most economists is for solutions that minimize interference with the market. And, given that some government regulation is necessary, there is a choice between reliance on discretionary actions taken by the supervisory officials and a system of rules that they must follow.

With respect to this latter choice, academic economists often have a preference for limiting the scope of discretionary judgements by the supervisory agencies. Obviously, the regulators feel differently, and have consistently argued for the broadest possible discretion.

As noted above, a major expansion of government regulation occurred following the banking collapse of the 1930s. Later, the Bank Holding Company Act came in the 1950s, and an expansion of regulation of deposit rates in the 1960s. The Bank Holding Company Act Amendment of 1970, which extended restrictions on multibank holding companies to those that controlled only one bank, brought us to the high-water mark of regulation (though perhaps only a local maximum). Regulation began to recede soon after, when the Penn Central crisis led to a removal of rate ceilings on large, negotiable CDs. That was eventually followed by the Depository Institutions Deregulation and Monetary Control Act of 1980 (which some do not view as deregulation, since it imposed reserve requirements for the first time on non-member banks) and the Garn–St Germain Act of 1982.

By the early 1980s it appeared clear that we were moving on the path of deregulation of the financial services industry. There was debate about priorities and what should come first—bank powers to provide additional services (securities, insurance, real estate), branching, interstate banking—but the trend seemed clear. The trend toward eliminating regulation seemed so clear, in fact, that in 1983 I presented a paper entitled "A Residual Role for Regulation" at the Federal Home Loan Bank of San Francisco Annual Conference (Horvitz, 1984). This paper was intended to stake out a reasonable middle ground between those who advocated free banking (Lawrence H. White, 1984) and those who were attempting to hold back the tide of deregulation.

The thrust of my argument was that federal deposit insurance is a nice device for solving some of the potential problems of financial fragility and instability. There have been several attempts in recent years to design private deposit insurance systems (Ely, 1993; Konstas, 1992). These schemes have economic merit, and Calomiris (1990) provides historical evidence in support of state insurance systems, but it seems unlikely that they will achieve political acceptability in the foreseeable future. If we rule out private deposit insurance, the existence of federal deposit insurance requires some amount of government regulation.[2] The hope of those who favor government insurance is that the necessary amount of regulation will result in only a minor degree of distortion of the operation of the banking system. Obviously, those who favor private deposit insurance, or no deposit insurance at all, believe that the distortions inherent in government insurance have adverse effects which outweigh the contribution of federal deposit insurance to financial stability. From either point of view, the key problem is to find the *minimal* amount of regulation sufficient to protect the government as operator of the insurance system. Horvitz (1984) argued that all that was needed was a monitoring system (i.e., bank examination), good information (reporting of the market value of assets and liabilities), a relatively high capital requirement, and the legal authority for the FDIC to take control over banks when they became insolvent.

We are not far from this now, but we still do not have market-value reporting, capital requirements are not truly high, and the legal authority to take over insolvent institutions may not be sufficient, if supervisors have incentives to delay action. Arguments still exist concerning the necessity for or usefulness of federal deposit insurance, the role of capital in bank supervision, the usefulness of forbearance as a supervisory tool, and the issue of "rules versus authorities" in bank supervision.

Debate over these long-standing issues became more intense during Congressional consideration of the FDIC Improvement Act in 1991, and has continued since passage of the legislation. Bankers, economists and regulators have expressed themselves on these issues, sometimes taking positions that appear to conflict with expected philosophical views.

Most of the issues have been well articulated in several articles and papers prepared by George Benston and George Kaufman, on the one hand, and Carter Golembe[3] and William Isaac,[4] on the other. Several of these have appeared in publications that may not be widely available, and deserve wider consideration than they may have received. The Shadow Financial Regulatory Committee has also put forth policy statements on several of the issues involved in this debate (Policy Statements Numbers 41, 43, 54, 65, 70, 76, 92, 101, in *Journal of Financial Services Research*, various issues.)

FDICIA involved some rather dramatic changes in the way deposit insurance is administered in the U.S. The substance of these changes is widely attributed to ideas advanced in papers by Benston and Kaufman, and to positions taken by the Shadow Financial Regulatory Committee (Benston and Kaufman, 1994; Golembe, 1994; Secura, 1993). Golembe (1994) finds it unusual for academic economists to play a significant role in shaping bank regulation, and analyzes in detail the circumstances that led to such a role. The influence of the academics, in this analysis, was due less to the intellectual power of their arguments than to a unique set of circumstances.

Golembe notes that "members of the academic community had been in the forefront of calling attention to the magnitude of the developing savings and loan crisis in the middle 1980s. Their predictions were often disputed by the S&L regulators and other government officials, so when the collapse finally came it gave to the academics credibility of the kind they had never enjoyed previously in Washington" (1994, p. 6). Moreover, the gain in credibility of the academics came at the expense of the regulators. The traditional ability of the bankers to weaken or prevent legislation they oppose was swamped by the Congressional desire to punish those they believed responsible for the huge cost of the S&L collapse.

The debate between the academic supporters of FDICIA and its banker-regulator opponents is on two levels: the need for federal deposit insurance, and, given federal deposit insurance, the need for detailed rules to be followed by bankers and regulators. Golembe approves of deposit insurance only as a means of "reimbursing unsophisticated depositors of modest means in the event of the disaster of a bank failure (1994, p. 2). This is reasonable if the banking system is sufficiently stable that there is little risk of systemic failure or bank runs. Curiously, it is Kaufman who has examined the historical record and concluded that the risk of contagious bank runs is not a serious one (1994), though Benston and Kaufman's paper for this Conference recognizes that "near simultaneous multiple failures of banks . . . have occurred in the past." It is this historical research by Kaufman that provides a necessary underpinning for Golembe's view that deposit insurance is not necessary to assure financial stability. There is also a reversal of stereotypes here: Golembe, the practical man of affairs, supports a complete reliance on the free market, while the academic scribbler, Kaufman, argues for a detailed set of regulations to correct presumed market failures.

Kaufman's basic conclusion is that movements from one bank to another merely shift reserves, and provide no basis for a collapse of the money supply, a flight into currency can be offset by actions of the Federal Reserve. However, these movements of deposits from one bank to another can be disruptive and costly, even if they do not lead to a collapse of the system. Deposit insurance protects against these costs, even if it is not needed to prevent systemic or linked bank failures.

Golembe's view is almost directly opposite: "Professor Kaufman views the portions of FDICIA for which he was most responsible as a significant reform of deposit insurance because, he believes, it will make that system work more smoothly, more rationally, and with least cost to the federal government." Golembe, on the other hand, is "not at all interested in seeing that the present system of deposit insurance works better but, rather, that it is reduced significantly in scope and importance." (1994, p. 2). But this is not the real policy issue, since there is no practical possibility that federal deposit insurance will be eliminated or reduced. The relevant issue is the scope and shape of the federal regulation that is necessary to make such insurance viable.

Golembe has two basic criticisms of FDICIA, and these may be somewhat conflicting. He objects to a number of provisions of FDICIA as representing inappropriate and unwarranted intrusions into the discretion to be exercised by management and supervisors. Some of this criticism has been focused on specific provisions of FDICIA, the so-called "tripwires," of Section 132 that deal with such sensitive issues as the setting of salaries.[5] Some of it has been aimed at more central issues, such as to primary role given to capital, or the requirement for "early intervention" by the regulators. The second criticism is that FDICIA just might work, and thereby preserve the system of government deposit insurance that Golembe believes should be more basically "reformed," i.e., eliminated.

The emphasis of FDICIA on capital has been attacked by Golembe and by Isaac, as well as by other bankers and regulators. In one sense it is odd that a chairman of the FDIC would complain about a high capital requirement. Supervisors, particularly the FDIC, have traditionally put heavy emphasis on increasing bank capital. Even before formal guidelines were established, it was FDIC policy to urge banks with below-average capital ratios to raise their ratios to the average. This unsuccessful effort to get all banks to have above-average ratios gave rise to the old joke about FDIC standing for "Forever Demanding Increased Capital."

The benefits of high capital are clear: capital is a cushion against loss that protects the FDIC and other uninsured creditors. Perhaps more importantly, a high equity position affects the attitude of owners toward risk-taking. Despite these considerations, Isaac and Golembe make a strong attack on the usefulness of capital ratios as a basis for supervisory action. They approvingly quote the FDIC to the effect that "capital is a lagging indicator of problems" (Secura, 1993). That is, capital does not decline until losses are incurred. Empirical support for this proposition is provided by Lemieux (1993, p. 18). She finds that "studies of capital levels at failed banks have found that deteriorating conditions were often times not signaled by a decline in capital ratios. . . . [F]or a majority of the banks that failed in 1989, reported capital levels gave no warning of impending failures." Similar results are reported by Gilbert (1993).

The principal objections of supervisors to the capital provisions of FDICIA go to the matter of discretion. FDICIA puts into place a system of "prompt corrective action," that is based on what Kaufman and Benston call SEIR (structured early intervention and resolution). The original Benston–Kaufman proposal (1988), endorsed by the Shadow Committee, provided for an automatic, mandatory, set of actions that the supervisors would take as a bank's capital ratio declined.

FDICIA does not quite go this far, leaving a fair amount of room for the agencies to decide what actions to take as capital ratios decline. FDICIA goes rather far, however, in removing discretion in the handling of "critically undercapitalized" banks. Prior to FDICIA, the powers of the FDIC to deal with failing but not insolvent banks were limited. The agencies had cease-and-desist powers, and the FDIC could remove deposit insurance coverage, but this was a long, drawn-out process.

Richard Pratt, Chairman of the Federal Home Loan Bank Board during the early 1980s, had taken the position that FSLIC could take over an S&L that was insolvent on the basis of financial statements prepared in accord with "Regulatory Accounting Principles" (RAP). RAP allowed savings and loan associations to carry assets on their books at values that exceeded the value that would be allowed under generally accepted accounting principles (GAAP).[6] It is easy to forget that many argued at the time that this was an overly aggressive position.[7] Roger Mehle, Assistant Secretary of the Treasury at the time, testified in the case of *Telegraph S&LA* v. *FSLIC* that there was no reason to close an S&L unless it was experiencing a liquidity crisis, i.e., unless it was insolvent in the traditional sense of an inability to meet obligations as they come due. Mehle was representing the Administration position on this issue (National Commission, 1993). Litigation involving Biscayne Federal in 1983 ultimately upheld the FSLIC authority to take over an institution that was RAP insolvent, but RAP insolvency generally meant a very large negative net worth on a market value basis (Black, 1993).

This problem was resolved by FDICIA. We would expect that FDICIA, by strengthening the ability of the agencies to take early action—while there was still an equity cushion to protect the deposit insurance system—would have been applauded by regulators. That was not the case, however.

It is not the authority to act that regulators are opposed to, but the obligation that they take action on the basis of financial data. The agencies believe that they have the ability to make judgements that go beyond reliance solely on capital ratios. "Forbearance" as a policy may have become politically incorrect, but supervisory officials believe that they can make correct judgements as to when forbearance is appropriate.[8] The extent to which the regulators should be able to exercise discretion as banks fall into lower capital adequacy tranches is the principal difference between the original Benston–Kaufman proposal, FDICIA, and its opponents. This is the battlefield on which meaningful debate will take place in the future. It is the area which is most crucial to the regulators, who want this discretion, and to the bankers, who believe that they will be able to make their case for forbearance to the agencies, as long as the agencies have discretion.

Benston and Kaufman had at least two reasons for taking the approach they did. First, discretion with respect to closure was an artifact of deposit insurance (Kaufman, 1994). In the pre-FDIC days, weakness or doubts about solvency led to liquidity problems for such banks (runs), and, if they were unable to meet claims against them, suspension was automatic.[9] With federal deposit insurance, banks were generally closed only following a determination by the chartering agency that the bank was insolvent (on a more-or-less book value basis after adjustments for losses found as a result of an examination). Because this definition is rather fuzzy, considerable discretion was left with the chartering agencies.[10]

The second reason was probably more convincing to Congress: during the 1980s the regulatory agencies made bad decisions in determining whether to take over weak institutions or allow them to continue in operation (i.e., grant forbearance). Benston and Kaufman argue that these decisions were biased in the direction of forbearance. Their analysis of the evidence was based on some theoretical considerations, primarily the work of Kane (1989). Kane has set forth a logical basis for believing that regulators will tend to delay taking strong actions that recognize losses that could otherwise be postponed.

Kane's interpretation is plausible, and is backed by some evidence. That is, if market-value insolvent thrift institutions had been closed in the early 1980s, the losses suffered by the insurance agencies would have been less. However, that is a particular outcome, resulting from the way the real estate market behaved in the 1980s. If the real estate market had performed better, forbearance might have looked good in retrospect. Moreover, examples of successful forbearance exist, though these are mostly anecdotal.[11] By some measures, the structured early intervention and resolution (SEIR) advocated by Benston and Kaufman might have required the recapitalization of Bank of America in the early 1980s (Hector, 1988) or Citicorp in the late 1980s. Perhaps intervention by the supervisors would not have impeded the ultimate recovery of these banks, but it would have imposed additional costs, and would have affected the distribution of the gains from their recovery.

It is agreed that thrift institutions were massively insolvent on a market-value basis in 1981. If all such institutions were liquidated at that time, the loss would have been about $150 billion (Brumbaugh, 1988; Kane, 1985; Kopcke, 1981). Allowing them to continue in operation avoided that loss (at least temporarily).[12] Moreover, several studies find that many thrifts that were insolvent at some point in the 1980s returned to solvency in a later year (Benston & Carhill, 1993).

After giving due recognition to these considerations, however, the weight of the evidence suggests that regulators are likely to be biased toward forbearance, and that is unlikely to be the correct policy, on average. The debate on this issue is very much like the "rules versus authority" debate over monetary policy. The classic statement in favor of a rule comes from Henry Simons (1936). That debate has continued to this day, and topics other than monetary policy have been analyzed in terms of this paradigm (Cagan and Bordo, 1984). Simons' arguments (except, perhaps, for those related to lags) seem relevant and timely to the issue of discretionary authority to deal with weak banks. The counterargument here, just as in the monetary policy debate, is that the authorities may have made mistakes in the past, but they have learned from those mistakes, and will not repeat them. Of course, those who would make the decisions very much prefer to have discretionary authority. An important reason why regulators want discretion is to deal with the "Too Big to Fail" (TBTF) problem. The regulatory authorities, particularly the Federal Reserve, have traditionally been extremely concerned that financial collapse could be triggered by the failure of a large bank. Fear of contagious failure was the basis for protecting depositors against loss not only in a truly large bank such as Continental Illinois, but also in banks as small as Bank of the Commonwealth or National Bank of Washington. Continued forbearance granted to Bank of New England was based more on such considerations than on an expectation that the bank could be turned around and restored to solvency. FDICIA does not conclusively lay TBTF to rest, though it does make protection of uninsured depositors in large banks much more difficult. While there have not yet been any cases to test how these provisions will work, my view is that no banker or depositor can have confidence that his bank will be considered TBTF.[13]

FDICIA also restricts the discretion of the FDIC in determining how to resolve bank failures. Before FDICIA, the FDIC was subject to a requirement that any resolution decision must result in lower cost to the FDIC than liquidation of the bank and payoff of insured deposits. FDICIA requires that the FDIC choose the least costly method of resolution (unless it triggers the TBTF process). Where there are large amounts of uninsured deposits, the least cost requirement will generally preclude purchase and assumption transactions that protect all depositors.

The thrust of FDICIA to reduce agency discretion reflects a lack of confidence in the bank supervisors. Golembe attributes this to a desire on the part of Congress to fasten blame for the thrift debacle and the (temporary) FDIC insolvency on someone other than Congress itself. That is certainly correct, though Golembe ignores the fact that the agencies do deserve some of the blame.

Golembe defends the supervisors as dedicated, able individuals, who do not deserve the criticism expressed in Kaufman's papers (particularly, "FDICIA: The Early Evidence," 1994).[14] In my years with the OCC and the FDIC, I was impressed, like Golembe, with the ability of career bank examiners and supervisors. Not every decision was correct, but attempts were made to reach decisions on the merits (as seen through the eyes of the supervisors) with virtually no role for political pressure. (Obviously, the FHLBB was different, both with respect to sensitivity to political pressure and to the role of supervisors.)

But the banking agencies were much smaller in those days, and bank failures were a rare event. In recent years it appears that the bank supervisory process has become increasingly sensitive to political pressures. The agencies seem to make decisions not solely on their judgement of the merits, but with one eye cocked on how a Congressional oversight committee would view the decision. This leads to an overly rigid posture, as it is not lost on supervisors that a capable Comptroller—sometimes called "the regulator from hell"—was not reconfirmed because he was not tough enough.

Golembe and others may idealize the concept of "independent" agencies exercising independent judgement. But the agencies are now too weakened to exercise independent judgement. Supervisors are afraid to make decisions that may subject them to criticism from Congressional oversight committees. Evidence of the politicization of the supervisory process can be found in the long delay in confirming the Clinton nominee as Chairman of the FDIC, and the lack of a permanent head of the Office of Thrift Supervision. Questions have been raised as to the independence of the Comptroller, and the temporary appointment of a Treasury official as head of the RTC has turned out to be a disaster. The Treasury has long believed that it should play the key role in bank supervision, but recent events may have convinced all that that is not such a good idea.

My evidence is anecdotal, but sufficient to convince me that basing banking supervision on the discretionary authority of public officials is not tenable. Deposit insurance is a reasonable way to minimize instability resulting from bank failures. Deposit insurance requires some government regulation to protect the insurance system. Regulation should be the minimum necessary to protect the system, and that need not involve restrictions on geographical expansion or on powers exercised by affiliated corporations. But that regulation should be specified with limited range for discretionary actions related to bank capital or closure by the supervisory agencies.

Some of the detailed provisions of FDICIA may be regulatory overkill,[15] but the reluctance of the agencies to impose use of market values to measure capital, or to impose a meaningful measure of interest-rate risk, suggests that some mandates are appropriately part of the statute.

I would not argue that FDICIA, or government deposit insurance, is essential to assure stability of the financial system. A well functioning central bank is probably sufficient. But deposit insurance is a nice way of preventing instability and reassuring the public. It need not involve excessive cost or risk to the taxpayer, and it need not entail all-encompassing government regulation. The basic thrust of FDICIA is an appropriate means of providing the necessary regulation to protect the taxpayer; it is correct in reducing the scope of the exercise of discretion by the supervisors.

Notes

1. 1893 may be an exception to the statement that financial panics under the National Banking Act did not spread to the real sector.
2. The collapse of state-sponsored deposit insurance systems in Ohio, Maryland, and Rhode Island during the 1980s makes it unnecessary to consider the revival of this approach to banking stability.
3. Golembe is an economist and bank consultant. He publishes a periodic newsletter, "The Golembe Reports," which frequently focuses on deposit insurance. Several of the articles discussed in this paper appeared in "The Golembe Reports."
4. Isaac is an attorney and former Chairman of the FDIC. He is now Chairman of the Secura Group.
5. The Shadow Financial Regulatory Committee suggested that these standards need not be onerous if interpreted as guidelines or indicators of potential problems, rather than rigid quantitative measures. On this basis, even the much-ridiculed provision relating to maintaining stock market value above book value may have merit as promoting the use of market price information. It appears that the regulators have adopted this approach in their implementation of the Section 132 provisions. There is room for difference of opinion as to whether these provisions are important to the substance of FDICIA. Golembe and other critics view this as unnecessary "micromanagement" of banks by regulators. Others might point to the long delay, and the weak results, in the banking agencies' work on a mandated capital requirement for interest rate risk, as an argument in favor of mandating such actions by the regulators.
6. For example, RAP allowed losses resulting from the sale of mortgage loans to be deferred, and allowed some fixed assets to be carried at values higher than historical cost.
7. The FSLIC was unsure of its legal authority to deal in 1984 with Empire Savings, an institution that reported high profits and adequate net worth on a RAP basis, but which was massively insolvent if its assets were valued at their fair value.
8. During the 1980s many economists, including the Shadow Financial Regulatory Committee, criticized the preference of the supervisory agencies and Congress for granting forbearance to weak institutions. It is interesting that as FDICIA has reduced the ability of the supervisors to exercise forbearance, the economic literature on the potential benefits of forbearance has grown. Much of this literature concerns the conditions under which forbearance can be optimal policy (Eisenbeis and Horvitz, 1994).
9. Kaufman (1994, p. 136) concluded that "runs caused few failures, so that the liquidity problem was not transferred into a solvency problem." Following an examination, a solvent bank was permitted to reopen.
10. The agencies also had the authority to close a bank for operating in an unsafe and unsound manner, but this is an even fuzzier (and less frequently used) basis for a decision.
11. One important issue is whether the supervisors are able to distinguish those institutions that will benefit from forbearance from those that will not. A study of the formal forbearance program initiated by the FDIC in the 1980s indicates that they cannot (Brinkmann, Horvitz & Huang, forthcoming). Even if they could, Kane argues that forbearance is inappropriate because the government does not capture its fair share of the gains from successful forbearance. That is, the decline in interest rates after 1981 reduced insurance agency losses. But the government did not capture all of the gains from falling rates, and it was the government that took all the risk if rates had increased.
12. Of course, prompt corrective action would not necessarily have led to a closing and liquidation of all such thrift institutions. That could have been avoided with recapitalization by existing owners, or sale to new owners. The magnitude of their insolvency makes that somewhat unlikely. More important, had Benston–Kaufman type policies been in effect, with market-value capital requirements, thrift institutions would probably never have taken the interest rate risk they did. And even if they did, corrective action would have been taken long before the exposure became anywhere near $150 billion.
13. While this should contribute to depositor discipline by leading large depositors to believe that they are truly at risk, the more recent passage of depositor preference rules may restore many depositors' confidence that they are not at risk in case of bank failure (Kaufman, 1993). It is interesting to note that Isaac, who as Chairman of the FDIC was responsible for engineering the protection of Continental Illinois depositors on TBTF grounds, has more recently stated that "The too-big-to-fail doctrine is alive and well, and we need to get rid of it" (Klinkerman, 1994). Also, Isaac (1994) has criticized FDICIA for reducing the scope of discretionary authority of the regulators. However, in a recent newspaper column he noted that "I never cease to be amazed by the extent to which government agencies confuse their interests with the public's."

14. Golembe is particularly critical of some of the language in this paper. For example, Kaufman says "In this instance, the regulators' self-interest outweighed their responsibility as delegated agents of the taxpayer. Through the use of scare tactics based on Congress' fear of systemic breakdowns, the regulators were successful in convincing Congress to permit them to retain more of their discretionary authority" (p. 55).
15. Former FDIC Chairman William Seidman proclaimed that FDICIA "produced the greatest overload of regulatory micromanagement seen anywhere in the world" (1993, p. 47).

References

Benston, George J., and Mike Carhill. "The Causes and the Consequences of the Thrift Disaster." In: *Research in Financial Services*, Vol. 6, New York: JAI Press. 1994, pp. 103–169.

Benston, George J., Robert A. Eisenbeis, Paul M. Horvitz, Edward J. Kane, and George G. Kaufman. *Perspectives on Safe & Sound Banking*. Cambridge, MA: MIT Press. 1986.

Benston, George J., and George G. Kaufman. "Is the Banking and Payments System Fragile?" *Journal of Financial Services Research* 9 (December 1995).

Benston, George J., and George G. Kaufman. "Regulating Bank Safety and Performance." In: *Restructuring Banking and Financial Services in America*. Washington, DC: American Enterprise Institute. 1988.

Benston, George J., and George G. Kaufman. "In Defense of FDICIA: Reply to Golembe." *The Golembe Reports* 7 (1994), 8–14.

Bernanke, Ben, and Mark Gertler. "Agency Costs, Net Worth, and Business Fluctuations." *American Economic Review* (March 1989), 14–31.

Black, William. "Examination/Supervision/Enforcement of S&Ls 1979–1992." Staff Paper No. 4, National Commission on Financial Institution Reform, Recovery and Enforcement, Washington, DC.

Brinkmann, Emile J., Paul M. Horvitz, and Ying-Lin Huang. "Forbearance: An Empirical Analysis." *Journal of Financial Services Research* (forthcoming).

Brumbaugh, R. Dan, Jr. *Thrifts Under Siege*. New York: Harper & Row, Publishers. 1988.

Cagan, Phillip. *Determinants and Effects of Changes in the Stock of Money*. New York: National Bureau of Economic Research. 1965.

Cagan, Philip, and Michael D. Bordo. "The Report of the Gold Commission." In: *Carnegie-Rochester Conference Series on Public Policy*. Spring 1984, pp. 247–273.

Calomiris, Charles W. "Is Deposit Insurance Necessary? A Historical Perspective." *Journal of Economic History* (June 1990), 283–295.

Dwyer, Gerald P., Jr., and Alton Gilbert. "Bank Runs and Private Remedies." *Review*, Federal Reserve Bank of St. Louis (May/June 1989), 43–61.

Eisenbeis, Robert A., and Paul M. Horvitz. "The Role of Forbearance and Its Costs in Handling Troubled and Failed Depository Institutions." In: *Reforming Financial Institutions and Markets in the United States*. Norwell, MA: Kluwer Academic Publishers. 1994.

Ely, Bert. "Financial Innovation and Deposit Insurance: The Cross-Guarantee Concept." Presented at Eleventh Annual Monetary Conference, Cato Institute, Washington, DC, March 19, 1993.

Gilbert, R. Alton. "The Effect of Legislating Prompt Corrective Action on the Bank Insurance Fund." *Review* (Federal Reserve Bank of St. Louis), 3–22.

Golembe, Carter. "Reflections on the Origins of FDICIA." *The Golembe Reports* 4 (1994).

Golembe, Carter. "Other Voices, Other Views." *The Golembe Reports* 7 (1994).

Gorton, Gary. "Bank Suspension of Convertibility." *Journal of Monetary Economists* (March 1985), 117–193.

Haines, Walter W. *Money, Prices, and Policy*. New York: McGraw-Hill Book Company. 1961.

Hector, Gary. *Breaking the Bank: The Decline of BankAmerica*. Boston: Little, Brown and Company. 1988.

Horvitz, Paul M. "Deposit Insurance After Deregulation: A Residual Role for Regulation." *Proceedings of the Ninth Annual Conference*, Federal Home Loan Bank of San Francisco Conference, 1984.

Isaac, William M. "Remarks on FDICIA." In: *FDICIA: An Appraisal*. Federal Reserve Bank of Chicago. 1993, pp. 495–500.

Isaac, William M. "A Bronx Cheer for the Credit Union Regulator." *American Banker*, October 6, 1994, p. 5.

Kane, Edward J. *The Gathering Crisis in Federal Deposit Insurance*. Cambridge, MA: MIT Press. 1985.

Kane, Edward J. *The S&L Insurance Mess: How Did It Happen?* Washington: The Urban Institute Press. 1989.

Kaufman, George G. "The New Depositor Preference Act: Time Inconsistency in Action." Working Paper, Loyola University of Chicago, November 1993.

Kaufman, George G., and Robert E. Litan. *Assessing Bank Reform: FDICIA One Year Later.* Washington: The Brookings Institution. 1993.

Kaufman, George G. "Bank Contagion: A Review of the Theory and Evidence." *Journal of Financial Services Research* (April 1994), 123–150.

Kaufman, George G. "FDICIA: The Early Evidence." *Challenge* (July/August 1994), 53–57.

Klinkerman, Steve. "Is Banking's Safety Net Big Enough?" *American Banker*, October 5, 1994, p. 4.

Konstas, Panos. "How to DIG ourselves out of the Insurance Mess." *Journal of Retail Banking* (Spring 1992), 16–24.

Kopcke, Richard W. "The Condition of Massachusetts Savings Bank and California Savings and Loan Associations." In: *The Future of the Thrift Industry*, Proceedings of a Federal Reserve Bank of Boston Conference, October 1981.

Lemieux, Catherine M. "The Role of Bank Capital in a Post-FDICIA World." *Financial Industry Perspectives* (Federal Reserve Bank of Kansas City) (November 1993), 15–23.

Minsky, Hyman P. "Can 'It' Happen Again? A Reprise." *Challenge* (July/August 1982), 5–13.

National Commission on Financial Institution Reform, Recovery and Enforcement. *Origins and Causes of the S&L Debacle: A Blueprint for Reform.* Washington: USGPO. 1993.

Secura Group. *Capital Based Regulation.* Bank Administration Institute. 1993.

Seidman, L. William. "The Banking Crisis in Perspective." In: *FDICIA: An Appraisal*, Federal Reserve Bank of Chicago, 1993, pp. 46–47.

Shadow Financial Regulatory Committee. *Journal of Financial Services Research*: Statement 70 (October 1991); Statements 41, 43, 54, 65 (August 1992); Statement 76 (September 1992); Statement 92 (September 1993); Statement 101 (April 1994).

Simons, Henry. "Rules Versus Authorities in Monetary Policy." *Journal of Political Economy* (February 1936).

White, Lawrence H. *Free Banking in Britain: Theory, Experience and Debate 1800–1845*, Cambridge: Cambridge University Press. 1984.

Journal of Financial Services Research 9: 381–391 (1995)
© 1995 Kluwer Academic Publishers

Regulatory Solutions to Payment System Risks: Lessons from Privately Negotiated Derivatives

DAVID L. MENGLE
Vice President, J.P. Morgan & Co. Inc., New York, NY 10260 U.S.A.

1. Regulators and the payment system

Payment system risks were the "major minor" banking policy issue of the 1980s. They were minor issues in that they were of interest mainly to the Federal Reserve System and to bank operations officers; they were major issues in that they supposedly involved significant risks and that they were a source of constant regulatory pressure on banks.

One of the salient characteristics of the regulatory response to payment system policy issues was the emphasis on specific, mandated solutions to perceived problems. Regulators cited huge interbank wire transfers as evidence of risks, and assumed that the risks represented a policy problem. They then enumerated possible solutions to the policy problem, and interpreted the failure of banks to implement those solutions as evidence of the need for a regulatory response. This is in marked contrast to the experience of privately-negotiated derivatives activity, in which privately-developed risk management solutions made government-developed regulatory solutions largely unnecessary.

It is the purpose of this analysis to consider why the development of risk management tools in the two areas, derivatives and large-value funds transfers, has taken divergent paths. That is, for large-value wire payments, risk-management solutions developed largely as the result of regulatory prodding; for derivatives, in contrast, risk management solutions developed as an integral part of the business. The analysis concentrates on the experience of the United States payment system on both the Fedwire and Clearing House Interbank Payments System (CHIPS), both of which are described in the Appendix, because that is where risk concerns first arose. But given the attention now being given to payment system issues internationally, particularly by the Bank for International Settlements and the European Community, the experience of the United States should have lessons for policy makers in other countries.

2. Comparing payment concerns with derivatives concerns

Despite the divergent development of risk management solutions for wire transfer systems and derivatives, similar concerns motivate policy discussions for the two areas. First, both payment systems and derivatives discussions routinely cite huge volumes involved, if not necessarily at risk. For example, in 1993 banks on the Clearing House Interbank

The views in this paper are those of the author and do not necessarily reflect the views of J.P. Morgan & Co. Incorporated or any of its subsidiaries or operating divisions.

Payments System (CHIPS) in the United States made payments totaling over $1 trillion per day; similarly, the notional principle of interest rate and currency swaps outstanding in 1994 was over $11 trillion world-wide. Both figures are misleading indicators of risk, however. In the case of CHIPS, actual exposures are measured as the net debit positions outstanding during the business day; data reported in Clair (1991) suggest that the upper bound of settlement exposures in 1989 was approximately 7 percent of daily volume. In the case of swaps, actual settlement exposures consist of the semiannual two-way payment of interest on the notional principle and principal flows on currency swaps on a particular day; daily settlement exposures on interest rate and currency swaps turn out to be approximately 0.1 percent of the notional amount outstanding.

A second similarity between concerns about payment system risks and concerns about derivatives risks is that both arise from the increasing interdependencies between institutions that characterize modern financial markets. Such concerns stress that interdependence enables disturbances to be transmitted between market participants more rapidly today than when institutions and markets operated more independently; the concerns do not always cite the corollary, however, that interdependence helps disperse the effects of disturbances instead of concentrate them on a small number of participants.[1]

A final similarity between the two issues is that both are cited as examples of low probability/high-cost risk situations that, if they were to occur, would threaten the stability of the financial system. Yet for both payment systems and derivatives, instances of actual or narrowly-averted losses that threatened the stability of the financial system are difficult to find.

One exception in the payment system area is Bankhaus Herstatt, a German private bank that failed in 1974 (Spero, 1980). This bank became a symbol of payment system risk because it showed the risks connected with foreign exchage spot markets. Because Herstatt was closed after the German market closed but the U.S. market had not settled, the U.S. banks did not receive the dollar leg of Herstatt's foreign exchange transactions. Whether or not the Herstatt failure actually threatened the stability of the system, it did lead to losses at individual banks and provided the impetus for improvements to CHIPS settlement procedures.

In the derivatives area, examples of threats to the system are even harder to find. The United States General Accounting Office (1994) pointed to the 1987 U.S. stock market crash, the 1990 failure of Drexel Burnham Lambert, and the 1991 failure of the Bank of New England as examples of how federal involvement *could* be necessary in the event of a derivatives disruption, although none of the examples actually involved systemic disruption. Since the GAO report, the failure of Barings PLC, a British investment bank, has cast further doubt on the notion that the financial system is prone to systemic disruptions.

3. Derivatives

The salient characteristic of derivatives risk management is that it has developed in advance of regulatory pressure, not in its wake. Indeed, today regulatory agencies and central bankers are recommending that financial institutions apply derivatives risk management tools to other, more traditional risks.

Here are some examples of risk control measures that derivatives dealers and users have developed. With regard to control of credit exposures, financial firms have upgraded their ability to monitor and evaluate the credit risks posed by counterparties. In addition, swap participants have developed and routinely use such credit exposure control methods as collateral and margin requirements, third-party credit guarantees, and early termination provisions. With regard to market risks, financial firms have developed measurement methodologies such as Value at Risk (VAR), which is a measure of the maximum loss within a specified confidence interval of a portfolio's value resulting from an adverse market move over a specified unwind period.[2] Measures such as VAR take account of the correlations between exposures and therefore help measure the risk of a firm's entire portfolio. And market participants have developed risk-reporting formats to monitor risks and position limits to control risks. Finally, derivatives dealers and user have set up internal risk monitoring units, responsible directly to senior management, to ensure that both credit risk and market risk policies are followed.

The derivatives industry has also acted collectively to limit risks. First, the industry has worked to change the legal environment to provide certainty to market participants with regard to the enforceability of swaps contracts and of netting provisions. Second, the industry detailed its "best practices," such as those in the preceding paragraph, in the Group of Thirty's 1993 report on derivatives (Group of Thirty, 1993). Finally, the International Swaps and Derivatives Association developed the ISDA Master Agreement, which limits risks in several ways: the payment netting provisions reduce settlement risks; the close-out netting provisions limit exposures to net instead of gross exposures in the event of bankruptcy; and the agreement defines precisely what constitutes default by a counterparty and thereby allows prompt remedial action when a counterparty gets in trouble.

4. Payment system regulatory solutions in the United States

The two major issues regarding payment system risk in the United States have been (1) daylight overdrafts and (2) systemic risks on net settlement systems. In both cases, and in contrast with the experience of derivatives, the solutions were either mandated by regulators or involved considerable prodding by regulators to attain a particular result.

4.1. Daylight overdrafts on Fedwire

Fedwire is the large-value wire transfer system run by the Federal Reserve System in the United States (see Appendix). Fedwire functions by means of transfers of balances among bank reserve accounts at Federal Reserve Banks. In the mid-1980s, a controversy arose over the practice of allowing Fedwire participants to let their reserve balances go negative so long as they are covered by the close of business, hence the name "daylight overdrafts." The risk of daylight overdrafts arises because the bank receiving the transfer gets immediate credit for the funds, which can then be made available to the beneficiary; the Federal Reserve Bank bears the risk that the sending bank will not cover the transfer. Stated another way, the Fed extends unpriced intraday credit to banks on Fedwire.

It is not clear why Fedwire permitted daylight overdrafts in the first place. Although it is tempting to surmise that they were an attempt by the Federal Reserve to allay the cost to banks of membership in the System, there is no evidence that they resulted from a conscious decision to extend unpriced intraday credit. Indeed, it is likely that daylight overdrafts existed in practice under the pre-1971 Federal Reserve funds transfer system that relied on manual accounting and teletype notification of transfers (Mengle, 1985). Under that system, the capability to determine in real time whether covering funds were in the sending bank's reserve account did not exist. And when the Federal Reserve moved to an automated wire transfer system in the 1970's, it did not move to real-time reserve accounting. In fact, the Federal Reserve did not have a real-time reserve accounting capability until late in the 1980s, and even then the funds transfer systems and reserve accounting systems were not completely integrated. Thus the most likely explanation for the existence of daylight overdrafts is that they resulted from the piecemeal automation of the Federal Reserve funds transfer system.

Whatever their origin, daylight overdrafts were seen as a problem for two reasons. First, because daylight overdrafts had a zero price, banks would demand more than the socially optimal amount of intraday credit. And second, because the Federal Reserve Banks bore the intraday credit risk, there was an implicit taxpayer subsidy to commercial bank risk taking (Mengle, Humphrey, and Summers, 1986). But there were other considerations that likely slowed the search for solutions. One consideration was the concern with costs of Federal Reserve System membership, as mentioned above. Another consideration was that attempts to restrict daylight overdrafts could make Fedwire vulnerable to competition from private sector alternatives.

The Fed acted in 1986 by imposing "voluntary" caps on intraday credit related to a bank's capital. At the time, pricing intraday credit was considered a radical solution. But eventually, sentiments turned toward rationing by price, and, since April of 1994, daylight credit has been priced. The effect of pricing on intraday credit levels should be known shortly, but it is likely that, other than the usual pains associated with implementing a change, daylight overdrafts are no longer perceived as a policy problem.

By its nature, the solution to the daylight overdrafts issue had to be an imposed regulatory solution: a public-sector institution provided unpriced intraday credit, and it has now changed from rationing by caps and limits to rationing by price. But ironically, using price to ration intraday credit is the type of solution one would expect if the market were left to its own devices.

4.2. Risks in net settlement systems

Of potentially greater interest to policy makers is the controversy surrounding risk controls on net settlement systems such as CHIPS in New York. CHIPS is a private sector institution, but it settles through the Fed at the end of each day. The existence of competition between the private sector and the Federal Reserve, which also has regulatory authority by virtue of its provision of net settlement services, make the issue even more complex.

The policy concern is that the unanticipated failure of a CHIPS participant to meet its settlement obligations could induce a chain reaction of settlement failures among otherwise solvent banks. An influential article by David Humphrey (1986) simulated the effect of a settlement failure on the ability of other CHIPS participants to settle; he found that, under a set of restrictive assumptions, over one-third of CHIPS participants could fail to settle. The simulation was a rough approximation, and made no attempt to allow for the difference between insolvency and illiquidity or for the unrealism of the assumption that failures would be totally unanticipated. But however implausible the results, the numbers put some meat on the bones of the vague concept of systemic risk, and evocations of the specter of systemic failure became a staple of subsequent payment system (and later derivatives) policy discussions.[3]

Similar to Fedwire, the initial solution was caps on each institution's net debits and bilateral limits on net credit exposures between institutions. But there was additional concern about the systemic consequences if a net settlement network were allowed to unwind its settlement after a failure; consequently, regulators pushed network participants to develop loss-sharing and collateralization arrangements that would determine how costs would be allocated after a settlement failure. In addition, finality of payment provisions were written into the Uniform Commercial Code, although not all agree that meaningful finality of payment or settlement yet exists because there are certain extreme cases remaining in which a settlement unwind can take place.

If there are substantial risks to payment system participants of a settlement failure, why did the private sector not adopt risk control measures on its own? Here is a partial list of alternative hypotheses that come immediately to mind:

- *Market failure I: Risk misperception.* The risks of systemic failure are substantial, but payment system participants systematically underestimate risks of settlement failures and therefore treat them as insignificant. Regulatory pressure is essential to bringing about the optimal solution.
- *Market failure II: Collective action problems.* The risks of systemic failure are substantial and perceived to be so, but it is in no bank's individual interest to devote resources to developing a solution. Regulatory pressure is essential to bringing about the optimal solution.
- *Policy failure I: Moral hazard.* The risks of systemic failure are substantial, but progress has been hampered by existence of an implicit central bank settlement guarantee. There is no incentive to develop risk control measures if the central bank will end up taking care of the problem otherwise. Regulatory pressure is essential to bringing about the optimal solution *unless the central bank explicitly and credibly abjures the settlement guarantee.* Commodity and financial futures and options markets seem to provide evidence in favor of the moral hazard argument because, lacking any central bank guarantee, they have on their own developed risk reduction arrangement such as margin requirements and loss-sharing arrangements.

- *Policy failure II: Ambiguity of regulatory response.* The risks of systemic failure are substantial, but there is ambiguity about how the central bank will react. Ambiguity leads to a "time inconsistency," which means the market expects that the central bank would guarantee settlement if faced with a crisis. Regulatory pressure is essential to bringing about the optimal solution *unless the central bank is explicitly and credibly abjures the settlement guarantee.*
- *Policy failure but no market failure.* The risks of systemic failure do not justify the cost of establishing the specific risk control measures demanded by the Fed (for example, finality of payment, collateral pools, and loss sharing arrangements). No additional measures are necessary or economically justified, and imposed solutions are suboptimal.

Consider the alternatives one at a time. Under risk misperception, it is not just the market that fails; some proposed regulatory and legal solutions, specifically receiver finality rules that require banks receiving funds transfers to make funds available to consumers whether or not the sending bank meets its settlement obligation, actually increase risk in the system (Mengle, 1990). In general, the risk misperception hypothesis is plausible for infrequent situations but difficult to defend for long-run situations involving vast numbers of transactions on a daily basis.

Second, the economic argument that the private sector did not respond because of a collective action problem is fraught with difficulties. Suppose a settlement failure occurs. There are three possible outcomes. The first is that the central bank takes a "hands off" attitude and lets the payment system participants sort out the resulting problems; clearly, participants would have incentives to develop measures to avoid or to mitigate the effects of future settlement failures. The second is that the central bank misses the failure and fails to act, so the participants are left to clean up the problems; again, participants have incentives to control risks. A third and most plausible outcome is that the central bank makes liquidity available to banks that are solvent but temporarily illiquid because of the settlement failure; this presumably would include the vast majority of banks in the system. But the banks will be required to pay back the loans, plus interest, to the central bank, so ultimately the losses will be borne by the payment system participants. Moral hazard exists only if the credit is underpriced. So in all three cases banks have incentives to control risks on their own whether or not the central bank were to provide liquidity.

The third hypothesis, moral hazard, implies that progress in risk management has been hampered by the existence of an implicit central bank settlement guarantee. Hal Scott (1990), for example, argues that "the presence of a widely perceived Fed guarantee gives inadequate incentives for risk reduction efforts by banks. . . . " The moral hazard hypothesis is a difficult one either to prove or disprove. It is consistent with observed behavior in that banks failed on their own to take what regulators perceived as adequate risk control measures. But as Scott goes on to argue, "for risk reduction efforts to actually be undertaken they must be efficient;" that is, the expected losses in the system must be sufficiently large to justify the expenditure on measures to reduce them. To accept the moral hazard hypothesis, one must first accept the premise that regulators were correct in asserting that expected losses were significant.

The fourth hypothesis, ambiguity about how the central bank will react, can work in two ways. One relates to a situation of "uncertainty" as distinct from "risk" as normally defined in economics. There is ambiguity about both the probability of failure and about the central bank's reaction. "Uncertainty aversion," however, implies that payment system participants would react conservatively and institute risk management measures on their own to avoid the costs of a systemic crisis (Hu, 1994). This did not happen.

The other way ambiguity can work is through inconsistency between policy makers' intentions and their choices at a later time (Mengle, 1990). That is, even if a central bank denies that it will bail out a failing payment system participant, the market may reason, correctly, that the central bank would, when faced by a potentially disruptive failure, act to bail out the failing bank in order to avoid taking the chance on a possibly worse outcome, namely systemic failure. That being the case, payment system participants are acting rationally by proceeding as if the central bank had assumed the risk. Thus the situation returns to that of policy failure and moral hazard.

The last hypothesis, which has received scant attention by policy makers, is that payment system participants acted efficiently in not taking active risk control measures on their own. One reason is that the central bank, as emergency lender of last resort, may be the most efficient channel through which to distribute settlement losses among payment system participants. Another reason is that the costs of implementing the risk management measures preferred by the Fed and embodied in the Lamfalussy Standards (Bank for International Settlements, 1990) may exceed the expected reduction in the costs of settlement failure the measures would bring about.

Consider first the possibility that the central bank is the most efficient channel for allocating risk by supposing that the central bank takes three actions: First, the central bank makes it clear that they will lend to illiquid but solvent banks after a settlement failure. Second, it charges a penalty rate on advances to illiquid banks in the event of a settlement failure. And third, the central bank adopts an explicit and credible policy of not lending to insolvent institutions, even when systemic risk fears are invoked. Assume now that a payment system participant fails, and the resulting default leads to liquidity problems for other participants sufficiently severe as to threaten their ability to fulfill their own settlement obligation that day. If the central bank were to lend to the illiquid participants, they would be able to fulfill their settlement obligations that day. The participants would then be obligated to pay back the loans at interest, and in the end the losses will have been apportioned among the participants who borrowed from the central bank.

The outcome would have been similar had payment system participants formed (either voluntarily or involuntarily) a collateral pool or a loss-sharing arrangement. A settlement failure would lead to a call on the collateral pool or an assessment on the members, regardless of how the failure affects their liquidity, and settlement would go on. In this case, losses would be distributed according to collateral put up by each member or, in a loss-sharing arrangement, according to the loss-sharing formula.

Payment system participants might prefer one of the above two arrangements over the other. But it is not clear why the central bank would prefer one over the other, unless it were reluctant to lend even at a penalty rate.[4] If the central bank were to adopt the policy outlined above, payment system participants could then choose collectively whether to institute collateralization and loss-sharing arrangements in order to reduce the expected costs from a failure.

Consider now the possibility that regulators may have discouraged private sector solutions by constraining the choices available. One of the factors increasing the costs to participants may be the tendency of regulators to specify the risk management measures they find acceptable instead of simply specifying the general result they want to achieve and allowing the private sector to develop specific solutions. The Lamfalussy standards, for example, outline a set of minimum standards for risk control arrangements. Although such standards may in themselves have great merit as means of achieving the objective of reduced risk, they could also reduce the range of methods available for achieving that objective. It is conceivable that narrowing the scope for innovation by relying exclusively on current concepts of risk management could raise the cost of managing risks and thereby reduce banks' incentives to control their risks voluntarily.[5]

A similar tendency shows up occasionally in derivatives policy discussions, when observers lament the failure of the derivatives market to move toward a centralized swaps clearing house (Folkerts-Landau and Steinherr, 1994). Currently, there is no centralized clearing arrangement for privately negotiated derivatives. Further, even the implicit subsidy in the zero risk-weighting given by risk-based capital requirements to exchange-traded derivatives does not appear to have quickened the pace of movement toward centralized clearing. But a closer look at derivatives transactions shows that the market has acted in its own way to manage credit risks of derivatives (Brickell, 1994). Specifically, parties to derivatives transactions reduce risks by netting under bilateral master agreements for single products—swaps against swaps, for example—and reduce still further by including other derivatives under the master. Netting across products—commodity swaps against equity options, for example—reduces potential exposures, even more than can single-product netting. Finally, and most fundamentally, credit risks in derivatives markets are supported by the capital of the dealers; in contrast, clearing houses use collateral contributed by members to support risks. It is not clear why regulators should prefer one form of intermediation over the other, so long as risk is managed.

5. Lessons from derivatives activity

To summarize the foregoing:

- Regulators perceived risks associated with large value interbank wire transfers, and pushed banks to adopt specific solutions.
- Banks perceived risks associated with their derivatives activities and developed tools to manage the risks; the tools were in place well in advance of significant regulatory concerns.

Why did the paths differ? Of the above explanations for the outcome in large-value payments, only two, moral hazard and optimal response by banks, survive as plausible. Both involve policy failure, not market failure. The lesson derivatives provide for payment system regulation is that the market works when it is allowed to do so and when regulators do not insist on specific solutions as opposed to policy results.

Allowing the market to work, however, does not eliminate the role of central banks or regulators. On the contrary, policy makers can work to decrease the level of uncertainty regarding the enforceability of contracts, they can work to make legal environments more uniform, and they can plan carefully and even announce publicly how they would perform their jobs in the event of a crisis.

In the past, central banks have tended to be vague (or, to use former New York Federal Reserve Bank President E. Gerald Corrigan's term, "constructively ambiguous") about their intentions in the event of a settlement failure. This is understandable in some regards because it is natural for officials to want to keep open their options how to react to a potentially difficult situation that no one has actually experienced. But greater candor about central bank and regulatory intentions would have the benefit of allowing the private sector to form expectations regarding the costs to them of a failure and then to act accordingly. In addition, it would encourage regulators to plan carefully how they would react to a failure, perhaps through "stress tests" similar to those used by derivatives dealers to determine how they would react to abnormal market conditions.

A common form of regulatory activity that should be approached with caution, how-ever, is drawing up detailed guidelines for how the private sector should manage risks. Even supposedly "voluntary" regulatory guidelines can often be the result of regulatory pressure. This is not to say that the individual points of the Lamfalussy guidelines, for example, do not have much to recommend them, but rather that there is an inevitable trade-off between detail and flexibility. The more the private sector sees itself as con-strained by specific recommendations, the less able it will be to develop solutions suited to their own situations. By enshrining a particular solution or set of solutions, regulators increase the costs faced by firms that must innovate in order to adapt to changing markets. A preferable approach is for regulators to concentrate on risk management objectives, and leave banks free to determine how best to attain the objectives at minimum cost.

Appendix: Large value wire transfer systems in the United States

Fedwire.   The main wholesale wire transfer network in the United States is Fedwire, which operates through bank reserve accounts at the twelve Federal Reserve Banks. Fedwire transfers are settled on a bilateral, trade-for-trade basis, also known as gross settlement.

Fedwire can be used to transfer both funds and book-entry United States government securities between banks and other depository institutions. During 1994 almost 287,000 Fedwire funds transfers totaling about $841 billion occurred on an average day. Mean transfer size was about $3 million. In addition, over 50,000 book-entry securities transfers amounting to about $576 billion occurred daily. The average book-entry transfer was about $11.5 million.

CHIPS.   The Clearing House Interbank Payments System (CHIPS) is a multilateral net settlement system. In a net settlement system, transfers are consolidated into net positions between banks or between banks and the network in order to reduce the actual number of interbank transfers that take place. In a multilateral (as opposed to bilateral) net settlement system, each bank's bilateral net positions against other banks are combined into a "net net" obligation between the bank and the other banks in the system. Settlement occurs at the end of the day, when banks in net debit positions send (over Fedwire) the funds they owe to a special CHIPS account at the Federal Reserve Bank of New York. CHIPS then wires funds from the account to banks in net credit positions.

   CHIPS is owned and operated by the New York Clearing House, a private organization. It transfers only funds and not securities, and is used largely, although not exclusively, in connection with international transactions such as Eurodollars and foreign exchange (Clair, 1991). During 1994 approximately 182,000 transfers totaling about $1.2 trillion took place on an average day on CHIPS. The average transfer size was $6.5 million. At the end of 1994, 115 depository institutions, many of them branches of non-U.S. banks, participated in CHIPS.

Notes

1. For a balanced argument that considers both sides, see Alan Greenspan (1995).
2. For detailed descriptions of the Value at Risk methodology, see Longerstaey (1995) and Beckström and Campbell (1995).
3. It might also be mentioned that the Federal Reserve Banks viewed CHIPS and other private sector large value transfer systems as competitors, and that the conflict between the Federal Reserve's role as provider and regulator in the payment system has been an ongoing source of controversy.
4. One reason occasionally cited is the difficulty during a crisis in distinguishing insolvent from illiquid banks. In a payment system in which large volumes are distributed over a large number of participants, this might be a persuasive argument. But in a typical system, the largest payments are concentrated among a relatively small group of participants, which are in turn likely to be monitored closely by the central bank. It is highly unlikely that a settlement failure of a large participant would occur and catch the central bank totally off guard.
5. Cf. Hayek (1972): "To make the best available knowledge at any given moment the compulsory standard for all future endeavors may well be the most certain way to prevent new knowledge from emerging." For an alternative approach, in which the recommendations are presented as a transfer of knowledge instead of as a set of standards, see Group of Thirty (1993).

References

Bank for International Settlements. *Report of the Committee on Interbank Netting Schemes of the Central Banks of the Group of Ten Countries.* Basel. 1990.

Beckström, Rod, and Alyce Campbell. *An Introduction to VAR*. Palo Alto: C•ATS Software, Inc. 1995.
Brickell, Mark C. "Clearinghouse Arrangements for Privately-Negotiated Derivatives." *Proceedings of the International Symposium of Banking and Payment Services*. Washington, DC: Board of Governors of the Federal Reserve System. 1994.
Clair, Robert T. "The Clearing House Interbank Payments System." In: *Research in Financial Services: Private and Public Policy*, Vol. 3. Greenwich, CT: JAI Press. 1991, pp. 63–94.
Folkerts-Landau, David, and Alfred Steinherr. "The Wild Beast of Derivatives: To Be Chained Up, Fenced In or Tamed?" In: *AMEX Bank Review Awards: Finance and International Economy*, Vol. 8. London: Oxford University Press. 1994.
Greenspan, Alan. Remarks at the Financial Markets Conference of the Federal Reserve Bank of Atlanta, Coral Gables, Florida, March 3, 1995.
Group of Thirty. *Derivatives: Practices and Principles*. Washington, DC: Group of Thirty, Global Derivatives Study Group. 1993.
Hayek, Friedrich A. von. *The Constitution of Liberty*. Chicago: Regnery. 1972.
Hu, Jie. "Information Ambiguity: Recognizing Its Role in Financial Markets." *Economic Review* (Federal Reserve Bank of Atlanta) 79 (July/August 1994).
Humphrey, David B. "Payments Finality and the Risk of Settlement Failure." In: A. Saunders and L.J. White, eds., *Technology and the Regulation of Financial Markets: Securities, Futures, and Banking*. Lexington, MA: Lexington Books. 1986.
Longerstaey, Jacques. *Introduction to RiskMetrics™*, 3rd ed. New York: J.P. Morgan & Co. Incorporated. 1995.
Mengle, David L. "Legal and Regulatory Reform in Electronic Payments: An Evaluation of Finality of Payment Rules." In: D.B. Humphrey, ed., *The U.S. Payment System: Efficiency, Risk and the Role of the Federal Reserve*. Boston, MA: Kluwer Academic Publishers. 1990.
Mengle, David L. "Daylight Overdrafts and Payments System Risks." *Economic Review* (Federal Reserve Bank of Richmond) 71 (May/June 1985), 14–27.
Mengle, David; David Humphrey; and Bruce Summers. "Intraday Credit: Risk, Value, and Pricing." *Economic Review* (Federal Reserve Bank of Richmond) 73 (January/February 1987), 3–14.
Oedel, David G. "Private Interbank Discipline." *Harvard Journal of Law and Public Policy* 16 (Spring 1993).
Scott, Hal S. "Commentary." In: D. B. Humphrey, ed., *The U.S. Payment System: Efficiency, Risk and the Role of the Federal Reserve*. Boston, MA: Kluwer Academic Publishers. 1990.
Spero, Joan E. *The Failure of the Franklin National Bank: Challenge to the International Banking System*. New York: Council of Foreign Relations, Columbia University Press. 1980.
U.S. General Accounting Office. *Financial Derivatives: Actions Needed to Protect the Financial System*. GAO/GGD-94-133. May 1994.

Journal of Financial Services Research 9: 393–407 (1995)
© 1995 Kluwer Academic Publishers

Systemic Stability and Competitive Neutrality Issues in the International Regulation of Banking and Securities

HARALD A. BENINK
Limburg Institute of Financial Economics (LIFE), University of Limburg, 6200 MD Maastricht, The Netherlands

DAVID T. LLEWELLYN
Department of Economics, Loughborough University, Loughborough Leicestershire LE11 3TU, United Kingdom

1. Introduction

The increasing globalization of banking and finance means that autarky (self-sufficiency at the national level) is no longer a feasible strategy in financial regulation: there is the potential for regulation determined at the national level to be undermined by developments in other regulatory jurisdictions, and regulatory requirements in one country have impacts in others. This creates a standard case for international regulatory cooperation, as, given the externalities involved, cooperative strategies have the potential to increase the effectiveness of regulation, and limit the scope for regulatory arbitrage.

The focus of this article is upon the international dimension to regulation in two areas (banking and securities business), which, while they have common considerations, also raise different issues. The focus is upon two issues in internationally cooperative regulatory strategies: *systemic stability* and *competitive neutrality*. Two central themes emerge. First, while in some areas there is a potential case for international coordination to increase the effectiveness of regulation for systemic stability reasons, issues of competitive neutrality might be dominant and, at times, in conflict with the requirements of prudential regulation for systemic stability. Second, specific examples of international coordination (the examples chosen are the 1988 Basle Capital Convergence Arrangements, with respect to banking, and the 1993 European Union's Capital Adequacy Directive, with respect to securities business) demonstrate that the approaches adopted may be inefficient in two respects: they do not achieve their systemic stability or competitive neutrality objectives, and the two objectives may be in conflict with the resultant compromise, being suboptimum for both.

The structure of the article is as follows. Section 2 considers the regulatory implications of the increasing globalization of banking and financial markets. Section 3 considers the

We would like to thank George Benston, Charles Goodhart, and other participants at the Financial Fragility Conference in Maastricht for helpful comments. Naturally, all remaining errors are our responsibility alone.

potential conflicts between systemic stability and competitive neutrality. Section 4 discusses the systemic stability and competitive neutrality dimensions of the 1988 Basle Capital Convergence Arrangements, with respect to banking, and the 1993 European Union's Capital Adequacy Directive, with respect to securities business. Section 5 summarizes the main conclusions.

2. International dimension to regulation

The internationalization of finance has accelerated as both suppliers and users of financial services increasingly have global options and are less restricted to purely domestic facilities. The international dimension of finance means that competitive pressures in banking, securities trading, and other financial services have become increasingly international. For these reasons, national financial systems have become subsets of a global system. In the process, something of a two-tier structure of banking and financial services has emerged, in which the corporate sector increasingly has global options, while financial services at the retail level are still more limited to within national financial systems. Nevertheless, as noted by Grundfest (1990, p. 350): "In today's internationalized securities market, even the smallest investor can treat national regulatory regimes as partially discretionary constraints on investment activity."

These trends imply that effective and efficient regulation in one country can no longer be applied independently of regulatory levels in other major systems. The international dimension to regulation has both competitive neutrality and systemic stability implications. First, given that financial institutions and markets compete globally, regulation in national systems has the capacity to confer competitive subsidies or disadvantages. Second, this can have the effect of inducing regulatory arbitrage. This, in turn, creates a third potential hazard: international competition in laxity. The *potential* danger is that the stability of the financial system (systemic stability) can be threatened because of a failure in a poorly regulated jurisdiction. Thus, partly through the international interbank market, risks can be spread, and the failure of an institution can have repercussions in other countries. The risk of widespread contagion or spillover effects is often referred to as *systemic risk*.

The word "potential" should be emphasized. Although international supervisors and regulators, such as the Basle Committee and the European Union, explicitly acknowledge the stability of the international financial system as one of the main reasons for international regulatory cooperation, this issue is not resolved. Corrigan (1992, p. 6) argues: "The speed, volume, value and complexity of international banking transactions have introduced new linkages and interdependencies between markets and institutions that have the *potential* to transmit problems and disruptions from place to place and institution to institution at almost breakneck speed" (italics added). Similarly, Steil (1992, p. 66) asserts: "Since any systemic effects of inadequate or misguided regulation in one jurisdiction cannot be contained within that single jurisdiction, the imposition of universal standards or modes of operation is likely to be the only effective response."

Against these positions, Benston (1994) sees no link between individual bank failures and the stability of a financial system in either a national or international context *as long as* central banks offset the reduction in total bank reserves associated with individual bank failures. The failure of an individual bank does not threaten the stability of the financial system if a liquidity crisis in the whole system is prevented by timely liquidity assistance from central banks. Moreover, according to Kaufman (1994), there is no evidence to support the widely held belief that, even in the absence of deposit insurance, bank contagion is a holocaust that can jeopardize solvent banks, the financial system, and even the macroeconomy, in domino fashion. It is also evident that two recent major bank failures (BCCI and Barings) did not produce either domestic or international systemic problems even though both were involved in international business.

In this article, we will not deal with this unresolved issue. Starting from the premise that international regulators *perceive* the preservation of systemic stability as a rationale for international regulatory cooperation, we analyze to what extent regulation with systemic stability objectives can be effective and consistent with competitive neutrality objectives of regulation in an international context.

The general problem in banking and securities regulation is that the jurisdiction of national regulators is smaller than the geographical area of regulated financial institutions and markets. There is no overriding international regulatory authority, as supervision and prudential regulation is conducted at the national level, while the issues have an international dimension. Different legal systems are involved, the powers and authority of individual central banks and bank supervisors vary considerably as do institutional structures in different countries. Steil (1992, p. 66) puts it as follows: "The global integration process in capital markets means that the system with which policymakers are concerned extends over a multitude of regulatory jurisdictions."

The central issues are the extent to which international factors undermine the power of exclusively national regulation, and whether, in an increasingly integrated global financial system, some or all of the objectives of regulation can only be achieved by abandoning the autarky of exclusively national legislation, implying that the design of effective regulatory structures can be met more effectively through various forms of international cooperation.

The collapse of BCCI in the summer of 1991 revealed several problems and weaknesses in the international dimension to banking regulation, namely, uncertainty over the division of responsibility between different national regulators; doubt about the quality of supervision in some jurisdictions; inadequate means of verifying the supervisory practices, effectiveness, and standards of regulatory authorities; the fact that complex company structures may make effective supervision more complicated; the importance, but absence of, consolidated supervision under a clear lead regulator; fraudulent exploitation of offshore banking centers with strict secrecy laws; and inadequate cooperation on the exchange of information among national supervisors. For a full description of the BCCI collapse, see Dale (1993), Hall (1991a, b, c; 1992; 1993) and Herring (1993).

The Basle Committee (with the endorsement of the central bank governors of the Group of Ten countries) subsequently responded with a series of proposals to reinforce the 1983 Concordat which governs the division of supervisory responsibility between parent and host supervisors of international banks. The objective is designed to "provide greater assurances that in the future no international bank can operate without being subject to effective consolidated supervision" (Basle Committee, 1992, p. 8). In particular, the Basle Committee recommended that: (1) all international banking groups and international banks should have a home country authority that capably performs consolidated supervision, (2) the creation of cross-border banking establishments should receive the prior consent of both the host country supervisor and their home country supervisor, (3) supervisory authorities should possess the right to gather information from the cross-border establishments of banks for which they are the home country supervisor, and (4) if a host country authority determines that any of the above minimum standards is not met to its own satisfaction, that authority could impose restrictive measures necessary to satisfy its prudential concerns consistent with the minimum standards. This last mentioned would include the prohibition of the creation of banking establishments. The key is that all international banks should be supervised by a home country supervisor "that capably performs consolidated supervision." This presupposes that national supervisory authorities are able in practice to monitor the quality of each other's supervision. Measures were also incorporated into the European Union's Second Consolidated Supervision Directive, including an extension to the information exchange requirement between supervisory agencies (see Benink, 1993; Hall, 1993).

3. Systemic stability and competitive neutrality

3.1. Systemic stability versus competitive neutrality

The specific rationale of international collaboration in regulation may focus upon one or more of three broad objectives: (1) to increase the efficiency of regulation in achieving its objectives of systemic stability and consumer protection *to the extent that* the international dimension to finance has the potential to undermine the effectiveness of nationally determined regulation, (2) to equalize competitive conditions between suppliers of financial services in different countries, or (3) to contribute towards the creation of a single market in financial services. The last mentioned is particularly relevant for the European Union, and this may require a greater degree of harmonization than would otherwise be the case. The type of collaboration will depend largely upon which of the three objectives is dominant. A central issue is the extent to which collaboration, including harmonization, is to extend beyond the requirements of systemic stability.

We focus on the two key issues of systemic stability and competitive neutrality which are considered in two areas, namely, banking and securities business. The *systemic stability* objective relates to internationally cooperative mechanisms to ensure the effectiveness of regulation to reduce the probability of default, and the potential for default of an institution in one country to threaten the stability of the financial system in others. This requirement arises to the extent that systemic stability considerations cannot be confined to individual countries, and hence countries have a mutual interest in each others' regulatory arrangements. However, international cooperation need not cover areas wider than those necessary to ensure the solvency of institutions. In particular, it does not in itself require harmonization of conduct of business rules. Thus, systemic stability need not be compromised if other countries have different conduct of business rules, providing that those regulations which relate specifically to systemic stability are effective. Conversely, systemic stability is potentially compromised if, for instance, a country has capital adequacy rules for banks which are less than those necessary for prudential reasons, as the lax regime may impose costs on other countries (e.g., because of the failure of banks in these countries). Thus, competition in regulation (while it has merits in some areas) should not apply to those regulatory requirements which specifically impinge on systemic stability. While the ultimate objective of international cooperation is to make such regulation effective, it does not have to extend to all aspects of regulation, as different countries may choose regulatory arrangements for a wider set of objectives than systemic stability. The question is how far, and into what areas, international corroboration is to extend.

The focus of the *competitive neutrality* objective is different. It implies international collaboration in those aspects of regulation (e.g., conduct of business rules) that have the potential to affect the competitive position of suppliers of financial services in different countries. The premise is that all forms of regulation have a potential impact on the cost of providing services. The issue arises as to whether competitive neutrality should relate to institutions (similar institutions in different countries operate under a similar regulatory regime) or functions, irrespective of which institutions provide those functions. The distinction between institutional and functional regulation arises because institutions may not be specialized, and institutional structures vary between countries. The obvious example is with respect to securities business, which is conducted both by banks and specialist securities firms. This aspect is discussed below.

A central issue relates to which areas of regulation are to be undertaken at the national level and which need overt international collaboration. In general, because of potential links between financial systems, regulation for systemic stability requires a higher degree of international collaboration in order to make it effective than does regulation with respect to conduct of business. While it is potentially hazardous to leave systemic stability issues strictly within the jurisdiction of national authorities, there may be considerable merit in allowing national differences in other areas where systemic stability considerations do not arise. Following the general principle of subsidiarity, regulation which does not have a systemic stability dimension is best left to the choices of individual countries.

Even so, there may be a case for extending international collaboration to wider aspects of regulation than purely systemic stability considerations. Two areas in particular arise: (1) where the objective is to create a single market in financial services across several countries, and (2) where cross-border transactions are undertaken, and a judgement is made that consumers may be unaware of differences in regulation and may assume that the same regulation applies as in their home country. The latter consideration is easier to handle when financial firms supply services to consumers by locating in the latter's home country. The generally accepted principle is that host country regulation applies with respect to conduct of business rules even though it is home countries that are responsible for prudential regulation.

Regulation for systemic stability relates to the probability of default and the social costs associated with it. Such regulation is not appropriate when, because of the nature of a firm's business, there is a low probability of failure or where, if failure does occur, the social costs are zero or are less than the costs of preventing the failure. This raises the issue of the uniqueness of banks as compared to securities firms. If the social costs of bank failure are positive or significantly higher than those associated with the failure of a securities firm, then it is appropriate, for instance, for capital adequacy requirements to be greater for banks than for securities firms. In other words, if the probability of failure and the social costs of failure are different, capital requirements also should be different. However, this may conflict with objectives related to competitive neutrality. In this case, while applying the same capital adequacy requirements for different firms (functional regulation) may satisfy the competitive neutrality objective, it would be suboptimum with respect to the systemic stability objective. In this case, competitive neutrality and systemic stability objectives are in conflict. Also, Mayer (1993) finds that systemic risks associated with securities activities are different in different countries, which implies that harmonized capital requirements are not appropriate. If, in general, capital requirements should be greater for banks, then meeting the competitive neutrality argument by applying the same capital ratio implies either that these requirements are set too low for banks or too high for securities firms. In the first case, there is a potentially greater danger of incurring social costs through bank failure, whereas in the latter case consumer welfare is impaired, because the costs of securities firms (in terms of the costs of required capital) are higher than are necessary to avoid the social costs of failure.

If, because of the unique position of banks and the higher social cost of failure, capital adequacy requirements are set higher for banks' securities business than are set for specialist securities firms, banks may be placed at a competitive disadvantage in this type of business. This is not necessarily an issue for regulatory authorites to the extent that they are concerned about systemic stability rather than industrial structure. If, by setting optimum capital requirements, business migrates to particular types of firms, then this may be regarded as an acceptable consequence of optimum capital adequacy requirements. Indeed, if higher capital requirements for banks were justified, because bank failures were more likely to impose systemic negative externalities, it would be socially desirable that banks lose securities business unless they can offset capital costs with savings from economies of scope.

3.2. Alternative forms of international collaboration

As international financial integration erodes the viability of autarky there is a prima facie case for at least a limited form of international collaboration. In highly interdependent systems, cooperative strategies can yield welfare benefits in terms of enhancing the effectiveness of regulation. In those cases were autarky is either not viable or less efficient than international collaboration, there is a spectrum of alternative forms of international collaboration, in which harmonization and competition represent two polar cases. The full spectrum of international regulatory collaboration encompasses what might be termed systemic harmonization, economic harmonization, international coordination, cooperation, extraterritorial enforcement, and international competition.

Systemic harmonization implies a high degree of harmonization of regulation for systemic stability reasons in order to make common regulatory objectives effective. It reflects the weakness of autarky in achieving regulatory objectives because of externalities at the international level.

The case for *economic harmonization* arises when there are differences in regulation which, while serving no regulatory or other objective and may simply be a product of history, impose unnecessary costs and inconvenience. The regulation of securities markets, for instance, is based on arrangements which vary considerably between countries (OECD, 1993). Harmonization in these cases, while not impairing any country's regulatory objectives or detracting from consumer welfare, could reduce the costs and inconvenience involved when suppliers and consumers operate under different regulatory regimes. Examples include arrangements with respect to information disclosure, registration procedures, accounting conventions, etc. While the case for reducing unnecessary or unchosen differences in regulation is strong, if the benefits of standardization are significant, the market should be able to devise its own mechanisms for securing regulatory convergence without the intervention of official regulatory authorities. Self-regulatory agencies are in a position to respond to market pressures if there are mutual advantages in standardization and no regulatory objectives are involved. This is one of the roles of IOSCO in the securities market.

Coordination aims not at harmonization but at establishing a common set of *minimum* regulatory standards above which individual countries can make choices, and the removal of evident inconsistencies and conflicts in regulation between jurisdictions.

Cooperative strategies relate to enforcement procedures and information sharing. With institutions conducting business in several regulatory jurisdictions, there can be advantages in sharing information between host and home countries. However, problems can be encountered, such as confidentiality and legal power to divulge information to foreign agencies. Such cooperative arrangements are well established in the banking sector through the Basle Committee, but fairly rudimentary in the securities industry, though IOSCO has made some contributions (e.g., establishment of a common code of conduct record). Cooperative strategies are also beneficial in enforcement where the cooperation of foreign regulatory authorities may be essential for the enforcement of home regulation and the prosecution of infringements. Regulatory authorities have a mutual interest in cooperation to secure enforcement and, where necessary, prosecution. This has been well developed by the Securities and Exchange Commission in the United States, which has successfully negotiated a network of treaties, communiqués, and accords with regulatory authorities outside the U.S.

A further option to address problems encountered with the international dimension to regulation is the application of *extraterritorial jurisdiction*. In some cases, though this may require the consent of host country authorities, a home regulator may require certain regulatory standards to be met by institutions under its jurisdiction even when the operations are being conducted by a foreign subsidiary of that institution which is formally under the jurisdiction of a host regulator. A host country would not normally allow a more lenient regulatory arrangement to apply, but in practice has no choice other than to acquiesce in more demanding standards being set.

In the absence of harmonized arrangements, *international competition* in regulation enables transactors to choose markets and institutions regulated under different regulatory regimes. This in particular applies to conduct of business rules where the case for harmonization is limited. Providing systemic stability is not put in jeopardy through non-harmonized regulation, diversity can enhance welfare and yield potentially valuable information. The counterargument, even when systemic dangers do not arise, is that consumers may not have access to the necessary information about different regulatory regimes, may assume that regulatory standards are universal, may be illequipped to make informed judgements, and may become confused. Furthermore, the institutions may be unwilling or unable to inform consumers of the differences.

In selecting the form of international collaboration, the ultimate focus needs to be on the objectives of regulation (systemic stability and consumer protection) and the extent to which they can be secured more efficiently through international collaborative strategies. There is a danger that, once the principle of collaboration is accepted, harmonization in particular will be pursued for its own sake and questions related to competitive neutrality will come to dominate prudential requirements and systemic stability. Such "international escalation" may take harmonization beyond the point where benefits (in terms of increased effectiveness in regulation) exceed costs. The original motive for the Basle Capital Convergence Arrangements for banks was related both to questions of safety and soundness of banks and systemic stability. Over time, however, the emphasis has shifted decisively towards requirements of competitive neutrality, with more emphasis on harmonization. In section 4, we will elaborate on this issue.

There are many reasons why, in some areas at least, differences in regulation between countries are both viable and desirable. They allow for different social choices to be made with respect to objectives, for different institutional structures and potential for systemic hazard, and for differences in externalities and the social cost of institutional failure. Competition in regulation can be beneficial providing that systemic stability is not impaired, that the externalities of one regime do not impose costs on others, that consumers have sufficient information about differences in regulatory regimes, and that the costs do not exceed the benefits of competition.

The principle of subsidiarity, which surfaced in the Delors Report on European Monetary Union (1989) and is related to the level at which general policy decisions are to be made in a monetary union, can equally be applied to regulation. For the reasons just outlined, the benefits that can be derived from competition, and questions of accountability of regulatory authorities, there is a strong case for regulation being framed at a local level except when its effectiveness is significantly impaired for systemic stability reasons, and where clear economic gains which exceed the benefits to be derived from local regulation can be made by international collaboration. The position has been highlighted by Grundfest (1990, p. 367): "The major challenge for regulators will, however, be to distinguish situations in which coordination is desirable from those in which diversity yields greater benefits." We add that decisions also relate to the particular form of collaboration, of which the fashion for harmonization is at one end of a spectrum.

4. Banking and securities business

4.1. Rules versus systems

The principal objective of regulation in banking and securities business relates to safety and soundness of institutions and systemic stability. Capital is the main focus of bank regulation for this objective and is the dominant aspect of international collaboration in regulation. The key issue is whether regulation for capital requirements for safety and soundness reasons is more efficiently based upon prescribed and internationally agreed *rules*, or banks' risk management *systems* coupled with use of market indicators.

Both nationally and internationally, the rules approach dominates. Although such rules have the advantage of being quantifiable and internationally agreed, in a later section we argue that precision may be a substitute for accuracy, and the capital requirements for banks based upon the 1988 Basle Capital Convergence (BCC) rules bear little resemblance to what would be derived from risk and portfolio analysis models. The BCC regime and the 1993 European Union's Capital Adequacy Directive (CAD) with respect to securities business hardly offer any advantage to banks with superior systems (Taylor, 1994).

An alternative approach is to abandon fixed rules and focus on banks' systems and efficiency with respect to identification and measurement of risks, banks' management of risks, the extent to which risks are hedged or externalized, and the way risks are combined and managed within the overall portfolio. The focus would be on whether banks have satisfactory risk-management systems, with imposed capital requirements being set in relation to the efficiency of systems. Thus, banks which demonstrate superior risk-management systems would be subject to lower capital requirements. This could act as an incentive for banks to develop superior risk-management systems, which is likely to contribute more to *systemic stability* than formal capital adequacy rules. It is pertinent to note that the collapse of Barings Bank in 1995 was a product of inadequate risk-management systems rather than a failure to adhere to capital adequacy requirements.

An advantage of a rules system (even though the rules may, to some extent, be arbitrary and not based upon actuarial assessment or risk) is that rules can be precisely quantified and internationally agreed. In this respect, they may serve the *competitive neutrality* objective of international collaboration. However, providing that systems effectively and efficiently contribute to systemic stability, competitive neutrality is of second-order importance. A focus on systems could alleviate a potential dual moral hazard of rules to the extent that the latter reduce the incentive both for banks to create effective risk-management systems, and for private monitoring of banks' behavior and balance-sheet positions.

At the international level, the focus of a systems approach would be international agreement on the assessment and monitoring of systems rather than on specific rules. This could create a new role for the Basle Committee, namely, monitoring the approach of national regulatory authorities with respect to risk-management systems of banks under their jurisdiction. International agreement would centre on the methodology and systems of risk analysis and management rather than on precise rules, as at present.

4.2. Capital for credit risks

The 1988 Basle Capital Convergence (BCC) arrangements, which established a common framework for capital regulation of banks, were designed to satisfy both systemic stability and competitive neutrality objectives. The primary objective was, as stated in the original document, "to strengthen the soundness and stability of the international banking system" (Basle Committee, 1988, p. 6). Competitive neutrality was addressed as follows: "The framework should be fair and have a high degree of consistency in its application to banks in different countries." The approach is highly prescriptive and capital adequacy is measured in terms of capital ratios against risk-adjusted assets. The approach generally can be criticized on the grounds that the "safety and soundness" of banks is determined not by fine capital calculations but by the quality of the asset book, the structure of the loan and asset portfolio, the banks' risk analysis and management systems, and internal control arrangements. The experience of Scandinavian banks in the early 1990s demonstrates that these were the reasons for bank failures other than failure to meet prescribed capital ratios (Benink and Llewellyn, 1994).

More specific weaknesses relate to the risk weight methodology applied. First, it cannot realistically be claimed that the risk weights applied to each category of assets are based upon actuarial assessments of true, absolute or relative, risk. Second, the largest category of most banks' assets is the portfolio of loans to the private sector, and yet all these loans are assigned a risk weight of unity. In practice, the differences in risk characteristics *within* the loan portfolio far exceed the differences between loans on average and other components of the asset portfolio. The largest single component of a bank's assets is not a homogenous category. Third, no allowance is made for the degree of diversification in the asset structure or for the way assets are combined in the total loan portfolio. Risks in a balance sheet are not additive, though this is the procedure adopted in the BCC methodology. Even accepting the validity of the basic methodology, if risk weights do not accurately reflect "true risk" suboptimum business structures and pricing strategies may emerge. There is a danger that, through the objective of seeking competitive neutrality, banks' pricing and other business decisions will come to be based upon a set of dubious and spuriously precise risk weights and conversion factors for off-balance-sheet business. This can have the effect of creating arbitrary and unwarranted distortions in business structures between different nationalities of banks, between banks and other institutions supplying "banking" services, within the asset portfolio, and between on- and off-balance-sheet business.

Because of the weaknesses embodied in the BCC risk-weight methodology, it is questionable whether BCC makes a significant contribution to systemic stability. At the same time, competitive neutrality seems to be important, since the Basle capital arrangements allegedly create competitively neutral capital positions through common capital adequacy requirements, definitions of allowable capital, risk weights attached to different assets, and conversion factors for off-balance-sheet items. Although competitive neutrality has been a dominant principle in the arrangements, they do not in practice create competitively neutral conditions. In a detailed comparison of U.S. and Japanese banks, Scott and Iwahara (1994) enumerate several examples of where different regulatory requirements are imposed on U.S. and Japanese banks and which undermine the competitive neutrality of BCC. The examples include the different role of the safety net and other non-BCC policies, imposed regulatory ratios in addition to those contained in BCC, differences in the scope of BCC requirements, differences in the definition of qualifying capital, differences in the risk weighting of some assets, and the manner in which BCC is enforced in the two countries. Differences in accounting procedures, the cost of capital, and in taxation also impinge on competitiveness in the two countries. In general, applying the principle of the second-best, harmonizing one aspect of regulation when other aspects are not equalized does not produce overall competitive neutrality.

4.3. Capital for market risks

The 1993 Capital Adequacy Directive (CAD) of the European Union seeks to apply common capital standards to banks (which conduct securities business) and specialist securities firms. The CAD seeks to harmonize regulation in four dimensions: by placing banks and securities firms under the same capital adequacy regime, by prescribing specific capital requirements with respect to market risk, by defining the form of regulatory capital for both, and by applying broadly similar consolidated supervision rules to both banking and investment groups.

The following three alternative approaches are applied by different regulators with respect to capital requirements against position risks: (1) the comprehensive approach which is applied by the Securities and Exchange Commission in the United States, (2) the building-block approach which is incorporated within the CAD, and (3) the portfolio approach which, in a simplified form, is used in the United Kingdom by the Securities and Futures Association (SFA). With the *comprehensive approach*, the capital requirement of a securities firm is set on the basis of a specified proportion of the value of its long positions plus a proportion of the value of its short positions. This has been the traditional method of setting capital requirements on securities firms both in the United States and elsewhere (though not in the United Kingdom). The *building-block approach* sets capital requirements partly on the net value (i.e., the extent of any net long or short position) of the trading book (representing market risk), and partly on the gross value of the book (representing specific risks). By distinguishing net and gross positions, this method at least recognizes that balanced books (i.e., those in which there is no net long or short position) provide partial hedging and therefore justify lower capital requirements. Under the theoretically superior *portfolio approach*, the setting of capital requirements is based upon a specific portfolio model which reflects the risk (volatility) of a firm's trading book, which, in turn, is influenced by the extent to which the portfolio is diversified. In other words, it sets capital requirements by reference to an explicit estimate of overall portfolio variability. The SFA in the United Kingdom applies a simplified version in that the model is based on a set of strong simplifying assumptions (Dimson and Marsh, 1994).

The Capital Adequacy Directive's approach to capital adequacy requirements for securities business and interest-rate risk favors the building-block approach, although there is little theoretical justification for it. With the building-block approach, only a partial offset is allowed for balanced trading books. For instance, the overall capital requirement is set equal to X percent of the gross position plus Y percent of the net position. These percentages are largely arbitrary and ad hoc, although some allowance is given for a balanced book. With respect to the CAD, the original idea was that X would be equal to 4 percent, and Y equal to 8 percent. Eventually it was agreed to impose arbitrary values of 2 percent and 8 percent, respectively, for large diversified portfolios.

Dimson and Marsh (1994) have tested the three alternative approaches based on the books of 58 British securities firms. The overall conclusion is that the simplified portfolio approach applied in the United Kingdom is superior to the comprehensive approach and the building-block approach in terms of economic efficiency and consumer protection. The others were rated poorly on these criteria. The authors conclude (p. 45): "The portfolio approach should be the preferred methodology for setting capital requirements. Yet international regulators have shown a marked preference for the building block approach."[1] It is also the case that the portfolio approach tends to give the lowest measure of capital requirements. This seems to suggest that international regulators are risk-averse and cautious in the setting of capital requirements, and in the process impair economic welfare to the extent that capital requirements are set in excess of what are needed for systemic stability. It also suggests that capital adequacy requirements are dominated by issues of competitive neutrality rather than the safety and soundness of institutions. Here seems to be an example where the motive of competitive neutrality has in practice taken precedence over efficiency of regulation, even though, as argued above, a set of regulatory requirements designed for competitive neutrality may not in practice be neutral.

Apart from the question of methodology of capital requirements, which was discussed above, there is the question of whether the securities activities of banks and securities firms should have the same capital requirements. In the European Union, in contrast to the United States, securities business is conducted both by banks and specialist securities firms, and the CAD seeks to apply a common capital adequacy regime for competitive neutrality reasons. However, there are substantial differences between banks and securities firms which have a bearing on the way in which they should be regulated, most especially with respect to capital-adequacy requirements.

Most, if not all, of the special characteristics of banks which give rise to the alleged case for regulation do not apply to securities firms: in the absence of deposit insurance and a lender of last resort, there is no moral hazard to be protected against; the systemic risk is less evident, and may not exist at all (Mayer 1993, p. 44); contagion is less likely, and the potential disruption of the payments system does not arise with securities firms. The main consideration, however, relates to the nature of securities firms' assets. Being readily marketable, they can be liquidated, albeit at the risk of a fall in prices, in the event of difficulty. Ultimately, securities firms can contract the balance sheet more easily than can banks, since they are not subject to the asymmetric asset and liabilities contracts that are a feature of banking. This in itself justifies higher capital requirements for banks than for securities firms.[2]

While systemic risks are less than with banks, they might not be totally absent. A default of a securities firm could have a *potentially* destabilizing impact on a financial system. A recent official study (OECD, 1993, p. 38) has opined as follows:

> . . . the rising importance of securities markets in the financial systems of OECD countries, the growing concentration in the securities industry, the effects of new

technologies, the nature of the risks now being borne by securities market intermediaries and the links between the securities market and the banking and payments system all suggest that the occurrence of serious misfunctions in the securities markets would have the potential to destabilize the entire financial system.

In the European Union's 1993 Capital Adequacy Directive (CAD), the choice was made for competitive neutrality rather than for systemic stability. Both banks and securities firms have to comply with the same capital requirements relative to their trading book position. In the case of banks, the mechanism devised is to isolate banks' trading books in securities from their portfolio holding of securities (i.e., that part of their securities business which is similar to that of specialist securities firms) and to apply the same capital requirements to the trading book position as are applied to nonbank securities firms. The trading book of a bank covers positions where market risk is a more accurate measure of exposure than credit risks, where the normal banking capital-adequacy requirements apply. The capital requirements in the CAD are less onerous than those applying to credit risks of banks in two respects: less capital is required and greater use can be made of subordinated debt capital to meet the capital requirements.

Overall, the potential danger implicit in the CAD, as far as the securities business of banks is concerned, is that the drive for a measure of competitive neutrality based on *functional* regulation makes banks potentially more vulnerable (too low capital requirements from a systemic stability point of view), more so than specialist banks that have no securities business. This seems to imply that, in order to achieve a common regulatory framework for banks and securities firms, bank supervisors have acquiesced in lower standards for banks than they would have ideally chosen. Overall, and given the unique position of banks, the drive for alleged competitive neutrality in the CAD results in treating as equal institutions what, at both the micro and systemic level, are not equal.

5. Conclusion

Our focus has been upon the international dimension of regulation and the interaction between systemic stability and competitive neutrality issues. Particular reference has been made to the 1988 Basle Capital Convergence (BCC) arrangements for banks and the 1993 European Union's Capital Adequacy Directive (CAD), with respect to the securities business of banks and specialist securities firms. The main themes may be summarized as follows:

- International cooperation in regulation focuses upon *systemic stability* and *competitive neutrality* issues. Although the two elements are interactive, the dominant objective in cooperative strategies should be systemic stability, while in practice the motivating force is predominantly competitive neutrality. There is a danger of harmonization being pursued for its own sake without reference to the ultimate objectives of regulation. The escalation of harmonization may take it beyond the point at which benefits exceed costs.

- Several specific problems arise when following competitive neutrality objectives in regulation: they may be in conflict with systemic stability objectives (e.g., securities activities of banks versus specialist securities firms); institutions which are not equal may be treated as if they are; different social choices may be denied through "escalating harmonization"; the potential benefits of competition between regulators may be lost; and harmonization within some areas may be insufficient to create overall competitive neutrality.
- The business of banks and securities firms is different, and, because the social cost of failure is different, this raises different systemic risks. The objectives and nature of regulation are different in the two sectors. Applying competitive neutrality principles to banks (with respect to their securities business) and securities firms may compromise systemic stability objectives of regulation.
- Notwithstanding the powerful international dimension in the design of optimum regulatory structures, *harmonization* in regulation is only one of several ways of incorporating international considerations. Financial integration does not in itself create sufficient conditions for total regulatory integration. Harmonization is a polar case along a spectrum, competition in regulation being the other polar case.
- Different approaches should be applied to different aspects of regulation, and there is no presumption in favor of harmonization. The general principle of *subsidiarity* is relevant in the design of regulatory structures: regulation is most effectively constructed at the national level, unless it is evidently more efficiently devised at a broader level.
- Specific examples of international coordination demonstrate that the approaches adopted may be inefficient in two respects: they do not achieve their systemic stability and competitive neutrality objectives, and the two objectives may be in conflict, with the resultant compromise being suboptimum for both. The BCC rules (the most detailed form of international regulatory cooperation) are seriously flawed with respect to both systemic stability and competitive neutrality objectives.
- Regulation and international collaboration have normally been conducted on the basis of rules. An alternative, superior approach is to focus upon financial firms' systems of risk analysis and management, and for the regulatory authorities to set capital requirements which reflect the efficiency of banks' risk analysis and management systems.

The ultimate objective of harmonization is to ensure the effectiveness of regulation. Questions of competitive neutrality raise fundamentally different issues from those of systemic stability, and the case for harmonization for competitive neutrality is considerably less and, under some circumstances, can be hazardous and welfare reducing. The central issue concerns what areas of regulation require international collaboration and what form such collaboration should take.

Notes

1. In April 1995, the Basle Committee announced a new proposal to calculate the capital that banks must set aside for market risks. The proposal gives banks a choice between applying the building-block approach or

using their own financial models to calculate the "value at risk." These models should meet certain regulatory quality standards (The Economist, April 15-21, 1995, pp. 70-71). The new approach is likely to be adopted by the European Union as well, which would require a modification of the CAD.

2. Benston (1989), analyzing the potential effects of a repeal of the Glass–Steagall Act's separation of commercial and investment banking in the United States (U.S.), sees, both from a theoretical and empirical point of view, no fundamental difference in terms of risk exposure and potential strain of the safety net (including deposit insurance) between commercial banks (U.S. model) and "universal" banks which combine commercial and investment banking (European model).

References

Basle Committee. "International Convergence of Capital Measurement and Capital Standards." Bank for International Settlements, July 1988.

Basle Committee. "Minimum Standards for the Supervision of International Banking Groups and their Cross-Border Establishments." Bank for International Settlements, June 1992.

Benink, H.A. *Financial Integration in Europe*. Kluwer Academic Publishers: Dordrecht/Boston/London. 1993.

Benink, H.A., and D.T. Llewellyn. "Fragile Banking in Norway, Sweden and Finland: An Empirical Analysis." *Journal of International Financial Markets, Institutions and Money* 4 (3/4) (1994), 5–19.

Benston, G.J. "The Federal 'Safety Net' and the Repeal of the Glass–Steagall Act's Separation of Commercial and Investment Banking." *Journal of Financial Services Research* 2 (1989), 287–305.

Benston, G.J. "International Harmonization of Banking Regulations and Cooperation among National Regulators: An Assessment." *Journal of Financial Services Research* 8 (1994), 205–225.

Corrigan, E.G. "Challenges Facing the International Community of Bank Supervisors." *Quarterly Review* (Federal Reserve Bank of New York) (Autumn 1992).

Dale, R. "Bank Regulation after BCCI." *Journal of International Banking Law* (1993), 8–17.

Delors Report. "Report on Economic and Monetary Union in the European Community." Office of Publications of the European Communities, Luxembourg, 1989.

Dimson, E., and P. Marsh. "The Debate on International Capital Requirements." City Research Project, London Business School, February 1994.

Grundfest, J. "Internationalization of the World's Securities Markets: Economic Causes and Regulatory Consequences." *Journal of Financial Services Research* 4 (1990), 349–378.

Hall, M. "BCCI: The Issues Raised." *Banking World* (September 1991a).

Hall, M. "BCCI: Yet More Questions." *Banking World* (October 1991b).

Hall, M. "BCCI: Latest Developments." *Banking World* (December 1991c).

Hall, M "BCCI: Spotlight on the Regulators." *Banking World* (July 1992).

Hall, M. "BCCI: The Lessons for Bank Supervisors." *International Journal of Regulatory Law and Practice* 3 (1993), 298–313.

Herring, R.J. "BCCI: Lessons for International Bank Supervision." *Contemporary Policy Issues* 11 (1993), 76–86.

Kaufman, G.G. "Bank Contagion: A Review of the Theory and Evidence." *Journal of Financial Services Research* 8 (1994), 123–150.

Mayer, C. "The Regulation of Financial Services: Lessons from the United Kingdom." In: J. Dermine, ed. *European Banking in the 1990s*. Oxford: Blackwell Publishers. 1993.

OECD. "Systemic Risks in Securities Markets." Paris, 1993.

Scott, H., and S. Iwahara. "In Search of a Level Playing Field." *Occasional Paper*. No. 46, Group of Thirty, Washington, DC.

Steil, B. "Regulatory Foundations for Global Capital Markets." In: R. O'Brien, ed., *Finance and the International Economy*, No. 6. Oxford: Oxford University Press. 1992.

Taylor, C. "A New Approach to Capital Adequacy Regulation for Banks." Centre for the Study of Financial Innovation, London, 1994.

The Economist. "Do-It-Yourself Regulation." April 15-21, 1995, 70-71.

G-21

G-28

Journal of Financial Services Research 9: 409–412 (1995)
© 1995 Kluwer Academic Publishers

215 - 18

Comment: Banking

CHRISTIAN DE BOISSIEU

Professor of Economics at the University of Paris I (Pantheon–Sorbonne), 75005 Paris, France, and member of the Committee for Banking Regulation (France).

1. The real cost of bailout and no-bailout

The optimization model built by F. Bruni and F. Paterno underlines, in the definition of the objective function and the constraints, some costs and benefits associated with the policy choice of bailout versus no-bailout. It would be of interest to introduce some other real costs, i.e., costs for the real economy. For example, the bailout policy could lead to systemic distortions (the "moral hazard" arguments) and to crowding-out effects generated by increased public expenditures. Conversely, the no-bailout policy could induce a cumulative loss of confidence, systemic repercussions, and short-run and long-run implications on investment, growth, employment, etc. In both cases, the policy has an impact on the real growth path. The channels and the intensity of this impact need to be analyzed more carefully by referring to dynamic models with a sufficient degree of integration of real and financial variables.

2. Interest rates and market discipline

Bruni–Paterno argue from theoretical and empirical considerations that market interest rates adjust pretty well to the level of risk and that markets foresee bank problems. The methodology and the empirical analysis are open to discussion. Nevertheless, the conclusion is of interest when looking at the possible working of the economic and monetary union in Europe. If, according to the Maastricht Treaty, the European Union introduces a single currency, what will be and must be the degree of coordination of national fiscal policies? Market discipline through interest rates and risk premia will be necessary in order to encourage highly indebted countries and institutions to adjust. But it is very likely that it will not be sufficient, and that some form of "multilateral surveillance" of fiscal policies at the European level, e.g., the monitoring of public sector deficits as organized by the Maastricht Treaty, will have to be introduced.

3. Some remarks on the analysis of optimal banking

The contributions of Bruni–Paterno as well as Horvitz belong to the burgeoning literature on optimal banking regulation. As was the case for the concept of equilibrium several decades ago, the debate about banking regulation has recently evolved from the existence problem to the optimality problem. As far as the existence of regulation is concerned, the arguments are well-known and largely accepted, namely, the necessity to contain the market power of some financial institutions, the existence of externalities, and information failures and asymmetries. The optimality problem raises numerous issues, many of them being aspects of the "rules versus discretion" debate.

1. Optimality often refers to the optimal *level* of a regulatory tool (such as, for example, the capital-to-asset ratio). But optimality considerations must also relate to the form of regulation. What I call the *structure* of regulation plays a crucial role. In particular, it is essential to fix the respective weights of three types (and levels) of regulation and monitoring:

    (ii) external regulation, namely, the implementation of more or less sophisticated rules by governmental regulatory authorities;

    (ii) self-regulation mechanisms, which may be very similar to those derived from external regulation, and through which decentralized markets introduce rules; and

    (iii) internal (i.e., within the firm) monitoring and control.

Some countries rely more on self-regulation, others emphasize external regulation. The issue of the optimal weighting of these three types and levels of regulation is crucial in two current debates: (a) the implementation of the new required capital ratios (which integrate counterparty risks and market risks); and (b) the attitude of the authorities vis-à-vis the growth of derivative instruments. As far as derivative markets are concerned, the development of intermediate forms between exchange-traded markets and OTC markets (e.g., OTC markets introducing clearing houses) illustrates a durable move, as does the extension of self-regulation procedures (segments of the OTC market resorting to deposits, margin requirements, etc., comparable to the ones on organized markets). For a couple of years, banks often have been asking for deposits and margin requirements from hedge funds.

2. The "regulatory dialectic," according to Edward Kane, emphasizes the interaction between regulation and financial innovation. It implies that the theory of optimal banking regulation must resort to dynamic models and face time-consistency problems. (Bruni and Paterno study one important variety of these models, which has nothing to do with the endogeneity of the menu of financial instruments, i.e., with the fact that regulation could generate the creation of some financial instruments.)

4. The regulation of a contestable market

The market for banking and financial services is becoming increasingly contestable as regards both entry and exit conditions. One of the justifications for regulation is "fair" competition (see, e.g., the adjustment of the new prudential ratios to the new competitive situation). Regulation could be necessary, but not sufficient, to enforce market rules and the search for a "level playing field." Two observations should be made:

1. The very notion of a "level playing field" is ambiguous and deserves deeper analytical and empirical discussion. Nevertheless, the search for such a competition condition could be more justified but also more demanding in a world of rapid diversification by financial institutions, which is justified in many cases by the existence of economies of scope in banking and financial activities. Diversification would require the implementation of functional control (i.e., control by activities) instead of the prevailing institutional control. For evident practical reasons, it is difficult to move to functional control.

2. An effective "level playing field" necessitates short regulatory lags, particularly short delays between changes in market conditions and consequent adjustments in the regulatory framework in order to keep the playing field level. The overall regulatory lag is the sum of a recognition lag and a decision lag, and both vary among countries. This is true within the European Union, despite the single market and extended regulatory convergence, and present divergences are going to persist at least in the short run. In order to make the regulatory framework adapt to rapidly evolving market conditions, it is crucial to shorten the regulatory lag. A permanent adjustment of regulation could create some instability and uncertainty for private agents. There is an optimum frequency of adjustments. For example, the weights embedded in the new capital ratios have to be updated, but not continuously.

5. Regulation and coordination

5.1. At the international level

In a world of perfect capital mobility and regulatory arbitrage, most countries are "regulation takers", since they have to adjust on the most favorable conditions. International coordination could be, in certain circumstances, the way to internalize externalities and avoid the adjustment to the least regulated market, i.e., competitive deregulation.

In this respect Bruni and Paterno are right when they emphasize the necessity of a greater coordination of national prudential policies within the European Union. According to the Maastricht Treaty, the future European Central Bank (ECB) is not given the "lender of last resort" (LLR) function. Monetary policy is going to be centralized at the European level, while the subsidiarity principle applies to prudential policy, which will remain decentralized. Since the LLR function and the monetary policy function are more and more intertwined, this decoupling of monetary policy and prudential policy might lead, under certain circumstances, to conflicts between the monetary policy goals of the ECB and the liquidity support for payment systems or other purposes from the national central banks. It does not necessarily correspond to a steady state.

An application of the rules versus discretion debate at the world level (more specifically, within the G10 at Basle) relates to the new capital adequacy rules. In the European directive adopted in 1993 and to be implemented as of 1996, a precise methodology is provided in order to harmonize the way financial institutions calculate their market exposure, e.g., their exposure to interest rate risk. Some countries outside the EU (but also within it) would prefer a more decentralized and flexible procedure, namely the free choice by the financial institutions of the methodology to be implemented. This debate illustrates strength and weakness of coordination of financial regulation.

5.2. At the domestic level

A greater coordination of regulatory authorities within each country is the logical consequence of the globalization of financial activities and the diversification by financial institutions. For example, the development of financial conglomerates requires increasing cooperation among banking, market, and insurance regulatory bodies. It must be recognized that in many countries—and not only the U.S.—persistent conflicts of interest explain why coordination between, e.g., banking and market authorities, could be more difficult to negotiate and implement than some international coordination exercises taking place in Brussels or Basle.

Journal of Financial Services Research 9: 413–419 (1995)
© 1995 Kluwer Academic Publishers

Comment: The Payment and Settlement Systems

CLAUDIO E.V. BORIO
Bank for International Settlements, CH-4002 Basle, Switzerland

To quote from the latest BIS Annual Report,[1] which devotes a whole chapter to the subject:

> Payment and settlement systems are to economic activity what roads are to traffic: necessary but typically taken for granted unless they cause an accident or bottlenecks develop (p. 172).

On both counts policymakers and market participants have had increasingly convincing reasons to pay closer attention to what constitutes the basic infrastructure of our economies. The Herstatt crisis of 1974, the global stock market crash of 1987, and the failure of Drexel Burham Lambert in 1990, for example, have all highlighted the potential of payment and settlement systems for propagating and amplifying financial shocks. At the same time, a spectacular growth in financial transactions has resulted in an unprecedented surge in the average size and overall value of payments, putting pressure on existing systems and radically altering the scale of the credit and liquidity risks involved. Against this background, public authorities and private agents in recent years have taken a broad set of initiatives with a view to improving the soundness of the arrangements. The fact that at least one-fifth of the program of the present international conference is devoted to payment system risks—something that would have been unthinkable a decade ago—is a clear indication of how keen the interest in the topic has recently become.

What I propose to do in the following pages is not so much to discuss in detail the two articles presented at the conference, but rather to provide a broad overview of the issues and initiatives taken. This should help to put in a better perspective the progress made in various areas and to understand the interrelationship between them. Where appropriate, I shall be making reference to the individual contributions to this conference.

First of all, what is special about payment system risks? In a fundamental sense, not much: the two basic types of risk—liquidity and credit risk—are those that lie at the core of much of the academic and policy discussions of fragility in financial systems more generally. The same conceptual and analytical toolkit therefore applies. On the other hand, the way we traditionally think of financial crises is to imagine that transactions have already taken place, that agents have achieved their desired portfolios and that then suddenly some "shock" occurs. By contrast, payment system risk concerns those liquidity and credit risks that are connected with the *process of executing transactions*: the forward replacement cost risk associated with any lag between trade and settlement (the "settlement lag"); the capital risk stemming from lags between the delivery and payment legs of trades; and the credit and liquidity risks run by the payment intermediaries that facilitate the execution of the transactions.[2] The corresponding exposures, albeit short-lived, can be very large in relation to on-balance-sheet ones and the capital of participants, especially for providers of payment services such as banks. They are also typically more opaque and less controllable. Add to this the fact that payment and settlement arrangements are the most pervasive connective tissue across institutions and markets and it becomes clear why their potential for propagating and amplifying disturbances is so large, as evidenced by the episodes of distress described in Professor Eisenbeis' article. At the heart of the propagation is the uncertainty[3] about the size and distribution of both *direct* and *indirect* settlement exposures, and hence the difficulties in ascertaining the condition of counterparties and in identifying the sources of liquidity demands. The result is an exacerbation of the tendency to withhold payments, ration funds and withdraw from transactions, which heightens and spreads the original disturbance.[4]

There are several dimensions in which action may be taken to reduce the risks inherent in the settlement process. One is improvements in the ability of participants to monitor and control their direct exposures to counterparties, possibly complemented by more centralized monitoring facilities. A second is a shortening of settlement lags commensurate with technical possibilities. A third is the reduction of "involuntary" credits arising from asynchronous payments and receipts or from lags between the execution of the delivery and payment legs of trades. A fourth, crucial one is the implementation of arrangements to limit the impact of a failure to settle by one participant on the ability of others to do likewise, commonly achieved through some form of risk-sharing. A fifth is ensuring that participants have the necessary incentives to control the risks they incur; limiting the reliance on central bank support to resolve a settlement failure is especially important in this context. A final dimension is the reduction of legal uncertainties which may impinge on the settlement process, such as those surrounding netting schemes and bankruptcy laws; this is a source of difficulties in its own right to the extent that it generates doubts about, or incorrect perceptions of, exposures and hence potential losses.

Action along all these lines had indeed been taken in recent years. But given the complexity of payment and settlement arrangements, the approach has been selective, focusing on four interrelated areas of significant concern: large-value interbank funds transfer systems (LVFTs), and the settlement of three types of transaction, namely securities, foreign exchange and, more recently, derivatives. Note that in the case of LVFTs only the *payment leg* of transactions is considered; particular attention is paid to the risks incurred by banks as payment intermediaries. In the other three cases, the main focus is on the *relationship* between the delivery and payment legs of the transactions themselves and hence on the risks incurred by counterparties. Although in practice counterparties and payment intermediaries are often banks themselves, the distinction is useful analytically. It helps to understand the interrelationships between the risk-reduction measures and their partial nature—aspects which do not emerge very clearly in the commendable effort of Eisenbeis. Let me spend just a few words on each of these areas.

LVFTSs are the lynch-pin of modern payment arrangements. Established or profoundly modified with the introduction of information technology during the 1980s, they handle the payment leg of the bulk of financial transactions. Settlement takes places on the books of the central bank. Traditionally, these systems have had relatively few safeguards against settlement risk and tended to rely excessively on the central bank to prevent or deal with a settlement failure. As Mengle reminds us; this is a very comfortable position for the banks, but hardly for the authorities.

Consider first those systems, the vast majority, that settle on a multilateral net basis at fixed intervals, at present generally at the end of the day. The lag implies an accumulation of funds transfer orders: any settlement failure necessarily affects the backlog of transfers. Until recently, most such systems were wholly open-ended: there was no built-in mechanism to ensure that the original transfer orders would indeed be settled. The orders were typically made conditional on successful settlement ("unwinding clauses") and no mechanism addressed the system-wide liquidity shortfall implied by the default of a participant. The result was that inordinate pressure was placed on the central bank to intervene in order to limit the risk of a chain reaction that would affect participating banks and any other market that relied on the system for the final settlement of its transactions.

The possible remedies? One is to retain discrete-time settlement but upgrade the safeguards: to shorten the fixed settlement lag somewhat; to introduce real-time monitoring of positions; to implement caps on the bilateral and multilateral exposures; and, above all, to put in place liquidity-pooling and loss-sharing arrangements aimed at ensuring settlement despite the failure of individual institutions. This means in effect attempting to decouple illiquidity from insolvency problems, i.e., to eliminate the cash-flow shortfall and allow the losses on the underlying contracts to be dealt with separately through the courts. By the same token, it also means shifting back the burden on to the participating banks. The history of CHIPS is just one illustration among many: between 1970 and 1990 all the above steps were taken.[5]

An alternative strategy is to move to real-time gross settlement (RTGS). In this case funds transfer orders are settled irrevocably and unconditionally ("finally") as soon as they have been sent provided that the sending bank has sufficient cover in its account with the central bank. The advantages: exposures become more transparent (setlement accounts and credit limits need to be monitored), more "voluntary" (if the sending bank is short of funds it must obtain an explicit credit)[6] and do not cumulate so easily; above all, the uncertainty surrounding unwinding provisions is eliminated and intraday finality made possible. The catch is that the tighter liquidity constraint may be *too* tight: if intraday borrowing facilities and procedures to manage the traffic of funds transfers are not well developed, orders may fail to be executed and generalized "gridlocks" with potential systemic consequences may arise. Failure to obtain sufficient funds may lead to default on settlement obligations and help to spread disturbances, especially given the difficulties in distinguishing between illiquidity and underlying insolvency problems. At the other end of the spectrum, if intraday central bank credit is unlimited, uncollateralized and at zero cost, all the risk is absorbed by the central bank, hardly a situation conducive to prudent behavior. Hence the risk-reduction program launched in 1986 in the United States with regard to Fedwire, introducing self-imposed caps and the pricing of overdrafts (April 1984). Elsewhere, intraday credit has generally been fully collateralized and more limited. Several countries have recently introduced or are planning to implement RTGS systems with due regard to risk management characteristics. The EC central banks have recommended the introduction of such a system in the shortest delay in each member state.

The foregoing analysis indicates that it is the delayed settlement and the uncertainty surrounding it that constitute the main reasons for introducing RTGS, a point noted by Eisenbeis. Legal uncertainties are one element of the story, but certainly not the most important one. Moreover, as emphasized by Mengle, the pressure for change has come primarily from the authorities, not from the banks. Indeed, it has often met with their resistance.

An area where private initiative has played a bigger role is that of securities transactions. Following the October 1987 global stock market crash the main strategy has been to shorten the settlement lag of trades and, more importantly, to eliminate the lag between the payment and delivery legs ("delivery versus payment", or DVP). Several reports by official, private, and quasi-private bodies have been written on the subject; the G-30 recommendations have been particularly influential. As discussed in detail in a recent report by the G-10 central banks, there are several ways in which DVP may be achieved. RTGS systems can be very useful in this context too, as a means of ensuring the irrevocability of the payment leg of the transactions and hence avoiding the risk of unwinding trades. In other words, real-time gross settlement can help to insulate the securities subsystems from problems that arise elsewhere in the payments arrangements.

Of greater concern, however, has been the risk stemming from the nonsimultaneous settlement of the two legs of foreign exchange transactions ("cross-currency settlement risk" or "Herstatt risk"): the amounts involved are much larger; the risk necessarily has a international dimension; it is more difficult to manage; and the trades giving rise to it are mainly between banks. The key constraint at the origin of the risk is that there is no effective overlap between the operating hours of the LVFTSs of the countries of the three most actively traded currencies (the US dollar, the Deutsche Mark, and the yen), while settlement typically takes place in the country of issue of each currency. Another, quantitatively even more important, source of risk is that market participants have failed to limit the exposures to the extent allowed by the settlement cycles of the domestic systems.

There are several ways to improve the management of Herstatt risk. First, the soundness of the settlement mechanisms of each of the two legs, essentially domestic LVFTSs, may be enhanced; the measures taken in CHIPS fall under this heading (see above). Secondly, the settlement flows between counterparties associated with the original trades can be reduced; it is in this context that netting of contracts is especially important: besides limiting the credit exposures implied by forward-dated transactions, it can also result in a significant reduction in the associated settlement flows. Bilateral contract netting arrangements are already in operation (e.g., FXNET and ICSI) and multilateral ones are planned (Multinet and ECHO). Thirdly, payment arrangements outside the country of issue can be used to limit cross-border flows; the Chase-Tokyo scheme mentioned by Eisenbeis is one such example. Finally, full DVP mechanisms can be implemented; this would generally call for the upgrading of central bank services as a complement to private initiatives.

The authorities have clearly recognized for some time the major contribution that private cross-border netting and settlement schemes can make to risk management. The concern has been that their potential benefits can remain beyond reach if they are poorly designed. The 1990 report on interbank netting schemes by the G-10 central banks (the "Lamfalussy Report") addresses these concerns. Besides setting out the principles for cooperative central bank oversight, it recommends a set of minimum standards for the operation of cross-border multi-currency netting schemes (see table 4 in Eisenbeis' article). It stresses the importance of a well-founded legal basis and the need for the schemes to ensure the timely completion of daily settlements in the event of the failure to settle by the participant with the largest net debit position. Given their compass, the standards have served as a blueprint for the assessment even of purely domestic settlement systems, including LVFTSs. They are hardly, in my view, an excessively detailed straightjacket that can hamper private initiatives, as Mengle appears to suggest.

As outlined in a recent report by the G-10 central banks, the upgrading of central bank services to support DVP mechanisms may take a variety of forms: introducing intraday final settlement in domestic LVFTs through RTGS; extending opening hours to eliminate time-zone gaps, as planned with Fedwire as from early 1997; conceivably, providing multicurrency settlement services directly, either individually or through an ad hoc international institution which would settle both legs of cross-currency trades on its books (a "common agent"). Such services, however, would represent a major departure from existing arrangements, call for much closer cooperation, and raise a host of difficult issues, ranging from the monetary policy implications to the need for agreement on the appropriate balance between public involvement and market discipline.

Turning next to the settlement of derivatives transactions, certain specific characteristics of the instruments merit attention. First, in contrast to spot transactions, where the settlement lag reflects technological and operational frictions, derivative contracts involve commitments to transfer cash or perform exchanges at future dates. The associated credit risk is the result of frictions only to the extent that the mandated future spot exchanges, if any, are themselves subject to settlement lags or not a DVP basis. Second, derivative transactions are generally structured so as to limit settlement flows, typically by avoiding the exchange of principal and relying extensively on netting; the actual settlement amounts are often tiny in comparison with notional trading volumes. Finally, this does not mean that settlement risk is unimportant; rather, its management is more difficult to disentangle from procedures aimed at limiting the forward replacement cost risk implied by the contracts. Indeed, as correctly highlighted by Eisenbeis, the sophisticated risk-management procedures of clearing houses for exchange-traded derivatives resemble, and may have inspired, those found in some LVFTSs: the posting of daily margins (shortening of settlement lags),[7] limits on members' positions (multilateral caps), the power to assess members (loss-sharing agreements), and back-up credit lines (interbank and central bank standing credit facilities).

A major current policy issue is the desirability and feasibility of extending such clearing house arrangements to over-the-counter (OTC) products. Indeed, the distinction between centralized and decentralized risk management should have merited attention in Mengle's piece, given the very different implications in terms of incentives and feasibility of spontaneous emergence in the markets. In principle, as the Lamfalussy Report concludes, provided the arrangements are properly designed they can yield considerable benefits. In practice, a number of obstacles hinder their extension. These pertain to the highly customized nature of most of the instruments, legal, and regulatory problems relating to cross-border trading and competitive considerations, most notably the fear on the part of the most creditworthy players to see their competitive advantage undermined.

Where, then, do we stand? Our understanding of the risks involved in payment systems has considerably improved in recent years. Nevertheless, academics have tended to shy away from a specific analysis of the issues involved. This is a pity, not only because the workings of payment and settlement systems are central to the understanding of the propagation of financial shocks, but also because the toolkit for the work, as argued before, is already there. How to contain risks without impairing, and possibly improving, the efficiency of the arrangements is a challenging question deserving careful study. From a welfare viewpoint, how far risk reduction should be pursued is another. More generally, a deeper understanding of payment systems can help to cast light on certain old but still quite topical issues: the specificity of "banks," the extent of their actual and prospective disintermediation, competition, and profitability. The role of banks as providers of payment services tends to be downplayed or neglected all too often.

At the policy level, a number of concrete steps have been taken or are planned to upgrade risk management. Yet progress has neither been easy nor uniform; the agenda for the future remains a charged one. Three sets of factors have contributed to slowing down progress, the first two of which, I feel, have been excessively downplayed by Mengle.[8] A first set has been of a purely economic nature: the necessary changes are costly; the costs are easily quantifiable and private; and the benefits less amenable to estimation and often a common good. A second set is of a psychological character: there is a pervasive tendency, especially in the markets, to underestimate the likelihood of worst-case scenarios. It typically takes a major shock to catalyse agents into effective joint action. A third set relates to the difficulty of adapting the legal framework to the new market realities, an aspect which finds ample space in Eisenbeis' discussion. There is considerable uncertainty surrounding the rights and obligations of participants, and uncertainty is the worst enemy of rational responses at times of difficulties.

It is therefore not surprising that progress has been slowest in the area of international transactions. It is there that competitive forces are strongest and voluntary cooperation indispensable, among both market participants and public authorities. It is there, too, that the tension between the borderless nature of finance and essentially national, not necessarily consistent, legal frameworks is most forcefully apparent. It may be worth recalling that it is now almost exactly 20 years since Bankhaus Herstatt failed. And yet, despite the phenomenal growth in the value of cross-border transactions since then, the mechanisms for settling foreign exchange trades are not fundamentally different from what they were at the time. This is an area where cooperative efforts between the authorities and market participants are absolutely essential in order to make good progress.

Notes

1. The following remarks draw extensively on that report. A more detailed and comprehensive analysis of the issues can be found in Borio and Van den Bergh (1993), which also includes an extensive bibliography.
2. To these one should also add the default risk on the settlement medium itself, a significant one given that settlement often takes place in inside money.
3. The situation is indeed one better characterized by "Knightian uncertainty" than simply "risk."
4. For a discussion of the three episodes mentioned, see also BIS (1994).

5. Real-time monitoring was a feature of the system since its inception. The system moved from next-day to same-day settlement in 1981. Bilateral and multilateral net debit caps were introduced in 1984 and 1986 respectively. A loss-sharing rule backed by collateral requirements was implemented in 1990.
6. Of course, as the discussion above illustrates, those pluses can also be achieved in properly designed net-settlement systems.
7. Actual settlement normally takes place on a next-day basis and in inside-money balances.
8. Even in the derivatives area, it should be recalled that the G-30 report mentioned by Mengle was in part a reaction to the voicing of policy concerns. In addition, the report leaves open the question of the enforceability of the best practices it recommends.

References

Bank for International Settlements. *Report on Netting Schemes*. Prepared by the Group of Experts on Payment Systems of the Central Banks of the G-10 countries, Basle, February 1989.

Bank for International Settlements. *Payment Systems in Eleven Developed Countries*. Prepared by the Group of Experts on Payment Systems of the Central Banks of the G-10 countries, Basle, April 1989.

Bank for International Settlements. *Survey of Foreign Exchange Market Activity*. Basle, February 1990.

Bank for International Settlements. *Large-value Funds Transfer Systems in the G-10 Countries*. Prepared by the Group of Experts on Payment Systems of the Central Banks of the G-10 countries, Basle, May 1990.

Bank for International Settlements. *Report of the Committee on Interbank Netting Schemes of the Central Banks of the G-10 countries*. Basle, November 1990.

Bank for International Settlements. *Delivery versus Payment in Securities Settlement Systems*. Report prepared by the Committee on Payment and Settlement Systems of the Central Banks of the G-10 countries, Basle, September 1992.

Bank for International Settlements. *Recent Developments in International Interbank Relations*. Prepared by a Working Group established by the central banks of the G-10 countries, Basle, October 1992.

Bank for International Settlements. *Central Bank Survey of Foreign Exchange Market Activity in April 1992*. Basle, March 1993.

Bank for International Settlements. *Central Bank Payment and Settlement Services with Respect to Cross-border and Multi-currency Transactions*. Report prepared by the Committee on Payment and Settlement Systems of the Central Banks of the G-10 countries, Basle, September 1993.

Bank for International Settlements. *Payment Systems in the Group of Ten Countries*. Prepared by the Group of Experts on Payment Systems of the Central Banks of the G-10 countries, Basle, December 1993.

Bank for International Settlements. *64th Annual Report 1993/1994*. Basle, June 1994.

Bank for International Settlements. *Cross-border Securities Settlements.* Report prepared by the Committee on Payment and Settlement Systems of the Central Banks of the Group of Ten Countries. Basle, March, 1995.

Borio, C.E.V., and P. Van den Bergh. "The Nature and Management of Payment System Risks: An International Perspective." BIS Economic Paper No. 36, Basle, February 1993.

Committee of Governors of the Central Banks of the Member States of the European Economic Community. *Issues of Common Concern to EC Central Banks in the Field of Payment Systems*. Prepared by the Ad Hoc Working Group on EC Payment Systems, Basle, 1992.

Committee of Governors of the Central Banks of the Member States of the European Economic Community. *Minimum Common Features for Domestic Payment Systems*. Prepared by the Ad Hoc Working Group on EC Payment Systems, Basle, November 1993.

227 - 30

Journal of Financial Services Research 9: 421–424 (1995)
© 1995 Kluwer Academic Publishers

Comment: International

CHARLES A.E. GOODHART
London School of Economics, London WC2A 2AE, England

Since Maastricht has become even more famous than it was beforehand, as the site of the eponymous Treaty a few years ago, it is a perfect place to consider issues of international political economy. Then British concern at the prospective embrace of European federalism led to our opt-out from monetary union. On the subject of banking and financial regulation, however, the British have been in the forefront of those seeking international cooperation, both at the European (Brussels) and international (Basle) levels.

This interest is typified by the fact that one of the authors of the main paper, "Systemic Stability and Competitive Neutrality Issues in the International Regulation of Banking and Securities," is my friend and colleague, David Llewellyn, coauthor with our host at this Conference, Harald Benink. In their paper, they focus on the two key issues of systemic stability and competitive neutrality. They tend to regard these two as alternative objectives, i.e., that there is often, or generally, a trade-off between the two. And they clearly believe that, in recent years, the trend in international negotiations has shifted much too far towards the pursuit of competitive neutrality, a level playing field, at the expense of systemic stability.

When I was a young undergraduate, my Department at Cambridge was called the Faculty of Political Economy. Now it is just called Economics. We have gained technical rigor, but lost some of our appreciation of the historical and political context. In this respect, I have very little criticism, and much agreement, with the *economic* analysis in the Benink–Llewellyn paper. The two particular issues that they analyse and dissect are the Basle Capital Convergence risk-weighting methodology, and, at rather greater length, the proposed attempts in Europe under the Capital Adequacy Directive to apply common, competitively neutral, capital standards between those (universal) banks which also conduct securities business and specialist securities firms. I agree wholeheartedly with the analytical criticisms made of both. I can only suggest that one takes the time to read these pages.

Where I tend to some doubt and disagreement is over the question of the political context which shaped these international accords and agreement. In particular, I want to argue that in the political context the objectives of systemic stability and competitive neutrality are not generally substitute, alternative objectives; instead they are, in my view, essentially *complementary* objectives at the international level. As the song goes, you cannot have one without the other. And by the same token, since Benink and Llewellyn do not view, in my eyes, the political context with sufficient clarity, they can not address the normative question of what can be done to overcome the economic failings of the present and proposed regulatory system with proper political realism and pragmatism.

Let me go back to the prior, initial question of why there is an international dimension to concern over regulation. Benink and Llewellyn suggest that this is quite largely because of the *international* ramifications of specific failures. Let me quote from their text:

> . . . international operations have the potential to increase systemic risk due to the increasing interdependence of national financial systems. The potential danger is that systemic stability can be threatened because of a failure in a poorly regulated jurisdiction. Thus, partly through the international inter-bank market risks can be spread and the failure of an institution can have repercussions in other countries.

An obvious example relates to banking where because of direct business links between banks (notably in the interbank market) and indirect contagion and confidence effects, the systemic costs of a bank failure can be significant. If this is true within a national banking system, it can also be true internationally though perhaps with less force as international links may be less than within a national banking system, and the factors behind bank failures may be perceived as being predominantly country-specific. The systemic stability objective of regulation may, therefore, require international collaboration.

While this may well be one part of the story, I doubt if it is the main key issue driving the perceived need for international collaboration. Instead, the key problem is the effect of regulatory arbitrage on the ability of *national* authorities to maintain the extent of regulation that they think appropriate *within their own national jurisdiction* in the face of international competition. As Charles Taylor wrote,

> there is one cause for systemic concern. And that is that competitive conditions will eventually lead all systemically significant core firms to operate without any "margin of safety" so far as capital is concerned.

Nowadays the crucial competitive conditions are international. Brian Quinn (the Executive Director responsible for Banking Supervision at the Bank of England) and Jerry Corrigan (then the President of the Federal Reserve Bank of New York) did not initiate the Capital Adequacy Requirement (CAR) exercise of 1988 because they were worried that the collapse of a foreign, say a Japanese, bank might cause systemic problems in their own countries; rather, they were concerned that the political and structural aspects of introducing 'appropriate' CARs *unilaterally* in their own country would have been unacceptable. To put it another way, in the global financial market, you will not be able to achieve *national* regulations for the achievement of systemic stability, *unless* there is an acceptable degree of competitive neutrality internationally. If your regulators want required capital ratios that are twice those of a major competitor, there will be an outcry that you are penalizing your own banking system, and to no good purpose, since increasingly footloose business will just move to the more laxly managed banking system abroad, making the whole global system weaker.

But how then do countries which want to tighten up their own regulations manage to "persuade" those with easier requirements to follow? How have we overcome the problem of international competition in laxity, where to quote Benink and Llewellyn, "In a highly inter-dependent global financial system the security of the whole is as secure as that of its weakest part"? The answer depends on the particular political circumstance. At the world level the exercise was based, I believe, largely on coercion, *not* voluntary agreement. The threat that was mainly made was that unless your country signs up, your banks may be excluded from the main international financial centres of the world. At the European level, the resolution of conflict is more akin to horse-trading. In order to build alliances in areas each member regards as essential to its interests, it has to compromise on others of lesser importance.

One consequence of this is that it is naive to expect an intellectually coherent and socially optimal set of regulations to come out of such a political process. For example, take the Basle accord zero-risk weighting on OECD government bonds. Exactly those same Central Banks were simultaneously engaged in the Delors/Maastricht Treaty exercise, one aspect of which was to seek to deny governments access to Central Bank financing. So with one hand the Central Banks were forcing government bonds to bear extra credit risk, while with the other they were denying that this was happening. The reason for this is *not* stupidity, but political sensitivities.

When they turn to the proposals raised in the aftermath of BCCI, Benink and Llewellyn state:

> The measures are designed to clarify supervisory responsibilities, and to ensure that international banks are supervised by a home-country regulator 'that capably performs consolidated supervision.' This requires that national authorities are able to monitor each others' quality of supervision and this may require some form of institutional mechanism for peer group review.

But is it likely that the national authorities would ever feel able to face the political uproar that would follow from a public censure of another country's supervision, in conditions that are inevitably uncertain and arguable?

Exactly the same point crops up, where they write:

> At the international level, the focus of a systems approach would be international agreement on the assessment and monitoring of systems rather than specific rules. This could create a new role for the Basle Committee: monitoring the approach of national regulatory authorities with respect to risk management systems of banks under their jurisdiction.

To censure the Cayman Islands or Netherlands Antilles is easy enough, but how about Luxembourg or Greece, to take two examples not entirely at random? Charles Taylor notes that "many of these efforts, for encouraging improved risk management, are guidelines of an exhortatory kind. This seems odd when one stops to think of the private gains and losses associated with disclosure." It seems less odd when one stops to think of the public political process of trying to achieve some commonality of international action.

Given the problems of international political diplomacy, I think that one has to accept two conclusions. First, that any meaningful international agreements will have to be expressed in terms of rather simple, even simplistic, quantifiable rules. Relying on subjective peer group judgment will not do. It will be exhortatory in form, and meaningless in practice, because of political sensitivities. Second, it is highly unlikely that those rules that *can* be agreed internationally under the political process will be economically optimal. Where does this leave us? With a three point program:

1. Require all deposit insurance to be the responsibility of the home-country supervisor, which will give the right incentives, but then allow the home country supervisor access to all host-country supervisory examinations of the subsidiary or branch, and reasonable forewarning of any closure plans.
2. Introduce on a worldwide basis the Benston/Kaufman structured early intervention and response capital ratios. The failure of the Basle accord to implement a graduated response to capital impairment was one of its worst failings.
3. Scrap all attempts at worldwide risk weighting. Encourage banks to develop their *own* internal risk-management systems, but we must recognize that this will have to be achieved primarily on a national basis by national authorities, since international peer group pressures will not amount to much.

Journal of Financial Services Research 9: 425–432 (1995)
© 1995 Kluwer Academic Publishers

Summary of Conference

ROBERT Z. ALIBER
University of Chicago, Chicago, IL 60637 U.S.A

One of the reasons for this Conference on Financial Fragility is Hy Minsky's continued attention over 40 years to the economic instability hypothesis: that the financial system in a market economy is inherently unstable. Hy more than any other economist in the last several generations has stressed the dependence of the real economy on the stability of somewhat fragile financial institutions.

The irony is that many of the participants in this conference have come to Maastrict to bury Hy rather than to praise him. Much of the attention at this conference appears to have been directed at refuting the economic instability hypothesis or attributing financial fragility to one or several different types of government regulation—deposit insurance, interest rate ceilings, and the historic U.S. emphasis on unit banking—rather than as an inherent feature of a market economy.

The organizers of the Conference are to be complimented for inviting a somewhat diverse group of individuals to this meeting. Several of us accept the financial fragility hypothesis, many of us reject it, and a few of us seek to join the issue and identify the optimal amount and form of regulation.

My intent in this session is to reflect on the Conference rather than to summarize each of the individual papers. One key theme is the relation of the financial economy and of changes in the financial variables to the real economy, i.e., to national income. A second theme involves the source or sources of financial fragility and the relation of fragility to the form of regulation.

The Conference was organized by type of financial institution. Think of a two-dimensional matrix, with the different columns representing each of several different types of financial institutions, while the rows represent causes of instability, private solutions, and public solutions. The participants in the Conference have wanted to talk about functional questions that span several different institutions—the roles of rules and authorities, the credibility of government commitments, the relation of the financial economy to the real economy, and the value of a level playing field for regulation of major banks headquartered in individual countries. Let me suggest a metaphor for the framework for the evaluation of the financial fragility hypothesis.

A few years ago, I flew to LaGuardia Airport and, after a day's meetings in Manhattan, I rented a car from Avis to drive to northwestern Massachusetts. Like everyone else in this room, I declined the insurance coverages, believing that they were greatly overpriced. It began to snow, gently at first, and then the snow became heavy and wet. Just after I crossed the state line into Massachusetts, the car slid down a hill and hit a parked vehicle on the side of the road.

My immediate reaction was that I had goofed; I should have bought the collision insurance. On reflection, I realized that since the price of the insurance was the same from one day to the next, the insurance was underpriced on snowy days and overpriced on sunny days. Perhaps this decision is one more example of the distinction between risk and uncertainty that has recurred in the discussion at this Conference. If I had checked both the weather report for the day and forecasting record of the weatherman, I could have converted an uncertain proposition into a probability distribution, and then made a reasonable decision about whether the insurance was overpriced relative to the probable loss from an accident.

The trade-off which I encountered at the Avis counter involved comparing two loss functions. One was the daily insurance premiums on the sunny days; this loss function might be called Type-I costs. The second loss function is one for the costs of repairing the damage whenever I might have an accident without having first purchased the daily insurance; this loss function might be called Type-II costs. The decision about whether to buy the insurance depends in large part on my comparison of the Type-I costs and the Type-II costs. More is involved then this comparison of financial costs, since my driving behavior may depend on whether I have acquired the collision insurance. I may drive faster if I have bought the collision insurance, and so I may have more time for more productive activities because less time is spent driving.

Each of these types of costs has a counterpart in the types of costs that various participants in this Conference highlight as they think about financial fragility and regulation. Minsky and several others are concerned with the costs to the real economy in the form of lower levels of employment and income from debt deflation associated with the collapse of financial institutions. These large infrequent costs are like the costs associated with the losses from the occasional auto accidents on the days the insurance hasn't been purchased. Most of the participants, however, are concerned with the costs to the real economy from the burden of regulation during the sunny days—and most of this group seem so enamored of these costs that they tend to disbelieve that there is any likelihood that there will be any accidents. These costs are like the Type-I costs associated with the daily payments for collision insurance; they raise the costs of the financial intermediaries, and, as a result, a smaller share of credit flows moves through these institutions.

The reason why I believe that so much of the discussion at this Conference has seemed misplaced is that each participant tends to highlight one set of costs, either Type-I costs or Type-II costs; the other set of costs is either ignored or slighted. The issue between those who accept the financial fragility hypotheses and those that reject the hypothesis has not been joined.

The central issue in a conference of this type should involve the comparison of these two types of costs. A related issue is the type of regulatory structure that would minimize the net present value of these two types of costs. The tension in any financial system is between the desire for financial stability and the desire for economic efficiency. A stable financial system can be readily engineered; high Chinese walls would separate the payments mechanism from the credit arrangements, and the credit arrangements would be designed to limit leverage. In contrast, an efficient financial system involves credit; a system that involves credit is potentially fragile if there is an implosion of asset values.

High capital requirements can be viewed as a partial compromise to "protect" an efficient financial system. The rationale is that the contagion effect of declining asset values can be more fully contained within the institutions that own these assets; fewer institutions would fail, and there would be fewer occasions when the assets of failed or failing institutions would be "flogged." The higher the capital requirements, the larger the wedge, between the interest rate that banks and other financial intermediaries earn on their assets and the interest rates they pay on their liabilities. and the smaller the share of credit flows that would go through these institutions rather than the market.

One of the arguments in the taxation literature is that the system "adjusts" to any changes in effective tax rates to minimize their costs. There must be a counterpart proposition in the regulation literature; agents and intermediaries adjust the composition of their assets and liabilities to reduce the real cost of regulation.

A large part of what should be the debate at conferences of these type involves both the evaluation of the externalities of regulation and the incidence of regulation. Just as corporations collect the funds for their income tax payments from their customers and their shareholders and their suppliers in some combination, so the banks and other financial intermediaries subject to regulation pass on the costs to both borrowers and depositors. In this sense, some types of regulations have an impact similar in direction to the impact of an increase in capital requirements; they increase the size of the wedge between the interest rates paid by borrowers and the interest rates paid to depositors. In contrast, other regulations might reduce the size of this wedge; access to a lender of last resort probably reduces the size of this wedge. The impacts on the real economy of changes in the size of this wedge in response to alternative regulatory regimes might be explored.

Minsky is greatly concerned with the impacts of debt deflation on the real economy and the impacts of declines in credit extant on the levels of prices, real interest rates, income, and employment. Almost certainly, he believes that the lender of last resort and deposit insurance have meant a more efficient pattern of financial flows on the sunny days as well as less frequent and much less severe snowy days. The critics of the fragility hypotheses rarely challenge these stories about the externalities.

Joining the issue between those who accept and those who reject the financial fragility hypothesis requires a distinction between the financial costs of regulation and the economic costs of regulation. The financial costs are primarily the payments made by the U.S. Treasury to keep depositors in guaranteed institutions whole; estimates of these costs from the S & L debacle are generally in the range of $130 billion to $145 billion. Some of these losses to the financial institutions and to the U.S. Treasury resulted from declines in asset values triggered by the surge in interest rates on U.S. dollar securities, and some of these losses resulted from fraud by Charles Keating and his colleagues.

Most of the losses to these institutions represented transfers of real income to the depositors of institutions that had negative net worth. The taxable incomes of many of these depositors were higher, and so tax payments were higher; the fiscal deficit was lower. Moreover, national income probably was higher in the years before the collapse of the S&Ls, because more individuals trusted and used the financial system. The economic costs associated with the regulation generally involved the impacts on U.S. national income of the pattern of financial transfers within the existing regulatory regime, relative to the estimates of U.S. national income with some alternative and presumably less comprehensive regulatory regime.

Let me now turn to some of the papers, beginning with Hy's, which is in two parts, one traditional. "Minsky I" develops a general theory of financial instability in terms of the relation between interest payments and cash flows. This is the taxonomy of the speculative, hedge, and Ponzi finance for different groups of borrowers. Periods of optimism lead to credit expansion at a rate that is not sustainable indefinitely, perhaps because the central bank seeks to forestall increases in the consumer price level. Alternatively, the lenders may realize that their loans to a particular group of borrowers have increased at such a rapid rate that these loans are becoming too large a part of their portfolios, and so the rate at which they will acquire more loans from these borrowers declines.

The decline in the rate of growth of loans may induce a period of pessimism that proves self-reinforcing because of the contagion impacts of debt inflation. During these periods individual borrowers are shunted among the three types of finance as their cash inflows decline relative to their interest payments. When the period of credit expansion slows, some of the firms that had been involved in Ponzi finance now encounter difficulty. They can no longer rely on newly borrowed funds to finance the interest payments on the outstanding loans. Some of the companies that had been involved in speculative finance now become involved in Ponzi finance because their cash inflows from their traditional activities are too small to finance the interest payments on their outstanding loans. Some of the firms that had been involved in speculative finance now become involved in the hedge finance.

Hy's general theory does not tell us why the rational agents become involved in processes that are not sustainable indefinitely, nor does it provide a story of the turning points. The lenders are now in great difficulty. Some of these lenders may be insolvent; some are illiquid. If the illiquid firms seek to sell assets, the prices of these assets will decline, and what had started as a liquidity crises may escalate into a solvency crises, as Bagehot noted 125 years ago.

Minsky suggests that the source of the recent problem was the Volcker shock of October 1979, which decapitalized the S&Ls, and made them easy takeover candidates for the Charles Keatings, and the other theft artists. This shock was inevitable given the 1970s inflation; Volcker is the Poincaré of this generation. There could not have been a decline in the U.S. inflation rate until the nominal interest rate on U.S. dollar securities increased above the U.S. inflation rate.

"Minsky II" seeks to explain why there was no debt deflation in the early 1980s in response to the very high real interest rates that resulted from the Federal Reserve's policy to reduce the U.S. inflation rate. "Minsky II" suggests that the willingness of the federal government to incur a large fiscal deficit meant that the recession led to a much smaller decline in the corporate profits, and hence fewer firms were shunted from speculative finance into Ponzi finance. Hy might have noted that the Fed reversed its contractive monetary policy in the summer of 1992 following the Mexican announcement that they could not pay the scheduled interest payments on their outstanding debt. It would be useful to know whether the stability of the economy in the early 1980s resulted from the surge in the fiscal deficit or the shift away from the contractive monetary policy.

One implication of "Minsky II" is that much of the system of financial regulation built up prior to the development of a large government and the potential for large and stabilizing fiscal deficits might now be redundant. It is a double irony that Minsky's critics may be right in their belief that there is too much financial regulation, even though few of them are likely to accept Hy's explanation for why some of this regulation may now be unnecessary.

A number of developments in different markets support Hy's view that the financial system in a market economy is inherently fragile—that certain processes are initiated that cannot be sustained indefinitely even though they may be sustained for an extended period. The surge in bank loans to the MBA countries—Mexico, Brazil, and Argentina—in the 1970s eventually led to very large losses for the bank lenders. For years the lenders failed to recognize that the ability of the borrowers to pay interest on a timely basis depended on the receipt of funds from new loans. The price of Midwest farmland increased sharply in the late 1970s as long as the inflation rate was accelerating. The failure of Continental Illinois Bank in 1984 (somewhat earlier touted as one of the five best managed firms in the United States) resulted because the senior officials had a view of oil price increases that was not sustainable; they—and we—also learned that real estate loans in Texas, Louisiana, and Oklahoma are oil loans "in drag." There was the junk bond debacle of the mid-1980s and the rise and fall of Drexel Burnham and Michael Milken; the daisy chain between a few S&Ls and Drexel Burnham was one element in the Ponzi scheme. There was a bubble in Japanese equities and Japanese real estate in the late 1980s and the early 1990s. The Norwegian and the Swedish banks in the last several years have become insolvent because of the implosion of a real estate bubble.

The paper by George Benston and George Kaufman reminds me of a chapter title in one of my favorite books: *Where Do the Problems Go When They're Assumed Away?* They present a pollyannish view of the banking system; financial fragility results because of some combination of the actions or the inactions of the central bank and bank regulations. They suggest that banks do not differ significantly from nonfinancial firms and that the failure of banks is not different from the failure of nonbanks. So, in effect, they deny the contagion effect. Indeed, they suggest that the failure of nonbanks can have more harmful impacts on local communities than the failure of banks, presumably because the local bank is acquired by some other bank. They might have been somewhat more careful in their distinctions between the failure of an individual bank and the failure of banks or nonbanks as a group. When a nonbank fails, the market share of its competitors increase, although these firms may be temporarily discombobulated by the liquidation of the inventories of the failed firm. When banks fail, the value of the assets of the surviving banks will decline, both because of the forced sale of their assets and because the level of economic activity will decline.

Benston and Kaufman fail to give adequate attention to the distinction between the level of financial regulation and changes in this level. A particular set of regulations can lead to bank failure. The failure of U.S. banks in the 1930s cannot be traced to the unit banking system; this system survived the 1920s. They suggest that the central bank can always provide reserves to forestall the rush to currency or gold or other threats to bank reserves. Presumably, a central bank could forestall generalized insolvency of the banks as a group by measures or policies that would minimize the decline in the prices of a significant part of bank assets.

The source of the problem is that the central bank has more targets than instruments; the stability of the banking system is not the only objective of the central bank. Benston and Kaufman earlier have made a significant contribution in the timely development of regulations based on bank capital adequacy. The implication of their paper is that the primary cause of bank failure are institutional and legal restrictions. They suggest that the banking system is not fragile and not subject to collapse.

The significant contribution of Charles Calomiris paper is the proposition that the speculative boom in agricultural land prices in Iowa, Kansas, and other midwestern states in the late 1970s was due to government lenders. These lenders apparently were dedicated to farmers, more so than the private banks were. What needs to be shown is whether the price of farmland increased because of the increase in the credit from these government lenders, or whether instead the price of land increased because agricultural incomes were increasing. Land is a stock, and presumably the price of this stock is the present value of the associated income. In this second case, the increase in the share of public credit may have resulted because it was less expensive than private credit.

There is much of interest in Frank Edwards's presentation, especially the attention to the Metallgesellschaft case. MG had apparently structured a set of hedge; it had sold oil forward for delivery in the distant future, and had covered these sales with purchase of oil futures contracts with shorter maturities. When the oil price declined, MG had an unrealized gain on its forward sale and a loss—to some extent realized—on its forward purchases. MG was asked to provide additional margin to maintain the equity in its forward purchases. Edwards suggests that a source of the problem was German accounting asymmetries; MG's gains on its delivery commitments could not be used to offset its losses on its purchase of oil futures. The New York Mercantile Exchange clearly acted in an irrational way. Edwards should explain why these private agents did not see through these accounting problems.

Franco Bruni highlights the fit between interest rates and credit ratings. This story confirms the view that credit rating agencies follow rather than lead interest rates. It would be useful to develop a time series approach to this proposition to determine whether interest rates or the rating agencies lead the authorities in determining when individual banks or other financial institutions are especially sensitive to liquidity and solvency problems.

Seha Tiniç provides evidence that the stock prices were more highly variable in the 1920–1940 decade than in other decades. This approach would be more valuable if it were extended by reducing the unit of observation from 20 years to three or four years, and if the variability of the stock prices were related to changes in the commodity price level and changes in the level of economic activity.

Charles Taylor highlights the importance of the protection of the core financial institutions. I remember buying shares in Continental Illinois in 1982. Fortunately, I sold these shares in 1993, and at a modest profit. One insight from this experience is that core financial institutions frequently get into trouble becuase of their loans to institutions at the periphery. Continental Illinois had acquired millions of dollars of poorly documented loans from borrowers in the oil industry from Penn Square, a small shopping center bank in Oklahoma. In the 1930s, the banks in Vienna had borrowed from German banks which in turn had borrowed from British banks. The 1931 crises began in Austria with CreditAnstalt; the Austrian authorities had the choice between seeking to maintaining the parity for the schilling and seeing the bank fail, or going off gold. In their effort to maintain the value of the schilling, they held to a high interest rate, which contributed to the failure of Credit Anstalt. Then, they broke the link between the currency and gold. The value of the credits of German banks to the Austrian banks declined when the CreditAnstalt failed. The value of the loans of the British banks to the German banks declined when the German banks failed. The 1992 exchange rate crises in the EMS began with the devaluation of the Finnish markka (necessitated by the collapse of the export markets in Russia); the EMS parity of the Swedish krona was then suspect.

One of the themes of this conference has been the continuing debate between rules and authorities. Several years ago my son and I had climbed Mt. Washington. Afterwards, we drove to the Mt. Washington Hotel, famous for the Bretton Woods meeting of 50 years ago. An auction was taking place. The RTC, which had acquired the hotel when the Eliot Savings Bank of Boston tanked (somewhat earlier this bank must have acquired the hotel from a borrower that had defaulted on a mortgage loan), was selling the hotel. As we left the hotel, we considered how many times this hotel—first constructed in 1902—had been bankrupt. Almost certainly in the early 1920s, and again in the early 1930s and as well in World War II.

Each time the hotel goes bankrupt, the lenders seek to attract a new owner. This sequence of recapitalization and bankruptcy is a metaphor for rules and authorities. When the uncertainties are large, the rules reach their limits and it becomes necessary to rely on discretionary authority. Rules serve two purposes. Rules prevent or limit the arbitrary policy changes by the authorities; rules also reduce small uncertainties. When the shock is large, the rules are likely to be abandoned; the key question is whether the rules should be abandoned sooner or later.

The paper by David Llewellyn and Harald Benink points to the issue of regulation in the international context, and especially to the idea of the "level playing field" associated with agreements negotiated at Basle. Most of us remember H. Ross Perot's assertions that the United States needs import tariffs on goods from Mexico to level the playing field between American workers and Mexican workers. Any economist who has heard this view would almost immediately reject it as inconsistent with comparative advantage. Yet most of those who would reject the idea of tariffs to level the playing field for trade in goods would be reluctant to apply this same principle to banking. There is one important difference; namely that the harmonization of capital requirements is not the same as the harmonization of wages, since the price of capital may still differ across countries. How banks are regulated with respect to capital adequacy is quite different from where individual banks undertake their productive activities.

In conclusion, I believe that this conference has suffered because there are too few participants who are involved in macroeconomics and who are concerned—as Hy is— with the impacts of changes in the pattern of financial flows on the real economy. The Minsky hypothesis has received less than a fair evaluation at this conference. Hy and many of his fans have failed to move beyond the generalities to substantiate the view that the costs to the real economy of occasional incidents of debt deflation are smaller than the costs of an abundance of financial regulation. Hy's critics have paid too much attention to the budgetary costs of failure of financial institutions, and too little attention to the real income gains both from a larger banking system and a higher level of real income.

One externality of this conference is that one leaves with an agenda for topics for the next conference. Some of the topics for papers for the next conference would be:

- The measure and incidence of the costs and benefits of the externalities from financial regulation;
- The costs of excess bank capital;
- The usefulness of bank credit analysis as forecasts of financial failure;
- When diversified bank portfolios are truly diversified;
- A taxonomy of causes of financial collapse;
- Type I error and Type II error;
- Causality and the insolvency of banks;
- Targets and instruments;
- Rules and authorities in the regulation of banks;
- Bank capital as a source of competitive advantage.

Journal of Financial Services Research 9: 433–444 (1995)
© 1995 Kluwer Academic Publishers

Supervision of Derivative Instruments

JERRY L. JORDAN
President and Chief Executive Officer, Federal Reserve Bank of Cleveland, Cleveland, OH 44101-1387 U.S.A.

1. Specialization in risk management

The financial press in the United States is having a great time telling readers about the risks associated with financial derivatives. The casual reader might think that some new risks have been invented or, at a minimum, that our financial system is riskier now than a few years ago. Neither conjecture is true. New risks have not been discovered, and the financial market is not a riskier place.

Nor is it true that an overriding policy priority today is the need for new legislation or new regulation to deal with derivatives. I realize that some people view the modern financial system as a house of cards that remains standing only when buttressed by wise regulation and other government interventions. Naturally, these people view financial innovations like derivatives as potentially destabilizing challenges to policymakers and regulators.

My own view is that financial innovation tends to be inherently stabilizing, not desta-bilizing. For those many of us who view modern financial systems—and, for that matter, market economies based on private property and price systems—as inherently resilient, financial innovations are welcomed as reinforcements of the natural discipline and sta-bilizing forces at work in a market economy.

Using derivatives to deconstruct risk into new categories does not create more risk. The revised risk catalogue, including systemic risk, credit risk, counterparty risk, settlement risk, Herstatt risk, market risk, legal risk, and operating or management risk, seems thicker, I know. For market experts, such terms as delta risk, convexity or gamma risk, and vega or volatility risk have become common. The naive conclusion seems to be that increasing the number of categories means increasing the amount of risk, and that legis-lators and regulators should be mounting a counteroffensive.

The Congressional hearings on derivative instruments reminded me of my paternal grandmother, raising a family in rural Texas about 70 years ago. Apparently, my father and my uncle were what you might call "adept at finding innovative ways of entertaining themselves." Recognizing this, my grandmother frequently would say to one of their older sisters, "Go find out what the boys are doing, and tell them to stop it!"

The writings of my Federal Reserve colleagues Alan Greenspan, John LaWare, William McDonough, Susan Phillips, and Peter A. Abken have been particularly useful in preparing this paper. Members of the staff of the Federal Reserve Bank of Cleveland, in particular Ed Stevens, have contributed significantly to the paper.

I detect a similar tendency among well-intentioned legislators, who want to say "Stop it!" as soon as they see that some participant has lost a bundle of money using financial derivatives. Such a reaction stems from the idea that market participants are propelling the financial system and the deposit insurance system into more risk. What needs to be understood is that we are seeing innovations in risk *management*, not innovations in risk itself. The underlying positions of participants always involve substantial risk, and there is substantial risk in any business endeavor. Innovations in risk management should be welcomed, as when wheat farmers first learned to lock in the price they would get for the current crop through the use of futures contracts.

In my remarks today, I want to make the following points:

1. Risk exists because there is uncertainty in the world. Successful innovations in risk management, such as derivative instruments, do not make financial markets riskier.
2. Increased specialization in the management of risks improves the functioning of markets; resource allocations will be wealth enhancing as comparative advantages evolve in identifying and managing risks.
3. Supervision of financial activity can strengthen the ultimate discipline coming from the marketplace; regulation of financial activity in a global environment can have unintended consequences by forcing activity out of natural channels and by socializing risk.

2. Specialization and risk

People often say they want to "reduce risk," "minimize risk," "eliminate risk," or "avoid risk." Such language suggests that risk is something undesirable, as it is for most people. However, individuals shed risk largely by passing it along to someone else. For the system as a whole, risk is unchanged—it is simply borne by someone else. This "someone" may be a specialist who is better equipped to manage it or, in the case of public policy, a citizenry that may or may not be aware that a risk has been socialized.

I find it helpful to think of financial innovations like derivatives in the context of Frank H. Knight's distinction between "uncertainty" and "risk," developed in his classic 1921 book, *Risk, Uncertainty, and Profit*.[1] At the heart of his analysis was a distinction between *uncertain* situations, in which the probabilities of possible outcomes simply are unknown, and *risk* situations, in which the probability distribution of potential outcomes of an event is known.

Following Knight's usage, entrepreneurs are specialists who use their expertise to transform genuine uncertainty about future events into risk—that is, from less well specified into better specified distributions of potential outcomes. Specialization allows entrepreneurs to calculate expected values as a basis for cost estimates, supply decisions, and market clearing prices. For example, farmers and bakers use the wheat futures market as the production technology for transforming uncertainty about the market price of wheat at harvest time into a known price and risky return when wheat is planted and when bread marketing and distribution arrangements are made. Bankers and insurance companies, as well as bond and stock mutual fund managers, use specialized knowledge and access to information, supplemented by the law of large numbers, as their production technology in transforming uncertainty about the outcome of unique business ventures into a risky return on a portfolio of assets.

Physicists say that matter can be neither created nor destroyed, but its form can be converted from liquids to solids to gas. Something similar can be said of uncertainty: it exists in nature and it can take a variety of forms. General uncertainty can be segmented into identifiable risks that, in turn, can be transformed into alternative forms. For example, interest rate risk can be converted into credit risk. Risk can be transferred from one party to another. Specific risks can be decomposed into component parts, allowing types of risk to be segmented or combined. Also, risk can be "managed."

Financial risk management has been evolving for centuries. For most of this time, the pace of evolution was gradual. With the coming of the industrial revolution, however, economic development was accompanied by financial development, reflecting more rapid accumulation of innovations in financial contracts, institutions, and markets. One index of financial development is the intermediation ratio, measuring the layering of wealth owners' claims on intermediaries, atop intermediaries' claims on borrowers, atop borrowers' claims to real capital. The seeming redundancy of claims was productive because banks, insurance companies, and other types of intermediaries each developed innovations, through unique specializations, that allowed them to make a profit while assuming risk and offering wealth owners a more assured return.

More recently, communications technology and computing power have changed the financial development process. Increasingly, derivative financial instruments allow risk to be transferred and better managed without adding new layers of intermediary claims atop the underlying real capital stock. Redistributing risk from less to more efficient specialists means, in general, moving toward a more efficient allocation of risk-bearing resources. Wealth is enhanced because, despite the trepidation of savers about interest-rate risk, for example, more houses are built as more mortgages are packaged into collateralized mortgage obligations and sold in the global capital market. As a result, less of something else may be built, but the world is a better place because markets have used the new financial technology to offer savers a higher return per unit of risk, and consumers a lower cost of consumption per unit of risk.

After all, if wealth were not being enhanced, why would anyone use the new technology? Two parties will enter into a contract only because each thereby realizes an increase in the present value of wealth. One party increases its present value by assuming a risk for which its specialization makes it fitted. The other party increases its present value by shedding that risk in return for a fee, or in return for a risk that is more congenial to its own specialization. Events are basically unchanged (ignoring, for the moment, any negative externalities and any feedback of efficiency on growth), but resources are allocated more efficiently. Old techniques for transforming uncertainty into manageable risks are pushed aside as new specialists penetrate more broadly and deeply into the market. The cost of risk-bearing falls for society, thereby enhancing wealth.

3. Derivative financial instruments

"Credit risk" management was the focus of attention in commercial banking in the 1980s. That followed a period in which "interest-rate risk" and "country risk" were the hot topics.

Now, financial engineers are radically altering the financial intermediary process, using finance theory and computer technology to divide risk into components that heretofore were inseparable from underlying assets. Beyond that, globalization of financial markets prevents anyone from monopolizing the benefits of derivatives, just as it cuts through monopoly and regulatory specializations based on old technology.

Financial derivatives came into formal being in the United States after the Commodities Futures Trading Commission ruled in 1976 that financial futures and options were not gaming contracts, and therefore were enforceable at law. Initially, most derivative financial contracts were traded on the organized commodities exchanges, so that holders of contracts were protected by the exchanges themselves, as well as by Securities and Exchange Commission (SEC) rules. The exchanges, as the counterparty to each contract traded, had a clear self-interest in promoting integrity of trading and delivery. Assuring truth and integrity remains the approach to supervision of exchange-traded derivative contracts today. The nature of contracts has expanded to include a variety of options indexed to financial-market measures like stock market price indicators and even the monthly average overnight federal funds rate.

The most rapidly growing instruments in the derivatives market, and the source of recent innovation, are over-the-counter (OTC) contracts. These are outside the purview of any exchange rules. They include ordinary currency and (largely) interest-rate swaps, plus a small portion in more exotic hybrid contracts. Typically, one or more of the counterparties to an OTC contract is a commercial bank, with the contract tailored to the idiosyncratic needs of the counterparties, much like a commercial loan. Most banks say they enter into contracts simply as end-users, to meet their own risk management needs. A dozen or so of the largest money center banks, however, are counterparties to a very large percentage of all OTC contracts because they act as dealers, tailoring contracts to the needs of any customer. These banks must manage the net risk that results from their dealer position, earning their income from a bid–ask spread.

Any user of derivative contracts, whether a dealer or end-user, should be able to demonstrate to management, directors, auditors, and shareholders qualitatively, if not quantitatively, the rationale for positions taken. This does not mean that all derivative positions can be designated as either a hedge or a speculation, because derivative contracts are not ordinarily isolated in a separate profit center.

Even a derivatives dealer will not necessarily try to run a riskless book of offsetting derivatives exposures, but instead may want to assume some risk, or use its dealer position to offset a risk exposure elsewhere on its books. For end-users as well as dealers, derivatives must be part of a larger risk-management strategy. Current accounting practices, of course, do not produce an integrated record of risk management. This is why some supposed losses from derivatives are not losses at all, but simply the offset to gains elsewhere in the business. Offsetting the gains and losses leaves the neutral position the firm was trying to ensure by off-loading certain types of risk. References to a firm's derivatives business as an actual or intended profit center, on the other hand, suggest an intention to do more than contribute an ingredient to risk management, perhaps by arbitraging some market niche, or simply by engaging in informed speculation.

4. Supervision and regulation

Derivatives are innovations that, like atomic energy and genetic engineering, can be used for good or ill, and be intended for good but have ill effects through mismanagement. An objective of government supervision is to ensure that innovation takes place in an open environment, so that those affected can see how innovations are being used and to what effect. Supervision in this sense stands in contrast to regulation, by which government seeks to ensure good results by directing or delimiting the actions of citizens.[2] The beauty of a market economy is that innovations like derivatives should be expected to have good results, as the "invisible hand" of the market mediates among the self-interests of potential users, preventing unintended gains and losses over time by driving the inept from the marketplace. This simple Smithian economic theory, however, seems at variance with the publicity being given to some spectacularly large losses attributed to derivatives activity in recent years. Current proposals to regulate derivatives are, at least in part, a reaction to those losses.

One reason for losses undoubtedly is inexperience with the new engineering of risk. Both experience and theory make good teachers, and the experience with derivatives has been teaching some valuable (or at least expensive) lessons. Some of these lessons have been more like refresher courses, such as the notions that interest rates are not a one-way bet, that leveraging a position leverages risk, and that undersupervised pockets of a large organization are bound to invite agency problems. Other lessons seem dumbfoundingly simple only with hindsight, like the fact that valuations of a derivatives position can be extremely sensitive to overlooked or untested assumptions about things like liquidity and cross correlations among asset returns.

Three additional important lessons are largely overlooked in the media. One is that derivatives redistribute risk from one counterparty to the other. This means that the counterparties to spectacular losers have been some substantial gainers who probably will be unable to continue laying off risk on as favorable terms in the future as in the past. A second lesson is that the recent spate of spectacular losses has been associated, for the most part, with so-called "exotic" derivatives that comprise only a very small fraction of the market. Of course, "plain vanilla" OTC currency and interest-rate swaps and futures can have very long maturities, so experience to date is not necessarily the whole story there. A third lesson is about the usefulness of capital in paying for an education. All but a slight fraction of losses on derivatives contracts *to date* have been absorbed from the capital of the exposed party, its parent, or its sponsor, and *not* from any haircut on the value of the contract to the party "in the money."

Market discipline can be a powerful educator, as long as the experience of both the gains and the losses from using derivatives remain with the contracting parties. Moreover, the potential for gain and loss provides the incentive for concerted action to change the infrastructure of markets. Law, accounting, and standard market practices devised in the past needed updating to cover the new derivative instruments. The 1993 recommendations of the Group of Thirty are one recent example of the self-interest of the participants in the OTC derivatives market seeking to allow more reliable evaluations of risks.

Government can help in strengthening institutional arrangements that promote market discipline. For example, markets operate best with reliable information, but most observers agree that reliable information is not yet consistently available about derivatives and derivatives positions. Supervisory authorities such as central banks are in a position to help market participants develop common forms of disclosure, even by such simple procedures, in the United States, as releasing CAMEL and BOPEC ratings.

"Better information" actually covers a wide range of possibilities where supervisors and participants have common interests. One opportunity for improvement is communication internal to a firm. Because banks are the dominant institutions in the OTC derivatives market, the existing bank examination process can serve as a useful check on some seemingly obvious, but often overlooked, matters where advice can substitute for painful experience. Supervisory authorities can ensure that fundamental questions are being addressed. Is a bank's strategy to be only an end user, or also a dealer in derivatives? Do staff, top management, and directors all have the same understanding of the bank's derivatives strategy? How consistently is that strategy being communicated to shareholders and the public?

Another aspect of information where the interests of supervisory authorities and market participants converge is in maintaining objective measures of risk and reliable interbank comparisons. Inclusive evaluations of management capability, based on something like the rating systems we use in the United States, are suitable for this function. Basle risk-based capital standards represent significant progress toward establishing global interbank comparability.

An obvious next step will be to incorporate off-balanace-sheet risks into firm-specific capital adequacy measures, and the federal banking supervisors in the United States have a proposal out for comment at the moment. In the case of exchange-traded contracts, risk is not so contentious an issue. Daily marking-to-market and margin requirements protect the exchange, while the strength of the exchange protects the in-the-money counterparty. OTC derivatives, in contrast, cannot be marked to market directly, so another method of monitoring exposures must be developed.

As the bank examination process evolves, I expect that the risk management of derivative instruments used or offered by a bank will employ firm-specific stress testing of the bank's capital adequacy. This will require a valuation model for OTC derivatives that includes consideration of duration, counterparty concentrations, and liquidity. Development of the appropriate simulation model should be left to the firm, but it must be well-documented, must provide a comprehensive representation of its exposures, and must also be flexible about the range of stress assumptions under which the model can be simulated. The advantage of a mutual market and supervisory interest in folding off-balance-sheet risk into capital adequacy is that supervisors will have the benefit of comparing many different methods, and of requiring answers to challenging questions.

Not all proposals for government action in the derivatives market are as benign as seeking better information. As a general rule, it is wiser to let market forces mete out losses as well as profits, than to force everyone to follow suboptimal rules and socialize losses. Perhaps the initial educational role of government supervision and examination will dwindle in importance over time. Certainly there can be no permanent detailed direction of derivatives practices from supervisory personnel whose technical expertise, while substantial, cannot be expected to match that of market players. Nonetheless, there is a crucial role for oversight by the chartering authority or, more significantly, by the provider of deposit insurance, in protecting the public trust and the public purse.[3] In Ronald Reagan's phrase about arms control, "Trust, but verify."

5. Systemic risk

Financial innovations in general, and derivative financial instruments in particular, may represent nothing more than new specializations being used to manage risk more efficiently. Like Adam Smith's pin maker, new risk specializations should increase economic efficiency and human well-being, as their benefits are realized through market trading. This assumes, however, that financial innovations have no negative externalities detracting from the benefits of the rapid spread of new financial technologies—that is, that the marginal private and social costs of risk bearing are identical.

There appears to be widespread apprehension that the social costs of derivatives exceed their private costs. Unrecognized in private cost, apparently, is the systemic aspect of potential market collapse, reflecting new interdependencies generated by derivatives among counterparties, risks, and markets.

Of course, for as long as counterparties have had counterparties, credit risk has had an element of interdependence: one party's repayment of debt to another was a function of someone else's ability to repay a debt to the first party. These interdependencies have been modeled according to three unique sources of potential difficulty. Two of these— manias and fragility—are viewed in much the same way today as they were by Walter Bagehot in 1870, in *Lombard Street*. The third, systemic risk, is a newer and still fuzzy concept of uncertain significance.

Manias and bubbles, including their consequent panics are one model of interdependence among market participants. This model recognizes that economic agents have a propensity for delusion about the return on particular investments, as a mass of investors mutually support each other's belief, first in the impossible, and then in the inevitable. Their common delusion is a misreading either of the likely real return to capital, or of the probability of cashing in a position before anyone else does. Walter Bagehot described the phenomenon as when owners of savings "find that . . . specious investments can be disposed of at a high profit, they rush into them more and more . . . So long as such sales can be effected the mania continues; when it ceases to be possible to effect them, ruin begins."[4] In modern jargon, this is known as "the bigger fool theory." A recent example was when the Nikkei average went to 40,000. Another is the popularity of the MMM enterprise in Russia, despite government assurances that it was nothing more than a Ponzi scheme.

The explosive growth of OTC derivatives contracts conceivably could be classified as a temporary mania, particularly from the point of view of those whose mismanagement has produced spectacular losses. With hindsight, marginal private cost was apparently seriously underestimated. Continued rapid growth of derivatives contracts at the pace of the past several years certainly would begin to raise the mania flag. Even in a global financial marketplace there must exist a finite limit to shiftable risk. For now, however, that point does not seem to be in sight.

The second model based on interdependence is *fragility*, in the technical sense used by writers like Hy Minsky. The fragility model produces debt/equity ratios that are higher than is socially efficient, and that rise as an economic expansion proceeds. Again, harking back to Bagehot, "And in so far as the apparent prosperity is caused by an unusual plentifulness of loanable capital and a consequent rise in prices, that prosperity is not only liable to reaction, but *certain* to be exposed to reaction. The same causes which generate this prosperity will, after they have been acting a little longer, generate an equivalent reaction."[5] That is, over the course of an economic expansion, financial markets become increasingly susceptible to instability in response to any random shock. Thus, fragility is an endogenous feature of modern market economies. The risk levels of all financial contracts are interdependent in that they jointly depend on the state of the aggregate economy.

Systemic risk, as that term has come to be used, is like the mania and fragility models in that interdependence creates the possibility of falling dominoes; all three models exhibit that common systemic characteristic. However, modern discussions of systemic risk do not emphasize the mass delusion of a mania, or the endogenous common association with the aggregate economy found in fragility. The systemic-risk model seems to postulate the existence of some new, third externality that makes private calculations of risk understate the true susceptibility of financial contracts to loss. In other words, absence of incentives for participants to internalize all costs associated with certain instruments creates a problem in the aggregate that is not apparent at the micro level. The presence of the externality invites governmental intervention to restore the equality of private and social marginal cost.

A major difficulty with the systemic risk concept comes in trying to identify the nature of this new form of externality that pushes private cost below social cost. Some have argued that borrowing is like an internal combustion engine, polluting the financial market atmosphere. When I lend to you by reducing my liquidity or otherwise accept greater risk, I increase the probability that I will be unable to meet my obligations to others. This would represent a negative externality from the point of view of my creditors, if they were unaware of my lending to you. The argument breaks down, however, to the extent that, acting out of self-interest, my creditors are able to internalize the supposed externality. Loan covenants, for example, protect a creditor from a debtor entering into unforeseen debt or credit relationships. More generally, the expectation of internalizing this potential externality is recognized in the eternal watchphrase, "Know thy counterparty!"

In the case of derivatives, a variant of the pollution argument has emphasized the concentrated dealer market. Each major dealer is the source of an interdependence among the exposures of its worldwide circle of end users. Evaluations of counterparty risk exposures to these end users should include a dealer risk, analogous to country risk, that would be too trivial to notice in a less concentrated market. Similar allowances might be made for interdependence arising from the use of common operations centers, payment networks, legal advisors, or credit rating services. Evaluating risk is not a simple matter; it involves compound probabilities and cross correlations.

In general, the interdependence envisioned in the systemic risk model seems to involve the sensitivities of many large counterparties to one another. Derivatives and globalization of markets may indeed be producing more complex compound probabilities of trouble. However, so, too, is the information age vastly expanding the ability to monitor counterparties and markets. If sophisticated financial engineering can produce complex derivative products, cannot the same sophistication estimate the resulting increasing complex compound probabilities of trouble?

The point is that there seems to be no reason to believe that the potential externality of increasingly complex financial relationships has outdistanced an increasingly powerful ability to internalize that potential externality. The commercial overhead of modern financial centers—including satellite-fed, on-line, worldwide information and monitoring systems, armies of legal talent, and even on-site monitors from the rating agencies—all reflect the substantial expenditures of firms trying to internalize their risk exposures. As long as economic agents are able to estimate compound probabilities of failures, systemic risk is indistinguishable from normal credit risk. Knowing your counterparty and your counterparty's counterparties, and even your counterparty's counterparties' counterparties, should lead to quality spreads in market prices, to prudent loan loss reserves and capital from which to absorb losses, and to equality of the private and social cost of risk.

Suppose that the wedge between private and social cost is not inserted by the inability to evaluate and control interdependency. Then, either there is no wedge—in which case there is no policy basis for concern about systemic risk—or the wedge originates from some other source.

Suppose that markets are perfectly able to, and do, price the risk of financial dominoes falling in a systemic collapse, but that politicians, acting for society, are unwilling to tolerate the consequent losses to individual constituents. Politicians therefore insert a wedge between private and social cost, raising the latter in the minds of legislators. It is the failure of markets to internalize this political cost that could lead to overproduction of specialized risk-management products. The problem would not be derivatives; the problem would be that politicians have a lower tolerance for risk than do market participants. The legislative and regulatory corollary would be the challenge to reduce losses without creating a moral hazard by subsidizing risk-taking.

6. Moral hazard

Perhaps the most troubling aspect of the widespread apprehension of the systemic risk consequences of derivatives is the seemingly equally widespread conviction that government—meaning central banks and deposit insurance providers—can be counted on to prevent a systemic collapse. Even if government had no such intention, the conviction that it would come to the rescue produces a growing externality in the form of unmonitored, compound probabilities of trouble. Systemic risk becomes real, though it need not be, but who bears the risk? Likely, it is taxpayers, through the earnings of the central bank, whose exposure would grow while private exposures would decline. More important, what is the direction of causation? Does growing systemic risk invoke central bank risk-bearing because it is socially more efficient, or has the apparent willingness of central banks to bear more risk allowed markets to adopt financial specializations whose systemic risk externalities are downloaded onto central banks?

Here is where central banks must tread very carefully. There is a moral hazard in reassuring markets that a lender of last resort will act, and at low cost, to prevent a contagious spread of broken promises. If systemic risk is becoming as worrisome as we are led to believe by some commentators, it seems at least as likely that the reason is not innovations in financial technology, but the moral hazard of central banks' implicit willingness to underwrite that risk.

Moral hazard can be a real danger in central banking, as was demonstrated during the last great spurt of financial innovation during the cash management revolution of the 1970s. Prophets long have foretold the coming of cashless transactions. What has been happening in the United States, however, is that both cash transactions and cash *balances* have been eliminated. Increasingly over the 1970s, reserve balances were created by central bank daylight credit, on demand, to accommodate transactions. Not until the early 1980s did the Federal Reserve discover the extent to which its free daylight credit, rather than someone's pre-existing, positive reserve balance, was the medium of wire payment; that a large chunk of private payment system risk had been transformed into Federal Reserve credit risk.

Efforts to reduce and manage Federal Reserve payment system risk in the past decade largely have involved digging out from under a mountain of daylight credit initiated during the cash management revolution. That story began with the central bank inadvertently absorbing the externality of payments system risk, rather than creating institutional mechanisms by which private parties would be led to internalize that risk.

Now a risk management revolution is in full swing. The specter of growing systemic risk is used to rationalize nonbank access to the discount window, to seek direct nonbank access to Fedwire payment finality, and to call for regulatory guidelines for derivatives contracts that could become the leverage for obtaining central bank assistance when they prove to be flawed. The regulatory challenge is to avoid these snares. Incentives must be created for participants to internalize risk. This is essential if we are to avoid socializing losses. As central bankers, our role is to supervise markets by spreading information that promotes knowledgeable risk-management structures, while avoiding wholesale reassurances that timely central bank money creation will prevent trouble.

7. Conclusions

Rapidly spreading use of derivatives suggests that they are expected to add value to those on both sides of contracts. Derivatives do not add to or subtract from the risks that are inherent in a modern financial system. They do, however, allow existing uncertainty to be borne more efficiently. Financial innovations are to be welcomed as basically wealth enhancing. As my colleague at the Federal Reserve, John LaWare, has said, "Derivatives have been used primarily to contain risk. . . . A useful definition of banking is that the banker essentially manages financial risk for customers. The job is to manage risk, not to avoid it."

"This is a scientific revolution," said former U.S. Secretary of State George Schultz in explaining the implications of the information age to Mikhail Gorbachev (too late, as it turned out). He went on, "There was a time when a government could control its scientific establishment and be basically successful. No longer. To keep up today and in the future means that scientists will have to be in constant touch with the 'thinking community' around the world. And this is an information revolution. The inability of one nation to be predominant in the international financial world is going to be repeated in field after field. The key is going to be knowledge-based productivity. . . ."[6]

To the extent that derivatives are not well understood, surprises should be expected and should be no cause for concern as long as information about derivatives use is not hidden, and is matched by attention to adequate liquidity and capital. A more significant danger is that we repeat the mistakes of the past, subverting market incentives for counterparty scrutiny with overly generous central bank assistance.

Some of the advocacy of new legislation or regulation has been based on the view that the entire financial system could be jeopardized by the losses sustained by a single large participant in derivatives markets. My view is that such vulnerability has not been established. In fact, I believe that certain proposals might actually increase systemic risk because they would penalize standard risk-hedging methods and change behavior to get around the regulations. Those who argue that financial innovation calls for new regulations should remember that new regulations are very often the stimulus for new innovation.

The ultimate regulator of any economic activity is the market. In the case of finance, the global marketplace is a powerful source of discipline. As we consider proposals for action by government authorities, I suggest that we establish a litmus test. Namely, in the words of Federal Reserve Chairman Greenspan, "The relevant question is whether private market regulation is enhanced or weakened by the addition of government regulation."

Notes

1. Knight (1971 [1921]).
2. The institutional implications of this approach are developed in more detail in Jordan (1993).
3. For a m ore detailed discussion of the roles of public authorities in supervision and regulation, see Jordan (1994).
4. Bagehot (1931), pp. 131–132.
5. Bagehot (1931), p. 146.
6. Schultz (1993), p. 893.

References

Abken, Peter A. "Over-the-Counter Financial Derivatives: Risky Business?" *Economic Review* (Federal Reserve Bank of Atlanta) 79 (2) (March/April 1994), 1–22.

Bagehot, Walter. *Lombard Street: A Description of the Money Market*, 14th ed. London: John Murray. 1931.

Greenspan, Alan. Testimony before the Subcommittee on Telecommunications and Finance of the Committee on Energy and Commerce, U.S. House of Representatives, May 25, 1994.

Group of Thirty, Global Derivatives Study Group. "Derivatives: Practices and Principles." July 1993.

Jordan, Jerry L. "A Market Approach to Banking Regulation." Remarks presented at the CATO Institute's Eleventh Annual Monetary Conference on Financial Deregulation in a Global Economy, Washington, DC, March 18–19, 1993.

Jordan, Jerry L. "Economic Forces versus Monetary Institutions." Remarks presented at the CATO Institute's Twelfth Annual Monetary Conference on Monetary Arrangements in the Americas after the NAFTA, Mexico City, May 25–26, 1994.

Knight, Frank H. *Risk, Uncertainty, and Profit*. Chicago: University of Chicago Press. 1971 (1921).

LaWare, John P. Remarks presented at the American Bankers Association's 1994 National Regulatory Compliance Conference, Washington, D.C., June 13, 1994.

McDonough, William J. "Financial Market Innovation—Practical Concerns," Remarks presented before the Money Marketeers of New York University, New York City, June 16, 1994.

McDonough, William J. Remarks presented at the Institute of International Bankers' Annual Meeting, New York, May 4, 1994.

Phillips, Susan M. "Derivatives and Risk Management: Challenges and Opportunities," Remarks presented at the Federal Reserve Bank of Atlanta Conference on Financial Markets, Coconut Grove, Florida, February 25, 1994.

Phillips, Susan M. Remarks before the Forum on Developing Country Access to Derivatives Markets. The World Bank, Washington, DC, June 30, 1994.

Schultz, George P. *Turmoil and Triumph: My Years as Secretary of State*. New York: Charles Scribner's Sons. 1993.

U.S. General Accounting Office. "Financial Derivatives: Actions Needed to Protect the Financial System." GAO/GGD-94-133, May 1994.

G 15

251-57

Journal of Financial Services Research 9: 445–451 (1995)

Coping with Financial Fragility: A Global Perspective

ANNA J. SCHWARTZ
National Bureau of Economic Research, New York, NY 10003, U.S.A.

Financial fragility means that the ability of the financial system to withstand economic shocks is weak. The basic reason that the system is held to be fragile by proponents of a financial-fragility interpretation is that the financial services industry is supposedly inherently unstable. On this view, a loss of confidence in the institutions in that industry is an imminent possibility, with disruptive consequences for the real economy. The situation, however, is even more dire, according to the proponents, because financial fragility is not limited to the domestic system. It is easily transmitted internationally.

I shall first comment on the belief that the financial services industry is unstable and then on the validity of the argument that authorities, presumably, necessarily must cope with financial fragility. I shall then review deregulation and liberalization changes in global financial markets, and ask whether it is true that the benefits are outweighed by added risk. I shall conclude by discussing the events of the past 15 years whch have been designated financial crises and thus serve as the hallmark of financial fragility.

Not to keep you in suspense, I believe instability of the financial services industry is attributable to destabilizing actions of monetary authorities and regulators; that the financial services industry is not inherently unstable; that the distress and failure of individual financial firms, whether owing to poor management or bad luck, is no threat to the system as a whole; that declines in asset prices of bonds, stocks, real estate, or artworks indicate wealth losses, not financial crisis; that a genuine financial crisis occurs only when the payments system is impaired. Finally, there has been no genuine financial crisis in the United States or globally despite stock market crashes, wide swings in prices of real estate, distress affecting individual commercial banks or banking systems, collapse of the U.S. savings and loans, failure of BCCI and the Maxwell conglomerate, and distressed insurance companies.

1. Instability in the financial services industry?

What produces instability in financial services? It is fashionable in academic circles nowadays to focus on the supposed problem of asymmetric information, that borrowers conceal from lenders the true prospects of the projects for which they seek financing and lenders are fooled—hence the instability of financial institutions (Mishkin, 1991). Adverse selection in financial markets is said to occur, when interest rates rise, because bad credit risks are most likely to be selected (Stiglitz and Weiss, 1981). A financial crisis supposedly occurs when the financial markets are no longer able to do the job of solving the information problems, and lending halts (Mankiw, 1986).

In my view, asymmetric information is not the central problem in studying instability in financial services. I believe lenders and borrowers both evaluate the prospects of projects in part by extrapolating the prevailing price level or inflation rate. A subsequent decision by monetary authorities to pursue contractionary policies will undermine the price-level assumptions of both lenders and borrowers. That is the common background leading borrowers to default and lenders to become distressed.

The usual suspects that are cited to account for financial instability include: (1) the difference in timing of debits and credits, (2) the illiquidity of assets, (3) the lack of recognition by regulators of insolvency, (4) the vulnerability of sound institutions to losses transmitted from relationships with other institutions experiencing difficulties, and (5) herd behavior, which results in bank runs (see unpublished papers for the Conference on Financial Instability, Jerome Levy Economics Institute, 1994).

Let me discuss each of the suspects in turn. How serious is the instability they are said to be responsible for?

1. The main concern related to differences in timing of debits and credits is associated with wire transfers in the United States. Intraday credit on both CHIPS and Fedwire involves a risk of default. Banks can send more funds than they have at hand at the time of the transaction. A bank that is unable to settle its overdrafts on CHIPS at the end of the day may affect other banks that have extended it credit. Since foreign banks clear through CHIPS, a failure of one of them could also disturb the domestic payments system. Payments made over Fedwire, however, are final when they are made, so public funds are at risk, not the private payments system. The single instance when a problem arose on wire transfers was occasioned by a computer breakdown at one bank. No financial crisis was involved even though the Fed made large temporary loans to settle commitments pending the restoration of computer services.
2. Illiquid assets limit the ability of banks to sell them at full value to meet immediate redemption demands from depositors. Since an increasing proportion of bank loans, mortgages, and company receivables is being packaged into marketable obligations and securitized, additional liquidity has been made available to banks.
3. The vulnerability of sound institutions to losses transmitted from troubled institutions is a fact, but emergency liquidity assistance to otherwise sound banks is a principle that has guided authorities for centuries.
4. If lack of recognition by regulators of insolvency is a problem, does this mean the CAMEL ratings, according to which regulators grade U.S. banks on their performance, are not reliable? The poorest CAMEL ratings, 4 and 5, are known promptly. Why should it be difficult to distinguish between an illiquid and insolvent bank?
5. Despite the emphasis on runs on banks, there is little evidence of contagion in the years since World War II. The influential Diamond–Dybvig (1983) model of bank runs is flawed because its bank has no capital. An adequately capitalized bank can prevent runs by reassuring depositors through the presence of its capital base. Since the bank

in the model is a monopoly, depositors who run necessarily shift to currency rather than redeposit their funds in another bank. Moreover, the model ignores a role for the central bank in offsetting the depletion of reserves in the event of a run.

2. Regulatory arrangements

I shall argue that it is regulatory misdeeds that have destabilized financial services institutions in the past 15 years. Let me note some examples of destabilizing regulatory arrangements.

One well-known problem with deposit insurance is that it distorts incentives. Deposit insurance encourages risky behavior by financial intermediaries ranging from the quantity and quality of assets which they acquire to the size of their capital.

When risks are known, instead of closing institutions with negative net worth, regulators may lower capital requirements, weaken accounting principles—as the Federal Home Loan Bank Board did—deter institutions from recognizing losses on loans, urge them to increase lending to delinquent borrowers so that interest payments are recorded as paid (as in the case of the nonperforming LDC loans in 1982), acquiesce in banks' retaining portfolios of nonperforming loans in the hope that eventually the outlook will improve for the projects the loans were for, fail to recognize fraud, and mismanagement.

A prime example of misguided regulation is the U.S. case of interest rate ceilings on thrift and bank deposits, belatedly eliminated. Prohibition of interstate banking is another example, now also about to be eliminated.

A regulatory lapse in the United States is exemplified by the recent legal requirement that by a fixed date savings and loan institutions had to sell their high-yield junk bonds (Yago, 1991, pp. 212–13). Technically, the thrifts had five years to sell the bonds, but, according to accounting regulations, securities to be sold before maturity must be marked to market before the end of the current quarter. The bonds therefore had to be sold by the thrifts within 90 days. As a result of the forced sales, losses were inflicted on those institutions and other bondholders, especially insurance companies.

My conclusion is that the problems of banking and financial markets in recent years are related to unstable monetary policies and bad regulatory actions rather than inherently unstable performance of the financial services industry.

3. Effects of globalization

Domestic financial markets have been integrated with markets across borders and with offshore ones, with an enormous increase in payments. Deregulation has eased, although not removed, restrictions on the combination of banking with underwriting and insurance. Financial instruments have proliferated thanks to information technology. Savings have been institutionalized, and the managers of these funds have diversified internationally.

These changes have improved efficiency in the allocation of resources and freed market forces in the financial sector. The concern raised by these changes is that internationalization will spread a financial crisis from one country to another. Market risks of losses from changing asset prices, and exchange and interest-rate fluctuations, it is feared, will lead to institutional distress or insolvency that will be transmitted to other solvent institutions not only domestically but across borders. The increase in the scale of financial transactions is regarded as heightening the system's vulnerability.

My response to these fears is the same as in the case of domestic financial markets. In the event of a collapse of a foreign bank with a subsidiary in another country, or of a bank in one country that is indebted to a bank in another country, the domestic central bank can offset any untoward effects in the home country by providing sufficient liquidity to maintain the money supply (Benston, 1994). Financial fragility is not a problem with stable monetary policies and regulatory policies limited to the imposition of capital requirement and closure of firms before their net worth turns negative (Benston and Kaufman, 1988).

4. Responses to financial crises since 1980

Severe shocks have been experienced by thrifts, banks, and the stock market since 1980, but none of them was a threat to the stability of the entire U.S. financial system.

5. Thrifts

In the case of the thrifts, when the Federal Reserve raised interest rates in the 1980–1982 period that reflected the inflation premium which the market imposed, it plunged the firms into market-value insolvency thanks to their badly designed structure of mismatched maturities of short-term demand liabilities and fixed-rate, long-term mortgages. The response to this crisis included deposit interest-rate deregulation to permit thrifts to retain deposits, broader thrift powers to enable them to acquire assets earning more than mortgages, higher deposit insurance coverage, and reduced supervision, all of which only exacerbated the problem of the mismatch. So that thrifts would not have to be closed and the losses which they had incurred would not bankrupt the Federal Savings and Loan Insurance Corporation, thrift capital requirements were reduced, indeed, almost eliminated. These measures encouraged thrift owners and managers to take risks at the expense of the thrift deposit insurance agency. Not until 1989 was a major effort made to close down hundreds of insolvent thrifts by liquidations or funding acquisitions, mainly at taxpayer cost that had been incurred earlier but recognized only at closure.

Runs on the state-chartered thrifts in Ohio and Maryland in 1985, after a failure of a thrift in each state, would not have occurred had authorities acted promptly to assure depositors that all their demands for cash would be met. The runs ended when both states imposed limits on withdrawals and the Federal Reserve provided loans to solvent thrifts with liquidity problems.

In any event, the runs would not have warranted concern as long as the Federal Reserve acted to prevent a decline in the money supply.

6. Banks

The first crisis for banks dated from mid-1982, when Latin American countries failed to make scheduled payments on their outstanding bank loans. Government policies after 1974 had promoted recycling of petrodollars to developing countries by the banks, while inflation lowered real costs of borrowing for the LDCs. Both the supply of and demand for bank loans rose. Acknowledgement of default on outstanding loans would have required write-downs that would reduce the legal capital of the banks involved and would undoubtedly have raised the cost of funds which they obtained in the open market, when it became evident that the government would not bail them out of their loan losses. Candid dealing with the problem that the banks faced was obfuscated.

The authorities rejected this course on the ground that confidence in the stability of the banking system would be shaken. Until 1987, they chose the subterfuge that all the loans would be repaid, and pressured the banks to reschedule principal and to provide an increase in lending sufficient to enable delinquent borrowers to maintain interest payments. In 1987, the banks abandoned the subterfuge and began accumulating large reserves to provide for substantial losses on their LDC loans, and arranging debt for equity swaps. In 1989, the Treasury stepped in, replacing the Federal Reserve as manager of the banks' LDC debt problems, pressuring them to negotiate with the debtor countries either lower interest rates or substantial principal write-downs.

In this episode, government was responsible for the troubles of both the LDCs and the domestic banks. Then Federal Reserve Board Chairman Burns praised the banks for providing loans to the LDCs in the 1970s, cautioning neither the borrowers nor the lenders, as the magnitude of the amounts extended escalated. The contractionary policies of the Federal Reserve from 1980 to 1982, which could not have been anticipated by the borrowers, undermined their capacity to repay. And government ultimately was responsible for the delayed resolution.

The run on Continental Illinois in 1984 led to its rescue on the presumption that its closure as insolvent before its net worth turned negative would have led to runs on its creditors. Not so. The institutions, foreign bank depositors, and creditors who ran on it redeposited their withdrawals in other institutions or bought financial assets to replace the certificates of deposit which Continental had issued and which the latter were no longer willing to buy or hold. Depositors ran from a bank that was troubled to untroubled banks or to safe securities. The payments system was never in jeopardy. Closing an insolvent bank would have prevented the too-big-to-fail syndrome that ensued.

By 1989, banks and even thrifts smaller than Continental achieved too-big-to-fail status, with protection extended to their uninsured depositors. Keeping large insolvent banks afloat was a costly policy. By delaying closure of failed institutions, losses borne by the FDIC and ultimately the taxpayers increased. Failure of bank holding companies in the late 1980s did not ignite contagion.

Dire predictions for the future of commercial banks by mid-1994 seem to have been misplaced. Banks have recapitalized and improved their efficiency. In the United States, geographic and product diversification is under way. International barriers have fallen, and economies of scale and scope have become possible. The globalization of financial markets has led to liberalization, another positive development for the future of the industry worldwide.

7. Securities markets

Market crashes in October 1987 and October 1989, the financial crises that raised apprehensions of effects on the real economy, far from precipitating a depression, did not bring on even a recession. The Federal Reserve responded to the crashes by promptly announcing its readiness to provide increased liquidity. The stock market is volatile, but it does not govern the economy, given appropriate behavior by the monetary authorities. Globalization of securities markets has increased the share of foreign equities traded on major exchanges throughout the world. What has to be a concern is the regulatory will of an international body of regulators to impose restrictions on innovative market activities.

8. Conclusion

Financial firms are no more imprudent than nonfinancial firms. Mismanagement and fraud are no more prevalent in finance than in industry in general. Individual bank insolvency need not have contagious effects on other solvent institutions. An effective lender of last resort can preclude panics. Monetary authorities that ensure price-level stability will also achieve financial stability. The only restraints on financial institutions needed as safeguards against excessive risk taking are capital requirements and closure of firms before their net worth turns negative. This is a prescription for individual countries and internationally.

References

Benston, George J. "International Harmonization of Banking Regulations and Cooperation Among National Regulators: An Assessment." *Journal of Financial Services Research* 8(3) (1994) 205–225.

Benston, George J., and George G. Kaufman. *Risk and Solvency Regulation of Depository Institutions: Past Policies and Current Options.* Monograph 1988-1, Salomon Center Monograph Series in Finance and Economics, New York University Graduate School of Business Administration, New York, 1988.

Diamond, David, and Philip Dybvig. "Bank Runs, Deposit Insurance, and Liquidity." *Journal of Political Economy* 91 (June 1983), 401–419.

Jerome Levy Economics Institute. Conference on Financial Fragility, Bard College, Annandale-on-Hudson, NY, 1994.

Mankiw, N. Gregory. "The Allocation of Credit and Financial Collapse." *Quarterly Journal of Economics* 101 (August 1986), 455–470.

Mishkin, Frederic S. "Asymmetric Information and Financial Crises." In: R. Glenn Hubbard, ed., *Financial Markets and Financial Crises.* Chicago: University of Chicago Press. 1991, pp. 69–108.

Stiglitz, Joseph, and Andrew Weiss. "Credit Rationing in Markets with Imperfect Information." *American Economic Review* 71 (June 1981) 393–410.

Yago, Glenn. *Junk Bonds: How High Yield Securities Restructured Corporate America*. New York: Oxford University Press. 1991.

Summary of Academic Conference

BARRY RILEY
Investment Editor, Financial Times, London, UK

For most of you it is the first day, but for me it is the third. Since Wednesday I have been confined in a roomful of academics discussing financial fragility. That might sound dull, and indeed it started quietly, but by the end the mood was getting quite heated and indeed tempers were occasionally getting fragile.

The use of the term fragility is indeed a little curious. It is the reverse of robustness or strength, and I suppose if this conference had been sponsored by banks or securities firms it would have placed a positive gloss on the subject and talked about financial strength. You could say it is another form of the old conundrum of whether a glass if half-full or half-empty.

I was slightly disappointed that the conference did not really attempt to define the term "financial fragility." It could refer to the risks of failure of individual financial institutions. In terms of the securities markets I suppose it refers to the possibility of extreme volatility, of price crashes such as we saw in October 1987. More generally we are talking about the extreme risks of systemic collapses such as engulfed many of the US savings and loan institutions in the late 1980s—a crisis which was, however, successfully isolated by the American regulators. One very academic definition offered this week was that financial fragility can be said to exist when financial factors create extra volatility compared to a neoclassical business cycle.

Well, I suppose a learned professor can get away with saying that kind of thing, but we journalists are a more sensational lot. So my initial response, at any rate to the early papers at the academic conference, was one of slight disappointment. Speaker after speaker expressed the view that the system was not fragile, that for instance there was no evidence of chain reactions, and that generally the risks were slight, at least so far as systemic problems were concerned. However, later it emerged that by no means all the participants were so confident; some fundamental areas of quite vigorous debate emerged.

At this point I have to make an apology to the participants. Originally I intended to attempt a proper summary of the various presentations, but when I found I was confronted with 12 rather densely argued papers running to a total of about 270 pages plus tables and charts, not to mention the formal contributions of discussants and many other points made in the course of the sessions, I had to abandon the idea of giving any kind of comprehensive report.

I shall have to skate journalistically over the subject, concentrating on four or five main themes, and if I leave out particular speakers or topics, as I say, I apologize. At the same time, if I steal ideas and insights and appear to present them as my own I will not pretend to be sorry about that; it is what journalists do all the time without scruple.

We began with Hyman Minsky. He, at least, is a self-proclaimed fragilist, and has been following this kind of theme, I believe, for some 40 years. He discussed his researches on

H. A. Benink (Ed.), Coping with Financial Fragility and Systemic Risk, 259–265.
© 1995 *Kluwer Academic Publishers. Printed in the Netherlands.*

the Great Depression and the widespread U.S. banking failures and associated severe contraction of the U.S. money supply in the 1930s.

Capitalist economies, he argued, are by their nature unstable. After long periods of growth confidence grows, and riskier and riskier financial structures become employed by financial institutions and companies. In a low-risk economy, notably one recovering from an economic slump, sound finance is the rule, and enterprises are financed with equity and long-term debt with no expected requirement for new capital. A riskier stage is when enterprises are covering their interest out of cash flow but need to roll over their shorter term debts from time to time. This Minsky considered to be speculative financing. Eventually, as confidence grows still further, and financiers become still less risk-averse, there is a widespread employment of what he described as Ponzi forms of financing, in which the investment cannot even return its servicing costs and relies on regular injections of capital to keep it afloat pending some speculative future payoff. This is what happens in real estate development booms, for instance. So over long periods of years the financial condition of growing capitalist economies moves from robust to fragile.

The potential costs of this fragility, if it leads to financial collapse, are huge. The government must be prepared to intervene, as indeed it did in the 1930s slump, very late, and, in the S & L crisis, in a more timely way. It is worth paying a high price for regulation, says Minsky, because the ultimate costs of another slump would be vast.

Now, I have rendered Hy Minsky's elegant exposition in my own crude and clumsy way, but it set the theme. Most of the other arguments, I thought, revolved around the questions of whether he was overstating the case and whether the costs and diseconomies associated with interfering with a free market were justified. These costs are quite important, as I shall discuss in a minute, and the full benefits are only realized at times of major financial crisis which may only come two or three times a century.

In any case, quite a few disagreed that there was any fundamental tendency towards fragility, and considered that modern economies are financial robust. At the same time, there was an argument that a certain amount of risk in the system was a tolerable and indeed essential feature. Weak institutions must be weeded out, and their sacrifice will strengthen the moral fibre of the remainder.

In summarizing this debate I will deal with four themes. First, some more thoughts on whether the system really is fragile or not; second, the balance between security and risk, given in particular the costs involved and the likelihood of introducing moral hazard; third, the nature of regulation, whether it should be based upon strict rules applied rigidly or discretionary intervention tailored to the particular institution and the particular circumstances; and last, the international dimension, which has become so important: are we suffocating international competition and imposing a damaging straightjacket by insisting on uniform ratios and controls around the world?

But first, one general point. I have to say that I was rather disappointed that the conference did not really live up to its subtitle, a global perspective. There was a lot of comment about America, and a certain amount about Europe, but almost no discussion of Asia or Latin America. Japan is a fascinating case. Many of the Japanese commercial banks are almost certainly insolvent on any realistic basis of accounting. Is this dangerous? What are the costs of propping up the Japanese system now, and who will bear the costs of working the banks into a solvent condition over a period of years? What would be the costs of *not* propping up the system, that is, of a panic? Is there too much attention paid to the American situation? We already have a financial system meltdown apparently under way in Venezuela, so that there is plenty of financial fragility in the world, but apparently not in any place anywhere near Chicago.

At any rate, the main paper on banking system fragility was very upbeat. It was produced by George Benston and George Kaufman (from Chicago). There is no reason, said the two Georges, to fear that banking is more fragile than any other industry. Their researches had shown that worries about contagion—a banking crisis spreading from one institution to another—were unfounded. Therefore banking failures have no economic significance. This does not mean, however, that bank failures are not costly to those directly affected by them. They certainly are. One might add that there is strong pressure on politicians to compensate innocent parties, certainly small personal depositors. At the same time, political interference such as through the geographical restrictions on branching by U.S. banks can actually increase the risks of failure, by reducing the opportunities for diversification of exposures.

So, say Benston and Kaufman, the market should be opened up (this, I should say, once again, is very largely a peculiarly American problem), and then the risks to the public can be almost eliminated by imposing a minimum capital requirement. This can be made more effective by installing a system of structured early intervention when danger levels are being neared. This is what the Americans now have (though it is not proven in practice). But it is something the Europeans have not got so far. I will come back to this subject under the heading of rules versus discretion.

But is the approach of Benston and Kaufman too optimistic? Outside the U.S. there are some uncomfortable examples. Virtually the whole of Scandinavia suffered a banking system solvency crisis in the late 1980s. David Llewellyn described the experience of Sweden, a country where just about all the banks became insolvent after credit deregulation followed by a property bubble that inevitably collapsed. There was a striking failure to assess risk properly. Llewellyn described the excuse of a Swedish banker. "Yes, of course we knew we were not charging a sufficient risk premium," he said. "We tried, but our customers would not pay."

Sweden has rescued its banks but this brings us to the next problem. The losses are real and have to be borne by somebody. After you have wiped out the shareholders and subordinated debt holders the depositors are next in line. If you decide to shelter them, for political reasons, the taxpayers have to foot the bill. But this can generate a dangerous fiscal crisis. Sweden is in a terrible financial mess, not likely to be helped by voting the Social Democrats back this month. Elsewhere, I have already mentioned the banking failures in Venezuela, which has ordered its solvent banks to bail out its insolvent ones. This could make them all insolvent.

The point to be made out of all this is a simple one. If the first line of defence, the capital requirements and other prudential regulations, fail, the system then depends upon the support of the lender of last resort, the central bank, or upon the Treasury directly. As Hyman Minsky put it at the end of his paper, the creditworthiness of the government must therefore be beyond question.

Let me touch on a more positive aspect of this fragility theme, however. In moderation, a little fragility does you good. At least, it does other people some good if your bank collapses. A dynamic capitalist economy needs to know about risk: the unlucky and imprudent must not be bailed out. Of course, this can sometimes be unfair: small institutions are permitted to fold while big ones are usually too important to be allowed to go.

But banks are not always conscious enough of the risks. Indeed, they may sometimes pursue them. This is not strictly part of the conference summary, but Harald Benink has drawn my attention to a very interesting paper just published by the Federal Reserve Bank of St Louis. Sangkyun Park, a senior economist at the bank, analyses the question of why U.S. banks appeared to adopt more risky strategies in the 1980s. He suggests that there may be three explanations. One is that the banks were affected by unexpected shocks in areas like Texas and New England. This is the regional problem again. The other two suggestions are more interesting. It may have become attractive for, first, stockholders and, second, managers to adopt higher risk strategies.

Let us look first at the owners of bank equity. They were affected by deregulation, which increased the level of competition in banking and reduced the franchise value of established banks. With the market value of the equity lowered, downside risk was lowered, and the upside potential arising from a risky strategy was more attractive. In theory this temptation should have been cancelled out by the higher deposit costs resulting from higher perceived depositor risk. But generous deposit insurance was available so depositors were largely indifferent to risk.

As for the managers, in a more competitive climate it became harder to make profits. This did not particularly disturb competent managers, who could still be successful, but less competent ones may have been tempted to take above-average risks in the hope of being lucky. Without taking these risks they could not have hoped to satisfy the requirements of the shareholders. The changed competitive conditions may have resulted in a change in manager incentives. Not all banks will have been affected in these ways, but a signficant minority may have been.

Now, the details of all this may be controversial, but the moral hazard and other adverse consequences of the regulations that are intended to reduce financial fragility certainly have to be very carefully considered. This is my second theme.

Particularly amongst the American participants of the academic conference there was a strong free-market bias. Deposit insurance is a case in point. It is a convenient device for politicians, providing help for those least able to afford losses. However, it undermines the incentives of banks to pursue prudent policies. And in the 1980s it became notoriously abused in the U.S., with individuals able to take advantage of $100,000 cover on a number of accounts with different institutions.

In fact, evidence was produced that deposit insurance operated by some individual states as far back as the 1920s encouraged damaging land-price bubbles, just as federal deposit insurance in the 1980s helped to generate another destructive boom and bust in commercial real estate. Moreover, high levels of free capital in banking balance sheets are required to protect the deposit insurance providers, notably the FDIC, which stands, some say, for Forever Demanding Increased Capital. The servicing of this capital then becomes an extra cost to the banking system. Moreover, with more capital at stake the owners of bank equity may become more risk-averse than before, the reverse of the situation I described before, and another distortion.

Now for the third theme which was hotly debated, rather surprisingly so to an outsider like myself. It concerned the details of banking regulation. I suppose it could apply to securities firms too. This was the issue described as rules versus discretion, or versus authority. We are used to discretion in banking regulation. In the UK the Bank of England Governor's eyebrows have traditionally been the main indicator of his concerns. If they are noticeably raised you must take the warning seriously. Sometimes, as with Johnson Matthey Bankers, the Bank decides on a rescue; at other times, as with BCCI, it lets the bank collapse. It all depends on circumstances; sometimes, the critics say, on whether the distressed bankers have white skins or brown skins. The Bank of England furiously denies this, but sometimes discretion can look like discrimination.

Rules can be crude, and lead to a suboptimal outcome, but their application might at least be seen as fair. There was Italian support from Franco Bruni for indiscriminate action here, rules, not discretion, on the grounds that otherwise regulation tends to become a largely political matter in which favors were done to political friends and supporters. That is, perhaps, a particularly Italian view, but some of the same concerns were expressed by Paul Horvitz. The U.S. regulators, he said, have become increasingly sensitive to political interference. The regulatory agencies were looking over their shoulders and were afraid to exercise their independent judgment for fear of criticism by Congressional oversight committees.

A response in the U.S. has been the introduction of a graduated system of intervention and controls as banks approach the critical area for balance sheet ratios, through the operation of various trigger points, an approach which was in fact devised by none other than Benston and Kaufman. This is an approach designed to reduce the need for discretion on the part of the authorities while at the same time allowing reasonably flexible regulation. Benston and Kaufman say this is producing a healthier industry. But these are early days.

Now for another contentious issue, the international level playing field. Harald Benink produced a paper with David Llewellyn. Their contribution had a strong and clear theme: that the objectives of the international regulation of banks and securities firms have become confused.

There are two objectives, the improvement of systemic stability, which may be threatened by cross-border inconsistencies as globalization proceeds, and the promotion of a level playing field, described in academic language as competitive neutrality. Stability requires the application of different rules to different kinds of banking and securities market institutions, the authors argued. But in fact competitive neutrality had become the dominant issue. The result was the imposition of inappropriate regulations which would distort the financial industry.

Other speakers put this in a slightly different way, saying that an excessive emphasis on harmonization would damage the ability of different countries to develop their own regulatory frameworks, and would block the benefits of comparative advantage in cross-border trade in financial services. But Charles Goodhart of the London School of Economics dismissed such suggestions, however justified in theory, as irrelevant. Rightly or wrongly, probably wrongly, the trade protection issue was dominant, he said. The political priority was seen as to defend domestic institutions against allegedly "unfair" foreign competition. The international rules were the result of horse-trading among leading countries. All the same—and this ties in with the previous theme on rules versus discretion—he thought it was a serious failure that the Basle Agreement had not implemented a graduated response to poor ratios. This failure meant that a high degree of discretion had to be maintained for bank regulators.

So much for the four issues. But I must not stop there, because you will be asking about the hot subject for fragility buffs, the theme of all finance directors' nightmares, the topic for all sensation-seeking financial journalists. I am talking, you will be aware, about derivatives.

In fact there was not much for the sensation-seeker to get his teeth into on Wednesday and Thursday. The main paper was given by Frank Edwards, and the message was clearly that this was no big deal. The foreign exchange markets had been in business offering forward contracts for maybe centuries. So why get so worried about swaps or other OTC contracts? Of course, individual companies had suffered losses, but there appeared to be little risk of a derivatives-induced systemic crisis. Here the monetary economics professors warmed again to their theme of the sacrificial victims. Let a few of them crash. Good for attitudes. Shake them up a bit. The risks are there, but that will encourage the prudent use of derivatives and lead to a healthy outcome. But although cases like the losses on derivatives by companies such as Procter & Gamble and Air Products can be written down to bitter experience, the crisis at Metallgesellschaft (MG) has been of a more serious magnitude, although you can argue that because it was trading in commodities derivatives, that is, various energy-based contracts, it is only a marginal example of a victim of the fragility of the financial system.

However, Frank Edwards drew some more general lessons from the MG experience. He argued that the company was actually trying to reduce its risks and it was only the mismatch of its long and short positions that got it into trouble. The errors were compounded in various ways. Part of the problem was that although the transactions were all done in New York, MG's parent is, of course, German and has to follow German accounting principles.

Now, my experience is that every international financial conference I go to ends up as a battle between the Americans and the Germans over accounting standards. I never thought the subject would pop up in a seminar on financial fragility, but here it is. The German principles required MG to report huge losses on its delivery contracts but it could not offset these with the unrealised gains on its forward delivery contracts. Edwards drew the conclusion that rigid and inappropriate accounting and disclosure conventions can kill you if you get involved in large and complex derivatives dealings. I should add that not all the academics swallowed this interpretation, arguing that sophisticated markets and bankers should be able to see through inappropriate accounting conventions, so there must have been more to this case.

Another failing at MG was the lack of communication between the executives and the supervisory board. So financial fragility can certainly result from the derivatives markets when they are used without proper understanding of the consequences of sharp price movements and without proper systems to control the risks being taken and to report these to the controlling board of directors.

As I say, I have been brutally selective and I have left out large areas of subject matter and ignored speakers regardless of their merits. Once again I apologize for that, but I hope that in abandoning comprehensiveness I have been able to put over to you an understandable snapshot of the issues that are concerning the academic world at this time. Stability, they say, definitely rules over fragility. But when they say that bank crashes are of no economic consequence I wonder whether we are all living in the same world. *Just on a different plane*, I suppose.

Now I look forward with great interest to hear the practitioners' views, and I wonder whether they will be preoccupied with the same themes or whether they will veer off at some sort of tangent. Thank you for listening to me.

G10

G20

Financial Fragility: Sources, Prevention, and Treatment

ANDREW D. CROCKETT
General Manager, Bank for International Settlements, Basle, Switzerland

1. Introduction

It is a pleasure to attend a conference which brings together so many well-known names in financial and monetary economics, particularly in a city whose name is so closely associated with European monetary and financial integration. At the same time, the intellectual standards of my fellow participants makes it an obligation and a challenge to try to provide some new insight or vantage point from which to view the subject of financial fragility.

As I embark on this task, I want to begin with a confession, an objective, and a warning. The confession is that much of what you are about to hear may not seem terribly original. T.S. Eliot, when accused of plagiarizing the 13th-century Italian poet Guido Cavalcanti, replied loftily "Immature artists imitate, while mature artists steal." You will have to be the judges of whether I am displaying maturity or immaturity in what I have to say, or possibly, simply misunderstanding earlier contributions. At any rate, I will try to use their insights, many of which have come from those present in this room, to reach some conclusions that are relevant from a policy perspective.

My objective is an ambitious one. I want to ask whether the tools available to central banks are adequate in coping with the types of financial fragility we are currently facing. There are several dimensions to this task. Coping with fragility presumably includes both limiting the danger of fragility emerging, and dealing with systemic problems should a crisis nevertheless arise. Moreover, in addressing the adequacy of central banks' instruments, both sufficiency and efficiency must be considered. In other words, we need to know not only whether financial crises can be avoided (this can sometimes be achieved by restrictions and regulations), but whether they can be avoided without undermining the efficiency gains obtained through the promotion of a competitive financial system and without increasing moral hazard problems that can make things worse, not better, over time.

My warning concerns the management of financial change. The objective of many governments, finance ministries, and central banks since the late 1970s has been to strengthen financial institutions through liberalization and deregulation. They have had considerable success in this. Nevertheless, in some cases, the result has sometimes been the opposite of what was intended; namely, greater rather than less direct government

H. A. Benink (Ed.), Coping with Financial Fragility and Systemic Risk, 267–277.
© 1995 *Kluwer Academic Publishers. Printed in the Netherlands.*

involvement in the control of financial institutions and weaker rather than stronger financial intermediaries. We should ask ourselves what guarantees we have that the next round in the transformation of our financial system does not result in a similar experience.

2. Definition

So much for preliminaries. Let me begin the main part of my lecture with a defintion of terms. There is, so far as I am aware, no generally accepted definition of what is meant by financial fragility, though quite possibly this conference may by now have advanced matters on this score.

I will take financial fragility to mean a level of debt, or a weakness of balance-sheet structure, across a range of economic agents that increases their vulnerability to economic shocks and significantly influences macroeconomic performance. By this definition, fragility can emerge both in the nonfinancial sector and in the financial sector (and, of course, can communicate itself from one to the other). Macroeconomic consequences can arise both because the behavior of economic agents is directly affected by their financial vulnerability, and because the policy actions of the authorities are constrained by the desire to avoid precipitating a financial crisis.

Much early discussion of financial fragility focused on the implications for the growth of aggregate demand of rising indebtedness in the corporate and household sector. This is an important and interesting subject, but it will not be my main concern today. Rather, I want to focus on the problems of fragility *within* the financial sector, and to ask how we can best mitigate their potential macroeconomic consequences.

This is certainly not just an academic question. Over the past 15 years or so, there have been a series of episodes in which unwise lending decisions have seriously impaired the profitability of financial institutions and raised wider questions about the stability of the financial system. These include the LDC debt crisis, the S&L debacle in the United States, the collapse of junk bond values, and the real estate lending crisis, to name just a few. There have also been worrying episodes of substantial market turbulence, such as the stock market crash of 1987 and the more recent erosion of bond values in early 1994.

Against this background, it is perhaps not surprising that many observers ask where the next shock is coming from, and whether individual institutions, and the system at large, are robust enough to withstand it. Much ink has been spilled recently, for example, on the potential dangers involved in the growth of derivative markets. The sheer size of the notional values involved, together with the inherent complexity of many of the instruments traded, has led many observers, especially those with a built-in suspicion of financial innovation, to conclude that derivatives must be a potential threat to systemic stability.

I shall have more to say on the subject of derivatives later. Let me simply note here that derivatives are like many other sophisticated pieces of new technology: efficient and safe if properly used, but dangerous in the wrong hands. As in other fields, the solution is not to ban or restrict the technology, but to ensure that practitioners understand its properties and use it appropriately.

3. Sources of financial fragility

The starting point for any assessment of how to improve the financial system's resilience must be an analysis of past episodes of financial stress. What caused them to arise? Were they avoidable? And having arisen, were they dealt with efficiently?

In considering some of the origins of financial distress, it can be useful to draw on Professor Frank Knight's classic distinction between risk and uncertainty. Risk was defined by Knight as an uncertain event in which the distribution of possible outcomes is assumed known, while uncertainty is associated with events in which the distribution of outcomes is completely unknown.

Many of the major innovations in financial theory made in the past 25 years concern the pricing of risk, including Markowitz's foundations of portfolio theory, Sharp's capital-asset pricing model, and the Black and Scholes model for the pricing of options. These innovations have allowed us to reduce diversifiable risk by knowing how to break down aggregate risk on various financial assets and price each of their components separately. Some discussions about the dangers involved with various modern financial products seem to forget that these products are specifically designed to permit a significant reduction in individual exposure to price and credit risk, and that they essentially transfer risk to those most willing—and presumably most able—to bear it. Without such instruments, risk-averse firms and financial institutions would be more exposed to asset price volatility and would be deprived of effective means of searching for the lowest cost of finance or the highest risk adjusted investment return.

Nevertheless, there is the legitimate question of whether these new instruments are always priced correctly by their suppliers and adequately understood by their users. Several of the sources of financial fragility since the 1970s in my opinion resulted from the improper pricing of risk. The causes of improper risk pricing are many; inadequate information, faulty specification of the underlying distributions of risk, lack of adequate technical sophistication, or simple incompetence. A current concern with the pricing of options, for example, is that the characteristics of the underlying distribution of price risk are not constant and may change significantly under particular market conditions. Fads, herd instinct, and bandwagon effects have in the past often characterized financial market behavior. Excessive enthusiasm in a bull market, as we have seen, has occurred with real estate and equity assets, causing some participants simply to ignore the underlying risks.

More often, however, financial fragility has its roots in Knight's concept of uncertainty, that is, in events for which we have no way of estimating the likelihood of their occurrence. A surprise shift in macroeconomic or political conditions which alters the expected value of long-term real and financial assets and the net worth of the private sector would be an example. Financial instability is particularly likely when some event occurs whose impact is common to all assets; in the Knight sense "uncertainty" might partly be defined in modern parlance as "undiversifiable risk." An interesting question in our internationally integrated financial environment is whether integration eventually reduces the opportunity to diversify away risk, so that a particular shock to a financial system becomes a non-diversifiable shock and a source of "systemic risk." (If there is anything to this, it constitutes another example of today's solution contributing to tomorrow's problem.)

Pursuing Knight's dichotomy, it is apparent that uncertainty is a more intractable source of vulnerability in the financial system than simple risk. Risk can be priced on the basis of historical experience, and the capital required to cushion residual risk can be relatively easily calculated. Mistakes will of course be made, and on occasion mistakes will be large ones. We have seen this with the well publicized losses on derivative contracts over the past couple of years. But the solution for such problems is relatively straightforward. Individual institutions need to have appropriate risk assessment and control mechanisms in place, together with an adequate cushion of capital. (I will come later to this issue of how these safeguards should be enforced.)

Uncertainty is more tricky because, by definition, it requires a judgment about the probability of future events that cannot be supported fully (or at all) by historical experience. Thus the calculation of an appropriate capital cushion requires difficult judgments by participators and regulators alike. Among the sources of uncertainty are unexpected shifts in economic policy, the working of the economic cycle, political events, and natural disasters.

Systemic stress generally arises when an unexpected event occurs against the background of pre-existing contractual behavior predicated on its non-occurrence. Moreover, the scope for stress has been magnified by developments in financial technology that permit greater leverage in financial positions. To put the matter in simple terms: economic agents can now make larger bets that favorable conditions will persist, so the losses they incur when an unfavorable event occurs are pro tanto larger.

4. Historical experience

It is instructive to briefly consider specific historical episodes in which unanticipated (and unforeseeable) events gave rise to financial fragility. Consider, for example, the combined effects of the shift in U.S. monetary policy in 1979 and the roughly contemporaneous rise in oil prices. Prior to these two events, banks had been engaged in substantial syndicated lending to developing countries. This lending made sense on two assumptions: first, that real short-term rates of interest would remain low or negative, and, second, that the global deflationary effects of external shocks would be offset by expansionary macroeconomic policies in industrial countries. Both of these assumptions were consistent with the economic policy responses following the first oil shock. In the event, however, the industrial countries decided to tighten monetary policy in a determined attempt to squeeze inflation out of the system. The result was a sharp increase in real interest rates and a worldwide recession. A number of LDCs found themselves unable to service their indebtedness, and the financial strains on the international banking system could well have provoked a serious global crisis, were it not for a timely and imaginative response by central bank supervisors and the IMF.

(Incidentally, I want to mention here the role of limited information in shaping the potential for crisis. The lack of adequate data on aggregate lending to certain LDCs caused credit to be extended when better information might have made lenders more circumspect about borrowers' ability to service their debt. I will return later to the role of inadequate transparency in generating fragility and the scope for disclosure to help prevent it.)

Quite apart from major changes in economic policy strategy, unanticipated developments in the economic cycle can also have repercussions for the position of the financial sector. For example, the severity of the 1991–93 recessions caught a number of financial institutions by surprise that had become exposed to highly leveraged companies. Quite a number of these companies, finding themselves in a squeeze between rising interest payments on their debt and falling profits and asset values, were forced into insolvency or debt rescheduling. None of this excuses the over-lending by financial institutions, who should certainly build the prospect of cyclical downturns into their forward planning. However, it does illustrate the capacity of financial decision-takers to be excessively influenced by their most recent loss experience and to pay insufficient attention to the lessons of more distant experiences.

The last example I want to consider is a political event: the collapse of communism in eastern Europe and the reunification of Germany. It is fair to say that the speed with which authoritarian regimes gave way to democracies in this region was unforeseen by almost everybody. Yet the consequences had important implications for asset values, interest rates, and payment flows. As is now well understood, the reunification process led almost inexorably to higher interest rates in Germany, which were communicated to the rest of Europe through the working of the Exchange Rate Mechanism. After the initial economic stimulus from unification wore off, the direct effects of higher interest rates together with the indirect effects of the ensuing recession put substantial pressures on financial institutions.

5. Coping with fragility: Prevention

The subject of this conference, and of my lecture, is "Coping with Financial Fragility." I have thus far approached the topic by noting, with examples, how institutions within the financial sector can find themselves in a vulnerable financial situation. But the operative question facing policy makers is how we can limit the build-up of financial fragility and, in the event that a crisis occurs, how we can contain its systemic consequences. I will deal first with the subject of prevention, and come later to the matter of treatment.

In considering prevention, a central question is the relative roles to be played by market discipline and regulatory intervention. This is a subject which has taxed the ingenuity of monetary authorities since the invention of modern central banking. There is probably no "right" answer that is appropriate for all times and all situations, and so it is appropriate to come to the subject with a sense of humility.

Most economists are likely to start with a predisposition to favor market solutions. Allowing competition to work reasonably freely should improve the efficiency of the financial system and increase "consumer surplus." At the same time, exposure to potential failure can be expected to sharpen the incentive for financial firms to run their affairs prudently, and for their customers to oversee the uses to which their resources are put. If, on the other hand, the authorities accept responsibility for assuring the stability of financial institutions, they immediately face the classic "moral hazard" problem, whereby economic agents increase their risk exposure beyond what would be justified by their own capital (implicitly allowing publicly provided capital to substitute for private capital).

I doubt, however, whether a pure laissez-faire solution provides a sufficient safeguard against the build-up of financial fragility. There are at least three reasons for this. First, there is the possibility of market failure. Market failure, in the technical sense of the term, can arise for several reasons, of which perhaps the most important is lack of adequate information. When economic agents do not have access to full and timely information about the balance sheet of a financial intermediary, their ability to exert market discipline is impaired. The same applies to the actions of the financial intermediary itself, if its knowledge of the position of those to whom it lends is incomplete. So any market-based approach to strengthening the financial system has, at a minimum, to include provisions for the disclosure of relevant information. And while the market will enforce the disclosure of certain types of information, comprehensive and consistent disclosure is unlikely to occur without official encouragement. (The same can be said for certain types of aggregate statistics; the market may not realize the value of aggregate data until an event occurs that shows the cost of its absence.)

A second reason for official involvement, which is perhaps more controversial, is what I would term a systematic tendency to misprice uncertainty. When an event that is uncertain (in the Knightian sense) has not happened for some time, economic agents are inclined to discount its recurrence by more than they should (so-called "disaster myopia"). After several years of economic upswing, for example, the possibility of recession may not be given adequate weight in financial decisions. In such circumstances, a common temptation facing both financial and nonfinancial companies is to bolster profits through increasing leverage. Managers may then face the unpleasant choice between lowering lending standards, on the one hand, and losing market share, on the other. In the absence of enforced standards, prudent financial institutions would lose business to less prudent ones willing to take greater risks or operate with a lower capital cushion.

It could be argued that this is a self-correcting problem in the longer run. Imprudent institutions will eventually fail, and greedy investors will learn their lesson. Eventually, therefore the price of uncertainty will rise to its proper level.

But this leads me to a third reason why a completely hands-off approach is likely to be unworkable: the political process is not willing to accept the consequences of the full application of market disciplines. Once the existence of contagion effects is taken into account, it has to be recognized that an external shock, coming against the background of financial fragility, could lead to a serial collapse of a number of institutions. Whether right or wrong, the Darwinian solution would not, I suspect, survive the test of political acceptability. Nor is this simply economic ignorance. It is far from clear that the discounted value of the future returns from a (putatively) more efficient financial system would outweigh the costs of an immediate financial collapse. At any rate, we should not reach this conclusion until we have considered other ways of strengthening financial efficiency with less severe consequences for the current functioning of markets and institutions.

If a certain element of official involvement in strengthening the financial system is difficult to avoid, how should it best be handled? In particular, how can it be made consistent with the efficient management of resources and the continued operation of market incentives?

Once again, it is helpful to use Knight's distinction between risk and uncertainty. As I said earlier, avoiding the danger that risk would lead to financial fragility is a matter of installing satisfactory systems of risk monitoring and control and maintaining an adequate cushion of capital to cover the risks that remain with the institution. In ensuring the adoption of appropriate risk-management systems, disclosure can have an important role to play. *If* (and it is an important proviso) financial institutions make plain to customers and shareholders the risk exposures they take on, and the techniques they use to manage risk, the market mechanism can probably be relied upon to play the major role in penalizing inappropriate risk management and rewarding prudent behavior. There is no compelling reason for the authorities to require a particular methodology to be employed. Indeed, if they did, it could well add to costs (if institutions have to duplicate proprietary risk-management techniques) and stifle innovation. However, it seems prudent to give supervisors a role in at least satisfying themselves about the resilience of risk-monitoring systems. Recent experience has shown that models designed to eliminate risk can, through faulty design, lead to significant losses.

As far as the size of the capital cushion to be held against risk is concerned, disclosure can also be a helpful discipline, though I am not convinced it is fully sufficient. There is always a trade-off between the added security which a higher level of capital provides, and the enhanced profitability that comes from sailing close to the wind. Minimum capital ratios provide a defence against competitive temptations to underprice risk. They thus help to level the competitive playing field. At the same time, ratios that are minimal do not prevent appropriate distinctions being made among institutions based on the additional security provided by higher capital holdings.

One substantive objection to uniform minimum capital requirements is that they do not differentiate adequately among the different assets the capital cushion is required to cover. It is indeed true that under present international standards, no distinctions are made within the broad category of claims that are 100% risk-weighted. But the alternative approach, in which bank supervisors would be required to distinguish different degrees of riskiness within particular classes of banks assets, poses even greater difficulties. It would be a major step toward transferring the credit assessment function from the financial institution to its regulator, with all the negative implications this would have for competitive efficiency and moral hazard. It seems to me preferable to follow the course of setting a uniform minimum capital standard (with different risk weights for major classes of assets), and continue to allow the market the task of distinguishing among institutions based on the quality of their specific portfolio decisions.

Thus far I have been talking mainly about preventing the financial fragility that arises from the Knightian concept of risk. Securing the financial system against uncertainty, the possibility of adverse events that cannot reasonably be foreseen, is, as I alluded to earlier, a more difficult matter. Since there is no measurable basis for assessing uncertainty, judgments about a prudent capital reserve are likely to vary widely. For reasons of competitive equity, as well as for systemic security, there seems no alternative for the authorities but to set a common safety margin which reduces to acceptable proportions the possibility that an unexpected shock will lead to systemic stress.

Note that there are two important qualifiers in this last sentence: the phrase "acceptable proportions" and the word "systemic." I use the term "acceptable proportions" because the complete elimination of financial vulnerability would be hopelessly uneconomic. This is a proposition which economists have little difficulty in accepting, but is harder for lay opinion to grasp. What we must seek to do is balance the costs of *preventing* financial instability from arising with the costs of *dealing* with instability after it has occurred. And the word "systemic" is important because it is no part of central banks' responsibility to intervene in support of an individual financial institution whose failure does not have wider consequences. Policy makers should be interested in externalities, not private costs.

Systemic protection involves the unglamorous but vitally important tasks of ensuring that clearing and settlement systems are robust, that the legal basis of market innovations is secure, and that mechanisms are in place to limit the propagation of financial difficulties across markets. Given the globalization of financial markets and institutions, strengthening what might be termed the financial infrastructure clearly has an important international dimension. I see the BIS as having a vital role in facilitating central bank cooperation in these fields.

Before leaving the subject of preventing financial fragility, I want to say a word about deposit insurance. Deposit insurance was originally introduced to prevent bank runs and in that respect it has been demonstrably successful. The potential danger of course is moral hazard, illustrated most graphically in the behavior of the U.S. S&L industry. The problem with deposit insurance is that by offering protection against the *consequences* of financial fragility, the disciplines against balance-sheet weakness are relaxed. Efficiency in resource allocation is therefore impaired and a major fiscal burden can be placed on the budget.

The answer to this problem has to involve the restoration of appropriate incentives to the customers and counterparties of financial institutions. In other words, deposit protection must not be such as to make depositors oblivious to the behavior of the firms with which they do business. Means other than full deposit protection must be used to limit the danger of contagion from one financial institution to another.

6. Coping with fragility: Treatment

Even if appropriate mechanisms to help prevent financial vulnerability are put in place, it cannot be excluded that certain external shocks will have systemic consequences, which in turn have implications for financial and macroeconomic stability. This takes us beyond the sphere of accident prevention, with which I have been dealing so far, into the realm of damage limitation. As I have noted earlier, the potential problem with damage limitation is that the short-term benefits may be purchased at the cost of longer-term moral hazard problems. Since I do not believe that the authorities cannot simply stand by and watch a systemic crisis unfold, how can this problem be minimized?

The classic answer, dating back to Bagehot, is that central banks should lend freely in a liquidity crisis, but refrain from intervening to support an insolvent institution. This dictum has much to commend it. It has the particular virtue of seeking to protect public funds since support will only be given where it is likely to be repaid. Nevertheless, I am not sure the liquidity/solvency dichotomy is a sufficient guide to how central banks should act in a crisis. In the first place, it is often not easy to distinguish between a liquidity crisis and a solvency crisis. Moreover, the former can turn into the latter as events unfold. Second, as far as systemic contagion is concerned, and this is the authorities' central concern, it may not matter very much whether the institution at the origin of the crisis is solvent or not. And last, it is not clear on incentive grounds that institutions should automatically be rescued from liquidity difficulties caused by their own mistakes.

So some additional guidelines are needed if the authorities conclude that official intervention is required to guard against systemic knock-on effects. No hard and fast rules are possible, but it is possible to set down a few broad principles that help to preserve market incentives. First, no rescue should be attempted unless a failure threatens the stability of the financial system more generally. This will lead to a measure of uncertainty about the authorities' response, but in this particular case some uncertainty may be no bad thing. Second, those who have exercised faulty judgment should pay an appropriate penalty. Managers of rescued institutions should forfeit their jobs, and shareholders should lose their equity. Third, caution should be exercised in providing protection to banks' customers and counterparties, beyond that which is contractually agreed. The objective of stabilizing the system in disturbed conditions should be achieved with the minimum of undesirable precedents for the future.

Before finishing on the subject of damage limitation, let me touch lightly on a topic that has acquired increasing prominence in the context of the debate on central bank independence. This is whether there is a potential conflict of interest between the regulatory authority and the monetary authority, which could be removed by separating the functions of banking regulation and monetary policy formulation. I do not want to take sides in the broader debate. However, two misconceptions should be disposed of. The first is that central banks can separate themselves entirely from concern over the financial state of major institutions. Since central banks are the lenders of last resort to the system, they must be fully aware of all relevant aspects of the management of any institution they may decide to support. The second misconception is that the potential conflict between monetary policy and financial system stability can be resolved by separating responsibility for the two objectives. The reason for the conflict is straightforward and not capable of simple resolution. It is that a single policy instrument affects two objectives. In such circumstances, as Tinbergen teaches, a trade-off is required. It may be, as some believe, that predominant weight should be given to the price stability objective and little or none to financial stability. Alternatively, it may be thought that financial stability has implications for monetary stability that must be given due weight. But decisions should surely be taken with full appreciation of the relevant trade-offs and interactions. Central bankers cannot avoid this trade-off through the simple expedient of saying that financial stability is somebody else's problem.

7. Derivatives

I want to end this lecture with some remarks on derivatives. I noted earlier that the most troublesome cause of fragility was uncertainty and that the essence of uncertainty is that you don't know where the next problem is coming from. Are derivatives destined to be the next source of a potential or actual financial crisis?

With derivatives, as with any new generic financial instrument whose market is closely interrelated to a variety of domestic and international cash markets, unfamiliarity with market size, use, and the distribution of risks are likely to raise concern among policy makers.

In approaching this subject I think it best if we broaden our perspective and ask in what context we are concerned with the growth of derivatives. For many I believe that context is one in which they believe that the changes in the financial system since the 1970s have increased systemic risk. These changes include the general liberalization of both domestic and cross-border financial transactions, together with the increased number and improved marketability of financial products. Add to this the greater institutionalization of private savings and the active management of portfolios which has led to an enormous growth in securities trading and payments flows, and you have the basic ingredients making up the "worry-basket" of central bankers, regulators, and supervisors. These concerns have been amplified as a result of the increase in private indebtedness in several countries and the greater competition in banking and the securities business.

Now enter derivatives. It is obvious that derivative products provide enormous benefits in the management of risk; by breaking down the different risk components associated with financial contracts, pricing these risk components separately, and redistributing risks according to the ability and desire of market participants to manage and absorb them. Markets have thus sprung up which aid both nonfinancial and financial enterprises to "lay-off" a particular price or, in some cases, pass credit risk on to another party. A market for risk coverage, or financial insurance, has evolved which has made both national and international financial markets more efficient.

But has it made markets safer? This question may appear as a non sequitur. How can systemic risk increase if the risk to individual market participants is reduced? The answer lies in the fallacy of aggregation. At any point in time each individual may indeed feel that his or her risk has been reduced with the aid of derivative instruments. But the ability of some derivative products to significantly increase the leverage of market participants may increase aggregate uncertainty. I would also conjecture that because of the fundamental lack of transparency of some financial products and the difficulty of evaluating risk associated with them (for example, embedded options), the resulting concentration in some derivatives markets creates "uncertainty externalities" in other closely related markets. As a result of the close cross-market linkages, the "uncertainty externalities" cannot easily be segmented in periods of market volatility and stress. As participants seek to shield themselves against the impact of an event whose timing or probability of occurrence cannot be estimated, markets may at times experience an erosion of liquidity possibly leading to difficulties in other markets.

Whether and to what degree derivative products heighten such a possibility is an open question, but we certainly cannot afford to dismiss the possibility. This concern has also been expressed by a number of informed market participants.

Let me make mention of a few reports which have raised specific concerns. In October 1992 a working group assembled by the governors of G-10 central banks highlighted three key features which seem to be reshaping interbank relations, partly as a result of the derivatives revolution: increased domestic and international linkages across markets; a greater sensitivity to credit risk; and a greater concentration in wholesale markets.[1] These concerns, together with a number of others (including the lack of transparency caused by new risk management techniques, the uncertainty created with a possible collapse of liquidity in the event of sharp price movements, and settlement and legal risks) were addressed last year by the Group of Thirty in their comprehensive study of derivatives practices.[2]

While I am in broad agreement with the Group of Thirty study, I would place the emphasis slightly differently in terms of the degree of concern to be expressed about certain practices and structure in the derivatives industry. I believe that the study may have gone a bit too far in trying to reduce worries about potential systemic risks. Its conclusions in this respect have not been completely accepted by all observers, private or public.[3]

The latest note of discord has been sounded by the U.S. General Accounting Office.[4] As the United States is a major player in all of the derivatives markets, the concerns of the GAO are of some relevance. One major area of attention is OTC (over-the-counter) derivatives activities. The GAO was particularly concerned by the fact that, at fiscal year-end 1992, five major securities firms and three insurance companies ("whose affiliates had the highest dollar amount in derivatives outstanding") comprised about 30% of the U.S. OTC dealers' total volume. And the GAO noted that neither the affiliates of securities firms nor insurance company affiliates engaged in OTC derivatives activities are subject to routine examination by oversight bodies or subject to capital requirements.

It is not my intent here to argue for or against examination or capital requirements for those OTC operators not currently covered by such regulations. This is a subject sufficient to warrant another lecture. What I would like to point to is the shape of public concern. Let me quote, for example, from the GAO report's executive summary: "The federal government would not necessarily intervene just to keep a major OTC derivatives dealer from failing, but to avert a crisis, the Federal Reserve may be required to serve as lender of last resort to any major U.S. OTC derivatives dealer, whether regulated or unregulated."[5] This is strong language. Requests for greater disclosure of derivatives activities by financial intermediaries, increased attention to improving internal risk control procedures, and advancements in derivatives clearing and settlement arrangements are all meant to avert the need for such an intervention.

In calling attention to possible areas of financial fragility one has to come somewhere between sounding strident, risking being dismissed for "crying wolf," and sounding so well-balanced as to lull oneself into a false sense of security. Let me simply conclude by saying that I think the financial disruptions since the 1987 equity market crash have made us all more reluctant simply to assume that the next crisis will be just one more "near miss." More needs to be, and is being, done. This conference should help us to both better focus and measure our concerns over financial fragility, and to find efficient means of reducing it.

Notes

1. "Recent Developments in International Interbank Relations," Bank for International Settlements, Basle, October 1992.
2. "Derivatives: Practices and Principles," The Group of Thirty, Washington DC, July 1993.
3. See "The Complacent Derivatives Industry," *Euromoney* (August 1993).
4. "Financial Derivatives: Actions Needed to Protect the Financial System," United States General Accounting Office, May 1994.
5. Ibid., p. 12.

Fragility in the Banking World

H. ONNO RUDING
Vice Chairman, Citicorp, New York, NY

1. General processes of change in the banking world

We are experiencing several general processes of change in the banking world:

1. *Concentration* in banking is leading to a reduction in the number of independent banks.
   a. In *Europe* this process started much earlier and is now largely completed in the individual countries. Examples include the Netherlands, but also the UK, France, Germany, etc. Recent developments in Spain reflect this trend.
   b. In the *U.S.* the situation is still fundamentally different as a result of legislation in the 1920s and 1930s, especially the ban on interstate branch banking. In recent years we have seen a partial lifting of this restriction to resolve the crisis in the savings and loan sector. Many S&Ls have been acquired by banks in other states. Also, there have been several mergers among both regional banks (NationsBank, Banc One) and money center banks (Chemical Bank). It now seems likely that Congress will finally lift the ban on interstate banking. This is welcome and long overdue. It will lead to many more mergers and acquisitions in the U.S. (However: Citibank is now less interested in making extensive use of this increased freedom than in the past!) I welcome this consolidation in U.S. banking. It will strengthen the banking industry and reduce its excessive fragmentation and fragility.
   c. *International, cross-border.* On the one hand we have seen several cross-border mergers and acquisitions or alliances. One of the biggest was the acquisition of Midland Bank by Hong Kong and Shanghai Bank. On the other hand, many efforts have failed. Examples include Netherlands-Belgium, AMRO-Générale de Banque, and ING-BBL. Concentration in banking is still largely a domestic activity, even in the EU. Acquisitions of U.S. banks by non-U.S. banks have in most cases been not very successful.
2. A second process is the *blurring of the separation between commercial banks and investment banks* or securities firms. This development has never been much of an issue in continental Europe, where banks traditionally perform both functions. They do this, in my opinion, in a satisfactory way which has not led to fragility of the banking system. In the U.S., however, this was and is a hot issue. The same for Japan. The Glass-Steagall Act of 1933 still stands, and the U.S. Congress still insists on this separation. I think that times have changed and that abolition of Glass-Steagall is long overdue. In fact, part of this separation has already disappeared as a result of the liberal

H. A. Benink (Ed.), Coping with Financial Fragility and Systemic Risk, 279–285.

interpretation of this law by the Federal Reserve. It has allowed a growing number of commercial banks to act as underwriter of bonds and—to a lesser extent—of (equity) shares. I welcome this development. If implemented properly it will remove elements of unfair competition against U.S. commercial banks and it will strengthen the position of these banks, not only against investment banks but also against foreign banks. In a time of growing disintermediation (industrial companies borrow less from banks and raise funds directly from investors through securities issues in the capital markets) the position of commercial banks in the U.S. would otherwise become unnecessarily restricted and fragile.

3. A third trend is the growing importance of *non-banks* as providers of loans to industry. In the U.S. and elsewhere *finance companies* play a growing role, especially in leasing and other asset-based lending. A large and successful case is General Electric Credit Corporation (GECC). As such this development is acceptable and an aspect of free competition. The only critical note I want to raise is that the authorities should provide a fair and "level" playing field. If a situation would arise where non-banks are free to do as they like because they are basically non-regulated whereas banks are constrained to perform the same activities because of rules set by their bank regulators, then there is reason for concern.

4. Finally the hotly debated issue of *bancassurance*: mergers, acquisitions, or alliances between banks and insurance companies, respective de novo activities of banks in insurance products, and vice versa. I take a relaxed and rather positive attitude towards this blurring of the borderlines between different financial industries. I simply note, however, that the U.S. Congress (and the Federal Reserve) continue to be strongly against bancassurance, and I expect no change in the foreseeable future. In Europe the situation is different. Both domestically and cross-border there is a movement towards bancassurance in the EU. The Netherlands is a clear case in point for both national mergers (Nationale-Nederlanden Insurance and NMB Bank/Postbank into ING Group) and cross-border mergers (AMEV and AG into Fortis). Provided that the problem of supervision of banks and insurance companies can be solved in a satisfactory way, I do not see why this trend would increase the fragility of the financial system.

> The above-mentioned trends could lead, however, to an unwanted increase in fragility if they result in an excessive degree of competition between financial institutions. This would be attractive in the short run for the customers of these institutions, but it would undermine the financial soundness and viability of the system in the long run. The other relevant observation is that these developments should not complicate the application of the level playing-field principle (financial institutions which perform similar activities should be regulated in a similar way).

2. Recent trends in U.S. bank markets

Many U.S. banks incurred severe losses, first in the 1980s in the aftermath of the Latin American debt crisis and later as a result of excessive lending to the real estate sector and the financing of highly leveraged buy-outs (LBOs). The question is whether the current situation contains similar, or other serious, risks for U.S. banks. Recently, several observers—and banks as well—have raised warning signals about an emerging trend in U.S. bank lending which can be characterized by:

- growing competition among banks; and
- more aggressive lending practices;

both leading to

- lower interest spreads;
- lower fees;
- longer tenors (maturities) of loans; and
- loan covenants with less stringent conditions.

Some wonder whether these developments signal a return to the dangers of the 1980s. In my view, there are indeed undesirable elements, although the recent practices in bank lending—fortunately—are not the same as in the 1980s.

Most U.S. banks have become more liquid and profitable and have strengthened their balance sheets and capital ratios. All of these welcome developments apparently are making many banks more willing to go for a larger share in a shrinking market of bank loans (shrinking because of the larger role for the capital markets: disintermediation). There now exists a substantial demand for finance as well based on a growing U.S. economy, a renewed wave of acquisitions and mergers in corporate America, and an increased level of refinancings of existing bank loans at terms more attractive to the borrowers.

Fortunately, the situation is different from the 1980s because the degree of leverage in the financing of U.S. corporations is less aggressive now, and because many mergers are now based on strategic considerations rather than purely financial motives. And, as I mentioned, most U.S. banks are much better capitalized now. This latter phenomenon presents a paradox. For years bank regulators have been urging many American banks—and rightly so—to increase their capital ratios, in line with the agreements reached internationally in the context of the Committee on Banking Supervision of the Group of Ten Countries in Basle: Tier I capital ratio minimum 4% of risk-adjusted assets and total (Tier I and Tier II) capital ratio minimum 8%. Most banks in the U.S. are now well above these minimums. These "BIS rules" have been very successful. This has reduced the fragility of the U.S. banking system.

The paradox is that U.S. bank regulators are about to worry whether many U.S. banks are not becoming overcapitalized, resulting from strong profits and raising of additional capital. Insofar as such a situation arises, banks may opt for higher dividend payouts or for share buyback programs. They may, however, also opt for increasing the denominator of their capital ratios: that is, increasing their assets either by making acquisitions or by autonomous growth through a larger loan portfolio. This, in turn, may lead to more aggressive lending practices by lowering the profitability (interest spreads) of lending and/or—worse—by accepting a higher degree of risk. Pessimistic voices raise the question whether particularly this latter aspect, accepting a too risky lending profile, will lead to the next bank crisis by way of nonperforming loans and future losses.

I consider this pessimistic scenario less likely because the lending practices—fortunately—are less risky than in the 1980s, because most banks are much better capitalized (larger buffer for losses), and because banks now are much more alert in avoiding excessive concentrations of risks. I do, however, share the concern that the prevailing extreme competition among the U.S. banks (and, to a lesser extent, between American and foreign banks) in domestic corporate lending poses dangers. Profitability in this sector of banking activity is becoming too thin and may make U.S. commercial banks more vulnerable if this trend continues.

3. What should be done?

If one wants to avoid financial fragility in the banking sector in the coming years, I think that the following aspects are relevant:

1. Sufficient *profitability* in the sense of earnings *before* the cost of credit: revenues minus non-credit expenses. The achievement of a satisfactory level of gross revenues is related to the above-mentioned factors of avoidance of excessive degree of competition, of a level playing field, and of adequate legislation and bank regulation.
2. Banks should be *well capitalized*. In most countries the present situation is satisfactory. Although the minimum international rules for bank capital ratios should continue to be conservative (BIS), I consider the prevailing rules sufficiently strict. There is indeed a potential danger of overcapitalization if banks were to become overly aggressive in their lending activities in order to achieve a satisfactory return on their high capital.
3. Banks should preferably try to spread their risks by a high level of *diversification* of their activities. I think of two desirable kinds of diversification within the traditional area of banking rather than diversification into non-banking activities such as insurance:
   a. *Geographically*. This means a relatively limited dependence on one country or one region in the world in order to reduce the vulnerability of heavy dependence on the economic and financial developments of a restricted geographical area. So this is more than mere internationalization, since a bank that has aggressively expanded its cross-border activities and local activities in countries outside its own can become overdependent on risks in one region (e.g., Latin America during the debt crisis).
   b. *Sectors of banking activity*. Diversification in the sense of dependence not solely on corporate (wholesale) activities or solely on consumer (retail) business but a balance between both offers advantages. One may add: also diversification within corporate banking by being active in both lending-oriented commercial banking and capital markets-oriented investment banking. This reduces vulnerability in revenues and risks. In many cases, a weak development in the one sector may be offset by a simultaneously strong result in the others. The reason is that the factors that determine profitability in corporate banking frequently are different from those in consumer banking.

   There is only one institution in the world that combines this dual diversification: Citibank. It is the only bank with a truly global network and a wide range of geographical activities. Simultaneously, it is well developed in both corporate and consumer banking. (In consumer banking the most profitable segment proves to be a huge credit card business rather than an extensive network of branches.)

4. A special factor that will reduce vulnerability and fragility in banking is a more active use worldwide of *netting* agreements. Netting serves to offset mutual financial claims that develop among counterparties resulting from a multitude of unrelated transactions between large institutions. Most important is netting between large financial institutions, but netting between banks and industrial companies is useful as well. The largest gross amounts in financial claims result from the rapidly growing trading activities, including derivatives. For netting to be legally binding, the requisite institutional and legal framework should be in place. This still differs from country to country. Much progress has been made, but more is necessary. Particularly the risk of a chain reaction of defaults is reduced if the losses resulting from gross claims on a defaulted bank or company can be reduced to losses related to net claims.

5. Another factor of crucial importance is the avoidance of heavy *concentrations of risk*. The total portfolio of a bank should not become overly vulnerable to losses in one particular component because of the excessive amount of a particular exposure. The issue is related to the above-mentioned diversification of banking activities. A solid anti-concentration policy not only focuses on rules setting limits for exposure on individual companies' or banks' counterparties; it also sets internal limits for exposures on individual

- countries or regions;
- industries (say, chemical, energy); and
- products or categories of products.

A bank becomes vulnerable if a relatively high portion of its total revenues comes, for instance, from trading. This became particularly clear in 1994. We at Citibank consider our trading activities (foreign exchange, derivatives, capital markets) of great importance, but we do not want them to become overwhelmingly significant in a relative sense, as a percentage of the bank's total revenues.

A sector that deserves special mention is real estate, particularly lending to the commercial property sector. Several banks, including Citibank, allowed their real estate exposure to grow too fast in the 1980s, in the U.S. and elsewhere as well. They looked at the perceived attractiveness of individual transactions without observing sufficiently that the bank as a whole was building up an excessive exposure to that particular industry. Hopefully, anti-concentration rules will be observed during the next cycle in real estate lending.

Fragility resulting from an incorrect risk policy is not limited to credit risks only. Banks may lose too much money not only as a result of lending but also because of noncredit risks, particularly market or price risks related to positions in financial products traded in markets: foreign exchange, capital markets, both bonds (interest rates) and shares, and commodities markets.

4. Derivatives

In recent years the rapidly growing markets for *derivative* products are attracting increasing attention and concern among regulators and politicians (especially in the U.S.) and in the media. I understand this growing interest; the management of banks are also paying much more attention to the risk aspects of their involvement in financial markets, particularly derivatives.

The basic risks include *price risk* (the potential impact on earnings of changes in the level of volatility of the underlying market factors such as interest rates, foreign exchange rates, commodity prices or equity prices); *credit risk* (the cost of replacing a contract should a counterparty default prior to settlement); *liquidity risk* (an institution's ability to access the market at any time and transact at the market price); and *operating risk* (the potential losses resulting from a failure in payments processing or other internal control systems).

It is true that the growing markets of, and exposure to, derivatives create additional risks for the participants in these markets (especially over-the-counter markets), both the intermediaries (banks) and the end-users (industrial and trading companies as well as institutional investors). The concerns focus on cases where the participants apparently are insufficiently aware of the precise risks embedded in these contracts, and on cases where the participants deliberately engage in aggressive risk-taking by entering into financial contracts which increase their risk (that is, their dependence on the movements of the underlying market variables such as interest rates or exchange rates). This applies particularly to highly leveraged derivatives. If industrial companies allow their treasury departments to act as "profit centers," warning signals should be raised.

However, one should not forget that the overwhelming majority of derivatives contracts are used to *reduce* the risk profile of the market participants: They enable the banks' customers to improve their risk management in a cost-effective and flexible manner. In other words, a proper use of derivatives may reduce financial fragility. One should not throw out the baby with the bathwater!

In my view, the best approach towards addressing the risks entailed in the growing use of derivatives is threefold:

1. First and foremost: adequate action by the banks (and end-users) themselves. This action should focus on:
   a. appropriate internal risk management and internal controls; and
   b. appropriate external disclosure on its activities (size, composition) in the area of derivatives.
2. An active role for the existing regulatory bodies which supervise banks, as well as other market participants.
3. No new legislation. Existing laws provide sufficient powers to enable supervisors to take any necessary action.

I add a few more detailed remarks on these important issues:

On internal risk management: Citibank, like most other banking institutions that act as large derivatives dealers for customers, has an extensive system of internal controls to monitor these risks. These include *independent* risk managers overseeing all trading businesses; marking the derivatives portfolio to market on a daily basis; placing strict potential loss limitations on derivatives business relative to forecasted revenues; employing independent audit and operational control units; utilizing rigorous qualification standards with potential derivatives customers; and putting into place comprehensive tracking and record-keeping functions.

On external disclosure: a working group of the Institute of International Finance (IIF) recently made an interesting and practical set of proposals, including one that banks and securities firms should disclose three things:

- The total replacement value of contracts, i.e., the amount they would have to spend to buy new derivatives contracts if companies defaulted on existing ones.
- The value of contracts in each category of derivatives, such as currency swaps and interest rate options, and a breakdown of maturity profiles, or the length of time contract have to run before expiry.
- Analysis of their methods of accounting, risk management, netting of contracts, and limits on trading. They would also have to describe management controls, an aspect of risk management which many supervisors have highlighted [*Financial Times*, September 9, 1994].

If new regulations are to be applied to the derivatives business, they should be structured in a manner which assures a "level playing field" among U.S. commercial banks and other financial intermediaries, especially investment banks, and among U.S. and foreign institutions. The nature of any new regulation should be based on expanding the level of disclosure and encouraging proper internal control mechanisms and not restricting the use of derivatives by the potential beneficiaries of these products.

One final general observation: Banks and bankers unfortunately have the bad habit of frequently repeating the same mistakes and of falling into the same traps again. It would be useful if young bankers are told to spend somewhat less time on studying the newest financial techniques and products and, instead, to analyze why certain losses (in their own bank or elsewhere) were incurred in the not-too-distant past and what should (or should not) be done to avoid similar risks and losses in the future.

Financial Fragility and Supervision: Discussion

MARIUS VAN NIEUWKERK
Deputy Executive Director Supervision, De Nederlandsche Bank, Amsterdam, The Netherlands

Before I discuss the relationship between financial fragility and supervision, I would like to explain that there are different layers to be distinguished with regard to supervision.[1]

The first layer is *microsupervision*, which is concerned with individual institutions. Are they for instance safe, sound, and stable? Is the management of the institution reliable and qualified?

The second is *macrosupervision*, which focuses on the stability of markets. In this connection a distinction can be made between the macroprudential aspect of supervision on the one hand, and the macrofinancial aspect on the other. The macroprudential aspect relates, among other things, to the lender-of-last-resort function of central banks (supervisory authorities) on the one hand, and the responsibility for the adequate functioning of the payment system on the other. The macrofinancial aspect notably focuses on the responsibility for the proper functioning of markets, or, in other words, on surveillance.

Finally, there is *monetary supervision*, which is concerned with monetary control, money creation, exchange rates, and inflation.

There are links between the above functions. This may be illustrated by comparing supervision to road traffic:

- microsupervision provides for the safety of individual cars, ensuring the safety of passengers (banks, deposit-holders);
- macrosupervision is concerned with the capacity and quality of the road system (financial system);
- monetary supervision regulates the size of the traffic flows and ensures that they proceed as smoothly as possible.

It goes without saying that monetary supervision and macrosupervision serve to promote a stable and sound environment for the players in the markets. This was not the case, for instance, in the Nordic countries during the 1980s. Monetary policy in those countries has contributed to relatively extensive lending, or has at least not obstructed the expansion of lending. This has fueled inflation in those economies. In addition, some critical remarks are in order with regard to macrosupervision in these countries. I will not address these issues here but refer you to a speech I gave earlier on this matter.[2]

Where these aspects are concerned, I agree with Anna Schwartz that inadequate monetary and macroeconomic policy *may* mess things up for the players in the financial

H. A. Benink (Ed.), Coping with Financial Fragility and Systemic Risk, 287–289.

markets. This does not mean, however, that these policy makers are to blame for everything that goes wrong, which is the impression one gets from her words. With that, I absolutely disagree.

First, in this day and age, the power of the financial markets, and notably that of the players in these markets, must also be taken into consideration. The fact that they have such power should make them more aware of their own responsibilities. Henry Kaufman, for instance, even holds the view that in a world of increasing integration or consolidation, large financial institutions must pursue a higher code of conduct in their business activities: "They must take account not only of their narrow private interests, but also of their public responsibilities." Some even see them as future public utilities, although this may be taking it too far. Nevertheless, I would like to quote a wise Dutch banker in this connection, Mr. Hazelhoff, who, in his farewell speech as Chairman of ABN-AMRO Bank, said: "A bank has its reputation. Its brand image. This takes decades to build, perhaps only days to destroy."

Second, history (always a favorite subject of Anna Schwartz) has taught us completely *different* lessons regarding the causes underlying financial institutions' failures, the ultimate expression of financial fragility. Empirical evidence in the United States and Europe shows that, even if adverse economic conditions may throw a bank off course, mismanagement or poor management, and often internal problems are the common denominator of failed and problem banks. Management-driven weaknesses play a significant role in the decline of 90% of the failed and problem banks. A great deal of the difficulties experienced by the banks resulted from inadequate loan policies, from inadequate problem loan identification systems, and from inadequate systems to ensure compliance with internal policies and banking law.

It is further evident from these studies that two more causes were related to poor management: insider abuse and even fraud. These two problems turn out to be significant causes underlying the decline of failed and problem banks. With regard to such insider abuse or fraud, directors, senior management, or principal shareholders were often involved. Related to their fraud was their failure to provide adequate oversight and control.

Furthermore, it is important to note in this connection that, without exception, *none* of the healthy banks which survived the bad economic circumstances experienced any significant insider abuse or fraud.

Another (often complementary) factor appears to be overly aggressive behavior on the part of the director or the management, which may result in imprudent lending practices and excessive loan growth, forcing the banks to rely on volatile liabilities and to maintain inadequate liquid assets.

The warnings emanating from these studies seem to be in line with Dr. Ruding's final remark during the speech he just held. What is really necessary is that banks learn from the lessons from the past. Strongly popularized, the experiences from the past result in the following "indicators" of financial institutions' financial fragility:

- excessive expansion of activities (excessive growth of balance sheet total);
- excessive development of new activities;

- mismanagement and conflict of interests;
- ego-building ("Napoleonic dreams") and high PR-expenditures; or
- moving to a new head office.

Notably, the *combination* of the above factors should alert the supervisory authorities.

I think that not only supervisors, but also the large number of auditors present here, may take these lessons to heart.

Notes

1. See Van Nieuwkerk, "Three Times around the World," Nijenrode University lecture, September 5, 1994.
2. See "The Real Estate Market, the Banking System and Supervision," a speech on the occasion of the second VOGON Symposium (Dutch Association of Real Estate Researchers), Amsterdam, November 1993.

Financial Fragility and Supervision: Discussion

PAUL J. RUTTEMAN
Partner, Ernst & Young, London, UK

To try to summarize the issues of "financial fragility" in ten minutes is a tall order, and I think you asked us all really to comment on the presentations of the speakers this morning and this afternoon. I hope you will forgive me, therefore, if I am selective in the issues I deal with.

First of all, you would expect me to comment that most of the presenters looked at financial fragility in the context of derivatives, because there has been so much discussion about them recently. Perhaps I may start there. At the opening of the conference André Bindenga referred to the rate of growth in derivatives in banks' balance sheets or in the notes to banks' balance sheets. In that context I was intrigued by the Bundesbank Report earlier this year which showed that off-balance-sheet activities accounted for 90% of the business volume of 827 banks studied in the middle of 1993, and that is up from 58% at the end of 1991. Those numbers include traditional forward foreign exchange contracts, and, if you exclude those derivatives, exposure accounted for 53% of business volume—still quite a lot. With such an expansion, therefore, you can understand that regulators and others are beginning to be concerned as to whether banks can control or even understand all the risks which are associated with derivatives.

We have heard that different regulators are concerned about the risks attaching to derivatives and that they feel something must be done about it. I found it interesting also that in the United States the General Accounting Office is questioning the accounting treatment of derivatives. The most significant aspect is that they question whether hedge accounting should ever be used because there is no such thing as a perfect hedge and most people are, in any case, coming to the conclusion that the proper way to account for all contracts of this kind is to mark them to market. You may have heard the comment that I have also heard about Metallgesellschaft where the use of hedge accounting was said to have masked the effect of the basis risk which actually caused their losses. Certainly, if they had not used hedge accounting, the problems would have been very much more apparent earlier. Some question whether Metallgesellschaft really had a loss at all. My own view is that it had a loss whichever way you looked at it, but you can form your own judgment from the circumstances which are spelt out in the booklet we have handed out today on derivatives (it is example 1 on page 12 of that booklet).

Anyway, enough of Metallgesellschaft for the moment. I would just comment that, while I favor marking to market, it is not always as easy as it sounds. So much of the growth in derivatives has been in over-the-counter products, and some of those in very exotic items which are notoriously illiquid and very difficult, therefore, to mark to market. There is a parallel in past banking crises. In the case of real estate for example, many banks thought that the valuations placed on real estate used as collateral were conservative, and

H. A. Benink (Ed.), Coping with Financial Fragility and Systemic Risk, 291–294.
© 1995 *Kluwer Academic Publishers. Printed in the Netherlands.*

that, based on those valuations, the lending was safe and that it was well covered. When a crash comes, of course, for whatever reason (and it is often external rather than anything to do with the banks themselves, monetary policy for example) the markets become less liquid and the values become meaningless. My concern, therefore, about the accounting for derivatives is with the liquidity and whether those marked-to-market figures are always very meaningful, particularly, in the area of over-the-counter products and some of the more exotic items.

I think there is a problem also in relation to disclosure. A number of people suggested this morning that there was a need for greater disclosure and I would support that view too, but there is a risk in seeing that as the solution to all the problems. Some banks are already providing extensive disclosure but often the readers understand very little of it. Notional amounts of swap transactions, for example, provide very large numbers but what exactly do they mean to the average reader. I was pleased to see, therefore, Onno Ruding's suggestion of what might be disclosed because I thought they were useful disclosures. He suggested, if I recall correctly, that we should disclose total replacement costs of contracts, the value of contracts by category, and explanation of the accounting policies used. Whilst I would support those suggestions, I think they too would require a fair amount of narrative, and even then it would be very difficult for the lay reader (and perhaps not all too easy for the specialist reader) to analyze the risks which lie behind those products and what would happen in the event of extreme volatility or just simply illiquid markets. What both the lay reader and the specialist might be interested in is the models those companies use, how far they have been stress tested and what would happen in the event of a crisis of one kind or another.

So that is the next point I wanted to say something about in the context of derivatives. I think it was Andrew Crockett who made the point that in the case of Granite there was a deficient model. What we have at present is the more sophisticated players in the market developing their own models. The question is, what should the regulators do about that. Right now the regulators leave it to the players in the market to develop their own models, accepting that it is the regulators job to make sure that there are adequate controls in force. Now that might be fine provided, of course, that the models are understood by the regulators and that their staff have the training and experience to understand them properly. I noticed, however, that Jerry Jordan made the point this morning that you cannot expect the regulators to have the same knowledge as the players in the market; surely this must apply to the models which are becoming increasingly complex. I wonder, therefore, whether it is realistic to expect the regulators to understand those models and to ensure they do not have any built-in faults. A key consideration of the models concerns stress testing. Our experience has been that by and large the players are trading on the basis of risk probabilities that are reasonable. Most of the time they make profits but occasionally they make losses too. There is nothing wrong with that because you would expect such players to recognize market risk and to run some of those risks, but the models are designed to limit the risk of making large losses. What has surprised a number of these companies is that on a number of occasions when they have made losses they have made enormous losses, far more than they had expected. This raises questions about the effectiveness of the stress testing. Certainly, the models are adequate to deal with the losses that can be expected to occur every 40 days or every 2 years, or whatever it may be, but the

292

real test is whether they can cope with the big one. It is here that we have to rely on the supervisors. My suggestion is that they should take particular notice of the effectiveness of the stress testing in these models.

Another point made today was that derivatives are fine provided they are used for the right purpose. I would agree with that. But the question is what is the right purpose. In the case of an end-user clearly derivatives are very useful as part of its hedging strategy, provided, of course, that there are adequate controls in place to make sure that those derivatives are clearly understood and that the hedges are effective. I am worried that derivatives are being increasingly used in the treasury areas of industrial companies and other end-users for profit enhancement. For a long time now a number of companies have seen their treasury areas as profit centers. In the case of a number of French companies for example, treasury departments have made up for falling profits in other areas by their profits on currency transactions. More recently, you will find insurance companies and other investment institutions trying to obtain an extra return by writing options. By writing the option they obtain a premium, usually small, while accepting a risk, often large, on the downside. The trouble is that recently the downside risks come home to roost too often. Most of the recent problems have had to do with end-users not appreciating fully the risk that they are taking in relation to their derivative products. There is, therefore, a question of how you deal with that. Today we have looked at derivatives very much in the context of the systemic risk for the investment bankers, but if in practice the major losses so far have been largely for end-users who are unregulated, the risks are rather more in the area of credit than is always appreciated.

Now I would like to move on to one or two other aspects of financial fragility. What intrigued me is that commentators have different views as to what is likely to be the main source of problems according to where they come from. Early this year CSFI (The Centre for the Study of Financial Innovation) in the UK asked commentators from different countries what they saw as the major banana skins for banks. Most were quite predictable, but what was intriguing is that there were different views from different countries. John Plender from the Financial Times in the UK picked up the same sort of points as Onno Ruding made earlier in the context of the U.S. scene. That did not surprise me too much; his concern therefore was "collective memory loss," as older bankers move on and younger bankers taking their place tend to overlook history. Bankers all too soon forget that property can go down in value as well as up, and the fear is, therefore, of over enthusiastic lending on real estate developments once more. It seems to happen every 10 years or so.

Personally, and looking at it from a UK perspective, I am concerned about something else. I suspect it might also apply in the U.S., and indeed I think Onno Ruding suggested as much earlier today. This is that banking capital ratios have now recovered to such an extent that banks are now in a position of surplus capital and flushed with cash rather than suffering from a capital shortage. At the same time, it is rather difficult to know what to do with this surplus capital; there are not the same lending opportunities that there were, at least not those of the sort of quality that banks set as their minimum requirements only a year or so ago. Moreover, nearly all banks are trying very hard to improve their return on shareholders funds, which in turn implies an increase in the return on assets. That is very difficult to sustain without accepting greater risks. My concern, therefore, is that in the race to maximize profits banks will increasingly accept greater risk. In the UK, as in the U.S., we are seeing a reduction of spreads and loans being made that might not have been considered acceptable a year or so ago. In the present recovery phase of the economy the risks of this policy are not so apparent, but I can see a pattern develop where banks once more will be basing their lending on the collateral rather than on cash flows. That and the weakening of covenants also referred to by Onno Ruding suggest a risk or reduction in loan quality.

In summary, therefore, while I do consider derivatives to be a dangerous area, I think most of the major banking players have already gone a long way to making sure that they have adequate risk management and I believe the supervisors have done their best to ensure that the controls are in place and that they understand the risks as well. The risks with derivatives are well recognised, but I wonder if the more conventional sources of financial fragility are as much in the public eye. Banks currently with their surplus capital and a need to produce an increased return on equity are finding it more and more difficult to find quality borrowers prepared to pay an adequate price for the funds. So we now come to the second danger: that they will be tempted to use the surplus capital to take over other banks or other companies. Onno Ruding made a similar point, but whereas he feels that this can actually help in terms of diversification of risk, I would like to raise a question mark. History has shown that acquisitions are not always successful. Credit Lyonnais, for example, had quite some difficulties in managing its investments overseas. Onno Ruding mentioned that banks who had invested in the United States have not always managed to find a very good return on equity there. As banks have reduced their costs, often by reducing layers of management, the question arises whether banks are in a strong position to acquire at present and whether they have the management spread to do so.

That is a thought, therefore, looking at the banking scene from the UK standpoint. Intriguingly, in the CSFI survey, people looking at it from the French point of view commented about the capital adequacy of banks being rather less than was needed, and the consequent requirement to increase the capital base. The problems were seen to be with privatization, when banks may be less keen to renew loans they were prepared to take on when they were state banks. Difficulties were seen in the relationship with industrial holding companies, which is traditionally the pattern of state banks in France. Cross holdings which might at one time have been seen as a source of strength could be seen as a sign of weakness.

In Germany, commentators were particularly concerned about derivatives, but there was also concern about increased competition. While it was recognized that universal banking may be a strength in terms of the diversification of risk, there was thought to be a weakness in the degree of transparency. Following the Metallgesellschaft and Schneider problems, some commentators have suggested that the traditional link between banks and industry are such that banks may no longer be able to support the collective problems of a large number of weak companies. Up to now that has not been a problem, but there are obviously risks in just that position. Looking at the situation through Japanese eyes, financial fragility is associated with the well-known problems of bad debts in the property sector and the large number of banks who are suffering significant losses. It will be some time before the asset quality problems are set straight and there is a requirement for restructuring of a number of banks. So far there is very little experience of that, but clearly there are risks in that situation.

FINANCIAL AND MONETARY POLICY STUDIES

FINANCIAL AND MONETARY POLICY STUDIES

*Published on behalf of the *Société Universitaire Européenne de Recherches Financières* (SUERF), consisting the lectures given at Colloquia, organized and directed by SUERF.

Kluwer Academic Publishers – Dordrecht / Boston / London